Ecopsychology

Ecopsychology

RESTORING THE EARTH
HEALING THE MIND

Edited by

Theodore Roszak

Mary E. Gomes

Allen D. Kanner

. . . .

Forewords by Lester R. Brown and James Hillman

SIERRA CLUB BOOKS · SAN FRANCISCO

The Sierra Club, founded in 1892 by John Muir, has devoted itself to the study and protection of the Earth's scenic and ecological resources—mountains, wetlands, woodlands, wild shores and rivers, deserts and plains. The publishing program of the Sierra Club offers books to the public as a non-profit educational service in the hope that they may enlarge the public's understanding of the Club's basic concerns. The point of view expressed in each book, however, does not necessarily represent that of the Club. The Sierra Club has some sixty chapters coast to coast, in Canada, Hawaii and Alaska. For information about how you may participate in its programs to preserve wilderness and the quality of life, please address inquiries to Sierra Club, 85 Second Street, San Francisco, CA 94105.

www.Sierra.org/books

Published by Sierra Club Books, in conjunction with Crown Publishers, New York, New York. Member of the Crown Publishing Group.

Random House, Inc., New York, Toronto, London, Sydney, Auckland
www.randomhouse.com

SIERRA CLUB, SIERRA CLUB BOOKS, and Sierra Club design logos are registered trademarks of the Sierra Club.

Printed in the United States of America on acid-free paper containing a min-imum of 50% recovered waste paper, of which at least 10% of the fiber con-tent is post-consumer waste.

Design by Amy Evans

Library of Congress Cataloging-in-Publication Data
Ecopsychology : restoring the earth, healing the mind / edited by
    Theodore Roszak, Mary E. Gomes, and Allen D. Kanner ; forewords by
    James Hillman and Lester R. Brown.
        1. Environmental psychology.   2. Nature—psychological aspects.
    3. Environmentalism—Psychological aspects.   I. Roszak, Theodore,
    1933– .   II. Gomes, Mary E., 1962– .   III. Kanner, Allen D., 1952– .
    BF353.N37E26   1995
        155.9—dc20   94-31179

ISBN 0-87156-406-8

10 9 8 7

Contents

Acknowledgments • *xi*

Ecopsychology and the Environmental Revolution:
An Environmental Foreword • *xiii*

LESTER R. BROWN: *Ecopsychologists are drawing upon the ecological sciences to re-examine the human psyche as an integral part of the web of nature.*

A Psyche the Size of the Earth: A Psychological Foreword • *xvii*

JAMES HILLMAN: *The "bad" place I am "in" may refer not only to a depressed mood or an anxious state of mind; it may refer to a sealed-up office tower where I work, a set-apart suburban subdivision where I sleep, the jammed freeway where I commute between the two.*

Where Psyche Meets Gaia • *1*

THEODORE ROSZAK: *Only follow where ecological science leads. . . . Somewhere within this emerging vision of biospheric wholeness lies a new, environmentally based conception of sanity.*

ONE: THEORETICAL PERSPECTIVES

Nature and Madness • *21*

PAUL SHEPARD: *Modern society continues to work. . . . But the private cost is massive therapy . . . and, perhaps worst of all, a readiness to strike back at a natural world that we dimly perceive as having failed us.*

Technology, Trauma, and the Wild · *41*

CHELLIS GLENDINNING: *Total immersion, loss of perspective, and loss of control tip us off to the link between the psychological process of addiction and the technological system.*

The Psychopathology of the Human–Nature Relationship · *55*

RALPH METZNER: *We have forgotten something our ancestors once knew and practiced—respect for the mysterious, and humility in relationship to the infinite complexities of the natural world.*

Are We Happy Yet? · *68*

ALAN THEIN DURNING: *The future of life on Earth depends on whether the richest fifth of the world's people, having fully met their material needs, can turn to nonmaterial sources of fulfillment.*

The All-Consuming Self · *77*

ALLEN D. KANNER AND MARY E. GOMES: *The urge to purchase an endless stream of material products has now reached such proportions that it is no longer a matter of whim or choice, but one of personal and cultural identity.*

Jungian Psychology and the World Unconscious · *92*

STEPHEN AIZENSTAT: *From the perspective of the world unconscious everything has psychic depth and is dreaming—animate and inanimate, human-made and non–human-made.*

The Ecopsychology of Child Development · *101*

ANITA BARROWS: *What if such states of communion, such dissolution of boundaries, were as valued as rational consciousness?*

The Rape of the Well-Maidens: Feminist Psychology and the Environmental Crisis · *111*

MARY E. GOMES AND ALLEN D. KANNER: *As our defensive walls of separation and domination start to disintegrate, we become open to a world of increasing richness, complexity, and beauty.*

The Wilderness Effect and Ecopsychology · 122

ROBERT GREENWAY: *We had gone out alone like heroes on grail quests in search of dramatic and important visions that would guide our lives and make our decisions for us. Instead, we found in tiny scale and modest simplicity perfection all around us.*

The Ecology of Grief · 136

PHYLLIS WINDLE: *Passion, commitment, creativity . . . we shall have none of these if we fail to grieve for the magnificent trees, the lovely animals, and the beautiful places that we are losing.*

TWO: ECOPSYCHOLOGY IN PRACTICE

Therapy for a Dying Planet · 149

TERRANCE O'CONNOR: *I have even, upon occasion, interrupted a client's self-absorbed soliloquy by asking, "Are you aware that the planet is dying?"*

When the Earth Hurts, Who Responds? · 156

SARAH A. CONN: *We have cut ourselves off from our connection to the Earth so thoroughly that even though we are "bleeding at the roots," we neither understand the problem nor know what we can do about it.*

Shamanic Counseling and Ecopsychology · 172

LESLIE GRAY: *At the dawn of the twenty-first century, as we teeter on the brink of global catastrophe, it is precisely a shamanistic worldview that is our greatest hope.*

The Way of Wilderness · 183

STEVEN HARPER: *The essence of wilderness practice is to be wilderness. The very idea that wilderness exists as something separate lets us know how much we have disowned of our internal as well as our external wildness.*

The Skill of Ecological Perception · 201

LAURA SEWALL: *If we are part of a communication system within the Gaian organism, then perception is our best channel for listening.*

Ecological Groundedness in Gestalt Therapy · 216

WILLIAM CAHALAN: *Know that the oxygen you and all animals are taking in at this moment is a gift of green plants, given off by them as they breathe in the carbon dioxide that we and other animals have exhaled.*

Restoring Habitats, Communities, and Souls · 224

ELAN SHAPIRO: *This art and science of helping the web of life in a particular place heal and renew itself can serve as a mirror and an impetus for individual and community renewal.*

Working Through Environmental Despair · 240

JOANNA MACY: *Just as grief work is a process by which bereaved persons unblock their numbed energies by acknowledging and grieving the loss of a loved one, so do we all need to unblock our feelings about our threatened planet.*

THREE: CULTURAL DIVERSITY AND
POLITICAL ENGAGEMENT

Ecopsychology and the Deconstruction of Whiteness · 263

CARL ANTHONY: *The success of ecopsychology will depend not only upon its ability to help us hear the voice of the Earth, but to construct a genuinely multicultural self and a global civil society without racism.*

The Politics of Species Arrogance · 279

JOHN E. MACK: *Psychologists of the environment must participate with committed citizens in a broad-based movement aimed at nothing less than the transformation of our political and economic institutions.*

The Spirit of the Goddess · *288*

> BETTY ROSZAK: *There is no Goddess in the sky; we are all the Goddess. Our saints and heroines are not dead; they live within us, and like the phoenix are renewed each day.*

The Ecology of Magic · *301*

> DAVID ABRAM: *It was as if my body were suddenly being motivated by a wisdom older than my thinking mind.*

Keepers of the Earth · *316*

> JEANNETTE ARMSTRONG: *The soil, the water, the air, and all other life-forms contributed parts to our flesh. We are our land.*

Suggested Readings · *325*

The Contributors · *335*

Acknowledgments

The editors would like to thank the following individuals for their support, encouragement, and advice: Betty Roszak; Jerry Mander; Sharon Thom; Michael Murphy; and Barbara Ras.

Acknowledgment is also extended to the following for permission to reprint previously published material: Pantheon Books for David Abram (provisionally entitled) *The Earthly Body of the Mind: Animism, Language, and the Ecology of Sensory Experience.* New York: Pantheon Books, in press. An earlier version of "The Ecology of Magic" also appeared in *Orion* (Summer 1991). Sarah A. Conn for "When the Earth Hurts, Who Responds?" *Peacework: A New England Peace and Justice Newsletter* (July–Aug. 1991). Alan Durning for "Are We Happy Yet? How the Pursuit of Happiness Is Failing." *The Futurist* (Jan.–Feb. 1993). Chellis Glendinning for "The Conversation We Haven't Had Yet." In Michael Thurman and Julia Sweig, eds., *Technology for the Common Ground.* Washington, D.C.: Institute for Policy Studies, 1993. John Mack for "Inventing a Psychology of Our Relationship to the Earth." In Sylvia Staub and Paula Green, eds., *Psychology and Social Responsibility.* New York: New York University Press, 1992. Joanna Macy from her book *Despair and Personal Power in the Nuclear Age.* Philadelphia: New Society Publications, 1983. Terrance P. O'Connor for "Therapy on a Dying Planet." *The Family Therapy Networker* (Sept.–Oct. 1989). Phyllis Windle for "The Ecology of Grief." *Bioscience* 42 (May 1992), 363–366. Copyright © 1992 *American Institute of Biological Sciences.*

Ecopsychology and the Environmental Revolution
An Environmental Foreword

LESTER R. BROWN

Environmentalists sometimes despair at the magnitude of the task their movement has taken on. When we consider all that remains to be done to bring a sustainable way of life to our global society, we can easily forget how much has already been accomplished. No more than a generation ago, most Americans had no idea what global warming was, or the ozone layer, or acid rain. The distinction between renewable and nonrenewable resources was all but unknown. Concepts like "endangered species," "recycling," and "carrying capacity" were known only to a handful of environmental specialists; they did not exist in the public vocabulary. No such thing as an "environmental impact statement" existed.

We have the hard work and political savvy of environmentalists to thank for overcoming this condition of terminal ecological illiteracy. Over the past forty years, the environmental movement has succeeded in turning the health of the planet into a major political issue in every industrial society. When it comes to raising the collective consciousness about the liabilities of industrial "progress," we have done a remarkably good job of sounding the alarm. The number of dangers and disasters we have identified is daunting to say the least; in many ways, the dimensions of the problem appear overwhelming.

It is easy to see how this has come about. The environmental movement has grown to become the largest, most densely organized political cause in human history. From lofty government agencies to grass-roots citizens' groups, it has engaged people at every social level. Everybody seems to be protecting some piece, big or little, of the biosphere—from the worldwide tropical rainforests down to the local streams passing through our communities. Everything we turn our hand to becomes infused with an impassioned sense of urgency. Each group that takes up the cause understandably addresses its issue as *the* issue, the problem that needs to be solved *first*. One of the weaknesses of the environmental movement is that few groups can stand back at a sufficient distance to see the big picture and establish priorities.

Every political movement has its psychological dimension. Persuading people to alter their behavior always involves probing motivations and debating values; political activism begins with asking what makes people tick. What do they want and fear and care about? How do we get and hold their attention? How much can people take—and in what order of priority? Have we overloaded them with anxiety or guilt? How do we make credible the threats we perceive? Movements that fail to think carefully about this may fail to persuade.

The environmental movement is no exception. Once upon a time, environmentalists seemed to be idealists who were fighting on the side of the angels—at least in the eyes of the general public, if not the corporate and governing establishment. Now antienvironmentalists seek to undermine the credibility of the environmental cause, and some politicians show signs of taking them seriously.

Ecopsychologists like those you will find in this book believe it is time for the environmental movement to file what Theodore Roszak has called a "*psychological* impact statement." In practical political terms that means asking: *are we being effective?* Most obviously, we need to ask that question with respect to our impact upon the public, whose hearts and minds we want to win over. The stakes are high and time is short.

From the global vantage point, we see a world economy that is unsustainable, one that is slowly destroying its underpinnings. We live on a planet that is deteriorating ecologically and inhabited by people who are psychologically troubled.

We know that we cannot continue to deforest the planet at the current rate without eventually getting into trouble. Similarly we cannot continue to lose topsoil far faster than natural soil formation without eventually facing impoverishment. If we continue to lose plant and animal species at the rate of the past few decades, we face eventual ecosystem collapse. We also know that we cannot continue to pump greenhouse gases into the atmosphere without eventually producing economically disruptive climate change. Nor can we continue to add ninety million people to the world each year without eventually destroying the natural systems and resources on which we depend for sustenance.

What we are now looking at is nothing less than an environmental revolution, an economic and social transformation that ranks with the agricultural and industrial revolutions. Like the agricultural revolution, the environmental revolution will dramatically alter population trends. Whereas the former set the stage for enormous increases in human numbers, this revolution will succeed only if it stabilizes population size, reestablishing a balance between people and nature. In contrast to the industrial revolution, which was based on a shift to fossil fuels, this new transformation will be based on a shift away from them.

The two earlier revolutions were driven by technological advances— the first by the discovery of farming and the second by the invention of the steam engine, which converted the energy in coal into mechanical power. The environmental revolution, while it will obviously use new technologies, will be driven primarily by the restructuring of the global economy so that this economy does not destroy its natural support systems.

The pace of the environmental revolution will be faster than that of its predecessors. The agricultural revolution began some ten thousand years ago, and the industrial revolution has been under way for two centuries. But if the environmental revolution is to succeed, it must be compressed into a few decades.

Ecopsychology addresses the problem of effective communication with the general public that will have to meet the demands of the environmental revolution. However, the issues it raises amount to more than a matter of public relations and personal therapy. There is an underlying philosophical issue. It has to do with our understanding of human nature—or, if you will, the nature of the soul. Psychology is, after all, the study of the soul in all its complexity and contradiction. It is the study of what people love and hate and fear and need. At some point, both psychologists and environmentalists need to decide what they believe our human connection is with the planet our species has so endangered.

Do we believe people want to do the right environmental thing? Do we believe people *care* about the future of the living planet? Ecopsychologists believe there is an emotional bond between human beings and the natural environment out of which we evolve.

The major contribution ecopsychology promises to make to environmental politics is the identification of the irrational forces that tie people to their bad environmental habits. For example, some ecopsychologists believe that our consumption habits are connected to deep addictive attractions. Little wonder. The advertising industry is a contingent of talented "pushers" working to make us compulsive consumers. That is psychology working *against* environmental sanity. Ecopsychology seeks to redress that balance. It wants to know how to free people from the addictions of the shopping mall and to encourage values that serve the life of the planet rather than imperiling it.

At its most ambitious, ecopsychology seeks to redefine sanity within an environmental context. It contends that seeking to heal the soul without reference to the ecological system of which we are an integral part is a form of self-destructive blindness. Ecopsychologists are drawing upon the ecological sciences to reexamine the human psyche as an integral part of the web of nature. Having the support of so influential a profession would be a welcome gain for the environmental movement.

At the heart of the coming environmental revolution is a change in values, one that derives from a growing appreciation of our dependence on nature. Without it there is no hope. In simple terms, we cannot restore our own health, our sense of well-being, unless we restore the health of the planet. It is against this backdrop that we find the emerging new field of ecopsychology so exciting.

Ecopsychology brings together the sensitivity of therapists, the expertise of ecologists, and the ethical energy of environmental activists. Out of this rich mixture may arise a new, more effective, more philosophically grounded form of environmental politics.

A Psyche the Size of the Earth
A Psychological Foreword

JAMES HILLMAN

There is only one core issue for all psychology. *Where is the "me"?* Where does the "me" begin? Where does the "me" stop? Where does the "other" begin?

For most of its history, psychology took for granted an intentional subject: the biographical "me" that was the agent and the sufferer of all "doings." For most of its history, psychology located this "me" within human persons defined by their physical skin and their immediate behavior. The subject was simply "me in my body and in my relations with other subjects." The familiar term that covered this entire philosophical system was "ego," and what the ego registered were called "experiences."

Over the past twenty years all this has been scrutinized, dismantled, and even junked. Postmodernism has deconstructed continuity, self, intention, identity, centrality, gender, individuality. The integrity of memory for establishing biographical continuity has been challenged. The unity of the self has fallen before the onslaught of multiple personalities. Moments called "projective identification" can attach distant objects to the "me" so fiercely that I believe I cannot live without them; conversely, parts of even my personal physical body can become so dissociated that my fragmented body image regards them as autonomous and without sensory feeling, as if quite "other." How far away is the "other"? Is it Wholly Other and therefore like a "God," as Rudolf Otto believed? Or, is the "not-me" an inherently related other, a "Thou" in Martin Buber's sense? If we can no longer be sure that we are who we remember we are, where then do we make the cut between "me" and "not-me"?

So long as we cannot ascertain where the "me" ends (is it with my skin? with my behavior? with my personal interfacing connections and their influences and traces?) how can we establish the limits of psychology? How do we today define the borders of this field—as we must, since the first task of psychology is to explore and give an account of subjectivity?

By "psychology" I mean what the word says: the study or order (*logos*) of the soul (*psyche*). This implies that all psychology is by definition a depth psychology, first because it assumes an inside intimacy to behavior (moods, reflections, fantasies, feelings, images, thoughts) and second, because the soul, ever since Heraclitus twenty-five hundred years ago, has been defined as immeasurably deep and unlocatable. I therefore see all psychologies as ultimately therapies by definition because of their involvement with soul.

A clear example from psychology's history may serve to show the arbitrariness of the cut between "me" and "not-me." French rationalist psychology following Descartes, Malebranche, and La Mettrie declared animals to have no consciousness, not even the sensation of pain. A radical cut separated them from humans. The cut gradually softened: Kant allowed animals to possess sensation but no reason. Darwin's work on the expression of emotion demonstrated deep similarities between humans and animals. The gap grew even narrower and more blurred with later theories of instinct and inborn release mechanisms that allowed animals limited reasoning power. Today more and more "human"-like attributes, some even superior to human consciousness, are being teased out of animals, so that the cut itself has come into question.

The question of establishing the limits to the psyche, and to psychology, is further complicated by the notion of the unconscious. We cannot accurately set borders to human identity since it trails off from the light of focused awareness into the shadows of dreams, spotty memories, intuitions, and spontaneous eruptions whose point of origin is indefinite. Since the "discovery of the unconscious," every sophisticated theory of personality has to admit that whatever I claim to be "me" has at least a portion of its roots beyond my agency and my awareness. These unconscious roots may be planted in territories far away from anything

I may call mine, belonging rather to what Jung called the "psychoid," partly material, partly psychic, a merging of psyche and matter. This psychoid source refers to the material substrate of life: like calcium, inorganic by category, but, like bones, animated by activity in living beings. From the material perspective the psychoid substrate has effects; from the psychological perspective these effects may be discussed as intentions. The pharmaceuticals, legal and illegal, we take to alter psychological conditions demonstrate the psychoid view of material intentionality, the "liveliness" of matter, to millions of ordinary citizens who would be hard-pressed to accept the idea as a theory. So, again, where does psyche stop and matter begin? For the pioneers of psychology as therapy, the deepest levels of the psyche merge with the biological body (Freud) and the physical stuff of the world (Jung).

I am reviewing these well-known basics of psychological theory to show that the human subject has all along been implicated in the wider world of nature. How could it be otherwise, since the human subject is composed of the same nature as the world? Yet psychological practice tends to bypass the consequences of such facts.

In *The Voice of the Earth,* an exploration of ecopsychology, Theodore Roszak does face these facts. He extends Jung's collective unconscious and Freud's id and draws the rational conclusion that what these terms imply is "the world." Adaptation of the deep self to the collective unconscious and to the id is simply adaptation to the natural world, organic and inorganic. Moreover, an individual's harmony with his or her "own deep self" requires not merely a journey to the interior but a harmonizing with the environmental world. The deepest self cannot be confined to "in here" because we can't be sure it is not also or even entirely "out there"! If we listen to Roszak, and to Freud and Jung, the most profoundly collective and unconscious self is the natural material world.

Since the cut between self and natural world is arbitrary, we can make it at the skin or we can take it as far out as you like—to the deep oceans and distant stars. But the cut is far less important than the recognition of uncertainty about making the cut at all. This uncertainty opens the mind to wonder again, allowing fresh considerations to enter the therapeutic equation. Perhaps working on my feelings is not more "subjective" than working on the neighborhood air quality. Perhaps killing weeds on my lawn with herbicides may be as repressive as what I am doing with my childhood memories. Perhaps the abuses I have unconsciously suffered in my deep interior subjectivity pale in comparison with the abuses going around me every minute in my ecological surroundings, abuses that I myself commit or comply with. It may be easier to discover yourself a victim than admit yourself a perpetrator.

We do need to see, however, that the cut between me and world, arbitrary as it is, nonetheless has to be made. It is a pragmatic convention that establishes the borders of a field, in this case the field of psychology. The field then develops its own paradigm of what takes place in the field. But the map called "psychology" is only part of the terrain of uncertainty; in fact, that map may be a gross enlargement of but a small section blown up way out of scale. Therefore, psychology is bound to encourage us to take human emotions, relationships, wishes, and grievances utterly out of proportion in view of the vast disasters now being suffered by the world.

The subjectivist exaggeration that psychology has fostered is coming home to roost, because the symptoms that are coming back to the consulting room are precisely those its theory engenders: borderline disorders in which the personality does not conform to the limits set by psychology; preoccupation with subjective moods called "addictions" and "recovery"; inability to let the world into one's perceptual field, called "attention deficit disorders" or "narcissism"; and a vague depressed exhaustion from trying so hard to cope with the enlarged expectations of private self-actualization apart from the actual world.

One could accuse therapeutic psychology's exaggeration of the personal interior, and aggrandizing of its importance, of being a systematic denial of the world out there, a kind of compensation for the true grandness its theory has refused to include and has defended against.

In brief, if psychology is the study of the subject, and if the limits of this subject cannot be set, then psychology merges willy-nilly with ecology.

For depth psychology this merger implies that alterations in the "external" world may be as therapeutic as alterations in my subjective feelings. The "bad" place I am "in" may refer not only to a depressed mood or an anxious state of mind; it may refer to a sealed-up office tower where I work, a set-apart suburban subdivision where I sleep, or the jammed freeway on which I commute between the two.

Environmental medicine and environmental psychiatry have begun
to look at actual places and things, like carpets and drapes, for their effects on human disorders. When some cancers are hypothesized to begin
in people suffering recent loss, what loss? Is it only personal? Or does a
personal loss open the gates to that less conscious but overwhelming
loss—the slow disappearance of the natural world, a loss endemic to our
entire civilization? In that case, the idea that depth psychology merges
with ecology translates to mean that to understand the ills of the soul
today we turn to the ills of the world, its suffering. The most radical
deconstruction of subjectivity, called "displacing the subject," today
would be re-placing the subject back into the world, or re-placing the
subject altogether with the world.

What I am saying here was said far better by Hippocrates twenty-five
hundred years ago in his treatise *Airs, Waters, Places*. To grasp the disorders in any subject we must study carefully the environment of the
disorder: the kind of water; the winds, humidity, temperatures; the food
and plants; the times of day; the seasons. Treatment of the inner requires
attention to the outer; or, as another early healer wrote, "The greater part
of the soul lies outside the body." As there are happy places beneficial
to well-being, so there are others that seem to harbor demons, miasmas,
and melancholy. The early Gestalt theorists, Kohler and Koffka, located
emotions such as melancholy in the field; a landscape could be sad by
its expressive formal qualities (its gestalt) and not because sadness is
projected onto it from the subject's interior. The strict thinkers of the
Direct Perception school of J. J. Gibson of Cornell University locate
memory as much in the world as in the interior brain of the subject.
Landscape affords information to an animal; it is not simply stored in the
mind. The animal—and we humans are animals—perceives what is
there in the environment, given with the environment if we attend to it
carefully. Do not these schools, as well as the recent publications of Edward S. Casey on the phenomenology of place, suggest a nonhuman subjectivity, precisely what non-Western cultures have known and lived by
for millennia, but which ours has denigrated as superstitious animism?

The paradigm shift in psychology places it at a crossroads. It may go
along the well-worn track, declaring subjectivity to consist essentially
only in human nature, thereby making its cut close to the skin and regarding as secondary what lies outside its bell jar. No doubt this path

has its virtues, for it allows a special culture to bloom in the bubble, a culture today called egocentric, self-referential, and narcissistic by critics, but valuable for the meticulous analysis of the psyche as narrowly defined. In fact, the narrow definition intensifies the culture within the bubble, making it all the more effective on the one hand, yet ironically, perhaps, all the more wrongheaded on the other. The traditional argument of psychology says: maintain the closed vessel of the consulting room, of the behavioral lab, of the field itself, for this tradition is born from nineteenth-century science, which continues to define psychology as the "scientific" study of subjectivity. And science works best in controllable situations, *in vitro*, under the bell jar, where it can carefully observe, predict, and thereby perhaps alter the minutiae of the subject.

Psychology may take the wider road, however, extending its horizon, venturing to the interior in a less literal manner: *no cuts*. The interior would be anywhere: anywhere we look and listen with a psychological eye and ear. The whole world becomes our consulting room, our petri dish. Psychology would track the fields of naturalists, botanists, oceanographers, geologists, urbanists, designers for the concealed intentions, the latent subjectivity of regions the old paradigm considered only objective, beyond consciousness and interiority. The wider road is also a two-way street. Besides entering the world with its psychological eye, it would let the world enter its province, admitting that airs, waters, and places play as large a role in the problems psychology faces as do moods, relationships, and memories.

Sometimes I wonder less how to shift the paradigm than how psychology ever got so off base. How did it so cut itself off from reality? Where else in the world would a human soul be so divorced from the spirits of the surroundings? Even the high intellectualism of the Renaissance, to say nothing of the modes of mind in ancient Egypt and Greece or contemporary Japan, allowed for the animation of things, recognizing a subjectivity in animals, plants, wells, springs, trees, and rocks. Psychology, so dedicated to awakening human consciousness, needs to wake itself up to one of the most ancient human truths: we cannot be studied or cured apart from the planet.

I write this appeal not so much "to save the planet" or to enjoin my fellow therapists to retrain as environmentalists. I do not wish to urge another duty on you, another region of phenomena for your care. Yes, I worry over the disruption of the natural environment—as a citizen, as a father and grandfather, as a human animal. My concern is also most specifically for psychotherapy, for all of psychology. I do not want it to be swallowed up in its caverns of interiority, lost in its own labyrinthine explorations and minutiae of memories, feelings, and language—or the yet-smaller interiorities of biochemistry, genetics, and brain dissection. The motivation behind this appeal to my colleagues is to keep our field from narrowing into a specialty only. Professionals do have specialized skills, but even a dentist cannot confine her or his focus to the mouth. Careful observation always leads beyond the immediately observed, and we must follow the phenomena, the pathologies, rather then be hemmed in by our own "cut." The way out of specialization and professionalism, the isolation they breed, and the unreality that eventually follows upon self-enclosure is to entertain fresh ideas. Today such ideas are blowing in from the world, the ecological psyche, the soul of the world by which the human soul is afflicted, to which the human soul is commencing to turn with fresh interest, because in this world soul the human soul has always had its home.

Ecopsychology

Where Psyche Meets Gaia

THEODORE ROSZAK

The Personal and the Planetary

When we think of environmentalism, we call to mind a vast, worldwide movement that deals in imponderably complex social and economic issues on the largest conceivable scale. The environmental movement holds its place in history as the largest political cause ever undertaken by the human race. It includes everybody, because there is nobody the movement can afford *not* to talk to. Its constituency even reaches beyond our own species to include the flora and fauna, the rivers and mountains. Whenever I turn to an environmental issue, I find myself intensely aware that other, nonhuman eyes are upon me: our companion creatures looking on, hoping that their bewildering human cousins will see the error of their ways.

On the other hand, when we think of psychotherapy, we think of human relations on the smallest and most personal scale: one-to-one or in intimate groups. Therapy is private and introspective; it deals in the hidden life—fears, desires, guilty secrets perhaps too deeply buried to be known even to the individual.

What can these two levels of cultural activity possibly have in common? What link can there be between the personal and the planetary?

One thought comes to mind at once: the scale on which both environmentalism and therapy are pursued diverges radically from political business as usual. Neither ecological nor psychotherapeutic problems can be fully solved, if at all, within the boundaries defended by the nation-state, the free-trade zone, the military alliance, or the multina-

tional corporation. The one transcends even the largest of these awk-
wardly improvised human structures; the other eludes their insensitive
grasp. Perhaps this is in itself an ecological fact of the highest importance. We are living in a time when both the Earth and the human species seem to be crying out for a radical readjustment in the scale of our
political thought. Is it possible that in this sense the personal and the
planetary are pointing the way toward some new basis for sustainable
economic and emotional life, a society of good environmental citizenship that can ally the intimately emotional and the vastly biospheric?

Until just a few years ago, possibilities like this would have gone un-
recognized by both environmentalists and therapists. The environmental movement went about its work of organizing, educating, and
agitating with little regard for the fragile psychological complexities of
the public whose hearts and minds it sought to win. As intensely aware
as environmentalists may be of the complexity of the natural habitat,
when it came to human behavior their guiding image was simplistic in
the extreme. They worked from a narrow range of strategies and motivations: the statistics of impending disaster, the coercive emotional force
of fear and guilt. As an environmental writer and speaker, I know how
easily one reaches for scare tactics and guilt trips; they come so conve-
niently to hand. After all, there is a great deal to be afraid of and a great
deal to be ashamed of in our environmental habits. Even though many
environmentalists act out of a passionate joy in the magnificence of wild
things, few except the artists—the photographers, the filmmakers, the
landscape painters, and the poets—address the public with any conviction that human beings can be trusted to behave as if they were the living
planet's children.

As for the psychologists and therapists, their understanding of human
sanity has always stopped at the city limits. The creation of urban intellect, and intended to heal urban angst, modern psychotherapy has never
seen fit to reach beyond family and society to address the nonhuman
habitat that so massively engulfs the tiny psychic island Freud called
"civilization and its discontents." For example, in the *Diagnostic and Statistical Manual*, the American Psychiatric Association's canonical listing
of every form of neurosis for which an insurance company can be billed
and which a court of law will accept as authoritative, the state of nature

puts in only a single appearance; one finds it hidden away there as "seasonal affective disorder," a depressive mood swing occasioned by gloomy weather—unless, that is, the depression is correlated with seasonal unemployment. The economic factor then takes precedence over the natural phenomenon.[1]

Now there are signs that this is beginning to change from both directions. A new generation of psychotherapists is seeking ways in which professional psychology can play a role in the environmental crisis of our time. One indication of that change is this book. Here you will find a sampling of the thinking being done by environmentally conscious psychotherapists, and a report on the techniques they are innovating, in a volume commissioned by the country's leading environmental publisher. Here too you will find the work of environmentalists who display a healthy curiosity about their need to find a more sustainable psychology, one that will appeal to affirmative motivations and the love of nature. It is a timely concern; there is an urgent need to address the amount of anger, negativity, and emotional burnout one finds in the movement. Recently, in a private letter, the Australian rainforest activist John Seed put it this way:

> It is obvious to me that the forests cannot be saved one at a time, nor can the planet be saved one issue at a time: without a profound revolution in human consciousness, all the forests will soon disappear. Psychologists in service to the Earth helping ecologists to gain deeper understanding of how to facilitate profound change in the human heart and mind seems to be *the* key at this point.

Similarly, in cautioning against the emotional toll that results from an exclusive reliance on blaming and shaming, Dave Foreman, one of the country's leading "ecowarriors," wisely reminds his colleagues that the greater goal of all they do is to "open our souls to love this glorious, luxuriant, animated planet." To forget that, he warns, is "damaging to our personal mental health."[2]

1. Earlier editions of the *Diagnostic and Statistical Manual* included one other reference to the nonhuman world: zoophilia, having sex with animals. The older, quainter term for this was "bestiality," but something like animal rape might have been better. Oddly enough, "zoophilia" precludes the possibility of a "normal" state that involves loving animals.
2. Dave Foreman, "The New Conservation Movement," *Wild Earth* (Summer 1991), 10–11.

Biophilia and Ecopsychology

There is one more significant current of change that deserves to be mentioned. The biologists have begun to pay attention to the psychological side of human evolution. In a recent work, the Harvard zoologist E. O. Wilson has raised the possibility that humans possess a capacity called "biophilia," defined as "the innately emotional affiliation of human beings to other living organisms."[3] He sees this as an important force working to defend the endangered biodiversity of the planet. Even an impressionistic survey of folklore and fairy tale and of the religious life of indigenous peoples would surely yield a great deal of support for the idea. Wilson's colleagues have been quick to suggest that the influence of biophilia might be offset in some degree by an equally innate "biophobia," but from the psychologist's viewpoint, both our love and our fear of nature are emotions; both merit study. And both, as they might be translated into devotion, respect, concern, or awe, can be used to rebuild our strained bonds with the natural environment. Those of us who feel trapped in an increasingly ecocidal urban, industrial society need all the help we can find in overcoming our alienation from the more-than-human world on which we depend for every breath we breathe. Is there, indeed, any more urgent measure of our alienation than the fact that we must speak of our emotional continuity with that world as no more than a "hypothesis"? Nevertheless, in the form of a hypothesis, biophilia has at least begun to generate the sort of behavioral research that passes muster in the academic world as scientific proof. In a sense, ecopsychology might be seen as a commitment by psychologists and therapists to the hope that the biophilia hypothesis will prove true and so become an integral part of what we take mental health to be.

"Ecopsychology" is the name most often used for this emerging synthesis of the psychological (here intended to embrace the psychotherapeutic and the psychiatric) and the ecological. Several other terms have been suggested: psychoecology, ecotherapy, global therapy, green therapy, Earth-centered therapy, reearthing, nature-based psychotherapy, shamanic counseling, even sylvan therapy. Such neologisms never sound euphonious; nor, for that matter, did "psychoanalysis" in its day. But by

3. E. O. Wilson and Stephen R. Kellert, eds., *The Biophilia Hypothesis* (Washington, D.C.: Island Press/Shearwater Books, 1993).

whatever name, the underlying assumption is the same: *ecology needs psychology, psychology needs ecology.* The context for defining sanity in our time has reached planetary magnitude.

Like all forms of psychology, ecopsychology concerns itself with the foundations of human nature and behavior. Unlike other mainstream schools of psychology that limit themselves to the intrapsychic mechanisms or to a narrow social range that may not look beyond the family, ecopsychology proceeds from the assumption that at its deepest level the psyche remains sympathetically bonded to the Earth that mothered us into existence. Ecopsychology suggests that we can read our transactions with the natural environment—the way we use or abuse the planet—as projections of unconscious needs and desires, in much the same way we can read dreams and hallucinations to learn about our deep motivations, fears, hatreds. In fact, our wishful, willful imprint upon the natural environment may reveal our collective state of soul more tellingly than the dreams we wake from and shake off, knowing them to be unreal. Far more consequential are the dreams that we take with us out into the world each day and maniacally set about making "real"—in steel and concrete, in flesh and blood, out of resources torn from the substance of the planet. Precisely because we have acquired the power to work our will upon the environment, the planet has become like that blank psychiatric screen on which the neurotic unconscious projects its fantasies. Toxic wastes, the depletion of resources, the annihilation of our fellow species; all these speak to us, if we would hear, of our deep self. Hence, James Hillman has urged us to bring "asbestos and food additives, acid rain and tampons, insecticides and pharmaceuticals, car exhausts and sweeteners, televisions and ions" within the province of therapeutic analysis. "Psychology always advances its consciousness by means of pathologized revelations, through the underworld of our anxiety. Our ecological fears announce that *things* are where the soul now claims psychological attention."[4]

Learning from Stone Age Psychiatry

I have been calling ecopsychology "new," but in fact its sources are old enough to be called aboriginal. Once upon a time all psychology was

4. James Hillman, *The Thought of the Heart and the Soul of the World* (Dallas, Tex.: Spring Publications, 1981), p. 111.

"ecopsychology." No special word was needed. The oldest healers in the world, the people our society once called "witch doctors," knew no other way to heal than to work within the context of environmental reciprocity. Some are quick to see elements of sentimentality or romanticism in our growing appreciation of the sacred ecologies that guide traditional societies. This is mistaken. There is nothing "mystical" or "transcendent" about the matter as we might understand these words. It is homely common sense that human beings must live in a state of respectful give-and-take with the flora and fauna, the rivers and hills, the sky and soil on which we depend for physical sustenance and practical instruction.[5] "The country knows," a Koyukon elder warns. "If you do wrong to it, the whole country knows. It feels what is happening to it. I guess everything is connected together somehow under the ground."

We acknowledge our lingering connection with that earlier stage of psychotherapeutic practice whenever we flippantly refer to psychiatrists as "shrinks." We recognize that our supposedly enlightened psychiatric science contains a good deal of mumbo jumbo. But might it not also be the case that something of value can be found in the supposedly superstitious practice of witch doctoring? The anthropologist Marshall Sahlins once studied the surviving hunting and gathering cultures with a view to reconstructing a "Stone Age economics." Is there a "Stone Age psychiatry" waiting to be mined for similarly heuristic insights?

I raise this point with the full and concerned awareness that there are uninvited New Age enthusiasts who are already ransacking and freely borrowing remnants of traditional and aboriginal cultures, often with little study or respectful preparation. In this volume, we have tried to make clear that ecopsychologists are acutely cognizant of how difficult it will be to bridge the gap between the dominant society and the surviving, often fragile and marginal primary cultures of the world. In generalizing about the sanity and madness of the modern world, ecopsychologists have learned to use the word "we" with the utmost discrimination. They recognize that the "we" that runs the industrial world is psychically estranged from the "*we*" that holds out in the rainforests,

5. For some recent studies of the ecological sensibility of traditional cultures, see David Suzuki and Peter Knudtson, *Wisdom of the Elders: Honoring Sacred Native Visions of Nature* (New York: Bantam, 1992); Jerry Mander, *In the Absence of the Sacred: The Failure of Technology and the Survival of the Indian Nations* (San Francisco: Sierra Club Books, 1991); Helena Norberg-Hodge, *Ancient Futures: Learning from Ladakh* (San Francisco: Sierra Club Books, 1991).

outbacks, and reservations by a distance that has to be calculated in light-years. And the unit of measurement is power: wealth, property, brute force, media, managerial control.

Even apart from issues of justice, some will see an immediate psychological obstacle to such a dialogue between the traditional and the modern. It has to do with the contrasting worldviews that divide the psychotherapy of industrial society from the original headshrinkers. Theirs was an animistic vision of the world, a sensibility that both Judeo-Christian doctrine and scientific objectivity have censored. In our culture, listening for the voices of the Earth as if the nonhuman world felt, heard, spoke would seem the essence of madness to most people. Is it possible that by asserting that very conception of madness, psychotherapy itself may be defending the deepest of all our repressions, the form of psychic mutilation that is most crucial to the advance of industrial civilization, namely, the assumption that the land is a dead and servile thing that has no feeling, no memory, no intention of its own? With the full authority of modern science, conventional sanity cuts us off from using Stone Age psychiatry as a therapeutic resource. Those who believe that this condition can be easily remedied, say by spending a few hours in a sweat lodge, are simply not in touch with the true dimensions of their own alienation.

But history, the mirror of our unfolding needs and aspirations, has its way with the most tenaciously rooted orthodoxies. Even in a dominant and domineering culture, both religion and science are subject to that sort of major transformation we have come to call a shift of paradigms. In the mainstream Christian churches today, there are environmental ministries that are encouraging an active discussion of planetary stewardship and creation spirituality; some even seek to undo the longstanding prejudice against "pagan" culture and its insights. A new Earth and Spirit movement is exploring the possibility of a religiously based biophilia.[6]

6. See, for example, the "creation spirituality" of Matthew Fox, especially *The Coming of the Cosmic Christ: The Healing of the Mother Earth* (Boston: Shambhala, 1988); Thomas Berry, *The Dream of the Earth* (San Francisco: Sierra Club Books, 1988). James A. Nash offers a critical survey of these and other efforts to develop an environmentally relevant theology in *Loving Nature: Ecological Integrity and Christian Responsibility* (Nashville: Abingdon, 1991). Also see the journal *Earth Letter*, published by the Episcopalian Earth Ministry of Seattle, 1305 NE 47th St., Seattle, Wash., 98105, and the work of the environmental ministry at the Cathedral of St. John the Divine in New York: 1047 Amsterdam Avenue, New York, N.Y., 10025.

   Meanwhile, at least along the fringes of modern science, we are witnessing the birth of a new cosmology grounded in an ever-deepening
vision of ordered complexity on the Earth and in the universe at large.
Scientists may remain reluctant to spell out the revolutionary philosophical implications of this emergent worldview, but the lineaments of
the new cosmos are becoming unmistakably clear: it is no longer a matter
of scientific necessity for us to regard ourselves as "strangers and afraid
in a world we never made." We now know that the periodic table of
elements, as it moves from heavy to light, from simple to complex, is
the language of our evolving collective autobiography. It is in its own
right a creation story. Hydrogen, as one astronomer has put it, is "a light,
odorless gas that, given enough time, turns into people."

The Vision of an Ecological Universe

In contrast to the atomistic materialism of nineteenth-century physics,
ecology is the study of connectedness. It began its intellectual history as
the holistic study of the myriad niches and crannies in which life has
taken hold on this planet, but its destiny was to be much greater. It has
eventually come to see the entire Earth as a remarkable cosmic "niche"
intricately connected with the grand hierarchy of systems we call "the
universe." As nature around us unfolds to reveal level upon level of
structured complexity, we are coming to see that we inhabit a densely
connected ecological universe where nothing is "nothing but" a simple,
disconnected, or isolated thing. Nor is anything accidental. Life and
mind, once regarded as such anomalous exceptions to the law of entropy, are rooted by their physiochemical structures, all the way back to
the initial conditions that followed the Big Bang.

   We now know that the elemental stuff of which we are made was
forged in the fiery core of ancient stars. In a very real sense, the ecologist's
web of life now spreads out to embrace the most distant galaxies. This
magnificent cosmology has led us to the greatest turning point in our
understanding of the human place in nature since our ancestors first
looked skyward to ponder the wheeling stars. It may yet become our
cooler, more analytical version of the animistic world on which our
ancestors drew for their sense of companionship with all the more-than-
human. Surely even the most rigorously skeptical mind must be hard
pressed to escape the wonder of that possibility.

Developments like these take us a long distance from the way the founders of modern science and psychiatry viewed the human condition. It is not beside the point that modern psychiatric theory was created with the unshakable intention of being "scientific" in an era when the dominant scientific model of the universe allowed no natural place for the human psyche. For Sigmund Freud, a typically doctrinaire materialist, life and mind were freakish events in an infinite and alien void that was tyrannically ruled by the second law of thermodynamics. In such a cosmos, death was more "natural" than life.

> The attributes of life [Freud reasoned] were at some time evoked in inanimate matter by the action of a force of whose nature we can form no conception. . . . The tension which then arose in what had hitherto been an inanimate substance endeavored to cancel itself out. In this way the first instinct came into being: the instinct to return to the inanimate state.[7]

At the turn of the century, when the foundations of modern psychiatry were being laid, the newly discovered law of entropy had achieved cult status as the final answer to the riddle of the universe. For many *fin de siècle* intellectuals, thermodynamic doom became irrefutable proof for the futility of life. Human consciousness was a transient accident destined for annihilation; ultimately, every chemical process in the universe would succumb to the great and final "heat death." After that, for all eternity, there would be nothing, nothing, nothing at all except the measureless waste of space sparsely littered with the wandering cinders of long-expired stars. Firmly under the spell of the inexorable second law, early twentieth-century humanists could see no better destiny for life than merciful extinction.

I realize full well that there is very little left in Freud's body of thought that has not been revised or reviled, disowned or deconstructed. Over the past century, many schools of psychological and therapeutic thought have arisen to challenge the old psychoanalytical orthodoxies. But one remnant of Freud survives significantly, if subliminally. His decision—and that of the behaviorists of his day—to model the study of the human mind on the objective stance of the "hard" sciences has left a lasting imprint on mainstream psychological theory. That imprint remains, even

---

7. Sigmund Freud, *Beyond the Pleasure Principle*, trans. James Strachey (New York: Bantam, 1959), p. 70.

though it is based on a scientific paradigm that is now as antiquated as many of Freud's ideas about history, anthropology, and sociology.

Freud, therefore, provides an instructive baseline for measuring how far we have traveled from that era of preecological science. There is, for example, no hint in his work that evolution unfolds as a tiered series of ecosystems, or of the role that life itself may play in orchestrating the complexity of these mutually supportive patterns. Instead we have the state of nature presented as a "naturally" lifeless arena in which a grim and meaningless struggle for existence plays itself out, and where beauty, nobility, and cooperation are nowhere in sight. Thanatos, the most conservative of instincts, lies at the foundations of the psyche, summoning consciousness back to the peace of "the inanimate state." Freud was not alone in seeing the world that way. Out of a misguided commitment to a sort of village-atheist godlessness, the finest minds of the early twentieth century subscribed to the same bleak vision.

The Boundaries of the Self

The preecological science of Freud's day that became embedded in modern psychological thought preferred hard edges, clear boundaries, and atomistic particularity. It was predicated on the astonishing assumption that the structure of the universe had simply fallen into place by accident in the course of eternity. Accordingly, the psychiatry of the early twentieth century based its image of sanity on that model. The normally functioning ego was an isolated atom of self-regarding consciousness that had no relational continuity with the physical world around it. As late as 1930, well after the Newtonian worldview had been significantly modified and the very concept of atomic matter had been radically revised, Freud, still a respected authority, could write in one of his most influential theoretical papers,

> Normally, there is nothing of which we are more certain than the feeling of our self, of our own ego. This ego appears as something autonomous and unitary, marked off distinctly from everything else. . . . One comes to learn a procedure by which, through a deliberate direction of one's sensory activities and through suitable muscular action, one can differentiate between what is internal—what belongs to the ego—and what is external—what em-

anates from the outer world. In this way one takes the first step towards the introduction of the reality principle which is to dominate future development.[8]

"One comes to learn a procedure. . . . " These are among the most fateful words Freud ever wrote. Whatever else has changed in mainstream psychological thought, the role Freud assigned to psychotherapy, that of patrolling the "boundary lines between the ego and the external world," remained unquestioned in the psychiatric mainstream until the last generation. Moreover, his conviction that the "external world" begins at the surface of the skin continues to pass as common sense in every major school of modern psychology. The "procedure" we teach children for seeing the world this way is the permissible repression of cosmic empathy, a psychic numbing we have labeled "normal." Even schools of psychotherapy as divergent as humanistic psychology could only think of "self-actualization" as a breakthrough to nothing more than heightened personal awareness. As for the existential therapists, they were prepared to make alienation from the universe the very core of our authentic being.

Linked together, a would-be "scientific" psychiatry and a metaphysically naive science had no difficulty obliterating any practical connection between psychotherapy and the natural environment. "Nature," Freud was convinced, "is eternally remote. She destroys us—coldly, cruelly, relentlessly."

What does the caring therapist do with ideas as cheerless as these? Distressed clients arrive bearing the wounds of unresolved infantile fears and longings, grinding insecurity, debilitating anxieties. Does their physician then drown them in the existential void? Even Freud's maverick student Carl Jung balked at endorsing his mentor's biomedical reductionism when it led to such a desolate conclusion. In search of a therapy that edified and inspired, Jung refused to join Freud in his disconsolate surrender to "the omnipotence of matter." But as a consequence, he soon found himself departing farther and farther from the scientific mainstream, until there was little left of physical nature in his psychology. At least in its most prominent interpretation, Jung's collective unconscious

8. Sigmund Freud, *Civilization and Its Discontents*, trans. James Strachey (New York: Norton, 1961), p. 14.

belongs wholly to the cultural realm; it is filled, not with the tracks of beasts and the vegetative energies, but with high religious symbols and ethereal archetypes. It is a conception that has more to do with Plato than with Darwin.

For Freud and most of his followers, the "reality principle" had to be the scientist's reality; it was the world "out there" as experienced by physicists and biologists from whose ideally objective sensibilities every last trace of emotional bonding, even with one's own body, had been purged. Even so, at one point in his theoretical ruminations, Freud admitted, with the sadly candid stoicism that colored all his thinking, that "our present ego-feeling is only a shrunken residue of a much more inclusive, indeed, an all-embracing, feeling which corresponded to a more intimate bond between the ego and the world about it."

Now this is an interesting concession. It might be seen as the remote origin of ecopsychology, defined as a refusal to settle for that "shrunken residue." Rather, ecopsychology is an effort to salvage the "more intimate bond between the ego and the world about it" as the raw material of a new reality principle.

Psychology as if the Whole Earth Mattered

In 1990, a conference entitled "Psychology as if the Whole Earth Mattered" was held at the Harvard-based Center for Psychology and Social Change. There a gathering of ecopsychologists concluded that "if the self is expanded to include the natural world, behavior leading to destruction of this world will be experienced as self-destruction." In one conference paper, Walter Christie, assistant chief of psychiatry at the Maine Medical Center, observed,

> The illusion of separateness we create in order to utter the words "I am" is part of our problem in the modern world. We have always been far more a part of great patterns on the globe than our fearful egos can tolerate knowing. . . . To preserve nature is to preserve the matrix through which we can experience our souls and the soul of the planet Earth.

Sarah Conn, a Cambridge clinical psychologist who had helped initiate a form of "ecotherapy," put it more dramatically. She contended that "the world is sick; it needs healing; it is speaking through us; and it speaks the loudest through the most sensitive of us."[9]

The environmental philosopher Paul Shepard has invoked this same psychology in speaking of "the self with a permeable boundary . . . constantly drawing on and influencing its surroundings, whose skin and behavior are soft zones contacting the world instead of excluding it. . . . Ecological thinking registers a kind of vision across boundaries."

In their effort to dignify the "soft zones" of the psyche as a new standard of sanity, most ecopsychologists draw in one way or another upon the evocative, though highly controversial, Gaia hypothesis. Developed by biochemist James Lovelock and microbiologist Lynn Margulis in the mid-1970s, the Gaia hypothesis began its career as a biochemical explanation for the long-term homeostasis of the planetary atmosphere. Lovelock and Margulis postulated that the biota, oceans, atmosphere, and soils are a self-regulating system that plays an active role in preserving the conditions that guarantee the survival of life on Earth. If their theory had been given a conventional scientific name (like Biocybernetic Universal System Tendency or BUST, as Lovelock once facetiously suggested) it might have passed quickly and quietly into the professional literature as a mildly interesting speculative exercise. But Lovelock wanted something more colorful. Struck by the fact that the biomass, in its long-term self-regulation, exhibits "the behavior of a single organism, even a living creature," he called the hypothesis "Gaia," borrowing the name of the ancient Greek Earth mother.[10]

The name at once lent the idea an astonishing popular appeal far beyond anything Lovelock and Margulis had wanted. Their brainchild soon became a major talking point among the Deep Ecologists, some of whom saw it as a compelling statement of the vital connectedness of all living things. While some Deep Ecologists express concern that the global perspective of the hypothesis—the image of the Earth as a single superorganism adrift in space—may undercut a sensuous experience of place, others find in it the basis for a quasi-mystical biocentric ethic.

9. Report in the *Center Review*, Center for Psychology and Social Change, an affiliate of the Harvard Medical School, Fall 1990.
10. James Lovelock, *Gaia: A New Look at Life on Earth* (New York: Oxford University Press, 1979).

Some ecofeminists have gone even farther. For them, Gaia represents scientific validation for a legendary "goddess culture" where, once upon a time, the more ecologically sensitive qualities that would later be assigned to women governed the lives of both sexes.

In its search for a theoretical foundation, ecopsychology need not go so far. Gaia, taken simply as a dramatic image of ecological interdependence, might be seen as the evolutionary heritage that bonds all living things genetically and behaviorally to the biosphere. Just that much is enough to reverse the scientific worldview and all psychology based upon it. In place of the inevitable heat death, we have the deeply ordered complexity of natural systems holding out indefinitely against entropic exhaustion. In place of cosmic alienation, we have life and mind as fully at home in the universe as any of the countless systems from which they evolve. More hypothetically, we have the possibility that the self-regulating biosphere "speaks" through the human unconscious, making its voice heard even within the framework of modern urban human culture.

In Search of the Ecological Unconscious

This is the line of thought I have pursued, suggesting that an "ecological unconscious" lies at the core of the psyche, there to be drawn upon as a resource for restoring us to environmental harmony.[11] The idea is speculative, though no more so than Jung's collective unconscious, Rank's birth trauma, Winnicott's pre-Oedipal mother, or Freud's fantasies about the primal horde. For that matter, even the behaviorists' description of the brain as a "meat machine" is no better than a shaky metaphor that obscures more truths than it reveals. Psychology, understood as the deep study of human nature, is inherently speculative; it has no choice but to work from hunches, inspired guesses, and intuition. It can never "prove," only persuade.

In psychology, theories are best seen as commitments to understanding people in certain ways. Whether one accepts or rejects the concept of an ecological unconscious, ecopsychology as a field of inquiry commits itself to understanding people as actors on a planetary stage who

11. Theodore Roszak, *The Voice of the Earth: An Exploration of Ecopsychology* (New York: Touchstone, 1993).

shape and are shaped by the biospheric system. Even if that commitment never qualifies as more than a hypothesis, it can make a significant political difference. By assuming a deep, abiding connection between psyche and Gaia, ecopsychology could produce a timely reappraisal of the environmental movement's political strategy. It might generate a new, legally actionable, environmentally based criterion of mental health that could take on prodigious legal and policy-making implications. To suggest with the full weight of professional psychological authority that people are bonded emotionally to the Earth reads a powerful new meaning into our understanding of "sanity," a meaning that might even achieve the same legal and policy-making force that now attaches to physical hazards like toxic waste.

At the same time, exploring the psychological dimensions of our planetary ecology also gives environmentalists a compassionate new role to play other than that of "grieving greenies" out to scare and shame the public. It makes them allies of the Earth in a noble and affirmative project: that of returning the troubled human soul to the harmony and joy that are the only solid basis for an environmentally sustainable standard of living. It makes them healers rather than hecklers.

The time is clearly at hand to draw up a psychological impact statement for the environmental movement. In its task of saving life on Earth, does this movement believe it has anything more to draw upon than the ethical resolution of a small group of overworked, increasingly frustrated activists who feel they must assume more and more coercive legislative control over the conduct of daily life? Do we believe there is an ecological dimension to the human personality that is both "natural" and universal?

Ecopsychology suggests that the environmental movement has other means to draw upon besides shocking and shaming the public it wishes to win over. Every political movement is grounded in a vision of human nature. What do people need, what do they fear, what do they want? What makes them do what they do: reason or passion, altruism or selfishness? Above all, *what do they love?* The question of motivation sets the tone and shapes the tactics of every political program. Start from the assumption that people are greedy brutes, and the tone of all you say will be one of contempt. Assume that people are self-destructively stupid, and your tactics are apt to become overbearing at best, dictatorial at worst. As for those on the receiving end of the assumption, shame has always been among the most unpredictable motivations in politics; it too easily slides into resentment. Call someone's entire way of life into question, and what you are apt to produce is defensive rigidity. It is elementary psychology that those who wish to change the world for the better should not begin by vilifying the public they seek to persuade, or by confronting it with a task that appears impossible.

Ecopsychology holds that there is a greater ecological intelligence as deeply rooted in the foundations of the psyche as the sexual and aggressive instincts Freud found there. Or rather, to rephrase an obviously inadequate spatial metaphor, the psyche is rooted *inside* a greater intelligence once known as the *anima mundi*, the psyche of the Earth herself that has been nurturing life in the cosmos for billions of years through its drama of heightening complexification. The "greening of psychology" begins with matters as familiar to all of us as the empathic rapport with the natural world that is reborn in every child and which survives in the work of nature poets and landscape painters. Where this sense of shared identity is experienced as we most often experience it, person to person, we call it "love." More coolly and distantly felt between the human and not-human, it is (at least) that sympathetic bonding we call "compassion." In either case, the result is spontaneous loyalty.

Let me return one last time to old Father Freud, who, for all his failings, remains among the richest theoretical talents modern psychotherapy has produced. In his otherwise tough-minded analysis of the inner life, Freud at last felt compelled to grant that our infantile sense of oneness with the world plays one major role in adult life. From it, he believed, arise the fires of Eros: the emotional force that binds the self to others. In its normal, sane relations with the world "outside," he observed,

> The ego seems to maintain clear and sharp lines of demarcation. There is only one state—admittedly an unusual state, but not one that can be stigmatized as pathological—in which it does not do this. At the height of being in love, the boundary between ego and object threatens to melt away. Against all the evidence of the senses, a man who is in love declares that "I" and "you" are one, and is prepared to behave as if it were a fact.[12]

12. Freud, *Civilization and Its Discontents*, p. 13.

Freud's language lacks the poetry his insight demands, but his concession is touched with a persuasive honesty. This is a tribute to the wisdom of the heart by one of the great stoical philosophers. *A man who is in love declares that "I" and "you" are one, and is prepared to behave as if it were a fact.*

But now enlarge that insight; let it reach beyond our social relations to embrace all we have learned of the intricate bond that exists between ourselves and the biosphere that gives us life. Let the "you" become the Earth and all our fellow creatures upon it. Only follow where ecological science leads in its honest effort to understand the uncanny intricacy that links us to our planetary habitat. Somewhere within this emerging vision of biospheric wholeness lies a new, ecologically based conception of the psyche. Freud, who borrowed so much from the poets, might have done well to read one poet more, in whose imagination the ecological unconscious was taking shape. His name was Walt Whitman:

> Was somebody asking to see the soul?
> See your own shape and countenance, persons, substances, beasts, the
>   trees, the running rivers, the rocks and sands.

PART ONE

THEORETICAL
PERSPECTIVES

A LTHOUGH STILL IN its early stages of development, ecopsychology has produced a wealth of new theoretical insights, often drawing upon potentialities that were waiting to be found in Deep Ecology and in existing schools of psychotherapy. In the section that follows, we survey the thought and work of several representative ecopsychologists and environmentalists who have come to share a common interest in understanding the hidden, often irrational sources of our ecological habits.

The range of inquiry is great; it includes Paul Shepard's psycho-historical interpretation of the invention of agriculture and Chellis Glendinning's analysis of technological addiction. Ralph Metzner discerns significant parallels between dysfunctional environmental behavior and familiar psychopathological patterns like denial, psychic numbing, disassociation, and post-traumatic stress disorder. New insights into our consumption habits are offered by Alan Durning and by Allen Kanner and Mary Gomes. Stephen Aizenstat reconfigures the Jungian Collective Unconscious into an ecologically connected "world unconscious"; Anita Barrows traces many of these problems back to our anti-ecological forms of child rearing; and Mary Gomes and Allen Kanner, drawing on ecofeminist insights, extend feminist psychology to include the natural world. Robert Greenway probes the stubbornly deep dualistic tendencies that challenge wilderness therapy; and finally Phyllis Windle, ecologist and pastoral counselor, shows what a scientist's experience of environmental bereavement can teach us about our sympathetic bond with nature.

There are no orthodoxies in ecopsychology. It is best approached as an open and developing field of inquiry where many ideas and techniques can flourish. What else would one expect of a study of the psyche that takes its cue from ecology, the science of inexhaustible diversity and unexpected connectedness?

Nature and Madness

PAUL SHEPARD

P AUL SHEPARD DESERVES to be ranked among the pioneers of eco-psychology. In his groundbreaking 1982 study *Nature and Madness*, he launched the first searching discussion of the interplay between human psychology and humankind's increasingly destructive environmental behavior. His analysis amounts to a radical re-reading of cultural history as well as of individual neurosis. In Shepard's view the ecocidal habits of our species are far from a contemporary aberration on the part of industrial society. He sees them as rooted in a form of "ontogenetic crippling" that reaches back to the invention of agriculture—the crucial point at which human culture achieved a false sense of separation from the natural habitat. Writing as both ecologist and psychologist, Shepard analyzes the changing patterns of child rearing that stem from the major cultural transformations of human history. In focusing upon the "fantasies of power and heroics" that dominate human—mainly male—adolescent development, Shepard substantiates insights about gender roles that have been investigated by ecofeminists and feminist psychologists. Yet, as deeply embedded as our collective madness may be, Shepard offers the hopeful possibility that "an ecologically harmonious sense of self and world is" equally intrinsic in our nature. It is, he tells us, "the latent possession of everyone; it is latent in the organism, in the genome and early experience."

My question is: why does society persist in destroying its habitat? I have, at different times, believed the answer was a lack of information, faulty technique, or insensibility. Certainly intuitions of the interdependence of all life are an ancient wisdom, perhaps as old as thought itself, that is occasionally rediscovered, as it has been by the science of ecology in our own society. At mid–twentieth century there was a widely shared feeling that we needed only to bring businesspeople, cab drivers, homemakers, and politicians together with the right mix of oceanographers, soils experts, or foresters in order to set things right.

In time, even with the attention of the media and a windfall of synthesizers, popularizers, gurus of ecophilosophy, and other champions of ecology, and in spite of some new laws and indications that environmentalism is taking its place as a new turtle on the political log, nothing much has changed. Either I and the other "pessimists" and "doomsayers" were wrong about the human need for other species and about the decline of the planet as a life-support system; or our species is intent on suicide; or there is something we overlooked.

Such a something could be simply greed. Maybe the whole world is just acting out the same impulse that brought an 1898 cattlemen's meeting in west Texas to an end with the following unanimous declaration: "*Resolved*, that none of us know, or care to know, anything about grasses, native or otherwise, outside the fact that for the present there are lots of them, the best on record, and we are after getting the most out of them while they last."[1]

But it is hard to be content with the theory that people are bad and will always do the worst. Given the present climate of education, knowing something about grasses may *be* the greedy course if it means the way to continued prosperity.

The stockmen's resolution might have been in response to newfangled ideas of range management. Conservation in the view of Theodore Roosevelt's generation was largely a matter of getting the right techniques and programs. By Aldo Leopold's time, half a century later, the perspective had begun to change. The attrition of the green world was

1. Hervey Kleckly, *The Masks of Sanity* (St. Louis: Mosby, 1976).

felt to be due as much to general beliefs as to particular policies. Naturalists talking to agronomists were only foreground figures in a world where attitudes, values, philosophies, and the arts—the whole weltanschauung of peoples and nations could be seen as a vast system within which nature was abused or honored. But today the conviction with which that idea caught the imagination seems to have faded; technology promises still greater mastery of nature, and the inherent conservatism of ecology seems only to restrain productivity as much of the world becomes poorer and hungrier. The realization that human institutions express at least an implicit philosophy of nature does not always lead these institutions to broaden their doctrines; just as often it backs them into a more rigid defense of those doctrines.

In the midst of these new concerns and reaffirmations of the status quo, the distance between Earth and philosophy seems as great as ever. We know, for example, that the massive removal of the great Old World primeval forests from Spain and Italy to Scandinavia a thousand years ago was repeated in North America in the past century and proceeds today in the Amazon basin, Malaysia, and the Himalayan frontier. Much of the soil of interior China and the uplands of the Ganges, Euphrates, and Mississippi rivers has been swept into their deltas, while the world population of humankind and its energy demands have doubled several times over. The number of animal species we have exterminated is now in the hundreds. Something uncanny seems to block the corrective will, not simply private cupidity or political inertia. Could it be an inadequate philosophy or value system? The idea that the destruction of whales is the logical outcome of Francis Bacon's dictum that nature should serve "man," or René Descartes's insistence that animals feel no pain since they have no souls, seems too easy and too academic. The meticulous analysis of these philosophies and the discovery that they articulate an ethos beg the question. Similarly, technology does not simply act out scientific theory, or daily life flesh out ideas of progress, biblical dogma, or Renaissance humanism. A history of ideas is not enough to explain human behavior.

Once, our species did live in stable harmony with the natural environment (and in some small groups it still does). This was not because people were incapable of changing their environment or lacked acumen; it was not simply on account of a holistic or reverent attitude; rather,

there was some more enveloping and deeper reason. The change to a
more hostile stance toward nature began between five and ten thousand
years ago and became more destructive and less accountable with the
progress of civilization. The economic and material demands of growing
villages and towns are, I believe, not causes but results of this change.
In concert with advancing knowledge and human organization it
wrenched the ancient social machinery that had limited human births.
It fostered a new sense of human mastery and the extirpation of nonhuman life. In hindsight this change has been explained in terms of necessity or as the decline of ancient gods. But more likely it was irrational
(though not unlogical) and unconscious, a kind of failure in some fundamental dimension of human existence, an irrationality beyond mis-
takenness, a kind of madness.

The idea of a sick society is not new. Bernard Frank, Karl Menninger,
and Erich Fromm are among those who have addressed it. Sigmund
Freud asks, "If the development of civilization has such a far-reaching
similarity to the development of the individual and if it employs the same
methods, may we not be justified in reaching the diagnosis that, under
the influence of cultural urges, some civilizations—or some epochs of
civilization—possibly the whole of mankind—have become neurotic?"
Australian anthropologist Derek Freeman observes that the doctrine of
cultural relativism, which has dominated modern thought, may have
blinded us to the deviate behavior of whole societies by denying nor-
mative standards for mental health.

In his book *In Bluebeard's Castle,* George Steiner asks why so many
men have killed other men in the past two centuries (the estimate is
something like 160 million deaths). He notes that, for some reason, periods of peace in Europe were felt to be stifling. Peace was a lassitude,
he says, periodically broken by war, as though pressures built up that
had little to do with the games of national power or conflicting ideolo-
gies. He concludes that one of those pressures found its expression in
the Holocaust, motivated by unconscious resentment of the intolerable
emotional and intellectual burden of monotheism. Acting as the frenzied
agents for a kind of fury in the whole of Christendom, the Germans
sought to destroy the living representatives of those who had centuries

ago wounded the mythic view of creation, stripping the Earth of divine being and numinous presences, and substituting a remote, invisible, unknowable, demanding, vengeful, arbitrary god.

Steiner approaches these seizures of extermination in terms of collective personality disintegration; his framework has something to offer the question of the destruction of nature. What *is* indicated by the heedless occupancy of all earth habitats; the physical and chemical abuse of the soil, air, and water; the extinction and displacement of wild plants and animals; the overcutting and overgrazing of forest and grasslands; the expansion of human numbers at the expense of the biotic health of the world, turning everything into something human-made and human-used?

To invoke psychopathology is to address infancy, as most mental problems have their roots in our first years of life, and their symptoms are defined in terms of immaturity. The mentally ill typically have infantile motives and act on perceptions and states of mind that caricature those of early life. Among their symptoms are destructive behaviors through which individuals come to terms with private demons that would otherwise overwhelm them. To argue with the logic with which people defend their behavior is to threaten those very acts of defense that stand between them and a frightful chasm.

Most of us fail to become as mature as we might. In that respect there is a continuum from simple deprivations to traumatic shocks, many of which act on fears and fantasies of a kind that normally haunt anxious infants and then diminish. Such primary fantasies and impulses are the stuff of the unconscious of us all. They typically remain submerged, or their energy is transmuted, checked, sublimated, or subordinated to reality. Not all are terrifying: besides shadows that plague us at abyssal levels with disorder and fear, there are chimeras of power and unity and erotic satisfaction. All send their images and symbols into dreams and, in the troubled soul, into consciousness. It is not clear whether they all play some constructive part in the long trail toward sane maturity or whether they are just flickering specters lurking beside that path, waiting for our wits to stumble. Either way, the correlation between mental unhealth and regression to earlier stages of mental life has been confirmed thousands of times over.

The passage of human development is surprisingly long and complicated. The whole of growth through the first twenty years (including physical growth) is our ontogenesis or ontogeny, our "coming into being." Dovetailed with fetal life at one end and adult phases at the other, ontogeny is as surprising as anything in human biology. Anyone who thinks the human creature is not a specialized animal should spend a few hours with the thirty-odd volumes of *The Psychoanalytic Study of the Child* or issues of *The Journal of Child Development*. In the realm of nature, human ontogeny is a regular giraffe's neck of unlikely extension, vulnerability, internal engineering, and the prospect of an extraordinary view from the top.

Among those relict tribal peoples who seem to live at peace with their world, who feel themselves to be guests rather than masters, the ontogeny of the individual has some characteristic features. I conjecture that their ontogeny is healthier than ours (for which I will be seen as sentimental and romantic) and that it may be considered a standard from which we have deviated. Their way of life is the one to which our ontogeny has been fitted by natural selection, fostering cooperation, leadership, a calendar of mental growth, and the study of a mysterious and beautiful world where the clues to the meaning of life were embodied in natural things, where everyday life was inextricable from spiritual significance and encounter, and where the members of the group celebrated individual stages and passages as ritual participation in the first creation.

This seed of normal ontogeny is present in all of us. It triggers vague expectations that parents and society will respond to our hunger. The newborn infant, for example, needs almost continuous association with one particular mother who sings and talks to it, breast-feeds it, holds and massages it, wants and enjoys it. For the infant as person-to-be, the shape of all otherness grows out of that maternal relationship. Yet the setting of that relationship was, in the evolution of humankind, a surround of living plants, rich in texture, smell, and motion. The unfiltered, unpolluted air, the flicker of wild birds, real sunshine and rain, mud to be tasted and tree bark to grasp, the sounds of wind and water, the voices of animals and insects and humans—all these are not vague and pleasant amenities for the infant, but the stuff out of which its second grounding, even while in its mother's arms, has begun. The outdoors is also in some sense another inside, a kind of enlivenment of the fetal landscape (which is not so constant as was once supposed). The surroundings are also that which will be swallowed, internalized, incorporated as the self.

From the start, the experience of such a world is one of constancy. Following an easy birth in a quiet place, the mother is always there, a presence in the tactile warmth of her body. For the infant there is a joyful comfort in being handled and fondled often, fed and cleaned as the body demands. His is a world of variation on rhythms, the refreshment of hot and cold, wind like a breath in the face, the smell and feel of rain and snow, earth in hand and underfoot. The world is a pungent and inviting place with just enough bite that it says, "Come out, wake up, look, taste, and smell; now cuddle and sleep!"

It is a world of travel and stop. At first the child fears being left and is bound by fear to the proximity of his mother and others. This interrupted movement sets the pace of his life, telling him gently that he is a traveler or visitor in the world. Its motion is like his own growth: as he gets older and as the cycle of group migrations is repeated, he sees places he has seen before, and those places seem less big and strange. The life of movement and rest is one of returning, and the places are the same and yet always more.

There is a constancy of people, yet it is a world bathed in nonhuman forms, a myriad of figures, evoking an intense sense of their differences and similarities, the beckoning challenge of a lifetime. Speech is about that likeness and unlikeness, the coin of thought. The child begins to babble and then to speak according to his own timing, with the cooperation of adults who are themselves acting upon the deep wisdom of a stage of life. Initially it is a matter of rote and imitation, a naming of things whose distinctive differences are unambiguous. Nature is a lexicon where, at first, words have the solid reality of things.

In this bright new world there are as yet few mythical beasts, but real creatures to watch and to mimic in play. Play is an imitation, starting with simple fleeing and catching, going on to mimic joyfully the important animals, being them for a moment and then not being them, feeling as this one must feel and then that one, all tried on the self. The child sees the adults dancing the animal movements and does it too. Music itself has been there all the time, from his mother's song to the melodies of birds and the howls of wolves. The child already feels the mystery of kinship: likeness but difference. Animals have a magnetic attraction for the child, for each in its way seems to embody some impulse, reaction, or movement that is "like me." In the playful, controlled enactment of these comes a gradual mastery of the personal inner zoology of fears, joys, and relationships. In stories told, their forms spring to life in the mind and are represented in consciousness, training the capacity to imagine.

The play space—trees, shrubs, paths, places to hide and climb—is a visible, structured entity, another prototype of relationships that hold fast. It is the primordial terrain in which games of imitating adults lay another groundwork for a dependable world and prefigure a household, so that, for these children of mobile hunter-gatherers, no house is necessary to structure and symbolize social status. Individual trees and rocks that were also known to parents and grandparents are enduring counterplayers having transcendent meanings later in life.

To be sure, there is discomfort that cannot be avoided. The child sees with pride that he can endure it, that his body profits by it so that on beautiful days he feels wonderful. He witnesses sickness and death, but they are right as part of things and not really prevalent (how could the little band of fifteen continue if there were dying every day?).

The child goes out from camp with playmates to imitate foraging and then with adults to actually forage. The adults show no anxiety in their hunting, only patience; one waits and watches and listens. Sometimes the best is not to be found, but there is always something. The world is all clues, and there is no end to their subtlety and delicacy. The signs that reveal are always there. One has only to learn the art of reading them.

In such a world there is no wildness, as there is no tameness. Human power over nature is largely the exercise of handcraft. Insofar as the natural world poetically signifies human society, it signals that there is no great power over other people except as the skills of leadership are hewn by example and persuasion. The otherness of nature becomes accessible to humans in fabulous forms of incorporation, influence, conciliation, and compromise. When the male juvenile goes out with adults to seek a hidden root or to stalk an antelope, he sees the unlimited possibilities of affiliation with the environment, for success is understood to depend on the readiness of the prey or tuber as much as on the skill of the forager.

The child is free. He is not asked to work. At first he can climb and splash and dig and explore the infinite riches about him. In time he increasingly wants to make things and to understand what he cannot touch or change, to wonder about that which is unseen. His world is full of stories told; hearing of a recent hunt, tales of renowned events, and epics with layers of meaning. He has been bathed in voices of one kind or another always. Voices last only for their moment of sound, but they originate in life. The child learns that all life tells something and that all sound, from the frog calling to the sea surf, issues from a being kindred and significant to himself, telling some tale, giving some clue, mimicking some rhythm that he should know. There is no end to what is to be learned.

The child does not yet philosophize on this; he is shielded from speculation and abstraction by the intimacy of his psyche with his environment. The child is free, much as the creatures around him—that is, free to be delicately watchful, not only of animals but of people, among whom life is not ranked subordination to authority. Conformity for him will be to social pressure and custom, not to force. All this is augured in the nonhuman world, not because he never sees dominant and subordinate animals, creatures killing other creatures, or trees whose shade suppresses the growth of other plants, but because, reaching puberty, he is on the brink of a miracle of interpretation that will transform those things.

At the end of childhood he comes to some of the most thrilling days of his life. The transition he faces will be experienced by body and ritual in concert. The childhood of journeying in a known world, scrutinizing and mimicking natural forms, and always listening has prepared him for a whole new octave in his being. The clock of his body permits it to be done, and the elders of his life will see that he is initiated. It is a commencement into a world foreshadowed by childhood: home, good, unimaginably rich, sometimes painful with reason, scrutable with care.

The quests and tests that mark his passage in adolescent initiation are not intended to reveal to him that his love of the natural world was an illusion or that, having seemed only what it was, it in some way failed him. He will not put his delight in the sky and the earth behind him as a childish and irrelevant thing. He will graduate not out of that world but into its significance. So, with the end of childhood, he begins a life-long study, a reciprocity with the natural world in which its depths are as endless as his own creative thought. He will not study it in order to transform its liveliness into mere objects that represent his ego, but as a poem, numinous and analogical, of human society.

Western civilized cultures, by contrast, have largely abandoned the ceremonies of adolescent initiation that affirm the metaphoric, myste-rious, and poetic quality of nature, reducing them to aesthetics and amenities. But our human developmental program requires external models of order—if not a community of plants and animals, then words in a book, the ranks and professions of society, or the machine. If the ritual basis of the order-making metaphor is inadequate, the world can rigidify at the most literal level of juvenile understanding and so become a boring place, which the adult will ignore as repetitive or exploit as mere substance.

Harold Searles's remark is to the point: "It seems to me that the *highest* order of maturity is essential to the achievement of a reality relatedness with that which is *most unlike* oneself." Maturity emerges in midlife as the result of the demands of an innate calendar of growth phases, to which the human nurturers—parents, friends, and teachers—have re-sponded in season. It celebrates a central analogy of self and world in ever-widening spheres of meaning and participation, not an ever-growing domination over nature, escape into abstractions, or existential funk.

The twenty-year human psychogenesis evolved because it was adap-tive and beneficial to survival; its phases were specialized, integral to individual growth in the physical and cultural environments of the emergence of our species. And there is the rub: it is to those environ-ments—small-group, leisured, foraging, immersed in natural surround-ings—that we are adapted.[2] For us, now, that world no longer exists. The culmination of individual ontogenesis, characterized by gracious-ness, tolerance, and forbearance, tradition-bound to accommodate a mostly nonhuman world, and given to long, indulgent training of the

2. Kenneth Kenniston, "Psychological Development and Historical Change," in Robert Jay Lifton, ed., *Explorations in Psychohistory* (New York: Simon & Schuster, 1974).

young, may be inconsistent in some ways with the needs of "advanced" societies. In such societies—and I include ours—the persistence of certain infantile qualities might help the individual adapt better: fear of separation, fantasies of omnipotence, oral preoccupation, tremors of helplessness, and bodily incompetence and dependence. Biological evolution cannot meet the demands of these new societies. It works much too slowly to make adjustments in our species in these ten millennia since the archaic foraging cultures began to be destroyed by their hostile, aggressive, better-organized, civilized neighbors. Programmed for the slow development toward a special kind of sagacity, we live in a world where that humility and tender sense of human limitation is no longer rewarded. Yet we suffer for the want of that vanished world, a deep grief we learn to misconstrue.

In the civilized world the roles of authority—family heads and others in power—were filled increasingly with individuals in a sense incomplete, who would in turn select and coach underlings flawed like themselves. Perhaps no one would be aware of such a debilitating trend, which would advance by pragmatic success across the generations as society put its fingers gropingly on the right moments in child nurturing by taking mothers off to work, spreading their attention and energy too thin with a houseful of babies, altering games and stories, manipulating anxiety in the child in a hundred ways. The transitory and normally healthful features of adolescent narcissism, oedipal fears and loyalties, ambivalence and inconstancy, playing with words, the gang connection, might in time be pathologically extended into adulthood, where it would be honored in patriotic idiom and philosophical axiom. The primary impulses of infancy would be made to seem essential to belief and to moral superiority, their repressive nature masked by the psychological defenses of repression and projection. Over the centuries major institutions and metaphysics might finally celebrate attitudes and ideas originating in the normal context of immaturity, the speculative throes of adolescence, the Freudian psychosexual phases, or in even earlier neonatal or prenatal states.

Probably such ontogenetic crippling carries with it into adult life some traits that no society wants but that ours gets anyway, because such traits are coupled in some way with the childish will to destroy and with other sometimes useful regressions, fellow travelers with ugly effects.

Perhaps there is no way to perpetuate a suckling's symbiosis with mother as a social or religious ideal without dragging up painful unconscious memories of an inadequate body boundary or squeamishness about being cut loose.

In our time, youthfulness is a trite ideal, while the idealization of youth becomes mischanneled into an adulthood of simplistic polarities. Adolescent dreams and hopes become twisted and amputated according to the hostilities, fears, or fantasies required by society. Retarded in the unfolding of his inner calendar, the individual is silently engineered to domesticate his integrity and share the collective dream of mastery. Changing the world becomes an unconscious, desperate substitute for changing the self. We then find animal protectionism, wild-area (as opposed to the rest of the planet) preservation, escapist naturism, and beautification, all of which maintain two worlds, hating compromise and confusing complicated ecological issues with good and evil in people.

The trouble with the eagerness to make a world is that, because the world is already made, what is there must first be destroyed. Idealism, whether of the pastoral peaceable kingdom or the electronic paradise of technomania and outer space, is in the above sense a normal part of adolescent dreaming, like the juvenile fantasies of heroic glory. Norman Kiell observes that the "pubescent" is called on to reform while his precognitive self is at the world center, and hence acts to "save mankind from his own nonhuman status"—that is, from the temporary identity vacuum in the transition from juvenile into adult life.[3] The difficulty for our time is that no cultus exists, with its benign cadre of elders, to guide and administer that transition.

And so we come to our own time. The same questions are asked: To what extent does the technological/urban society work because its members are ontogenetically stuck? What are the means and the effects of this psychological amputation? We inherit the past and its machinations. White, European American, Western peoples are separated by many generations from decisions by councils of the whole, small-group nomadic life with few possessions, highly developed initiation ceremonies, natural history as every person's vocation, a total surround of non–human-made (or "wild") otherness with spiritual significance, and the

3. Norman Kiell, *The Universal Experience of Adolescence* (New York: International Universities Press, 1964).

"natural" way of mother and infant. All these are strange to us because we are no longer competent to live them—although that competence is potentially in each of us.

The question of our own disabilities of ontogeny cannot be answered simply as the cumulative momentum of the past coming to bear on the present. The culture of urban technicity works out its own deformities of ontogenesis. Some of these are legacies, while others are innovative shifts in the selective perpetuation of infantile and juvenile concerns. Many aspects of the urban hive are shaped by the industries of transportation, energy use, and state-of-the-art synthesis of materials and products. On the other hand, the city is shaped, designed consciously and unconsciously, by identity cripples, who are deprived in various social and ecological dimensions, yet who are also cripples in the sense of potential capacity, the possibilities of personal realization in the archaic and magnificent environments of the deep past.

Whether blindness is pathological to those living in a cave depends on whether you think of it in terms of personal adaptability or of the inherent potentialities of every member of our species. My view is the latter, but adaptability is the more vaunted trait—adaptability, that is, in the sense of flexibility, a readiness to change jobs, addresses, or beliefs—celebrated by the technocratic ideal of progress in convenience, comfort, safety, insulation, and the stimulus of novelty. This kind of adaptability is not of a citizenship that transcends place and time, but of not yet being adapted, of never finding one's place or time.

Cultural anthropology has often been used as evidence of this contemporary notion of heroic flexibility. A great many ethnographic studies do impress us with the various ways of being human, but few of them emphasize the inexorable direction in all human societies: what all cultures seek is to clarify and confirm the belongingness of their members, even at the expense of perpetuating infantile fears, of depriving their members of the object of their quest for adaptedness, and making their only common ground their nonrootedness.

In this connection it is no surprise that the "adaptability society" celebrates childhood, admires youth, and despises age, equating childhood with innocence, wisdom, and spiritual power. Its members cling to childhood, for their own did not serve its purpose. To those for whom adult life is admixed with decrepit childhood, the unfulfilled promise cannot be abandoned. To wish to remain childlike, to foster the nostalgia for childhood, is to grieve for our own lost maturity, not because maturity is synonymous with childhood, but because then it was still possible to move, epigenetically, toward maturity.

Wide-eyed wonder, nonjudgmental response, and the immediate joy of being are beautiful to see; I hope some kernel of them remains in the heart of every adult. They are sometimes presented as appropriate models for adult attitudes toward nature. But the open ecstasy of the child has its special purposes: a kind of cataloging, preconscious order finding, and cryptic anthropomorphizing that have to do with personality development—at least for the child with a good mother bond. The poorly bonded child, even though troubled, goes through this nature-wonder period, for it is a new "maternal" reality and perhaps is therapeutic. In any case, there is no figurative nature for the child; all is literal. Even in pretending, there is only one reality. The children playing delightedly on the green grass or in awe at an owl in the woods will grow up oblivious to the good in nature if they never go beyond that momentary fascination. When, as adults, they will weigh the literal value of the owl (already realized, for it taught them the name and owlness) against other literal values, such as replacing the forest with a hospital, a sewage system, or an oil well, their judgment is likely to be for progress. With poor initial mother symbiosis, with an inadequate or lackluster place-and-creature naturizing, or without the crucial adolescent religious initiation that uses the symbiotic, literal world as a prefigured cosmos, the adult cannot choose the forest and the owl. The self is still at the center of a juvenile reality. It may be true that the purpose of the childlike pleasure in the outdoors is an end in itself; it is also necessary to the further work of the self going beyond the self.

But I have oversimplified the choices in order to make a point. There is not a choice between the owl and the oil well at all. In our society those who would choose the owl are not more mature. Growing out of Erik Erikson's concept of trust versus nontrust as an early epigenetic concern and William and Claire Russell's observation that the child perceives poor nurturing as hostility—a perception that is either denied and repressed (as among idealists) or transferred in its source so as to be seen as coming from the natural world instead of from the parents (as among cynics)—there arises an opposition that is itself an extension of infantile duality. Fear and hatred of the organic on one hand, the desire to merge with it on the other; the impulse to control and subordinate on one hand, to worship the nonhuman on the other; overdifferentiation on one hand, fears of separation on the other—all are two sides of a coin. In the shape given to a civilization by totemically inspired, technologically sophisticated, small-group, epigenetically fulfilled adults, the necessity to choose would never arise.

The effects of the historical march away from nature, resulting in socially assimilated deprivation, can be seen in key elements of the European American personality. The American is not the profligate anti-European; he is, in respect to certain characteristics, the full embodiment of Western, classical, Christian human, enabled by the colossal richness of an unexploited continent to play out the wrenching alienation that began five to ten thousand years ago, with the advent of agricultural practices. Careless of waste, wallowing in refuse, exterminating enemies, having everything now and new, despising age, denying human natural history, fabricating pseudotraditions, being swamped in the repeated personal crises of the aging preadolescent: all are familiar images of American society. They are the signs of private nightmares of incoherence and disorder in broken climates where technologies in pursuit of mastery create ever-worsening problems—private nightmares expanded to a social level.

All Westerners are heir, not only to the self-justifications of recent technophilic Promethean impulses, but to the legacy of the whole. We may now be the possessors of the world's flimsiest identity structure, the products of a prolonged tinkering with ontogenesis—by Paleolithic standards, childish adults. Because of this arrested development, modern society continues to work, for it requires dependence. But the private cost is massive therapy, escapism, intoxicants, narcotics, fits of destruction and rage, enormous grief, subordination to hierarchies that exhibit this callow ineptitude at every level, and, perhaps worst of all, a readiness to strike back at a natural world that we dimly perceive as having failed us. From this erosion of human nurturing comes the failure of the passages of the life cycle and the exhaustion of our ecological accords.

In the city-world of today, infinite wants are pursued as though the environment were an amnion and technology a placenta. Unlike the cultures of submissive obedience, those of willful, proud disengagement, or those obsessed with guilt and pollution, this made world is the home to dreams of omnipotence and immediate satisfaction. There is no mother of limited resources or father of rigid discipline, only a self in a fluid system.

The high percentage of neuroses in Western society seems often to be interpreted as a sign of a highly stressful "life-style." If you add to it— or see it acted out as—the insanities of nationalism, war, and biome busting, it seems a matter less of life-style than of an epidemic of the psychopathic mutilation of ontogeny. Characteristic of the schizoid features of this immature subjectivity is difficulty differentiating among fantasy, dream, and reality. The inability to know whether one's experiences originate in night dreaming, daydreaming, or veridical reality is one of the most familiar disabilities of seriously ill mental patients. Drug use and New Age psychedelic athletics in search of a different reality, even the semantics of using "fantasy" as synonymous with creative imagination and "dream" with inspiration, suggest an underlying confusion. They are like travesties of the valid adolescent karma that expresses the religious necessity of transcendence. The fears associated with this confusion in adults are genuinely frightening. The anguished yearning for something lost is inescapable for those not in psychiatric care or on weekend psychic sprees, but who live daily in time-serving labor, overdense groups, and polluted surroundings. Blurry aspirations are formulated in concealed infantilisms and mediated in spectator entertainment, addiction to worldwide news, and religious revivalism.

Much of this has been said before, but not so often in terms of the relationship of the human to the nonhuman. Even as socially intense as we are, much of the unconscious life of the individual is rooted in interaction with otherness that goes beyond our own kind, interacting with it very early in personal growth, not as an alternative to human socialization, but as an adjunct to it. The fetus is suspended in water, tuned to the mother's chemistry and the biological rhythms that are keyed to the day and seasonal cycles. The respiratory interface between the newborn and the air imprints a connection between consciousness (or wisdom) and breath. Gravity sets the tone of all muscle and becomes a major counterplayer in all movement. Identity formation grows from the subjective separation of self from not-self, living from nonliving, human from nonhuman; it proceeds in speech to employ plant and animal taxonomy as a means of conceptual thought and as a model of relatedness. Games and stories involving animals serve as projections for the discovery of the plurality of the self. The environment of play, the juvenile home range, is the gestalt and creative focus of the face or matrix of nature. Initiatory ordeals in wilderness solitude and the ecological messages conveyed by myth are instruments in the maturing of the whole person.

Only in the success of this extraordinary calendar does the adult come to love the world as the ground of his being. For the child, immersed in the series of maternal/ecological matrices, there are inevitable normal anxieties, distorted perceptions, gaps in experience filled with fantasy, emotional storms full of topical matter, frightening dreams and illusions, groundless fears, and the scars of accident, occasional nurturing error, adult negligence, and cruelty. The risk in epigenesis is that the nurturers and caretakers do not move forward in their role in keeping with the child's emerging stages. If such deprivations are severe enough, the normal fears and fantasies can become enduring elements of the personality. The individual continues to act from some crucial moment in the immense concerns of immaturity: separation, otherness, and limitation. Wrestling with them in juvenile and primary modes, even the adult cannot possibly see them holistically. Some of these omissions and impairments enhance the individual's conformity to certain cultures, and the culture acts to reward them, to produce them by interceding in the nurturing process, and so to put a hold on development. In this way, juvenile fantasies and primary thought are articulated not only in the monosyllables of the land scalper, but in philosophical argument and pontifical doctrine. Irrational feelings may be escalated into high-sounding reason when thrown up against a seemingly hostile and unfulfilling natural world. The West is a vast testimony to childhood botched to serve its own purposes, where history, masquerading as myth, authorizes men of action to alter the world to match their regressive moods of omnipotence and insecurity.

The modern West selectively perpetuates these psychopathic elements. In the captivity and enslavement of plants and animals and the humanization of the landscape itself is the diminishment of the Other, against which people must define themselves, a diminishment revealing schizoid confusion in self-identity. From the epoch of Judeo-Christian emergence is an abiding hostility to the natural world, characteristically fearful and paranoid. The sixteenth-century fixation on the impurity of the body and the comparative tidiness of the machine are strongly obsessive-compulsive. These all persist and interact in a tapestry of chronic madness in the industrial present, countered by dreams of absolute control and infinite possession.

There are two ways of seeing this overall sequence. One is as a serial amputation of the maturing process, in which the domesticated world deflects adolescent initiation and rigidifies the personality into clinging to the collective loyalties, feats of bravery, and verbal idealism of pubertal youth. The era of Puritans and machines fixated on childhood anxiety about the body and its products. The urban/industrial age keyed on infantile identity diffusions, separation fears, and the fantasies of magic power. These truncations of epigenesis are progressive amputations, first at infancy and finally at adolescence.

Alternatively, the initial domestication may be seen as a calamity for human ontogeny, against which subsequent history is marked by cultural efforts to recover a mature perspective without giving up the centralization of power made possible by unleashed fecundity and urban huddling. In this sense, history is characterized as the self-contradictory will to recover the grace and poise of the mature individual, initially reduced to a shambles by the neolithic, without giving up the booty. For example, the psychology of self-actualization, group dynamics, and personal therapy, aimed at healing individuals deprived of appropriate adolescent religious experience, though helpful to the individual, is basically antagonistic to the modern state, which needs fearful followers and slogan-shouting idealists. Thus, the culture counters these identity therapies, and the philosophical realism of a cosmopolitan and sophisticated kind that could result from them, with prior wounds—damage to the fetus and neonate in hospital birth, through the anxieties of the distraught mother; asphyxiation; anesthetics; premedication; the overwhelming sensory shock of bright lights, noisy surroundings, and rough handling; impairment of delivery by the mother's physical condition and delivery posture; and separation of the infant from the mother—all corroding the psychogenic roots of a satisfactory life in a meaningful world.[4]

What can one say of the prospect of the future in a world where increasing injury to the planet is a symptom of human psychopathology? Is not

4. Joseph Chilton Pearce, *The Magical Child* (New York: Dutton, 1977), pp. 45–50, 56–60.

the situation far worse than one of rational choices in an economic system or the equilibration of competing vested interests?

In some ways the situation is far more hopeful. An ecologically harmonious sense of self and world is not the outcome of rational choices. It is the inherent possession of everyone; it is latent in the organism, in the interaction of the genome and early experience. The phases of such early experiences, or epigenesis, are the legacy of an evolutionary past in which human and nonhuman achieved a healthy rapport. Recent societies have contorted that sequence, have elicited and perpetuated immature and inappropriate responses. The societies are themselves the product of such amputations, and so are their uses and abuses of the Earth.

Perhaps we do not need new religious, economic, technological, ideological, aesthetic, or philosophical revolutions. We may not need to start at the top and uproot political systems, turn lifeways on their heads, emulate hunters and gatherers or naturalists, or try to live lives of austere privation or tribal organization. The civilized ways inconsistent with human maturity will themselves wither in a world where children move normally through their ontogeny.

I have attempted to identify crucial factors in such normal growth by showing what might have been lost from the past. Some of this, such as life in a small human group in a spacious world, will be difficult to recover—though not impossible for the critical period in the individual passage. Adults, weaned to the wrong music, cut short from their own potential, are not the best of mentors. The problem may be more difficult to understand than to solve. Beneath the veneer of civilization, in the trite phrase of humanism, lies not the barbarian and the animal, but the human in us who knows what is right and necessary for becoming fully human: birth in gentle surroundings, a rich nonhuman environment, juvenile tasks with simple tools, the discipline of natural history, play at being animals, the expressive arts of receiving food as a spiritual gift rather than as a product, the cultivation of metaphorical significance of natural phenomena of all kinds, clan membership and small-group life, and the profound claims and liberation of ritual initiation and subsequent stages of adult mentorship. There is a secret person undamaged in each of us, aware of the validity of these conditions, sensitive to their right moments in our lives. All of them are assimilated in perverted forms in modern society: our profound love of animals twisted into pets, zoos, decorations, and entertainment; our search for poetic wholeness subverted by the model of the machine instead of the body; the moment of pubertal idealism shunted into nationalism or otherworldly religion instead of an ecosophical cosmology.

We have not lost, and cannot lose, the genuine impulse. It awaits only an authentic expression. The task is not to start by recapturing the theme of a reconciliation with the earth in all of its metaphysical subtlety, but with something much more direct and simple that will yield its own healing metaphysics.

Technology, Trauma, and the Wild

CHELLIS GLENDINNING

CHELLIS GLENDINNING, a clinical psychologist, speaks of herself as a "neo-Luddite" social critic, by which she means someone who explores the full impact of industrial technology on humanity. She has been a pioneer in applying the psychological concepts of trauma and addiction to the ecological crisis. In her book *My Name Is Chellis and I'm in Recovery from Western Civilization*, she explores our disconnection from the Earth as the "original trauma" that has been interwoven with subsequent traumas, such as child abuse or the genocide of indigenous peoples. In her work, she seeks to reclaim the wisdom of native peoples and reconnect the psyche to the primal matrix of the Earth. In this essay, she shows us how the qualities that are hallmarks of substance abuse can be seen in urban-industrial society's addiction to technology. Her diagnosis has significant implications for environmental politics. If people cling to technology and its products in the same way alcoholics cling to liquor, then their behavior is more complex than simple "greed." Ecopsychologists like Glendinning are finding persuasive new ways to change the lives of people in industrial society.

> *That millions of people share in the same forms of mental pa-*
> *thology does not make those people sane.*   ERICH FROMM

I met with a young political activist for conversation last week at my favorite cafe. A profeminist man and founder of an antiwar youth organization during the Gulf War, this twenty-one-year-old lives to explore social issues and act on his convictions. His burning question of the hour concerned technology. "Has television made people less intelligent?" he wondered, and he based his conclusion on the deconstructionist dictate that one speak only from personal experience. His answer was, "Decidedly not." Indeed, this young man's mental capacity was as substantial and his wit as sharp as I had seen in anyone of any age. But I could not help noticing that even before a quadruple *espresso latte* had exploded into his brain cells, my young friend was ranting at 120 words per minute, vibrating in his seat like a rocket poised for takeoff, hurling about words like VPL and Macromind, and answering his own questions in quantum leaps across paradigms unintegrated by any coherent worldview, physical reality, or moral obligation to life.

Like my friend, most of us who inhabit mass technological society find it difficult to understand technology's impact on social reality, let alone on our psyches. Like the tiny aerobic bacteria that reside within computer hardware, we are so entrenched in our technological world that we hardly know it exists. Yet widespread radioactive contamination, cancer epidemics, oil spills, toxic leaks, environmental illness, ozone holes, poisoned aquifers, and cultural and biological extinctions indicate that the technological construct encasing our every experience, perception, and political act stands in dire need of criticism. Further, such a critique requires integration by a coherent worldview, physical reality, and moral obligation to life.

At this point in history, it is essential that we ask difficult and searching questions about the place of technology in our lives. What is the essence of modern technology? How does it structure our lives? Our perceptions? Our politics? How does it shape our psyches? What does it say about our relationship to our humanness and to the Earth? Unfortunately, obstacles to answers are entrenched, like concrete piers at a freeway exchange, in both our social and psychological reality.

I discovered the scope of such obstacles while I was on a promotional tour for my book *When Technology Wounds*. The book is based on a psychological study of technology survivors: people who have become medically ill as a result of exposure to some health-threatening technology. I interviewed Love Canal residents, atomic veterans, asbestos workers, DES daughters, electronics-plant workers, Dalkon Shield users, homeowners whose groundwater had been contaminated, and Nevada Test Site downwinders, as well as sufferers of cancer, environmental illness, chronic fatigue, immune dysfunction, and many other problems.

By all accounts, this population is on the rise. Forty-one thousand Louisiana residents are exposed to 3.5 million tons of toxic landfill along the industrial corridor between Baton Rouge and New Orleans. Thirty million U.S. households, or ninety-six million people, live within fifty miles of a nuclear power plant. One hundred and thirty-five million residents in 122 cities and counties breathe consistently polluted air, while 250 million Americans—every one of us—are exposed to 2.6 billion pounds of pesticides each year, in addition to all the radioactive fallout ringing the globe from Hiroshima, Chernobyl, and the nuclear test sites in Nevada and Kazakhstan.[1]

On the book tour, I suggested that since people everywhere are getting sick from technological exposure, we had best enter into an informed and reasoned conversation about technology. Such a conversation was not forthcoming. In a debate on National Public Radio with MIT Professor Marvin Minsky, the inventor of artificial intelligence, I was asked if I had any objections to computers. I expressed concern that the deadly chemicals used to manufacture computers contaminate the biosphere. I mentioned Yolanda Lozano, a thirty-six-year-old worker from a GTE plant in Albuquerque who died of cancer after being exposed to

---

1. David Maraniss and Michael Weisskoff, "Corridor of Death along the Mississippi," *San Francisco Chronicle,* January 31, 1988; Jay Gould, *Quality of Life in American Neighborhoods* (Boulder, Colo.: Westview, 1986), 2:117–20; Critical Mass Energy Project, "The 1986 Nuclear Power Safety Report" (Washington, D.C.: Public Citizen, 1986); Daniel F. Ford, *Three Mile Island* (New York: Penguin, 1982); *Aerometric Information and Retrieval System: 1988, with Supplemental Data from Regional Office Review* (Washington, D.C.: Environmental Protection Agency, July 1989); *Unfinished Business: A Comparative Assessment of Environmental Problems* (Washington, D.C.: Environmental Protection Agency, Office of Policy Analysis, February 1987), pp. 8–86; Lawrie Mott and Karen Snyder, "Pesticide Alert," *Amicus Journal* 10, no. 2 (Spring 1988), 2; and *Information Disease Almanac, 1986* (Boston: Houghton Mifflin, 1986), p. 129.

chemicals on the job. Professor Minsky replied, "It doesn't matter." Elsewhere on my tour, the conversation ended almost before it began. "Get this woman off the air! She's the stupidest guest you've ever had!" shrieked one talk-show listener. "I can't give up my mammogram!" howled another. "As soon as we take care of this environmental thing," insisted one man at a book fair, "we've got to colonize Mars. It's *imperative* for our belief in the future."

Techno-Addiction

As a psychologist, I compare today's public awareness of the impacts of technology to people's views of alcoholism in the 1950s. Back then, everybody drank. It was more than socially acceptable to drink; it was required. Alcoholics Anonymous was twenty years old and growing, but its members still considered it an embarrassment to belong. In the past forty years, a major revolution has occurred in our awareness of the destructive potential of alcoholism. I see a similar necessity in the coming decade to rethink another dangerous attachment: our addiction to technology.

It is not a new idea that we who live in mass technological society suffer psychological addiction to specific machines like cars, telephones, and computers, and even to technology itself. But the picture is bigger and more complex. As social philosopher Morris Berman says in *The Re-Enchantment of the World*:

> Addiction, in one form or another, characterizes every aspect of industrial society. . . . Dependence on alcohol, food, drugs, tobacco . . . is not formally different from dependence on prestige, career achievement, world influence, wealth, the need to build more ingenious bombs, or the need to exercise control over everything.

The editor of *Science* magazine describes the nation's dependence on oil as an addiction, while Vice-President Al Gore claims that we are addicted to the consumption of the Earth itself.[2] In *Steps to an Ecology of Mind*, evolutionary philosopher Gregory Bateson points out that addictive behavior is consistent with the Western approach to life that pits mind against body. Bateson concludes, "It is doubtful whether a species

2. D. E. Koshland, "War and Science," *Science* 251, no. 4993 (February 1, 1991), 497; Al Gore, *Earth in the Balance* (Boston: Houghton Mifflin, 1992).

having both an advanced technology *and* this strange polarized way of looking at its world can survive."

To clarify this notion that contemporary society itself is based on what I call "techno-addiction," we would do well to remember that no machine stands alone. In other words, we will forever be trapped in a narcissistic "but I want my mammogram" analysis as long as we view technology only as specific machines that either serve us individually or do not. What Lewis Mumford calls the "mechanical order" or the "megamachine" is an entire psycho-socioeconomic system that includes all the machines in our midst; all the organizations and methods that make those machines possible; those of us who inhabit this technological construct; the ways in which we are socialized and required to participate in the system; and the ways we think, perceive, and feel as we attempt to survive within it.

What I am describing is a human-constructed, technology-centered social system built on principles of standardization, efficiency, linearity, and fragmentation, like an assembly line that fulfills production quotas but cares nothing for the people who operate it. Within this system, technology influences society. The automotive industry completely reorganized American society in the twentieth century. Likewise, nuclear weapons define global politics. At the same time, society reflects the technological ethos. The social organization of workplaces, as well as their architecture, reflects the mechanistic principles of standardization, efficiency, and production quotas.

From our everyday experience within mass technological society, we will note that "normal" acts like standing in line, obeying traffic signals, or registering for the draft all constitute acts of participation in this grand machine. Regarding our minds and bodies as disconnected in health and disease, or thinking that radioactive waste buried in the Earth won't eventually seep into the water table, are symptoms of the fragmented thinking that emerges from such a mechanical order.

Technology and society are completely interwoven. "Technology has become our environment as well as our ideology," writes the Dutch social critic Michiel Schwarz. "We no longer use technology, we live it."[3]

3. Michiel Schwarz and Rein Jansma, eds., *The Technological Culture* (Amsterdam: De Bailie, 1989), p. 3.

Vine Deloria, a Sioux Indian and author of many books on Indian history and politics, describes the results of this social-technological imbrication as "the artificial universe":

> Wilderness transformed into city streets, subways, giant buildings, and factories resulted in the complete substitution of the real world for the artificial world of the urban man. . . . Surrounded by an artificial universe when the warning signals are not the shape of the sky, the cry of the animals, the changing of seasons, but the simple flashing of the traffic light and the wail of the ambulance and police car, urban people have no idea what the natural universe is like.[4]

Langdon Winner, in *Autonomous Technology*, moves the idea further, arguing that the artifacts and methods invented since the technological revolution have developed in size and complexity to the point of canceling our very ability to grasp their impact upon us. The socially structured scientific-technological reality that now threatens to determine every aspect of our lives and encase the entire planet is out of control, he asserts.

Total immersion, loss of perspective, and loss of control tip us off to the link between the psychological process of addiction and the technological system. Addiction can be thought of as a progressive disease that begins with inner psychological changes, leads to changes in perception, behavior, and life-style, and then to total breakdown. The hallmark of this process is the out-of-control, often aimless compulsion to fill a lost sense of meaning and connectedness with substances like alcohol or experiences like fame.

Throughout the technological system, the recognized symptoms of the addictive process are blatantly evident. They are obvious in the behavior of those who promote technology to maintain control over society or to inflate their own bank accounts and egos. And they are evident for us all because our experience, knowledge, and sense of reality have been shaped by life in the technological world. Symptoms of the addictive process to be discussed here include denial, dishonesty, control, thinking disorders, grandiosity, and disconnection from one's feelings.

4. Vine Deloria, *We Talk, You Listen* (New York: Delta, 1970), p. 185.

Denial

A hallmark of any addiction is the presence of denial. The practicing alcoholic pretends that everything is normal and holds up appearances at all costs. Similarly, with regard to technology and environmental destruction, a societywide stance of "business as usual" pervades our lives. Denial abounds. The automotive industry at home and abroad keeps cranking out new models of polluting cars. Television runs ads for them. We continue to buy them. The U.S. government denies a link between technological development and global warming, while one president after another calls for more technological development as the answer to environmental disaster. The plastics industry inundates world markets with petroproducts, even using the idea of park benches made from recycled plastic as an excuse for further production. The medical establishment denies the existence of environmental illness. Corporations deny the environmental impact of toxic manufacturing processes.

Technology survivors suffer further pain as they encounter widespread denial that their illnesses are caused by technology—denial by the insurance industry, the justice system, the medical establishment, the media, and even by friends and family. As Love Canal activist Lois Gibbs told me,

> I went to my son's pediatrician, and I said, "Look, there are eight patients who have you as their doctor. All of them are under the age of twelve, all of them have a similar urinary disorder. Why is this? What do you make of the fact that you have eight patients who live within a few blocks of Love Canal who have *the same disease?*" He said, "There is no connection."[5]

Dishonesty

This symptom is acted out by the alcoholic in secret drinking, sneaky behavior, and lying about feelings and activities. With respect to technology addiction, dishonesty reveals itself most blatantly in the behavior of corporations and government agencies whose self-interest lies in purveying offending technologies. We know, for example, that officials at A. H. Robins, the makers of the Dalkon Shield, knew in advance of the

---

5. Chellis Glendinning, *When Technology Wounds* (New York: Morrow, 1990), p. 66.

potential medical risk of their product. Nonetheless, they sent it to market, and when reports and studies indicating ill effects became public knowledge, A. H. Robins claimed complete ignorance.[6]

Control

Addicts need to control their world to maintain access to the source of their obsession. A workaholic I know who directs a small institute is incapable of negotiating even the smallest agreement, because input from others upsets her sense of control. Likewise, today's multinational corporations display an obsession with controlling the world's resources, consumer markets, workers' behavior, and public opinion toward their products.

Let us also consider the very structure of modern technology. The kinds of technologies a society develops are not as absolute or preordained as our ethos of linear progress would have us believe; they express a society's goals, both conscious and unconscious. In mass technological society there exists a striking resemblance between the kinds of technologies produced and tyrannical modes of political power. We could, in theory, focus our technological efforts on inventions that would permit us to meet basic human needs in as sustainable a manner as possible. Instead we strive to develop technologies, from dams to anti-aging creams, that allow us an increasing degree of control over the natural world.

This desire for control often backfires when humans assume a position of extreme dependence on technical artifacts, and the lines blur between who is master and who is slave. What happens to our lives when cars break down or telephones go out? What happens when you don't own a fax machine, a computer, or a car? Technology's mastery over our lives translates into political disempowerment as well. The very conception, invention, development, and deployment of new technologies involves a highly undemocratic social process that is rationalized as "progress." The life experience of technology survivors attests to this fact: they are usually exposed to technological events that rob them of their health and livelihood without any warning or choice.

If the particular kinds of technologies in our midst exist to promote

6. Morton Mintz, *At Any Cost: Corporate Greed, Women and the Dalkon Shield* (New York: Pantheon, 1985), chapter 3.

mastery and power, we might ask, for whom? And over whom? Wind-mills and tepees express democratic and ecological values because the very people who invent, produce, and maintain them are the same people who use them. By contrast, the technologies disseminated in mass society reflect a mentality of control over the natural world, space, other people, and even ourselves. As Jerry Mander points out, running a nuclear power plant requires tight, centralized control by both gov-ernment and industry, first to produce such a capital-intensive project, then to master public opinion, and finally to provide military backup in case of sabotage, accidents, or public protest. The presence of nuclear, biological, and chemical weapons in a nation's arsenal not only controls that nation's enemies; it also frightens and intimidates, and thereby con-trols that nation's own citizens.

Thinking Disorders

Alcoholics and other substance abusers typically employ modes of thought that serve the immediate needs of the addiction, rather than the long-term well-being of the person. This is seen, for instance, in the al-coholic who drinks to alleviate the physical and emotional pain of the hangover.

Likewise, much thinking in mass technological society is dysfunc-tional. Many people embrace the "technological fix" as the answer to so-cial, psychological, and medical problems caused by previous technological fixes. For instance, a proposed government program seeks to cover the oceans with polystyrene chips that, it is hoped, will reflect "unwanted" sunlight off the Earth's surface and save us from global warming. Likewise, some scientists suggest orbiting hundreds of satel-lites around the planet to block the sun's light.[7] This is techno-addictive thinking at its most convoluted.

Grandiosity

The practicing alcoholic's delusion of inflated power is well known. The delusion of grandeur that fuels technological development is less appar-ent, more assumed. This grandiosity insists that mass technological so-ciety is superior to all other social arrangements. It implies that human

7. Jerry Mander, *In the Absence of the Sacred: The Failure of Technology and the Survival of the Indian Nations* (San Francisco: Sierra Club Books, 1991), p. 179.

evolution is linear and always progressive, and that all societies should be judged by the yardstick of technological achievement.

Technological society's main organ of socialization, public relations, purveys the grandiosity of technology. "Master the Possibilities," teases the MasterCard ad. "What Exactly Can the World's Most Powerful and Expandable PC Do? Anything It Wants," promises the Compaq Desk-pro. At the same time, the "smart weapons" unleashed during Desert Storm and televised at home advertise that American technology, and America, are "Number One." Behind this all-too-earnest insistence lies the out-of-control, often aimless compulsion to create ever-increasing expressions of grandiosity—and the hallmark of the addict, to return continually to the source of aggrandizement. We *need* more cars, more televisions, more dams, more new technologies to prove our grandiosity.

Disconnection from Feelings

Alcoholics are brimming with emotions, but they can't express themselves directly or constructively. Instead, their feelings are hidden from view in the shadows of their unconscious minds, and so they deny their feelings and live in a state of frozen emotion.

Likewise, survival in the technological system requires that we act "cool" and behave like machines. The hallmark of technological education is to learn mathematics to quantify reality, and to master fragmented thinking to function in a mechanistic world. Every subject we learn in school seems unrelated to the others.

Mass technological society is structured "top-down," its fragmented nature keeping most of us from ever grasping an understanding of the whole. The Manhattan Project that built the bombs that killed hundreds of thousands of people in Hiroshima and Nagasaki was constructed according to a mechanistic military model. The project included thirty-seven installations scattered across the United States and Canada, each providing one fragment of the production process.[8] At the Los Alamos Laboratory, work was purposefully accomplished with a compartmentalization of tasks and a censoring of communication between scientists that enabled everyone involved to lose his or her sense of vulnerability

8. Richard Hewlett and Oscar Anderson Jr., *The New World, 1939–1946: A History of the Atomic Energy Commission* (University Park: Pennsylvania State University Press, 1962), p. 3.

and to engage in activities the consequence of which could neither be felt nor understood.

The upshot of such an approach to life is that feelings, experiences, and perceptions become disconnected from each other, and the unconscious mind becomes the receptor of repressed feelings. As a result, many of us tend to reside in a semiconscious state: the hideous and subterranean violations around us catalyze our feelings, but unacknowledged and unwelcome by the mechanistic world, we act them out in behaviors we neither feel nor understand. Like dropping the atomic bomb.

We must recognize systemic addiction in mass technological society if we are ever to achieve a state of psychological and technological well-being. The twelve-step recovery movement says that the addict must make "a searching and fearless moral inventory" of him- or herself. On the personal level, this includes claiming responsibility for instances in which we have violated another person's integrity. On the collective level, we would claim responsibility for technological society's uncounted violations against humanity, animals, the plant world, and the Earth. But lest our bleeding hearts overtake the process, let us be alert. As psychotherapist Terry Kellogg tells us, addictive behavior is not natural to the human species. It occurs because some untenable violation has happened *to* us.[9]

And indeed, we have undergone an untenable violation: a collective trauma that explains the insidious reality of addiction and abuse infusing our lives in mass technological society. The *Diagnostic and Statistical Manual of Mental Disorders* defines trauma as "an event that is outside the range of human experience and that would be markedly distressing to almost anyone."[10] The trauma endured by technological people like ourselves is the systemic and systematic removal of our lives from the natural world: from the tendrils of earthy textures, from the rhythms of sun and moon, from the spirits of the bears and trees, from the life force itself. This is also the systemic and systematic removal of our lives from

9. Terry Kellogg, "Broken Toys, Broken Dreams" (Santa Fe, N.M.: Audio Awareness, 1991). Audiotape.
10. *Diagnostic and Statistical Manual of Mental Disorders,* 3d ed. (Washington, D.C.: American Psychiatric Association, 1987).

the kinds of social and cultural experiences our ancestors assumed when they lived in rhythm with the natural world.

Vine Deloria rightfully asserts that we technological people "have no idea" about much of anything residing outside "the artificial technological universe with which [we] are familiar." Human beings evolved over the course of some three million years and a hundred thousand generations in synchronistic evolution with the natural world. We are creatures who grew from the Earth, who are physically and psychologically built to thrive in intimacy with the Earth. A mere three hundred generations ago, or 0.003 percent of our time on Earth, humans in the Western world began the process of controlling the natural world through agriculture and animal domestication. Just five or six generations have passed since the industrial societies emerged out of this domestication process. Our experience in mass technological society is indeed "outside the range of human experience," and by the evidence of psychological distress, ecological destruction, and technological control, this way of life has been "markedly distressing" to almost everyone.

Though largely ignored, evidence jumps from the pages of anthropological texts suggesting that the very psychological qualities so earnestly sought in today's recovery, psychological, and spiritual movements; the social equalities for which today's social justice movements struggle valiantly; and the ecological gains sought after by today's environmental movements, are the same qualities and conditions in which our species lived for more than 99.997 percent of its existence.

Nature-based people lived every day of their lives *in the wilderness.* We are only beginning to grasp how such a life served the inherent expectations of the human psyche for development to full maturation and health. In nature-based people who today maintain some vestiges of their relationship to the Earth and their Earth-based cultures, we can discern a decided sense of ease with daily life, a marked sense of self and dignity, a wisdom that most of us can admire only from afar, and a lack of the addiction and abuse that have become systemic in civilization.

The loss of these psychological and cultural experiences in the face of an increasingly human-constructed and eventually technology-determined reality, and the loss of living in fluid participation with the wild, constitute the trauma we have inherited.

The hallmark of the traumatic response is dissociation: a process by which we split our consciousness, repress whole arenas of experience, and shut down our full perception of the world. Dissociation results not only from direct traumatizing experience, but also from the kinds of social changes that took place in the historical process of domestication. In *Nature and Madness,* Paul Shepard describes this process as the initiation of a heretofore unheard-of tame/wild dichotomy in which all things considered tame (domesticated seedlings, captured animals, and the mechanical and controlling mentality required to keep them alive) are prized and protected, while all things considered wild ("weeds," wild animals, and the fluid, participatory way of being human) are considered threatening and to be kept at bay.

This split between wild and tame lies at the foundation of both the addictive personality and technological society. Ultimately, such a split imprisons us in our human-constructed reality and causes all the unnecessary and troublesome dichotomies with which we grapple today—from male/female and mind/body, to secular/sacred and technological/Earth-based.

Technological society's dislocation from the only home we have ever known is a traumatic event that has occurred over generations, and that occurs again in each of our childhoods and in our daily lives. In the face of such a breach, symptoms of traumatic stress are no longer the rare event caused by a freak accident or battering weather, but the stuff of every man and woman's daily life.

As human life comes to be structured increasingly by mechanistic means, the psyche restructures itself to survive. The technological construct erodes primary sources of satisfaction once found routinely in life in the wilds, such as physical nourishment, vital community, fresh food, continuity between work and meaning, unhindered participation in life experiences, personal choices, community decisions, and spiritual connection with the natural world. These are the needs we were born to have satisfied. In the absence of these we will not be healthy. In their absence, bereft and in shock, the psyche finds some temporary satisfaction in pursuing secondary sources like drugs, violence, sex, material possessions, and machines. While these stimulants may satisfy in the moment, they can never truly fulfill primary needs. And so the addictive process is born. We become obsessed with secondary sources as if our lives depended on them.

Today the world is awash in a sea of both personal and collective addictions: alcoholism, drug abuse, sex addiction, consumerism, eating disorders, codependence, and war making. In her book *Co-Dependence*, psychotherapist Anne Wilson Schaef points out that beneath these behaviors lies an identifiable disease process "whose assumptions, feelings, behaviors, and lack of spirit lead to a process of nonliving that is progressively death-oriented." While her words describe the addictive process of individuals, they also characterize the techno-addiction of a civilization. Society is addicted to specific technologies like cars, supercomputers, and biological weapons, all of which facilitate an unhealthy propensity to control, numb the psyche from pain, and momentarily feed a craving for power.

Techno-addiction is also an addiction to a way of perceiving, experiencing, and thinking. As the world has become less organic and more dependent on techno-fixes for problems created by earlier techno-fixes, humans have substituted a new worldview for one once filled with clean rushing waters, coyotes, constellations of stars, tales of the ancestors, and people working together in sacred purpose. But the ancestors from the Western world took on the crucial task of redefining their worldview in a state of psychic dislocation, and so they ended up projecting a worldview that reflects the rage, terror, and dissociation of the traumatized state. They dreamed a world not of which humans are fully part, but one that we can define, compartmentalize, and control. They created linear perspective, the scientific-technological paradigm, and the mechanistic worldview.

Life on Earth encased in the product of such a construction is, to quote the Hopi, hopelessly *koyaanisqatsi,* or out of balance. As a psychologist, I believe that to address this imbalance at its roots will require more than public policy, regulation, or legislation. It will require a collective psychological process to heal us technological peoples who, through a mechanized culture, have lost touch with our essential humanity.

The Psychopathology of the Human-Nature Relationship

RALPH METZNER

RALPH METZNER IS AMONG the leading theorists of "green psychology." In this essay, he critiques the many ideas that have been put forward to explain the alienation between the human species and the natural world. His survey is an instructive example of how standard psychological categories (addiction, dissociation, autism, amnesia) might be used as "diagnostic metaphors" to illuminate a central ecological question: how to identify the historical transition that accounts for human beings' peculiar capacity to distance themselves from their habitat—especially as that distancing has been exaggerated in the religious and scientific beliefs of Western society.

―――――――――――

Several different diagnostic metaphors have been proposed to explain the ecologically disastrous split—the pathological alienation—between human consciousness and the rest of the biosphere. None of these psychological diagnoses have been made by psychologists, who seem to have taken no interest in this question thus far. From one point of view these concepts are metaphors, analogies transferred from the realm of individual psychopathology to society or even to the entire species and its relation to the nonhuman natural world. From another, they are diagnostic tools that could be applied to the realm of collective or mass psychology, on a par with Wilhelm Reich's *Mass Psychology of Fascism* or Lloyd deMause's psychoanalytic interpretations of (mostly modern) historic events. In any case, the purpose of such diagnostic speculation is the same: to discern the nature of the psychological disturbance that has *Homo sapiens* in its grip, so that we can apply psychotherapeutic techniques and treatments to the amelioration of the present eco-catastrophe.

Paul Shepard in his book *Nature and Madness* was the first person to articulate a psychopathological metaphor for our destructive and exploitative treatment of the natural world. Drawing on the work of psychoanalytic developmental psychologists such as Erik Erikson and Harold Searles, Shepard brilliantly dissected the cultural pathology of Western Judeo-Christian civilization as a case of arrested development, or what he called "ontogenetic crippling." He traced the progressive distortion of normal developmental pathways, which could still be seen in surviving hunter-gatherer societies, through four historical stages: agricultural domestication, the desert fathers, the puritans, and the founders of mechanistic science.

A particularly interesting feature of Shepard's analysis is his discussion of the interplay between neoteny, the extended period of immaturity and dependency of the human child, and the ontogenetic support provided by culture. This long developmental process makes the growing child particularly vulnerable. In the case of a species with such marked neoteny as the human, the failure or disappearance of culturally provided developmental supports would have devastating consequences. In his use of paleolithic hunter-gatherers as models of ecologically balanced societies, Shepard says that with the advent of domestication, approximately twelve thousand years ago, civilized humanity began to pervert or lose the developmental practices that had functioned healthily for hundreds of thousands of years.

He sees two stages in which ancient patterns of development may have become chronically incomplete: infant/caregiver relationships and adolescent transition rites. The distorting process "first began with a slight twist in the life of the child, with events that may only have marred his capacity for elderhood and judgment. . . . The history of Western man has been a progressive peeling back of the psyche, as if the earliest agriculture may have addressed itself to extenuation of adolescent concerns while the most modern era seeks to evoke in society at large some of the fixations of early natality." Shepard argues that agriculture increased the distance between the growing child and the nonhuman or "wild" world of nature: "By aggravating the tensions of separation from the mother and at the same time spatially isolating the individual from the nonhumanized world, agriculture made it difficult for the developing person to approach the issues around which the crucial passages into fully mature adult life had been structured in the course of human existence."[1]

In Erikson's developmental model, adolescence is the time when the child is enmeshed in a conflict between "identity and identity diffusion." The notion of a species-wide fixation at the stage of early adolescence fits with the kind of boisterous, arrogant pursuit of individual self-assertion that characterizes the consumerist, exploitative model of economic growth, where the short-term profit of entrepreneurs and corporate shareholders seems to be not only the dominant value, but the only value under consideration. It also fits with the aggressive and predatory militarism and emphasis on the values and ideals of male warrior cults that have characterized Western civilization since the Bronze Age. Adolescents who have difficulty negotiating the turmoil of this stage often become, as Erikson writes, "remarkably clannish, intolerant and cruel in their exclusion of others who are 'different' in skin color or cultural background." Erikson points out how totalitarian doctrines have a special appeal to youths looking for solid identity structures: "The tempestuous adolescence lived through in patriarchal and agrarian countries . . . explains the fact that their young people find convincing and satisfactory identities in the simple totalitarian doctrines of race, class or nation."[2]

Rites of passage in traditional societies provided guiding structures for negotiating the transition from the family matrix to the larger society. The progressive deterioration and loss of adolescent rites of passage in the modern age is well known. Robert Bly has pointed out how even the

1. Paul Shepard, *Nature and Madness* (San Francisco: Sierra Club Books, 1982), pp. 16, 40.
2. Erik Erikson, *Identity and the Life Cycle* (New York: Norton, 1980), p. 98.

minimal father-to-son apprenticeship bonding that used to exist prior to the Industrial Revolution has eroded. Some of the only remnants of manhood transition rites involving elders are the boot camp and combat initiations by the military. Beyond that, there is only the stunted futility of attempted peer-group initiation, whether in the pathetic form of college fraternity hazing or in the casual violence of juvenile street gangs, where twelve-year-olds carry handguns to school to avenge imagined insults to their "home" band.

Besides the loss of adolescent initiation rites, Shepard points to the "unity pathology" that develops if the earliest stage of infant/caregiver bonding is disrupted or disturbed. Erikson identifies this as the stage where the child's developing sense of self deals with issues of "basic trust vs. mistrust." If this stage is not negotiated successfully, we may have, at best, an attitude of chronic insecurity and, at worst, the disposition to suspicion and violence of the paranoid psychotic. As Shepard says, "The social skills of the newborn and the mother's equally indigenous reciprocity create not only the primary social tie but the paradigm for existential attitudes."[3] Jean Liedloff's studies of mother-infant bonding among the Amazonian Indians and her "continuum concept" support Shepard's assertion that babies and parents in hunter-gatherer societies have an intense early attachment that leads not to prolonged dependency but to a better-functioning nervous system.

Shepard summarizes his theory of ontogenetic crippling by stating that "men [presumably he means "Western industrialized humans"] may now be the possessors of the world's flimsiest identity structure—by Paleolithic standards, childish adults."[4] One of the worst consequences of this collective pathology is "a readiness to strike back at a natural world that we dimly perceive as having failed us." Adults who have basic trust that the world of nature and society can provide for their needs are not likely to be attracted to a worldview that demands a relentless struggle for competitive advantage. Government leaders and opinion makers in the United States are now in the habit of promoting "competitiveness" as the value that the educational system should develop in the nation's children. We are suffering, Shepard says, from "an epidemic of the psychopathic mutilation of ontogeny."

3. Shepard, *Nature and Madness*, p. 85.
4. Shepard, *Nature and Madness*, p. 124.

A related psychopathological metaphor put forward by theologian-turned-*geologian* Thomas Berry is that the human species has become "autistic" in relationship to the natural world. He traces the origin of this autism to Descartes's invention of the mechanistic worldview: "Descartes . . . killed the Earth and all its living beings. For him the natural world was mechanism. There was no possibility of entering into a communion relationship. Western humans became autistic in relation to the surrounding world." Like autistic children, who do not seem to hear, or see, or feel their mother's presence, we have become blind to the psychic presence of the living planet and deaf to its voices and stories, sources that nourished our ancestors in preindustrial societies. This situation can be remedied only by "a new mode of mutual presence between the human and the natural world."

The current version of the diagnostic manual of the American Psychiatric Association, the DSM-III-R, describes autism as a "pervasive developmental disorder" characterized by "qualitative impairment in reciprocal social interaction . . . qualitative impairment in verbal and nonverbal communication and in imaginative activity (such as role-playing, fantasy) . . . and markedly restricted repertoire of activities and interests." Stereotyped movements and behavior, restricted range of interests, obsessive routines, preoccupation with parts of objects, absence of imaginative play and lack of awareness of the feelings of others are all typical of autistic children. These characteristics can readily be observed in many adults of industrial society when compared to those brought up in oral cultures.

The cause of infantile autism is not known; earlier views that it was caused by deficient mothering have given way to the general belief that it is a biochemical brain disorder. Some autistic children respond to vitamin B6 therapy; others to heroic and prolonged efforts by caregivers to dissolve the perceptual-affective barriers. Most are untreatable. It is clearly an extreme form of developmental deficit — and if this diagnosis of our cultural malaise is indeed correct, the prospects for humanity are not good.

A third metaphor from psychopathology that offers considerable insight is the model of *addiction*. We are a society whose scientists and experts have been describing for forty years, in horrifying and mind-numbing detail, the dimensions of global eco-catastrophe. Just think of some of the book-titles: *Silent Spring, The Population Bomb, The Death of Nature, The End of Nature.* Our inability to stop our suicidal and ecocidal behavior fits the clinical definition of addiction or compulsion: behavior that continues in spite of the individual knowing that it is destructive to self, family, work, and social relationships. This metaphor of addiction or compulsion, on a vast scale, also parallels in many ways the teachings of the Asian spiritual traditions, especially Buddhism, which acknowledge suffering as an inevitable dimension of human consciousness and desire as the root of suffering.

One of the first to develop the addiction diagnosis was the Deep Ecologist and mountaineer Dolores LaChapelle in her book *Sacred Land, Sacred Sex.* In a chapter entitled "Addiction, Capitalism and the New World Ripoff," she analyzes the interrelationships between the pursuit of addictive substances, including gold, silver, sugar, and narcotics, and the insidious global spread of the capital-accumulating, growth-oriented industrial society from the sixteenth century to the present. Several other authors have also pointed to the addictive quality of our relationship to fossil fuels, another major force of unrestrained industrial growth and ecological destruction. More generally, one can see the spread of consumerism and the obsession with industrial-economic growth as signs of an addictive society. Chellis Glendinning, drawing on ideas from Louis Mumford and Jacques Ellul, has analyzed the "techno-addiction" that characterizes industrial civilization, with its own compulsive craving for better machines, its pervasive denial, and the blatant attraction to "re-traumatization."

Descendants of the pirate bands of the seventeenth and eighteenth centuries, the modern transnational corporations are operating essentially as high-tech bandits, plundering the biosphere, focusing exclusively on the highest profit rate for their investors. As corporations, they are legal fictions, capital accumulation machines, with not even human interests, values, or ethics to restrain them, much less any concern for the intrinsic value of nonhuman beings. Buckminster Fuller called the multinationals the modern incarnations of mythic suprahuman giants. Nevertheless, since they are giants created by humans, there does exist the somewhat hopeful possibility of humans dismantling or transforming these corporate giants—presumably this is the self-appointed task of the "corporate responsibility" movement.

Yet another analogy is the notion that we as a species are suffering from a kind of *collective amnesia*. We have forgotten something our ancestors once knew and practiced—certain attitudes and kinds of perception, an ability to empathize and identify with nonhuman life, respect for the mysterious, and humility in relationship to the infinite complexities of the natural world. It may be that at several crucial turning points in the history of human consciousness we chose a particular line of development and thereby forgot and neglected something—with fateful consequences. Paul Devereux and his collaborators, in their book *Earthmind*, write, "For a long time now, we have been unable to remember our former closeness with the Earth. Due to this amnesia, the ecological problems now thrust upon us have come as a shock. . . . We notice the emergence of an amnesia that is really a double forgetting, wherein a culture forgets, and then forgets that it has forgotten how to live in harmony with the planet."[5]

As an elaboration of the amnesia metaphor we might consider the possibility of a *"traumatic amnesia."* We know from studies of the effects of child abuse and rape, of combat, of accidents and natural disasters, that where the person experiencing the trauma is in a completely helpless position, the memory of the experience can be completely lost—even though physical effects on the body and symptoms, such as nightmares and panic attacks, may remain. Such buried memories can often be recovered with hypnosis or psychedelic psychotherapy. If this metaphor applies to humanity's amnesia of prior knowledge of our interdependent relatedness, then perhaps there was some event that in a terrifying way threatened our sense of belonging and harmony.

The psychoanalyst Immanuel Velikovsky, in his book *Mankind in Amnesia,* proposed a brilliant theory explaining such a trauma. He argued that planetary near-collisions in prehistoric times caused massive and violent earth changes, leading to almost total amnesia and permanent fear and insecurity among humans. Even if we do not accept his theory of cosmic catastrophe, there are plenty of candidates for extremely violent natural cataclysms, such as volcanic and seismic events, with widespread loss of life and forced migrations, during the last four to five thousand years, as well as earlier. In the fifteenth century B.C., for ex-

5. Paul Devereux, John Steele, and David Kubrin, *Earthmind* (New York: Harper & Row, 1989), pp. 2–3.

ample, a volcanic eruption on the island of Thera in the eastern Mediterranean, accompanied by earthquakes and tidal waves, obliterated the highly advanced ancient Minoan culture—and may have provided the historical prototype for the legend of sunken Atlantis. Other possible events causing traumatic amnesia may have been periods of prolonged rain and freezing, prolonged drought and aridity, sudden weather changes, or invasions by marauding warrior-bands. In medieval Europe it is not difficult to imagine the traumatic effect of Christianity's prolonged onslaught on the pagan nature cults, as well as the Black Death, which wiped out one-third of the population in the fourteenth century. In Chellis Glendinning's view, as in Paul Shepard's, the original trauma leading to human separation from the rest of life was domestication, when "the human relationship to the natural world was gradually changed from one of respect for and participation in its elliptical wholeness, to one of detachment, management, control, and finally domination."[6]

The amnesia metaphor is more hopeful than some of the other models, since it is easier to remember something that we once knew than it is to develop an entirely new adaptation. We can also see that the indigenous peoples of the Fourth World, whether in North and South America, Southeast Asia, or Australia, have been trying for some time to help us remember certain vital attitudes and values that they have preserved and maintained in their own ways of life.

Theodore Roszak, in his book *The Voice of the Earth,* has argued that ecology and psychology need each other and that "repression of the ecological unconscious is the deepest root of the collusive madness in industrial society; open access to the ecological unconscious is the path to sanity."[7] Roszak points out that Jung's idea of the "collective unconscious" originally included prehuman animal and biological archetypes, but later came to concentrate primarily on panhuman religious symbols. He proposes that we take the original meaning and call it the "ecological unconscious" as "the living record of cosmic evolution." This may turn out to be a terminology that has a wide appeal, although I personally prefer Robert Jay Lifton's idea of a "species self." Calling some image or

6. Chellis Glendinning, *My Name Is Chellis and I'm in Recovery from Western Civilization* (Boston: Shambhala, 1994), pp. 70–71.
7. Theodore Roszak, *The Voice of the Earth* (New York: Simon & Schuster, 1992), p. 320.

understanding "unconscious," or even more, reifying it as "the unconscious," may function to keep it unconscious. After all, we are trying to foster ecological *consciousness,* or "ecological conscience," to use Aldo Leopold's term.

Roszak wants to rehabilitate the Freudian *id*: instead of the predatory, lecherous beast of the founder of psychoanalysis, he sees it as the repository of ancient ecological wisdom. "The id [is] the Earth's ally in the preservation of the biosphere . . . [and] Gaia gains access to us through the door of the id." But I do not believe this idea will do what Roszak wants it to do. While it is true that our Western modern child-rearing practices effectively stifle any innate ecological sensibility the child may have, it is also true that in traditional societies ecological knowledge and respect for nature is passed on from parents and elders to children and without such training does not just emerge. This is one of the reasons why the disruption of traditional cultures has been so environmentally devastating. "Open access to the ecological unconscious," whatever that may mean, is not going to be sufficient for a path to sanity, unless supplemented by a recovery of ancient traditions of initiation and ritual celebration and a strong dose of ecological literacy.

In contrast to the Freudian and post-Freudian view of the centrality of repression in the creation of "the unconscious," there has been in recent years a revival of interest in the concept of *dissociation*. Dissociative disorders, such as "post-traumatic stress disorder" (PTSD) and "multiple personality disorder" (MPD), are being diagnosed much more frequently, though it is not known whether this is because of an increase in the actual occurrence of such disorders or because of improved recognition of conditions previously misunderstood. Dissociation is a normal and natural cognitive function, the opposite of association. Dissociation plays a role in hypnotic and other forms of trance, when we progressively disconnect perception of the external world in order to attend to interior images, memories, and impressions. Even the simple act of focusing or concentrating attention clearly involves some degree of dissociation.

In the Freudian view, psychic material (thoughts, images, feelings, etc.) that is in the repressed unconscious (also called *id*) is disorganized, primitive, and childish, functioning according to the "pleasure principle"; whereas the conscious mind (*ego*) functions according to the "reality principle" and is capable of adjusting or adapting to the "demands" of reality in a rational, organized manner. The dissociationist view, as originally put forward by Freud's contemporary Pierre Janet and later in the neo-dissociationist theory of Ernest Hilgard and others, involves a "vertical" separation of strands of consciousness that may be equally well organized, rational, and in touch with reality. For example, the mental and emotional components of a painful experience may be dissociated, so that we remember what we saw and thought, but not what we (appropriately) felt; or conversely, a certain stimulus may trigger a feeling state of panic, but the cognitive memory of what happened remains dissociated. In multiple personality disorder, which has been shown in 99 percent of cases to have developed as a self-protective response to repeated sexual and physical abuse in early childhood, two or more fragments of identity, sometimes called "ego-states" or "alters," are created; these fragments maintain a continuity of their own, often with different names and different personality characteristics. As Hilgard says, "The concealed (or dissociated) personality is sometimes more normal or mentally healthy than the openly displayed one. This accords better with the idea of a split in the normal consciousness rather than with the idea of a primitive unconscious regulated largely by primary process thinking."[8]

The notion of "splitting" of two or more equally rational and organized psychic fragments or identities was also used by Robert Jay Lifton in his analysis of the Nazi doctors, who were able to enjoy listening to Beethoven in the garden and play with their children after a day of torturing and killing people. I believe that this concept of dissociation or splitting provides a more accurate and more useful understanding of the collective human pathology vis-à-vis the environment than the notion of a repressed and primitive "ecological unconscious." The entire culture of Western industrial society is dissociated from its ecological substratum. It is not that our knowledge and understanding of the Earth's complex and delicate web of interdependence is vaguely and inchoately lodged in some forgotten basement of our psyche. We have the knowledge of our impact on the environment, we can perceive the pollution and degradation of the land, the waters, the air—but we do not attend

8. Ernest Hilgard, *Divided Consciousness* (New York: John Wiley, 1986), p. 83.

to it, we do not connect that knowledge with other aspects of our total experience. Perhaps it would be more accurate, and fair, to say that individuals feel unable to respond to the natural world appropriately, because the political, economic, and educational institutions in which we are involved all have this dissociation built into them. Dissociative alienation has been a feature of Western culture for centuries or, in some respects, even for millennia, if Paul Shepard is right.

Elsewhere, I have argued that due to a complex variety of social and historical reasons, a core feature of the Euro-American psyche is a "dissociative split between spirit and nature."[9] We have a deeply ingrained belief that our spiritual life, our spiritual practices, must tend in a direction opposite to our nature. Spirit, we imagine, rises upward, into transcendent realms, whereas nature, which includes bodily sensations and feelings, draws us downward. In some versions of this core image, the contrast between the two realms is even sharper: spirit is not only separated from nature, but incompatible and opposed. The human spiritual is then always regarded as superior to the animal natural.

Paul Shepard calls this the "central dogma of the West" and traces it to the Christian desert fathers, who retreated to the desert the better to mortify the flesh and thus raise the spirit. (Susan Power Bratton on the other hand has argued that the desert fathers were the first ecologically conscious Christians.) Earlier foreshadowings of this idea can be found in the Hebrew Old Testament, in the following passage from Isaiah (55:8), for example: "My ways are not your ways, says the Lord; just as heaven and earth are apart, so are my thoughts separate from yours."

Whenever this dissociative split originated, clearly by the time of the Protestant reformation, the idea was firmly implanted in almost everybody's mind that we have to overcome our "lower" animal instincts and passions and conquer the body in order to be spiritual and attain "heaven" or "enlightenment." This image says that to enter into the city of God, the divine realms, you have to work against your nature; this was called the *opus contra naturam*. In the modern psychological, Freudian version of the ancient split, the conflict is between the human *ego* consciousness, which has to struggle against the unconscious body-based, animal *id,* in order to attain consciousness and truly human cul-

9. Ralph Metzner, "The Split between Spirit and Nature in European Consciousness," *The Trumpeter* 10, no. 1 (Winter, 1993).

ture. Our conflicted relationship with the natural, what Freud called *das Unbehagen in der Kultur,* the discontent of culture, was for him the price we had to pay for the possibility of civilization.

The similarity of the two formulations, the religious and the psychological, lies in this dualism: we could say that throughout the history of Western consciousness there has been a conception of two selves—a natural self, which is earthy and sensual, and tends downward, and a spiritual or mental self, which is airy and ethereal, and tends upward. Perhaps its most vivid formulation is by the eighteenth-century German poet-philosopher Goethe, who formulated this core dualistic image in a famous passage in his drama *Faust.* "Two souls, alas, are dwelling in my breast, and one is striving to be separate from the other." One "holds to the world, with sensual, passionate desire"; the other "rises from earthly mist to the ethereal realms." The story of Faust, with his restless and ruthless quest for knowledge as personal power, strikes us as somehow a mythic key to the European psyche.

The ecologically disastrous consequences of this dissociative split in Western humans' identity become clear when we reflect upon the fact that if we feel ourselves mentally and spiritually separate from our own nature (body, instincts, sensations, and so on), then this separation will also be projected outward, so that we think of ourselves as separate from the great realm of nature, the Earth, all around us. If we believe that in order to advance spiritually we have to go against, to inhibit and control, the natural feelings and impulses of our own body, then this same kind of antagonism and control will also be projected outward, supporting the well-known Western "conquest of nature" ideology. For most people in the West, their highest values, their noblest ideals, their image of themselves as spiritual beings striving to be good and come closer to God, have been deeply associated with a sense of having to overcome and separate from nature.

It does not take much imagination to see how the consequences of this distorted perception have been played out in the spread of European civilization around the globe. And it *is* a distorted, counter-factual image: we human beings are not, in fact, separate from or superior to nature, nor do we have the right to dominate and exploit nature beyond what is necessary for our immediate needs. We are part of nature; we are *in* the Earth, not on it. We are like the cells in the body of the vast living organism that is planet Earth. An organism cannot continue to function healthily if one group of cells decides to dominate and cannibalize the other energy systems of the body.

Furthermore, the idea that the spiritual and the natural are opposed or that spirituality must always transcend nature is a culturally relative concept not shared by non-monotheistic religions or traditional societies. In indigenous cultures around the world the natural world is regarded as the realm of spirit and the sacred; the natural *is* the spiritual. From this follows an attitude of respect, a desire to maintain a balanced relationship, and an instinctive understanding of the need to consider future generations and the future health of the ecosystem—in short, sustainability. Recognizing and respecting worldviews and spiritual practices different from our own is perhaps the best antidote to the West's fixation on the life-destroying dissociation between spirit and nature.

Are We Happy Yet?

ALAN THEIN DURNING

EVERY PSYCHOLOGY HAS a theory of what makes people happy. Ecopsychology raises the following question: is human happiness inevitably in conflict with the needs of the planet? Or are there sources of satisfaction that flourish in harmony with the natural world? In recent decades in the developed world, people have sought happiness in an increasing array of consumer products. This has had a devastating impact on the Earth. In fact, it is widely agreed that consumerism is one of the central roots of the environmental crisis, rivaled only by population growth. In this essay, Alan Durning examines the place of consumerism in modern life. He suggests not only that consumerism is failing in its promise to deliver contentment, but that by diminishing our free time and distracting us from relationships, the consumer culture is actually making us *less* happy.

―――――――――

High rates of economic growth are regarded as signs of economic success, but overconsumption is depleting the planet's resources, creating massive waste, and often making people miserable.

Consumption is almost universally seen as good—indeed, increasing it is the primary goal of U.S. economic policy. The consumption levels exemplified in the 1970s and 1980s are the highest achieved by any civilization in human history. They manifest the full flowering of a new form of human society: the consumer society.

This new manner of living was born in the United States, and the words of an American best capture its spirit. In the age of U.S. affluence that began after World War II, retailing analyst Victor Lebow declared: "Our enormously productive economy . . . demands that we make consumption our way of life, that we convert the buying and use of goods into rituals, that we seek our spiritual satisfaction, our ego satisfaction, in consumption. . . . We need things consumed, burned up, worn out, replaced, and discarded at an ever increasing rate." Most citizens of Western nations have responded to Lebow's call, and the rest of the world appears intent on following.

But the consumer society's exploitation of resources threatens to exhaust, poison, or unalterably disfigure forests, soils, water, and air. The consumers of the world are responsible for a disproportionate share of all the global environmental challenges facing humanity.

Ironically, high consumption is a mixed blessing in human terms, too. People living in the 1990s are on average four and a half times richer than their great-grandparents were at the turn of the century, but they aren't four and a half times happier.

Psychological evidence shows that the relationship between consumption and personal happiness is weak. Worse, two primary sources of human fulfillment—social relations and leisure—appear to have withered or stagnated in the rush to riches. Thus many in the consumer society have a sense that their world of plenty is somehow hollow—that, hoodwinked by a consumerist culture, they have been fruitlessly attempting to satisfy with material things what are essentially social, psychological, and spiritual needs.

How much is enough? When does having more cease to add appreciably to human satisfaction?

Unless we see that more is not always better, our efforts to forestall ecological decline will be overwhelmed by our appetites. We will likely fail to see the forces around us that stimulate those appetites, such as relentless advertising, proliferating shopping centers, and social pressures to "keep up with the Joneses." And we may not act on opportunities to improve our lives while consuming less, such as working fewer hours to spend more time with family and friends. Ultimately, sustaining the environment that sustains our humanity will require that we change our values.

Not since the Roaring Twenties had conspicuous consumption been so lauded as it was in the 1980s in the United States. Personal debt matched national debt in soaring to new heights, as consumers filled their houses and garages with third cars, motorboats, home entertainment centers, and whirlpool baths. Between 1978 and 1987, sales of Jaguar automobiles increased eightfold, and the average age of first-time buyers of fur coats fell from fifty to twenty-six.

Rather than making their owners happy, these things apparently engendered severe nervousness: to protect their possessions, Americans spent more on private security guards and burglar alarms than they paid through taxes for public police forces.

By the consumerist definition, satisfaction is a state that can never be attained. For decades, *Harper's* editor Lewis Lapham, born into an oil fortune, has been asking people how much money they would need to be happy. "No matter what their income," he reports,

> a depressing number of Americans believe that if only they had twice as much, they would inherit the estate of happiness promised them in the Declaration of Independence. The man who receives $15,000 a year is sure that he could relieve his sorrow if he had only $30,000 a year; the man with $1 million a year knows that all would be well if he had $2 million a year. . . . Nobody ever has enough.

If human desires are in fact infinitely expandable, consumption is ultimately incapable of providing fulfillment—a logical consequence ignored by economic theory. Indeed, social scientists have found striking evidence that high-consumption societies, just as high-living individuals, consume ever more without achieving satisfaction. The allure of the consumer society is powerful, even irresistible, but it is shallow nonetheless.

Measured in constant dollars, the amount of goods and services that the world's people have consumed since 1950 is equal to that consumed by all previous generations put together. Yet this historical epoch of titanic consumption appears to have failed to make the consumer class any happier. Regular surveys by the National Opinion Research Center of the University of Chicago reveal, for example, that no more Americans report they are "very happy" now than in 1957. The "very happy" share of the population has fluctuated around one-third since the mid-1950s, despite near doublings in both gross national product and personal-consumption expenditures per capita.

Studies on happiness indicate that the main determinants of happiness in life are not related to consumption at all; prominent among them are satisfaction with family life, especially marriage, followed by satisfaction with work, the leisure to develop talents, and friendships. Oxford University psychologist Michael Argyle's comprehensive *Psychology of Happiness* concludes: "The conditions of life which really make a difference to happiness are those covered by three sources—social relations, work and leisure. And the establishment of a satisfying state of affairs in these spheres does not depend much on wealth, either absolute or relative."

Indeed, some evidence suggests that social relations, especially in households and communities, are neglected in the consumer society; leisure likewise fares worse among the consumer class than many assume. In other words, the very sources of satisfaction tend to get squeezed out as individuals pursue their high-consumption lifestyles.

The fraying social fabric of the consumer society, though it cannot be measured, reveals itself poignantly in discussions with the elderly. In 1978, researcher Jeremy Seabrook interviewed scores of older people in the English working class about their experience of rising prosperity. Despite dramatic gains in consumption and material comforts their parents and grandparents could never have hoped for, they were more disillusioned than content. One man told Seabrook, "People aren't satisfied, only they don't seem to know why they're not. The only chance of satisfaction we can imagine is getting more of what we've got now. But it's what we've got now that makes everybody dissatisfied. So what will more of it do—make us more satisfied, or more dissatisfied?"

The elders Seabrook interviewed felt isolated from their neighbors and unconnected to their communities. Affluence, as they saw it, had broken the bonds of mutual assistance that adversity once forged. In the end, they were waiting out their days in their sitting rooms, each with his or her own television.

Mutual dependence for day-to-day sustenance—a basic characteristic of life for those who have not achieved the consumer class—bonds people as proximity never can. Yet those bonds have been severed with the sweeping advance of the commercial mass market into realms once dominated by family members and local enterprise. Members of the consumer class enjoy a degree of personal independence unprecedented in human history, yet hand in hand comes a decline in our attachments to each other. Informal visits between neighbors and friends, family conversation, and time spent at family meals have all diminished in the United States since midcentury.

The consumer society fails to deliver on its promise of fulfillment through material comforts because human wants are insatiable, human needs are socially defined, and the real sources of personal happiness are elsewhere. Indeed, the strength of social relations and the quality of leisure—both crucial psychological determinants of happiness in life—appear as much diminished as enhanced in the consumer class. The consumer society, it seems, has impoverished people by raising their incomes.

Yet, while consumption fails to make us happy and even contributes to our unhappiness, many of the forces "compelling" us to consume, such as advertising, cultivate and prey on our unhappiness. Even if television commercials or magazine ads fail to sell a particular product, they sell consumerism itself by ceaselessly reiterating the idea that there is a product to solve each of life's problems, indeed that existence would be satisfying and complete if only we bought the right things. Advertisers thus cultivate needs by hitching their wares to the infinite existential yearnings of the human soul.

Entire industries have manufactured a need for themselves. Writes one advertising executive, ads can serve "to make [people] self-conscious about matter-of-course things such as enlarged nose pores [and] bad breath." Advertisers especially like to play on the personal insecurities and self-doubt of women. As B. Earl Puckett, then head of the Allied Stores Corporation, put it forty years ago, "It is our job to make women unhappy with what they have." Thus for those born with short, skinny eyelashes, the message mongers offer hope. For those whose hair is too straight, or too curly, or grows in the wrong places, for those whose skin is too dark or too light, for those whose body weight is distributed in anything but this year's fashion, advertising assures us that synthetic salvation is close at hand.

Another human cost of the consumer society appears to be an acceleration of the pace of life and subsequent loss of true leisure time. In *Good Work*, renegade economist E. F. Schumacher proposed an economic law: "The amount of genuine leisure available in a society is generally in inverse proportion to the amount of labor-saving machinery it employs." The more people value time—and therefore take pains to save it—the less able they are to relax and enjoy it.

Leisure time becomes too valuable to "waste" in idleness, and even physical exercise becomes a form of consumption. In 1989, Americans devoted the wages of one billion working hours to buying such sports clothing as Day-Glo Lycra body suits, wind-tunnel-tested bicycling shorts, rain jackets woven from space-age polymers, and designer hiking shorts. Leisure wear has replaced leisure as the reward for labor.

Most consumers work more than they wish to. More and more people find themselves agreeing with American industrial designer William Stumpf, who says, "We've got enough stuff. We need more time." Harvard University economist Juliet Schor writes in *The Overworked American*:

> Since 1948, the level of productivity of the U.S. worker has more than doubled. In other words, we could now produce our 1948 standard of living in less than half the time. Every time productivity increases, we are presented with the possibility of either more free time or more money. We could have chosen the four-hour day. Or a working year of six months. Or every worker in the United States could now be taking every other year off from work—with pay.

Instead, Americans work the same hours and earn twice the money.

But that attitude appears to be shifting the other way. Schor found that workers in all the core regions of the consumer society express a strong desire for additional leisure time and a willingness to trade pay increases for it.

Although cynics predict that shorter workdays would simply translate into more time watching television, there is abundant reason to believe otherwise. For many people, television is something to do when their creative energy is low, when they are too tired to do something more rewarding. Europeans both work less and watch less television than Americans; Japanese both work more and watch more television.

No one can say yet how strong this preference is for free time over extra consumption. Indeed, the present generation of young Americans believes that being good parents means providing lots of goodies rather than spending time with their children. (According to the survey research of Eileen Crimmins and her colleagues at the University of California, Los Angeles, American high school seniors express a strong desire to "give their children better opportunities than they have had," but not to "spend more time with their children." In high schoolers' minds, "better opportunities" apparently means "more goods.")

Still, in theory, if everyone consistently chose free time over additional money, normal gains in labor productivity would cut consumer-class working hours in half by 2020, giving us abundant time for personal development and for family and community activities.

In transforming the consumer society into a *non*consumer society, or an economy of permanence, we should start by asking ourselves what we really want: for example, do we really want telephone books, newspapers, or magazines for their own sake? Or do we merely want access to the information they contain? In an economy of permanence, that information might be available to us for the same price on durable electronic readers. That would enable us to consult the same texts, but eliminate most paper manufacturing and the associated pollution.

Likewise, people do not necessarily want cars as such; they buy them to gain ready access to a variety of facilities and locations. Good town planning and public transportation could provide that access equally well. In every sector of the economy, from housing to food, there are vast opportunities to disconnect high resource consumption from a high quality of life.

The basic value of a sustainable society, the ecological equivalent of the Golden Rule, is simple: each generation should meet its needs without jeopardizing the prospects for future generations to meet their own needs. We can curtail our use of those things that are ecologically destructive, such as fossil fuels, minerals, and paper. And we can cultivate the deeper, nonmaterial sources of fulfillment that are the main psychological determinants of happiness: family and social relationships, meaningful work, and leisure. Or we can abrogate our responsibilities and let our life-style ruin the Earth.

Lowering consumption need not deprive people of goods and services that really matter. To the contrary, life's most meaningful and pleasant activities are often paragons of environmental virtue. The preponderance of things that people name as their most rewarding pastimes are infinitely sustainable. Religious practice, conversation, family and community gatherings, theater, music, dance, literature, sports, poetry, artistic and creative pursuits, education, and appreciation of nature all fit readily into a culture of permanence—a way of life that can endure through countless generations.

The first step of reform is uncomplicated. It is to inform consumers of the damage they are causing and how they can avoid it. New values never arrive in the abstract. They come entangled in concrete situations, new realities, and new understandings of the world. Indeed, ethics exist only in practice, in the fine grain of everyday decisions. For instance, an environmental ethic will have arrived when most people see a large automobile and think first of the air pollution it causes rather than the social status it conveys, or the frustration it will cause them when they get stuck in traffic or spend precious time hunting for a parking place, rather than the convenience of personal transportation.

For those who choose to live simply, the goal is not ascetic self-denial, but a sort of unadorned grace. Some come to feel, for example, that clotheslines, window shades, and bicycles have a functional elegance that clothes dryers, air conditioners, and automobiles lack. These modest devices are silent, manually operated, fireproof, ozone- and climate-friendly, easily repaired, and inexpensive.

At present, living simply may be an unattainable ideal for most people in the consumer class. People's choices are constrained by the social pressures, physical infrastructure, and institutional channels that envelop them. Most would be immobilized if they abandoned their cars while still living amidst mass-transit-less, antipedestrian sprawl. Few workers have the option of trading extra salary for reduced working hours because few employers offer it, and they could not accept it quickly anyway, with mortgage and car payments, insurance premiums, college tuition, utility bills, and so forth, making demands on their incomes. Thus, a strategy for reducing consumption must focus as much on changing the framework in which people make choices as it does on the choices they make.

The future of life on Earth depends on whether the richest fifth of the world's people, having fully met their material needs, can turn to nonmaterial sources of fulfillment; whether those who have defined the tangible goals of world development can now craft a new way of life at once simpler and more satisfying.

In the final analysis, accepting and living by sufficiency rather than excess offers a return to what is, culturally speaking, the human home: to the ancient order of family, community, good work, and good life; to a reverence for skill, creativity, and creation; to a daily cadence slow enough to let us watch the sunset and stroll by the water's edge; to communities worth spending a lifetime in; and to local places pregnant with the memories of generations.

The All-Consuming Self

ALLEN D. KANNER AND MARY E. GOMES

F REUD CALLED DREAMS the "royal road into the unconscious." In highly industrial society, consumption habits have taken on the dimensions of a vast fantasy life that now rivals the dream as a way of gaining insight into the irrational depths of everyday life. As these fantasies are elaborated through the mesmerizing power of the media and the advertising industry, they grow into a vast collective realm of projected desires, fears, and aspirations. For ecopsychologists, our behavior in the marketplace and the shopping mall represents a rich new field of diagnostic material. In this essay Allen Kanner and Mary Gomes analyze the powerful psychic forces and economic interests that underlie "the all-consuming self." Their conclusions are part of an ambitious ongoing analysis of the narcissistic foundations of the American psyche.

———

During the 1992 global environmental summit conference held in Rio de Janeiro, Brazil, representatives from several Third World countries approached President George Bush to ask him to consider reducing the consumption habits of the United States. They contended that a major cause of the current ecological crisis was the enormous demand for consumer goods emanating from the United States and other industrialized nations. Moreover, it seemed unfair to them that they should be asked to manage their natural resources in a more sustainable manner—often to the detriment of the short-term interests of their economy—while relatively minor concessions were being asked of the richer industrialized nations.

Bush's reply was terse and to the point: "The American way of life is not up for negotiation." To Third World countries, Bush's intransigence was disappointing and discouraging. But the strongest reaction that rippled through the conference, and then around much of the world, was one of outrage at the arrogance behind this statement. What was so holy about the American way of life? How was the rest of the world to deal with such an unyielding position?

Within the United States, however, something quite different was happening. Although some protest was heard, by and large the media and the public were quiet. Bush had struck a nerve. Americans *do* feel as if they have a right to the material comfort and convenience that their superior technology and science have produced. So strong is this feeling that psychologist Paul Wachtel, in his book *The Poverty of Affluence*, writes that "having more and newer things each year has become not just something we want but something we need. The idea of more, of ever increasing wealth, has become the center of our identity and our security, and we are caught by it as the addict by his drugs."[1]

The American addiction to unbridled consumerism only promises to get worse. As plans for the implementation of multimedia technology take form—the so-called information superhighway touted by Vice-President Gore—priority is being given to the technology necessary for around-the-clock interactive shopping. Television sets are being transformed into electronic mail catalogues. The goal is to allow viewers to buy anything in the world, any time of day or night, without ever leaving their living rooms.

But why is this fantasy of effortless consuming so attractive? Why is it that when environmentalists speak of the need to reduce consumption

1. Paul Wachtel, *The Poverty of Affluence* (Philadelphia: New Society, 1989), p. 71.

they arouse such intense anxiety, depression, rage, and even panic? Why is the consumer way of life nonnegotiable?

Fantasies of endless comfort and convenience, of every wish instantly becoming the world's command, are part of a syndrome that psychologists call narcissism. Narcissism is characterized by an inflated, grandiose, entitled, and masterful self-image, or "false self," that masks deep-seated but unacknowledged feelings of worthlessness and emptiness. Narcissistic individuals constantly strive to meet the impossibly high standards of their false self, frequently feeling frustrated and depressed by their inability to do so, but also avoiding at all costs recognizing how empty they truly feel.

Psychologist Philip Cushman has explicitly linked narcissism to consumer culture in the United States. He sees recent historical factors such as urbanization, industrialization, and secularization as having created an increasingly isolated and individualistic American self that bears the dual trademarks of narcissism: appearing "masterful and bounded" on the outside, yet "empty" underneath. American consumer habits reflect both the grandiose and the empty side of narcissism. In terms of the arrogant false self, Americans feel entitled to an endless stream of new consumer goods and services. Material abundance is not only an assumed privilege and a right of the middle and upper classes but proof of the cultural and political superiority of the United States.

At the same time, consumer practices serve to temporarily alleviate the anguish of an empty life. The purchase of a new product, especially a "big ticket" item such as a car or computer, typically produces an immediate surge of pleasure and achievement, and often confers status and recognition upon the owner. Yet as the novelty wears off, the emptiness threatens to return. The standard consumer solution is to focus on the next promising purchase. Perhaps the satisfaction will be more lasting and meaningful the next time. As Cushman describes it, the empty self

seeks the experience of being continually filled up by consuming goods, calories, experiences, politicians, romantic partners, and empathic therapists in an attempt to combat the growing alienation and fragmentation of its era. This response has been implicitly prescribed by a post–World War II economy that is dependent on the continual consumption of nonessential and quickly obsolete items and experiences. In order to thrive, American society requires individuals who experience a strong "need" for consumer products and in fact demands them.[2]

By placing consumerism within the context of narcissism, Cushman has highlighted the psychological aspects of this culturewide problem. We can broaden his work to include an ecopsychological perspective by recognizing that First World consumer habits are one of the two most serious environmental issues the world faces. As Alan Durning states in his extensively researched book *How Much is Enough?*:

> Only population growth rivals consumption as a cause of ecological decline, and at least population growth is now viewed as a problem by many governments and citizens of the world. Consumption, in contrast, is almost universally seen as a good—indeed, increasingly it is the primary goal of national economic policy.[3]

It is no coincidence that population growth has been recognized as a global ecological problem while consumerism remains in the good graces of so many governments and individuals. The situation would look quite different if billions of dollars a year were poured into sophisticated advertisements advocating the untold advantages of having many children. Imagine a world with billboards on all the highways depicting grandparents being joyously supported and loved by hordes of adoring children and grandchildren. Consider the impact of thousands of commercials parading the sexiest, happiest, most successful, and most talented people alive deliriously engaged in the daily ecstasy of huge extended families. In such a society, every nook and corner would bear a reminder of the wonders of population growth.

This, precisely, is the situation today regarding advertising and consumerism. Corporate advertising is likely the largest single psychological project ever undertaken by the human race, yet its stunning impact remains curiously ignored by mainstream Western psychology. We suggest that large-scale advertising is one of the main factors in American society that creates and maintains a peculiar form of narcissism ideally

2. Philip Cushman, "Why the Self Is Empty: Toward a Historically Situated Psychology," *American Psychologist* 45 (1990), 599–611.
3. Alan Durning, *How Much Is Enough? The Consumer Society and the Future of the Earth* (New York: Norton, 1992), p. 21.

suited to consumerism. As such, it creates artificial needs within people that directly conflict with their capacity to form a satisfying and sustainable relationship with the natural world.

Advertising, Technology, and Narcissism

It is far from clear that consumerism occurs naturally or spontaneously in humans. According to Christopher Lasch in *The Culture of Narcissism*, industrial leaders in the United States during the 1920s realized that the desire for non-essential goods and products was so weak that it needed active and ongoing cultivation: "The American economy, having reached the point where its technology was capable of satisfying basic material needs, now relied on the creation of new consumer demands—on convincing people to buy goods for which they are unaware of any need until the 'need' is forcibly brought to their attention by the mass media."[4] Creating such false needs was not such an easy task. To do so, comments Benjamin Hunnicutt in *Work Without End*, American industry had to lean ever more heavily on

> the hard work of investors, marketing experts, advertisers, and business leaders, as well as the spending examples set by the rich . . . .[Realizing] this, the business community broke its long concentration on production, introduced the age of mass consumption, founded a new view of progress in an abundant society, and gave life to the advertising industry.[5]

As it stands today, the drenching of the psychological and physical environment with commercial messages has become so complete that people are largely numb to it. According to *Business Week*, the average American is exposed to about three thousand ads a day.[6] Commercials continue to invade areas of life that were once immune to their presence. Movie producers are now routinely paid to place name-brand items in highly conspicuous spots in their films. Cosmonauts are hired to be filmed drinking a popular soda pop while in orbit. Ads are being printed

4. Christopher Lasch, *The Culture of Narcissism: American Life in an Age of Diminishing Expectations* (New York: Norton, 1979), p. 137.
5. Benjamin Hunnicutt, *Work Without End: Abandoning Shorter Hours for the Right to Work* (Philadelphia: Temple University Press, 1988), pp. 42–43.
6. Mark Landler et al., "What Happened to Advertising?" *Business Week*, September 23, 1991.

on hot dogs in Chicago and on eggs in Israel.[7] If corporations could find
a way to sponsor dreams, we are sure they would.

Media analysts have documented the growing control of all commercial outlets (including television, radio, and newspapers) by fewer and
fewer giant, multinational corporations. These corporations, who advertise through the media they own, are also exerting greater influence
on the programs they sponsor, which include public broadcasting. As a
result, programs increasingly reflect values consistent with consumerism
and themselves become a subtle form of advertising. This process is especially blatant on children's cartoon shows, in which many of the toys
being sold during the advertisements are based on the program's animated characters. Perhaps even more disturbing, many schools are now
showing weekly broadcasts of "Channel One," a watered-down news
program with commercials. The implicit school approval of the ads further legitimizes the consumer values they portray.

But what is actually being sold by this cascade of commercials? As
Alan Durning observes,

> People actually remember few ads. Yet commercials have an effect nonethe-
> less. Even if they fail to sell a particular product, they sell consumerism itself
> by ceaselessly reiterating the idea that there is a product to solve each of life's
> problems, indeed that existence would be satisfying and complete if only we
> bought the right things. Advertisers thus cultivate needs by hitching their
> wares to the infinite yearnings of the human soul.[8]

To cultivate consumer needs, advertisers need to create a false image
of the ideal consumer, one which people will wish to emulate. The actors
and luminaries who star in commercials are well suited to this task, as
they are chosen to represent paragons of virtue, sexiness, success, or any
other characteristic that marketers determine desirable. Ads are then designed to convince us that these superior people owe their success,
beauty, and happiness to the purchase of the right product.

Researchers and practitioners in the social sciences have played a major role in the advertising industry as marketing consultants. When psychologists offer their services to corporations, their statistical skills and
therapeutic insights are used to manipulate people for economic gain

7. Durning, *How Much Is Enough?*, p. 118.
8. Durning, *How Much Is Enough?*, p. 119.

rather than to foster well-being. Yet consumerism is so ingrained in American society that this outright abuse of psychological expertise receives no mention in the ethical code of the American Psychological Association.

These marketing efforts create not simply an impulse to buy, but far more seriously, a "consumer false self," an ideal that is taken to heart as part of a person's identity. Many Americans have now been exposed to daily commercials since infancy. Even if they "know better" on an intellectual level, the message of consumerism has gotten through.

We speak of a consumer *false* self for two reasons. Advertisements do not simply exaggerate or distort the truth, they lie. No one's success in business, athletics, or love ever depended on their toothpaste. Modern marketing techniques rely on the strategy that Joseph Goebbels, Nazi Germany's minister of propaganda, called "The Big Lie." Repeat any falsehood frequently enough, and no matter how absurd it is, people will believe it. Project the image of the totally happy consumer in countless commercials, and the false consumer self becomes fully internalized as an impossible goal to which Americans "spontaneously" aspire.

Even more disturbing, the consumer self is false because it arises from a merciless distortion of authentic human needs and desires. From our understanding of narcissism we know that a false self is formed when a child attends to external demands and rewards in order to obtain parental approval and love. When these external pressures conflict with the child's own feelings, these feelings are ignored, until the child comes to believe that the parents' wishes are her or his own. In a similar fashion, American children come to internalize the messages they see in the media and in society at large. They learn to substitute what they are told to want—mounds of material possessions—for what they truly want. By the time they reach adulthood, their authentic feelings are so well buried that they have only the vaguest sense that "something" is missing. Having ignored their genuine needs for so long, they feel empty.[9] But the emptiness is constantly denied. It is far easier, in the short run, to listen

9. The Buddhist term *sunyata,* which refers to the underlying "no thing" from which all else springs, is sometimes translated as "emptiness," but also as "bursting with fullness." We find it striking that consumerism can be understood as stuffing oneself to the point of bursting in order to avoid an inner emptiness that is horrible to behold. Here we wish to distinguish our use of emptiness from sunyata, although understanding these various meanings of emptiness and fullness seems worthy of further pursuit.

to the commercials, which are always beckoning, always promising, always assuring that this time, with this product, it will be possible to fulfill the heart's desire.

Beyond instilling a belief in the wonders of consumption, corporations have worked hard to foster in Americans a fascination with acquiring the very latest commodities. To this end, commercials emphasize the status afforded those who own recently produced items. In 1990 this meant that 12,055 new products were introduced to American drugstores and supermarkets alone, a rate of thirty-three per day, many of them indistinguishable from one another except for packaging. The ecological destruction involved in manufacturing, transporting, marketing, packaging, and storing so many barely discernible items is, of course, immense.

The advertising industry thus subverts the broad and multifaceted human need for novelty by confining it to the narrow realm of new, or at least repackaged, consumer products. In the process it creates an environmentally damaging compulsion among Americans to own "brand new" products, regardless of their true quality. The emphasis on sheer newness also produces a psychological aversion toward technologies and products that are old, used, repaired, or recycled. The satisfaction and intimacy that come from carefully maintaining well-made objects are replaced by the short-lived, impersonal glamour of shiny plastic and gleaming metal.

Modern advertising also promotes an almost religious belief among Americans in the ultimate good of all technological progress, through its claim that there is a product to solve each of life's problems. By implication, material solutions can supplant social, psychological, and spiritual ones, and the cumulative output of multinational corporations represents the pinnacle of all human accomplishment. The United States considers itself the greatest nation on Earth in no small part because of its role as the industrial leader of the twentieth century.

Yet most people will never understand how their computer works nor be able to design an automobile engine. Thus they cannot directly participate in the great technological adventure. Advertisements cleverly offer a way around this predicament. They indicate that through owning sophisticated technology it is possible to identify with the scientific and engineering genius it took to produce it. Buying something is the next best thing to making it. Each new purchase is a chance to ride on the cutting edge of human achievement. In this way the act of consuming technology becomes embedded in the consumer false self as a substitute for real creativity.

Ironically, the marketing industry has become so powerful that it now influences the direction of technological progress. It is a driving force behind the development of interactive media, which has been heralded as the next culture-transforming technology. Corporations are merging madly in order to control the huge markets that are anticipated once televisions, telephones, and computers have been successfully integrated and plugged into global electronic networks. The interactive nature of the media itself promises to be more engaging and convincing than television ever hoped to be. The potential impact of a virtual advertisement, which would create an irresistible multisensory experience for the viewer, is a marketer's dream.

Communication expert Mary King has been tracking the selling of interactive media to the American public. She writes that this new technology

> is being promoted as a Sleeping Beauty story of imagination long dormant, woken by the kiss of a surprisingly affectionate human-computer interface. Among its many promoters, multimedia promises to wake us from our routine, uncreative existence, long cursed by one-way television, boring classroom lectures, stifling corporate hierarchy. Interactive media makes utopian promises about liberating the creative potential in all its users. In a weird sort of Pygmalion twist, it—the technology—is going to animate us—the humans.[10]

These are among the most grandiose claims for a new technology ever made. Beyond convenience and speed, interactive media will reach into our depths to free the imagination.

Not mentioned are the many social and psychological dangers of this technology. People will be vulnerable to a massive invasion of privacy. Huge inequities in access to the information superhighway will occur. Particularly disturbing is the practice of equating "virtual" experience with real life. Newspapers report "computer romances" between individuals who have never met in person, as if this were desirable. Children

10. Mary King, "Interactive Media and the Rhetoric of Empowerment," unpublished manuscript.

are drawn away from playing with their neighborhood friends in order to log on and interact through networks. Educators anticipate interactive programs that will eventually supplant teachers. They equate the computer's ability to match the learning pace of an individual student and instantly provide huge amounts of information with the warmth, care, and presence of an actual adult. Technology is not merely augmenting but *replacing* real human contact. Already Americans are alarmingly comfortable with this idea.

Similar trends are discernible for human interactions with the natural world. Interactive simulations of natural settings are being designed to be so convincing that they can substitute for truly "being there." Children brought up with this technology could easily come to prefer virtual nature to the real thing.

In short, the potential for manipulating the human mind through multimedia technology is likely to be greater than anything that has preceded it. The rational approach would be to proceed extremely carefully and slowly. But the false consumer self is emotionally incapable of such caution. The lure of fantastic new technologies that will propel American society to greater heights is too seductive.

Yet the pace of technological innovation is already so rapid that it is virtually impossible to stay abreast of it, even if one could afford to. We are no longer speaking of "keeping up with the Joneses," but of staying current with the combined output of the multinational corporations, who are far ahead of the Joneses. As a result, Americans chronically experience a sense of material inadequacy that is but momentarily alleviated by any given purchase. The gap between what society offers and what people can afford continually widens.

This gap is dramatically illustrated in a recent *San Francisco Chronicle* article on the growing number of Americans who earn over $100,000 annually but "can't make ends meet." By "making ends meet," of course, they mean maintaining a standard of living that the rest of the world would see as luxurious. But skyrocketing mortgages, taxes, children's college tuitions, and a sagging economy are all making this impossible.

Visibly successful in their careers, by all accounts these high earners should be financially comfortable. Instead, their monetary struggles leave them feeling bitter and ineffective. The most common complaint is that their life choices are severely restricted. Typical is one family who moved fifty miles from Manhattan in order to afford a new suburban home. Now the father spends nearly three hours a day commuting, frequently works Saturdays, and feels terrible that he has so little time for his two daughters. Many in the six-figure bracket spend all of their income each month, leaving them with no savings and constant angst about job security. Others overspend as a way to deny the limitations of their high incomes, and then feel trapped by enormous debt. On top of all this, there is external pressure to buy more. The wife in one couple with a newborn finds having an infant far more expensive than she had been told. She adds: "And then there are those fun gadgets, marketed in such a spectacular way. It makes you feel your child can't live without that Barney sleeping bag."[11]

These "poor" well-to-do Americans, whose earnings are in the top 4 percent in the country, demonstrate how fully ingrained the consumer false self has come to be. In a moment of considerable triumph, the advertising industry has created false needs so potent that the most successful individuals in the richest country in the world perennially scramble to increase their ability to consume. They do so feeling frustrated and angry, but without seriously considering whether the enormous material wealth they already accumulated is truly satisfying. As a crowning touch, the number of products available continues to increase, upping the number of items "necessary" to maintain a good standard of living, and these highly successful people fall even further behind.

At the other end of the economic spectrum, in *Outlaw Culture,* bell hooks speaks to the devastating effects of "systems of representation," such as advertising and other forms of media, on poor people:

> Socialized by film and television to identify with the attitudes and values of privileged classes in this society, many people who are poor, or a few paychecks away from poverty, internalize fear and contempt for those who are poor. When materially deprived teenagers kill for tennis shoes or jackets they are not doing so because they like those items so much. They also hope to

11. Ilyce Glink, "Farewell to Easy Street," *San Francisco Chronicle, This World,* December 19, 1993, p. 5.

escape the stigma of their class by appearing to have the trappings of more privileged classes. Poverty, in their minds and in our society as a whole, is seen as synonymous with depravity, lack, and worthlessness.[12]

A sense of worthlessness, we would add, that fits precisely with our understanding of media-induced narcissistic injury. Within these poor communities, we again find an injured self striving to overcome the humiliation of material lack, yet so caught up in this struggle that it fails to challenge the consumer ideal of the dominant culture.

Further, hooks suggests that pervasive media images of the American Dream have stripped away the sense of dignity and integrity in living simply that was present in her parents' and grandparents' generations. This ability to find meaning and grace in a materially humble life is a hallmark of ecological sanity that has been undermined and nearly destroyed by the messages of corporate advertising.

Thus, no matter where we look, from the frantic and unhappy scrambling of successful professionals to the insult added to injury among the oppressed and disadvantaged, the media-induced consumer false self continues to wreak psychological havoc across the American landscape.

Beyond Narcissism

For American society to become ecologically sustainable, the narcissistic wounding of the public by the advertising industry will have to stop. The currently lost capacity to live in balance with nature will need to be rediscovered and revitalized. Does this mean that every consumer needs to see a therapist? We think not. But by applying our understanding of narcissism to consumerism, ecopsychologists can join forces with the environmental movement on a number of different levels, and in so doing enhance the efforts of both psychologists and activists.

When working with individual narcissists, therapists engage in an intricate three-step process. This involves alternatively challenging the lies of the false self, empathically understanding and "containing" the pain and panic that arise as the false self crumbles, and helping clients to identify, awaken, and nourish long-dormant needs, abilities, and inclinations buried and denigrated by the false self.

12. bell hooks, *Outlaw Culture: Resisting Representations* (New York: Routledge, 1994), pp. 168–69.

A similar multifaceted approach could be used to inspire people to free themselves from the grip of the false consumer self. First, such a program would involve drawing public attention to the massive psychological damage being done by corporate advertising. We would suggest focusing particularly on the vulnerability of American children, who are growing up in an environment of commercial lies and manipulations that is tantamount to corporate child abuse. It would also mean recasting the American love affair with technology as a form of dependence that limits creativity and narrows experience.

As important as these efforts are, there are pitfalls to focusing exclusively on the downside of consumerism. As we have noted, as consumers Americans have already been made to feel deeply inadequate. This sense of inadequcy in turn drives them to continue consuming so outrageously. When they are then criticized for excessive materialism, there is a danger that these admonishments will primarily increase their overall sense of failure rather than significantly alter their environmental habits. We see this today as Americans recycle and support environmental legislation, yet continue to purchase far beyond their means, all the while feeling inadequate both as environmentally responsible citizens and as consumers.

As Theodore Roszak has noted, the environmental movement may have overutilized "shame and blame" tactics in its approach to the public. After years of discouraging news about the state of the environment and dire predictions for the future, people are feeling numb and overwhelmed. In such a state they are particularly vulnerable to right-wing attempts to engineer a "green backlash." The backlash serves as an opportunity for people to avoid guilt and helplessness and to attack the activists who make them feel that way. The same pattern occurs on an individual level when a therapist too aggressively confronts narcissistic beliefs or is insensitive to the pain of a deteriorating false self. When this happens, clients will take any excuse to reembrace their grandiose beliefs, go back into denial, and vilify both therapists and therapy.

It is here that the second step is needed. Concomitant with publicly challenging the consumer false self, ecopsychologists can provide supportive and "guilt-free" contexts in which people can address the complex emotional side of environmental change. There is a great deal of loss involved in giving up the fantasy of a consumer paradise or in falling out of love with technology. Alternative, more sustainable ways of living are bound to appear boring and perhaps even depressing in comparison. Doubt and despair will emerge as people ponder whether change is possible or worth the effort.

As we have discovered in ecopsychology workshops, in a nonjudgmental environment people have much to say about their consumption habits, and do so eagerly. Participants have described a variety of ways that shopping meets, albeit poorly, a host of nonmaterial needs. Especially for women, senior citizens, and adolescents, malls are among the few safe public places to be with other people. Shopping is a less-than-satisfying substitute for actually making things. It is something to do to alleviate depression or celebrate good news, although afterward people frequently wish they had not splurged. We have also heard fascinating speculations about whether malls and supermarkets are the only remaining outlets for satisfying the ancient impulse for gathering food, which for most of human history was the primary means by which people fed themselves. In modern supermarkets, however, gathering is an activity divorced from the cycles of nature, the sources of the food itself, and from the community.

As consumption habits become a legitimate psychological issue, we will learn much more about the ambivalence that many Americans harbor regarding the materialistic nature of their society. At present we hear many stories of therapists reducing their clients' environmental concerns to the "human-only" world, such that dreams about ecological destruction or anxiety concerning pollution and toxic waste are "interpreted" as being symbolic of relationships with parents or important others. In the process, genuine concerns about the natural world are dismissed or simply ignored. Similarly, therapists fail to take seriously the substantial amount of increased stress and depression during the holiday season that is *directly* attributable to the environmentally disastrous commercialization of the last two months of the year. We suspect that the holiday "blues" would be far less severe if people could be freed from expensive obligatory gift giving and instead develop more heart-felt—and ecological—ways to celebrate with their friends and families.

This brings us to the third part of our multifaceted approach to the consumer false self: ecopsychologists can identify and nurture dormant qualities of the self that flourish when connected with the natural world.

The range of untapped capacities is immense. Many forms of pleasure that have been numbed by urban living, from bodily to perceptual to aesthetic to spiritual, come back to life in natural settings. These experiences can form the basis for an expanded sense of self, or what Deep Ecologists call an ecological self. There are many forms the ecological self can take, as we know from the enormous variation in cultural identity found among indigenous peoples.

We can anticipate that, in actively fostering an ecological self, people will experience periods of guilt and shame over their previously negligent or destructive environmental behavior, as well as a desire to make amends. Similar reactions toward past transgressions are quite common in therapy as individuals begin to change. However, when "environmental remorse" arises as part of a healing process and in direct response to a strengthening bond with the land, it leads to more substantial and pervasive change than that induced by moral condemnation and other types of external coercion.

It is common for ecopsychologists whose work includes long wilderness trips or intense urban restoration projects to report dramatic breakthroughs that shake individuals to their core. When the natural world reawakens in every fiber of our being the primal knowledge of connection and graces us with a few moments of sheer awe, it can shatter the hubris and isolation so necessary to narcissistic defenses. Once this has happened, ongoing contact with nature can keep these insights alive and provide the motivation necessary for continued change. It is these experiences that will ultimately fill the empty self and heal the existential loneliness so endemic to our times.

Jungian Psychology and the World Unconscious

STEPHEN AIZENSTAT

O F ALL THE MAJOR schools of modern Western psychotherapy, none has placed greater trust in the autonomous healing capacity of the human psyche than Depth Psychology, the movement initiated by C. G. Jung. The collective unconscious, as Jung formulated it, is the inherited psychic storehouse of the human species. It is filled with the archetypal wisdom we find expressed in our greatest cultural and spiritual treasures. As they make themselves known in dreams, the archetypes, if carefully heeded, can have an authentically therapeutic effect. Stephen Aizenstat is among those who are seeking to carry Jungian theory to still greater depths beyond the realm of human culture. He and his colleagues aim to reconnect the estranged psyche to a more inclusive ecopsychological level Aizenstat calls the "world unconscious." "The new generation of Depth Psychologists," he tells us, "is opening to a reality in which all creatures and things are animated by psyche."

As industrial culture charges on, irreparably damaging the planetary ecosystem, many of us create ever-more-ingenious ways to avoid confronting this threatening reality. We may seek to escape to protective interiors—into our enclosed shopping malls with programmed sound and conditioned air, into our domed stadiums with artificial grass and fluorescent light, into our interior selves. Or we may seek to escape to the outside—to theme parks or an electronic "virtual reality" of our own making and liking. But to retreat, whether to the inside or the outside, avoids the necessary head-on confrontation with the problem of here and now. Avoiding our relationship with nature only hastens the inevitable: the death of the natural world. To face the challenge anew we need, yet again, to hear the question: "What is being asked of us now?"

I remember that, as a boy, I was deeply nourished by the wilderness. I felt comforted by the land, engaged by the animals, touched by the sky, the stones, the canyons, the rivers. Today, I am aware of how the natural world informs my work as a Depth Psychologist. I believe I am being asked to tend the psychic relationships that exist between the creatures and things of our world—to facilitate, in particular, interaction between the psyche of nature and the human psyche. That is the task, the call. Only when there is communication between human beings and the creatures and things of the world will human institutions be responsive to the beauty and splendor that is nature's dream. I believe Depth Psychology has a pivotal and, as yet, unexercised role to play in helping to preserve our natural world.

Through the lens of Depth Psychology, I have discovered that human behavior is rooted most deeply in nature's intentions—that our actions are fundamentally expressions of nature's desire. The rhythms of nature underlie all of human interaction: religious traditions, economic systems, cultural and political organization. When these human forms betray the natural psychic pulse, people and societies get sick, nature is exploited, and entire species are threatened.

Perhaps Depth Psychologists today are being asked to act in the personal and the collective world as naturalists might—naturalists of the inner and outer psyche, witnessing and responding to our relationship with our environment. Perhaps what is being asked of us now is to create an alignment between natures, between souls in persons and soul in the world, a correspondence necessary for the health of all who live on planet Earth.

The Tradition of Depth Psychology

The field of Depth Psychology focuses on bringing conscious reflection to psychic processes, attending particularly to the unconscious. "Depth" refers to an imagined direction—down, behind, underneath. As a method of inquiry, its primary access to the psychic depths is the dream. The two major schools of Depth Psychology are Freudian and Jungian. Both perspectives seek to "uncover" (Freud) or "make conscious" (Jung) the inner unconscious life of the psyche. However, in their attempts to work the inner psychic landscape, both have placed emphasis on the *human* psyche, without giving much attention to the psyche of the world.

Freud postulated the "personal unconscious," the container of one's personal psychological history. The contents of the personal unconscious include instinctual drives such as sexuality and aggression, as well as memories of personal experiences that have been forgotten or repressed. Freudians understand dreams as reflections of the content of the personal unconscious and, therefore, of the dreamer's previously experienced personal life circumstances.

Jung went beyond the notion of the personal unconscious, with its focus on the individual psyche, and offered the possibility of a broader, shared human psyche that he called the "collective unconscious." The collective unconscious is made up of universal psychological forms known as archetypes. The term "archetypes" refers to psychological patterns that appear throughout human experience and can be seen in the motifs of age-old myths, legends, and fairy tales found in every culture throughout the history of the human species. Archetypes, the symbolic forms of the unconscious, can also be seen in the imagery of the dream. Examples of archetypes are "the wise old man/woman," "the tree of life," "the journey," and "home."

Both Freud and Jung, in their extraordinary investigations of intra-psychic reality, emphasized the psychology of the *human* experience. This emphasis also extended to their systems of dream work. Freud's primary interest was the interpretation of the dream image back to the developmental stages of the personal unconscious; Jung's emphasis was on consideration of the dream in terms of the archetypal patterns of the collective unconscious. The approach to the dream in each instance was intended to explore psychic life as it related to the experience of the individual.

It is important to note, however, that Jung, in other areas of his work, reached outward toward the psyches of phenomena of the world. He believed that the central archetype, "the self," had a universal quality, imagined as extending beyond the personal-particular. Also, when discussing the psychological concept of synchronicity (meaningful coincidences of outer and inner events), and the idea of the psychoid phenomenon (the notion that at a certain level the archetype exists in both psychic and physical states), Jung referred to the relationship between the inner human experience and the phenomena in the world. Yet even though Jung broadened his work toward this more inclusive vision of psychological life, contemporary Jungian psychological practice continues to center almost exclusively on the consideration of the human psyche (personal and/or collective)—attending to persona, developing a relationship to anima/animus, realizing the presence of shadow influences, and making conscious the unconscious process of individuation.

From Collective Unconscious to World Unconscious

Although both Freud and Jung developed intricate systems of psychological thought, neither brought particular emphasis to the interconnectedness between human experience and the creatures and things of our world. I believe the task of Depth Psychology today is to extend the work of Freud and Jung to include consideration of the psyche of non-human experience. This more inclusive understanding of psychic reality is currently being explored by a new generation of Depth Psychologists, including James Hillman, Robert Sardello, Robert Romanyshyn, Mary Watkins, and myself, among others. Our broader view of Depth Psychology includes the psychic realities of all phenomena, emphasizing the part of the Depth Psychological tradition that honors psyche in the world. In my work, I have come to call this more inclusive ecopsychological realm of psyche the "world unconscious."

The world unconscious is a deeper and wider dimension of the psyche than that of the personal or the collective unconscious. In the realm of the world unconscious, all creatures and things of the world are understood as interrelated and interconnected. Although there are clear differences in orders of complexity, I make the assumption that all the phenomena in the world possess intrinsic unconscious characteristics—subjective inner natures. I use the term "unconscious" realizing that, for the most part, it is *we* who are unconscious of these inner natures of the world's other inhabitants. These inner natures of the world's organic and inorganic phenomena make up the world unconscious.

At the dimension of the world unconscious, the inner subjective natures of the world's beings are experienced as dream images in the human psyche. In addition, I believe dream images are real, have imaginal weight and body, and act in dreams on behalf of themselves. For example, the elephant that appeared in my dream last night was fully engaged in his activity, not mine. In the dream, I watched as he looked intently at me with shiny black eyes and wide flopping ears. He used his trunk to spray dirt and tiny rocks over his fine-haired rump, his tail all the while swatting flies from his sagging hindquarters. After a time he plodded back to join the rest of the herd. This dream elephant, like all dream images, is alive, has body, and moves about according to his own inner nature.

The idea that all phenomena in the world possess subjective inner natures must be distinguished from the *ego*centric concepts of anthropomorphism (attributing human qualities to nonhuman forms of life), animism (humans attributing living soul to inanimate objects and natural phenomena), and personification (attributing personal characteristics to phenomena in the world). Rather, the idea that all beings are ensouled, in and of themselves, locates the life spark *in* the entity, outside of personal human psychic ownership. In this wider view the human experience exists in a field of psychic relationships, one among the many. Seen through the "eyes" of the world unconscious, the dream image is an independent presence in a broader psychic ecology, a dreamscape where there is room for many beings to "walk around" and be regarded by one another. The elephant that appeared in "my" dream had a life of its own; it visited to interact with me as a fellow creature of the "dreamtime"—perhaps to heighten my awareness of the plight of elephants in the world. From the perspective of the world unconscious, the dreamscape is the worldscape.

The new generation of Depth Psychologists is taking this wider view of psychic life into consideration and opening to a reality in which all creatures and things are animated by psyche. This change in orientation requires a move beyond the personal-particular human psyche into an active psychological relationship with the other species and things on our Earth. Our traditional focus on the relationship between ego and self, with its emphasis on the individual person or culture, is expanding to include contemplation of self and world. From the perspective of the world unconscious everything has psychic depth and is dreaming— animate and inanimate, human-made and non–human-made. Even such things as buildings and tables were first imagined, then constructed out of the dream that moves through us. Dreams, the hallowed windows into the depth of the human psyche, now also provide access to the inner life, the soul, of the creatures and things of our world. Working with dreams, the Depth Psychologist helps cultivate the capacity to hear, from the inside, the voices of those species and objects who help shape our experience, provide the source of our imagination—and who are in need of us.

Another way to hear these voices is to discover, or rediscover, the part of the natural world that is the most authentic source of our individual areas of expertise. The aviator, for example, can find the likeness in nature that feeds his yearning to fly. Perhaps the flight of wild geese is the model for this age-old imperative to take to the skies. Similarly, the engineer can remember how her craft is patterned after activities found in the natural landscape—how she is inspired by the ingenuity of so many of nature's creatures who engage daily in the work of planning and construction, such as the beaver, the termite, the mud swallow.

Underpinning the creative process of human invention are the archetypal patterns of the natural world. As individuals and as professional people, we are called to rediscover the elemental forces that generate and give form to our vocational expression. Once these connections are rediscovered, each of us will know, in a deep and essential way, what part of the restoration of the natural world we have access to and what part we are responsible for preserving.

What would result is a heartfelt empathy between the correspondent creatures and systems in the ecosphere. Imagine a world in which carpenter knows beaver, lawyer knows eagle, philosopher knows the silence of the deep night. With this connection between human consciousness and the natural world reestablished, people will feel compelled to make the journey back to the source in nature that inspires their work and teaches what contribution is asked in return.

Depth Psychological Advocacy

Again let us raise the question, "What is being asked of us now?" In order to build a respectful and sustaining relationship with the world, we must first recover a sensibility that is informed by the psyche of nature, an awareness that our essential psychological spontaneities are rooted most deeply in the psyche of the natural world. We are born out of the rhythms of nature and to destroy nature's psyche is, ultimately, to end our own. The responsibility of the Depth Psychologist is advocacy on behalf of all who share our world. There are at least four general areas in which the Depth Psychologist can play a significant role.

1. Depth Psychology can contribute new knowledge to the contemporary field of applied psychology. The guiding question is: "What would a psychology look like that is based on an *eco*centric worldview rather than an *ego*centric one?" An ecopsychological perspective would demand additions to established notions about psyche, projection, pathology, and treatment. From an ecopsychological point of view, for example, the concept of projection might be seen as working the other way around—with human life carrying the projections and personifications of the soul that reside in the creatures and things of the world. The activity of projection would be imagined as occurring in an intersubjective field that includes the phenomena in the world—a field in which an object, plant, or animal could project its particular subjectivity onto us. Pathology, too, would be resituated in a wider ecopsychological perspective. Depression, for instance, could be viewed as a natural response to the manic condition of the world. Another possibility is to reenvision depression as "ingression," a time of turning inward. As an adjunct to more traditional therapeutic approaches focused on getting over or fixing depression, a person could be encouraged to imagine a soul journey through a winter landscape, finding solace and new possibilities in nature's season of silence. Once "placed" in a psychic landscape mirroring the natural world, an individual would feel located in "a place to be," capable of receiving what nature has to offer.

2. Depth Psychology's research methodologies, particularly phenom-
enological approaches, can be utilized to explore how the human being
interacts with the "voices" of others who share the Earth. Inner psychic
processes such as dreams, visions, and affective states would be investigated and listened to from an *eco*centric perspective. In exploring these
receptive, nonverbal states, the researcher would learn to differentiate
without separating self from world. In fact, the state of mind one brings
to the world very much determines what one experiences of it. Cultivating different ways of listening would foster the ability to hear the diversity of nonhuman phenomena. Special care would be taken to listen
in ways that allowed the voices of Earth's inhabitants to be heard in the
full range of *their* sound.

3. Depth Psychologists would advocate that because the ills of our
world are inextricably tied to our personal pathology, psychotherapy
must be conducted in a context that considers one's relationship to the
plight of the world. To this end, Depth Psychologists can work with the
American Psychological Association (APA) and the American Medical
Association (AMA) to articulate our conviction that the suffering in the
world is reflected in, and interactive with, the suffering of human beings.
The time has come to move beyond the widely held belief that psychological health is solely a function of individual wholeness and nurturing
human relationships. Although this view has obvious therapeutic use-
fulness, it exists within a framework that perpetuates the separation of
person from world and that denies the essential importance of an individual's surroundings. As Depth Psychologists, we must advocate a re-
imagining of psychopathology that takes into account the other
presences in our world.

4. Depth Psychology, with an ecopsychological emphasis, would contend also that physiological illness is connected to our damaged relationship to nature. Our alienation from the rhythms of the natural world
contribute, in a direct way, to our physical suffering. For example, a therapist working from a Depth Psychological perspective would recognize
that for a person struggling with cancer, it is life-affirming to find a way
back to nature's rhythms. From an *eco*centric point of view the goal is
not to imagine the cancer as an entirely alien force to be eradicated at
any cost (like weeds in a garden requiring ever-more pesticides), but

rather, to see the cancer as one part of nature's ecology. From the perspective of the psyche of nature, cancer, too, has an important role to play. Yes, it has the capacity to make us suffer in horrible ways, even kill us; nevertheless, when viewed as one of nature's processes, cancer can be reimagined in a manner that acknowledges and respects its intended function. From a Depth Psychological point of view the goal is not to "get rid" of cancer in order to sustain life in service of a tenacious ego. Rather, this condition is reexperienced in relationship to the principles of nature—where health and disease, life and death are related parts of a continuing cycle. When cancer *and* death are seen as part of nature's design, both are given a sense of place. We do not work so hard resisting, at all costs, the "alien intrusion" of disease, or denying the existence of life's other side, death. Once we are resituated in this wider, ever-transforming ecology of nature, we reconnect with the natural resource and the rhythm that live inside of us. Realignment with nature's harmonic provides a potent complement to well-considered medical care.

As an individual and a Depth Psychologist, I am mindful of the psyche that lives in nature. My study of psychology is rooted in the consideration of psyche's nature, a nature evolving most fundamentally out of the organic life processes of the natural world. Nature's diversity keeps the human imagination alive, the creative processes animated, the tolerance for difference possible. When Depth Psychologists turn to the question, "What is being asked of us now?" they remember the source the psyche draws upon. They remember that the human psyche moves to the rhythm of nature. Depth Psychology has an opportunity to make a serious inquiry into these essential rhythms. We are part of a tradition founded on the study of people's dreams. I believe we must also attend to nature's dreaming, for nature is always dreaming, unfolding herself in each moment. We dream also—each day imagining ourselves into our own inner nature. In the meeting place between natures, a window opens and we are deeply touched. We remember, for a time, our psychic inheritance, an endowment rooted most essentially in the rhythms of nature.

The Ecopsychology of Child Development

ANITA BARROWS

I N A SENSE, all psychology is "child psychology," the critical study of our inherent nature, how the gifts we are born with flourish or wither, what nourishes or starves the potentialities we bring to the world. In his essay, Paul Shepard speculated that, despite the many distortions culture heaps upon each newborn generation, "there is a secret person undamaged in every individual" waiting to reconnect with nature. Here, Anita Barrows asks why that possibility of reconnection has been ignored by mainstream developmental psychology and how it might be recovered. Like Shepard, she believes we can discern in every child remnants of "a porous, permeable, sensitive essence intertwined with all other such essences, affecting and affected by them with its every breath." She suggests that some psychological theories, for example, that of D. W. Winnicott's object relations, lend themselves to a deeper environmental interpretation than they have so far enjoyed. Developmental psychology, blended with the insights of Deep Ecology, may yet offer us the chance to keep our children as sane as they were when they were born.

I live my life in widening circles
That reach out across the world.
RILKE, The Book of Hours

Our developmental theories have tended to focus on the growth of the child's psyche in relation to other people, the coming of the child into human society: learning its signs, its rules, its values; separating and developing autonomy; and consolidating what are known as the "executive functions of the ego" so as to take a place in the world of bounded, independent, individual selves. But there are cultures alive in the world today in which a child's development is not conceived of only in terms of his family or his initiation into human culture. In some tribal societies each person is accompanied through life by a totem animal, whose name a child might be given along with other names, and whose function is to embody the child's link with the natural world. A threat to the totem animal is also a threat to the person believed to share its essence. The relationship between the child and the natural world is honored in the southwestern United States by the Hopi, in a ritual reenacting their belief that newborns emerge from the underworld through the *sipapuni*, or Earth navel. For the first twenty days the infant remains in the darkness of this transition; then, at dawn, he is carried to the east and presented to the rising sun, while his mother says, "This is your child." Thus the Hopi's dependence on the cycles of nature, the diurnal rhythms, is acknowledged; the infant joins not only the human community, but the community of Earth.

The psychological theories that frame our late-twentieth-century grasp of the human condition were evolved, as Theodore Roszak has pointed out, in urban settings by urban theorists. In Freudian and post-Freudian formulations, the child's world is limited to the people who live within the walls of her house; indeed, animals, as in Freud's famous account of Little Hans, are stripped of their power and perceived as symbols of inter- and intrapsychic dynamics. Little Hans was the five-year-old son of a man Freud was analyzing; Freud never met Hans, but it was upon the father's description of his son's fear of horses that Freud first based his famous theory of the "Oedipus complex." In Freud's interpretation, the horses that Hans feared so much represented his father's sexual prowess; Hans's fear was his fear of his own feelings.

Elsewhere in psychoanalytic interpretations, the great dinosaurs become the devouring mother, and the five-year-old's fascination with them reflective not of his awe at these magnificent primitive beings, but of salient Oedipal conflicts. Bears, alligators, and snakes as they appear in our dreams and fantasies are reduced to symbols telling us of our preoccupation with human affairs—the only preoccupations deemed valid or even possible. Depending on which theory one adheres to, the animals represent internal or external events; along with other aspects of the natural world—mountains, the sea, the moon—nonhuman creatures are stripped of their intrinsic value and integrity. Thus, in psychology no less than in the postindustrial political and commercial milieu, nature is understood to serve human beings, to be utilized by them. If an affective relation to nature is taken into account at all, it is most often in the context of the postromantic notion of the lonely individual making his way through life against the background of indifferent, unloving nature, that is, as the forces of consciousness against the wild, irrational spirit of the natural world. Western psychology, in this regard, bears the legacy of imperialist civilization's vision of "the primitive" in the Victorian era.

As part of a growing movement to shift the paradigm of a bounded, isolated self toward a vision of a self that is permeable, interconnected not only with other human selves but with all living beings and processes, a new theory of child development must be evolved. Such a theory must take into consideration that the infant is born into not only a social but an ecological context. It must acknowledge that, from the earliest moments of life, the infant has an awareness not only of human touch, but of the touch of the breeze on her skin, variations in light and color, temperature, texture, sound. No one who has spent time watching an infant could fail to know this; yet the theorists on whose work our current understanding (and therapies) have been based fail to account for its importance—indeed, even for its presence. The "holding environment" is the mother and the domestic extensions of her caretaking: the shapes, colors, and rhythms of her body, her voice, her handling of her infant. If this were so, and carried to its extreme, one might imagine a healthy, balanced child growing up in a totally isolated, sterile room, so long as mother was there. That this example seems as ludicrous as it does is evidence of how deeply we know that the parent-child relationship does not proceed in a vacuum. The awakenings of sensuousness, desire, and pleasure that the mother (caretaker) facilitates in her child are contingent upon, and contained and interpenetrated by, the world into which she has given birth. Some ecofeminists have described rituals whereby they take their infant children out into a garden or park, sometimes during the first few days of life, to introduce them to rosebush, squirrel, wisteria, hummingbird. This is something I remember doing spontaneously when each of my daughters was born, and which a number of friends have told me they did as well; but our Western religions have rituals (baptism, briss) only to initiate children into the particular human community into which they are born. And our psychologies reflect an identical worldview.

I am writing this lying in the shade of a grove of live oak in the high desert mountains of southern California. My groundcloth is stretched over dry, pointy oak leaves and grass burnt yellow by the desert sun. Beside me, minnows swim in a spring-fed pond, birds rustle in tall reeds. The wind that has just come up tells me it's midday; I need no other clock. Now an artists' colony, before that this was a privately owned tract of land where a critically ill professor of physics came to heal himself (and lived forty years longer), and before that a place sacred to native peoples. Walking the trails, discovering wildflowers and natural springs, one experiences the sacredness of this place even today, when from the top of the hills a newly built mall is visible a mile or so down the highway. I have come to this place to spend ten days writing. In the four days since I've been here, I've done all of my work outdoors, even at night, by the light of a Coleman lantern. It strikes me that nature has always been a "holding environment" for me; there is something comforting to me, when I descend into the often terrifying blankness from which I draw my poetry, in being outdoors, in being surrounded by warm air, bird song, trees. My earliest memory is of lying in one of those enormous, high carriages popular in the 1940s, looking up at the leaves of the linden trees that lined the boulevard where we lived in Brooklyn. Those moving leaves, the shadows they cast on the inside of the carriage as the warm summer breeze moved through everything—these remain with me always. They are what I come home to when I take my notebook and pens outside.

I have allowed myself this digression because it feels important to me that the thoughts I have had for this essay—germinating in me for some time now—have come to shape themselves finally here; and that I have realized, working in this place, how utterly safe I feel struggling with the demons of writing when I am outdoors. I say this to underline the very real sense in which nature—ever since those first encounters with the linden leaves—has been identical for me with being held, has permitted me a free flow of creative energy that being indoors often doesn't.

Having said this, I am struck by the complexity of the task that faces the infant. This task is riddled with paradox: the child must simultaneously build enough of a membrane around herself to be able to function in her culture and allow that membrane to be permeable enough, receptive enough to sensation, feeling, communion. Our culture's insistence on independence, mastery, and competition has led to the popularity of a psychology that emphasizes only the first aspect of the child's task: the theory of Margaret Mahler, for instance, which traces the development of the child as a process of separation and individuation. The bounded, autonomous self (achieved, if the child is healthy, sometime around age three and a half) is the goal.

It is an inherent paradox of organic matter that both structure and permeability, containment and yielding, are essential to survival. In this context it should be possible to describe an understanding of development that gives weight to both these aspects of being, privileging neither and acknowledging the ways in which one potentiates the other. The Swiss child psychologist Jean Piaget, who began his career as a biologist, pointed to this in his formulation of assimilation and accommodation as the manner in which adaptation and learning are established. His cognitive/constructivist psychology, susceptible as it is to criticism about the areas of human experience it fails to account for, does, however, account quite extensively for the developing child's passion to discover his environment. The study of Piaget, I think, still serves as a healthy balance to theories of development centered only on the child's intrapsychic and family situations, although Piaget does seem to focus on the child's manipulation of, rather than her interaction with, the things around her perhaps too exclusively.

Piaget and others whose theories inform our work now may serve as a bridge to a more ecologically based understanding of child development. In *Children as Individuals,* Michael Fordham, the British Jungian,

posits a self that begins in an undifferentiated state and gradually "pro-
trudes" what he calls "de-integrates"—much as, over time, islands might
begin to define themselves from under a sea where they have constituted
a single land mass. These de-integrates become, in Fordham's conception, the ego, which finds its way into the world, still connected to the
original substrate but retaining only the vaguest memory of it. This central self is inarticulable, nonrational, and deeply responsive to archetypal
patterns in the world.

Daniel Stern, in his work based on empirical studies of newborns, also
suggests that there exists in each of us what he names a core self, a self
consisting of sensations and capable of being moved by inchoate perceptions of sound, rhythm, light. In that he does not see this state as
needing to be transcended or left permanently behind—in that he suggests, rather, that this matrix of sensation is a central cortex around
which the rings of further development will construct themselves, and
in that this core self is potentially accessible to the rest of the personality
throughout life—Stern's work may be an important step toward con-
ceiving of a developmental process not exclusively founded in the world
of social relationships.

D. W. Winnicott, the British object-relations theorist, formulated for
us the concept of transitional phenomena, essentially the investment of
subjective meaning in objective phenomena, a shadowy area of experience where there is neither me nor not-me, but rather a dynamic interpenetration between the self and something in the world. From the
child's capacity to impart meaning—usually, at the earliest, to something
quite inanimate—Winnicott suggests that the human capacity for creativity, culture, and spirituality evolves. The child first experiences such
phenomena in the context of the early caretaking relationship, then extends its realm of experience outward, into the world. That this world
is known as the "outside," the "not-me," is a phenomenon of Western
dualistic thought; as Thomas Berry, Theodore Roszak, Joanna Macy, and
others have pointed out, it is only by a construct of the Western mind
that we believe ourselves living in an "inside" bounded by our own skin,
with everyone and everything else on the outside. The place where transitional phenomena occur, then (to use Winnicott as a sort of bridge to
a new formulation), might be understood, in this new paradigm of the
self, to be the permeable membrane that suggests or delineates but does

not divide us from the medium in which we exist. It is in this realm that distinctions between subjective and objective begin to blur and inter-subjectivity is possible. Interestingly, this is also the realm of interbeing described by Buddhist teacher and poet Thich Nhat Hanh.

What evidence do we have of the existence of this "ecological self" in childhood? Certainly the infant's delight in his body and his sensuous reactions to the world—warm bathwater, cat's fur, cool grass—is some indication. No one watching a baby explore the world could deny his pleasure in it; yet, if we take the position of many analytically oriented theorists, we would have to say that all exploration is sublimation, the infant's search for the body of the mother. At its most reductionist, analytic theory would trace all experience of oneness, merging, interpenetration, and awe to preverbal experience of the personal mother.

That children's stories abound with animal protagonists speaks to the bond we perceive between children and animals; though analysts like Bettelheim have sought to interpret fairy tales as allegories of instinctual conflict, I think the attraction children have for fairy tales set in nature and populated with animal characters may also be explained by children's instinctually based feelings of continuity with the natural world. That so many contemporary children's books anthropomorphize and sentimentalize animals is again a manifestation of our utilitarian vision of nature and our elevation of the rational mind over all other modalities of living.

When my daughter Viva was small enough to be carried in a backpack, I used to walk with her almost daily in the open hills of Tilden Park, on the east side of San Francisco Bay. It struck me one day that her babbling hushed to a whisper as we entered a grove of Monterey pine. Under the spun light of pine needles, in the cool summer afternoon, I, too, felt hushed; but Viva's response seemed to me to be entirely her own, and I noticed it many times thereafter, as though something in her resonated instinctually with the changed air, the canopy of branches, the mysterious flickering of shadow.

The presence of an ecological self has implications for the way in which we practice therapy. If we see the child as inextricably connected not only to her family, but to all living things and to the earth itself, then our conception of her as an individual, and of the family and social systems in which she finds herself, must expand. How does our limited vision shape what we see, what we subtly encourage and discourage? How would an expanded vision alter our efforts to affect the child's environment, to look beyond her object relationships for the sources of depression, agitation, apathy, violence, or chronic illness? An ecological conception of development brings with it political imperatives, imperatives for social action; for protecting our children and facilitating their growth means broadening our vision to wider and wider contexts.

As we become increasingly aware of our inextricability from the web of life, the many ways in which the ecological self develops alongside the object-related self will, I believe, reveal themselves. A developmental theory embracing both would describe a sequence of stages that might appear rife with internal contradiction, but that would embrace the full experience of growth rather than a single aspect of it. What we have perceived, for example, as serving the process of separation might also be understood as serving the child's sense of connectedness to the world: the toddler who takes his first steps away from his mother makes active forays into the world. Thus mobility leads not only to increased autonomy, but to an enhanced capacity to approach and make connections with the environment. While this interface of child/world is implicit in many developmental theories, their predominant narrative is that of Adam in the garden, of the future dragon-slayer surveying his terrain, or of the victory of Logos over the forces of the irrational. In a sense, what I am suggesting amounts to a simple shift in point of view—to see, to continue with my example, that what the toddler is moving toward is as critical to him as what he is moving away from. This might result in our understanding that development does not necessarily rupture a oneness that is henceforth to be mourned, longed for but unattainable; rather, it can make an increasingly widening circle of oneness possible. In a much deeper and more radical sense, then, an ecologically based theory of development will acknowledge two fundamental movements of being—the tendency to cohere and the tendency to dissolve, the tendency to consolidate into a given shape and the tendency to yield and be yielded into—as equally valent and equally essential.

Ecophilosopher Arne Naess has suggested, in fact, that the process of maturing as a human involves a gradual broadening of one's identification. Psychoanalytic theory, with its pathologizing of experiences of merger, falls short precisely in that it envisions health as a narrowing and drawing-in of the experiences constituting the self. The conventional construct of the self is useful for us to function in the world, as are many of the other constructs we live with and take for granted—time, for instance, which to ancient and tribal peoples has meant something very different from what it means to us; or consciousness, which to the West means logos but to many people includes the reality of dream consciousness and the wisdom of the body. Certainly no one would suggest that a child could develop well without achieving some concept of "identity," some place from which to move forth, some container that gives structure to her experience. At the same time, however, it is limiting to assume that this is the sum, the consummate attainment, of healthy development. Even as consolidation is gradually achieved, another essential stratum takes shape in the child, having to do with the timeless, egoless forces around him, which penetrate him and create his reality in ways that the culture does not articulate or even acknowledge.

Frances Tustin, the British child analyst, sees the "awareness of bodily separateness" as the tragedy underlying human existence. But bodily separateness, we might argue, is an illusion; my skin is not separate from the air around it, my eyes are not separate from what they see. I would alter Tustin's statement to say that it is indeed the illusion of bodily separateness that is the genuine sorrow, that accounts for our loneliness, that isolates us and leads us to exploit and violate one another, the world we live in, and, ultimately, ourselves. Our conventional developmental theories have lent support to this illusion that we live wholly within this slender envelope of flesh that encloses the soft, vulnerable organs—that we are irrevocably cut off from everyone and everything else, and that much of our suffering arises from the yearning to repossess some primitive state of merger where neither need nor yearning had to exist. To make up for this loss, conventional theories posit an aggressive "taking in," a penetrating activeness, as our best and fundamental stance vis-à-vis the world. We are stewards or masters or conquerors, but nothing ever truly satisfies our vast and restless longing. This sorrowful illusion of separateness is expressed in Judeo-Christian thinking as estrangement from God; it is what the fruit of the tree of knowledge—consciousness—condemns us to.

Mystical experience, in both Eastern and Western traditions, has often centered on the dissolution of this perceived separateness. But the

loosening of boundaries provokes, in many of us, nearly intolerable anxiety. Nonattachment and interconnectedness receive far less validation
by competitive consumer culture than the neediness and greediness of
the little screaming ego. When—by grace or accident or even by
intention—something like what Freud described as the "oceanic feeling"
does arise in us, our response is often terror, as though it signified the
brink of madness. We defend against such loosening of boundaries as
though our very survival were threatened; and the numbing which we
ensure by our addictions to drugs, alcohol, entertainment, and so forth,
prevents us from experiencing not only the depths of our anguish, but
the potential we have for real communion with our world. What if such
states of communion, such dissolution of boundaries, were as valued as
rational consciousness? What if, from the beginning of life, nature were
perceived as teacher, guide, source, as important to us as our families?
How differently would we live?

The French Catholic philosopher Jacques Maritain said, "We awaken
to ourselves at the same moment as we awaken to things." A new developmental theory would take into account this double-faceted process,
which emphasizes not only the consolidation of a narrative of memory
that becomes the child's functional "I," but also the wordless stratum of
the child's being, which is not only the son or daughter of these particular parents in this particular time and place, but rather a life-force made
manifest, a porous, permeable, sensitive essence intertwined with all
other such essences, affecting and affected by them with its every breath.
I believe we need only look, holding this in mind, to perceive that it is
so, and that it is our task to enable the child to experience it as fully as
possible. It is our task to learn not to fear it or diminish it, not to deny
it or pathologize it. It is as critical to our development as human attachment is; unless it is nourished, a vital area of being is foreclosed.

The Rape of the Well-Maidens

Feminist Psychology and the Environmental Crisis

MARY E. GOMES AND ALLEN D. KANNER

GENDER IDENTITIES DIE HARD. Even in societies in which feminist values have had considerable impact, boys are still raised to be dominant and independent leaders; girls are still expected to be nurturing and receptive caregivers. The new school of feminist psychology has raised penetrating questions about the subtle ways in which even "modern" societies continue to shape their children. Why do men engulf others rather than acknowledging their dependence on them? How are the dynamic feminine qualities of inspiration, chaos, and ecstacy suppressed in partriarchal cultures? How would human relationships change if they were more fully egalitarian? Ecopsychologists have begun to see that questions like these have more than a purely social significance; they transcend the family and the individual. In this essay, Mary Gomes and Allen Kanner review the relevance of feminist psychology to environmental sanity, showing how "despoiling the Earth and subjugating women are intimately connected."

━━━━━━━

There is an old Grail story, "The Tale of the Well-Maidens," that speaks to many of our current environmental dilemmas. The story goes as follows:

Long, long ago, even before the reign of King Arthur, the land was blessed with enchantment and great fertility. Throughout the realm, maidens stood guard over the sacred wells, offering their healing waters in golden cups to any journeyers who might pass. Indeed, some say that these were the very waters of inspiration, offering transport between the worlds. The maidens themselves may have been Otherworldly, but the tale does not say. In those days, when the veil between the worlds was thinner, these distinctions were not so sharp.

All was well, with the land bounteous and the people content, until the King conceived a desire to possess one of the well-maidens. He stole her sacred cup, carried her off, and raped her. His men followed his example, raping the other maidens. In response to these unheard-of acts, these violations against nature itself, the maidens withdrew themselves and their magic from the world. The wells dried up, and the regenerative powers of the land were destroyed, leaving it barren and devoid of enchantment. By seeking dominion over others, the King and his men had diminished the world.[1]

This story illustrates a key insight of ecofeminism: that the despoiling of the Earth and the subjugation of women are intimately connected. It is not a coincidence that when women are raped, the land becomes parched and desolate, and when "feminine" qualities are oppressed, the human mind is cut off from participation in mystery and left with a disenchanted world. In patriarchal cultures, it is common to find patterns of domination and control aimed at both women and the land. Ecofeminists have suggested that these same patterns can be found on the individual level, both interpersonally and intrapsychically.

This observation is supported by the work of feminist psychologists, who in recent years have made enormous advances in our understanding of gender-role development and male-female relationships. While elucidating the psychology of domination, they have uncovered numerous patriarchal assumptions concerning human motivation and personality that have informed Western psychology since at least the time of Freud. Their work is currently among the most vibrant and productive in the social sciences.

Nevertheless, feminist psychology has focused almost exclusively on relationships among humans. Taking a cue from ecofeminism, we will extend the work of several feminist psychologists to incorporate the nat-

1. Adapted from Caitlin Matthews, *Arthur and the Sovereignty of Britain: King and Goddess in the Mabinogion* (London: Arkana, 1989).

ural world. The resulting synthesis, we believe, leads to a number of exciting and unanticipated insights that enhance both endeavors and promise future cross-fertilization.

Domination and Dependence

Theodore Roszak, in *The Voice of the Earth,* states that "there is no question but that the way the world shapes the minds of its male children lies somewhere close to the root of our environmental dilemma."[2] How are the minds of our male children shaped so that many find themselves powerfully drawn to fantasies of conquering lands, nations, or women? From the perspective of feminist psychology, part of the problem is that men are told, from early in life, that to be respected and admired as men they must be separate from others.

According to feminist psychoanalyst Nancy Chodorow, this push toward separation can be traced back to the very beginnings of life. In her theory, to the extent that women are responsible for the care of infants and young children, boys will receive a subtle message that, to be properly male, they must pull away from the intensity of this first intimate relationship. Instead, they are expected to identify with a father who often plays a distant role in the daily rounds of family life. As a result, boys come to base their sex-role identity on the ability to disconnect and to deny relationship.

There are many women as well as men who base their identity and self-worth on a sense of "heroic autonomy." Since "masculine" attributes, such as independence and disconnection, are valued in our culture more than those considered "feminine," separation is seen as a route to respect, strength, and status for women as well as men. But for many women this message will be buffered by a contradictory message: to be respected *as persons* they must take on "masculine" qualities, but to be respected *as women* they must adopt the less valued "feminine" qualities.

Radical autonomy is a cultural ideal that does not allow for other forms of growth, especially those based on relationship and connection. Absolute separation, however, is an illusion. While we can certainly act from our own center, it is impossible not to interact with and depend on the people, trees, rocks, and wildlife around us, the air we breathe,

2. Theodore Roszak, *The Voice of the Earth* (New York: Simon & Schuster, 1992), p. 242.

and the patterns of the seasons. These connections, potentially the joy and meaning of our lives, are experienced as threats due to the insistence that we *should* be separate. In *From a Broken Web*, feminist theologian Catherine Keller uses the term "separative self" instead of "separate self" to highlight that we are talking about an *attempt* to separate—an attempt that can never succeed. She describes the separative self as "an ego armored against the outer world and the inner depths."

> To sustain its sense of independence, such a subject is always liberating itself from its bonds as though from bondage. Intimacy, emotion, and the influence of the Other arouse its worst anxieties, for somehow it must keep relation external to its own being, its "self." . . . However much the ego feels single and apart, this feeling may represent not truth but denial. It is less precise to call this ego separate than separative, implying an activity or intention rather than any fundamental state of being.[3]

Thus, those who would fully separate find themselves in a double bind. Faced with a culture that defines worth, especially masculine worth, in terms of radical autonomy, they must constantly interact with a world in which such total isolation is impossible. One solution to this dilemma is to dominate the world so thoroughly that the autonomy of all else is wiped out. Ellyn Kaschak illuminates this process in the lives of women and men in *Engendered Lives*. One of her main points is that the separative self creates a false sense of independence through a form of domination characterized by engulfing the Other.

> It would seem that men have just as much difficulty separating and individuating as do women, and that the ideal of separation and individuality is a somewhat unnatural act which must be accomplished largely by illusion. If men define women, children, and even physical aspects of the environment as extensions of themselves, then their own difficulties with separation are made invisible.[4]

As Kaschak points out, this engulfing dynamic can be seen in the shocking and extreme acts of sexism with which we are all familiar, such as rape, incest, and domestic violence. The unique contribution of her work, however, lies in her analyses of the myriad everyday violations

3. Catherine Keller, *From a Broken Web: Separation, Sexism, and Self* (Boston: Beacon, 1986), pp. 8–9.
4. Ellyn Kaschak, *Engendered Lives: A New Psychology of Women's Experience* (New York: HarperCollins, 1992), p. 136.

that pass unnoticed in a patriarchy. For instance, the male boundary problems Kaschak describes permeate the "traditional" marriage. In this arrangement, a man relies on his wife to take care of his physical needs by cooking, performing household chores, and caring for the children. Rather than experiencing his dependence as a humiliating failure to be autonomous, he incorporates his wife into his ever-expanding self. Often, even her name disappears—a potent symbolic reminder that her identity has been merged into his.

In other words, domination becomes a way to deny dependence, a dependence that has been culturally defined as a failure and a humiliation, rather than as a natural and inevitable part of life.

From an ecopsychological perspective, the same process can be seen in the relationship between humans and the Earth in urban-industrial societies. It is clear that we depend on the Earth for our life: for the air that we breathe, the water and minerals that constitute our bodies, the plants that miraculously transform the energy of the sun into living substance. Yet we in urban-industrial civilization have centered our identity as a species around the renunciation of this truth. Human dependence on the hospitality of the Earth is total, and this is extremely threatening to the separative self. By dominating the biosphere and attempting to control natural processes, we can maintain the illusion of being radically autonomous. The living system, on which we depend and of which we are a part, is engulfed and made into a servant.

A related insight of feminist psychology concerns the parasitic quality of relationship that comes from the denial of dependence. By acknowledging our dependence, we allow gratitude and reciprocity to come forth freely and spontaneously. This is especially true when power in a relationship is fairly equal, as in a close friendship. When we deny our dependence on another person, we threaten not only to engulf them but to feed on their strength and vitality, often until we have used them up. This pattern is taken to its extreme in sadistic individuals, who thrive on breaking the spirits and will of others. A striking parallel is seen in the physical destruction of ecosystems, as we humans rush blindly to fill our "needs" for oil, landfill space, and consumer products, using up the Earth itself while maintaining a puzzling lack of awareness of the results of our actions. The unacknowledged dependence makes us act as parasites on the planet, killing off our own host.

Attitudes about access to women and access to wild places also illustrate the way in which women's subjugation by men parallels the Earth's subjugation by humans. As Marilyn Frye points out in *The Politics of Reality,*

> Differences in power are always manifested in asymmetrical access. . . . The resources of the employee are available to the boss as the resources of the boss are not to the employee. . . . The parent has unconditional access to the child's room; the child does not have similar access to the parent's room. . . . The slave is unconditionally accessible to the master. Total power is unconditional access.[5]

In the case of gender relationships, this pattern can be seen in the widespread sense that men are entitled to have access to women more than the reverse. Women who systematically deny men access—either generally, through a separatist life-style, or in specific instances, such as women's colleges or activist organizations—arouse extreme discomfort and suspicion in many men. In a similar vein, industrial society assumes a right of access to the entire planet. No place is considered by its own rights off-limits to humans. If a mountain is difficult to climb, it is considered all the more heroic to "conquer" it. It is not surprising that mountain climbers, in their eagerness to overcome natural limits and obstacles, often ignore their impact on the land. As a result, we see the ecological devastation of some of the most awe-inspiring lands in the world. Few people realize that K2 in Pakistan, the second-highest mountain on the planet, is also possibly the most polluted. Similarly, houses are built in the floodplain of the Mississippi River and on major fault lines in California. Rather than respecting these difficult natural features, people blame the "cruelty of nature" when the inevitable tragedies occur.

When environmentalists suggest that humans respect the integrity of uninhabitable or unwelcoming lands, they provoke outrage similar to that expressed by a domineering husband whose wife decides, without his permission, to spend her Friday nights at, say, a women's ritual circle. Both these examples threaten the status quo; they call into question some deeply held beliefs about status hierarchies and rights of access: humans over nature and men over women.

5. Marilyn Frye, *The Politics of Reality: Essays in Feminist Theory* (Freedom, Calif.: The Crossing Press, 1983), p. 103.

From the Separative Self to the Self-in-Relation

In mainstream male-centered psychology, healthy development has been conceptualized as a process of increasing autonomy and independence, thus lending an aura of authority to the separative tendencies of Western culture. While theorists such as Keller and Kaschak have provided an understanding of the engulfing and dominating tendencies of the patriarchal mind, psychologists at the Stone Center at Wellesley College have been working on alternative models of human development. Through their "self-in-relation" model, the Stone Center theorists have challenged this traditional view and stressed the primacy of human interconnection. Rather than equating healthy development with increasing autonomy, relational theory suggests that as we mature, we move toward greater complexity in relationships.

Since it is inevitable that we are in relationships, a crucial distinction is made between those connections that are empowering to the individual, fostering growth and creativity, and those that are diminishing, binding people into predictable and repetitive patterns. Janet Surrey, one of the creators of relational theory, describes healthy relationships in the following terms:

> An increase in energy, power, or "zest," and a sense of effectiveness based on [an] ability to contribute to everyone's greater awareness and understanding. . . . In this process each participant's voice is acknowledged, so that he or she . . . feels affirmed and empowered as a relational being. The joining of visions and voices creates something new, an enlarged vision. . . . Thus the sense of connection and participation in something larger than oneself does not diminish but rather heightens the sense of personal power and understanding.[6]

Relationships based on competition and hierarchy ultimately sap vitality and reduce power, even for those who are the apparent "winners" in the struggle to become fully independent. Since full autonomy is an illusion, hyperindividuality is a type of relationship that denies and often destroys the larger context, whether this is a friendship, a family, or an ecosystem. When these larger systems are destroyed, everyone ulti-

6. Janet L. Surrey, "Relationship and Empowerment," in J. Jordan, A. Kaplan, J. Baker Miller, I. Stiver, and J. Surrey, eds., *Women's Growth in Connection* (New York: Guilford Press, 1991), p. 172.

mately suffers the consequences, dominators as well as the dominated. We are beginning to see this process in the late twentieth century, where it appears that human beings are on the brink of finally conquering the planet.

On a physical level, this dynamic is seen in the increase in illnesses, such as cancer and immune-system disorders, resulting from the breakdown of ecosystems. In addition to the suffering among individuals, these illnesses have social costs, as more resources are directed toward medical treatments, insurance payments, and long-term care. On a psychological level, we see the deadening and depression that have become so widespread in modern societies. To live with the repeated violation of the natural world and the harsh environment that has resulted, we shut down much of our sensitivity. This closing off is vividly experienced when we come back to our cities after extended forays into wilderness. When we reenter, many aspects of modern culture are experienced as shattering to a sense of inner calm and as a direct assault upon the newly awakened senses (see Robert Greenway, this volume).

Like most psychological theories, the self-in-relation model has, thus far, focused largely on relationships among people. But it could easily be extended beyond the human realm to include an ecopsychological perspective. To quote Catherine Keller again, by defining "relationship" more inclusively, we can create "places of inner and outer freedom in which new forms of connection can take place. Liberated from relational bondage, we range through an unlimited array of relations—not just to other persons, but to ideas and feelings, to the earth, the body, and the untold contents of the present moment."[7]

Ecopsychology and the Dynamic Feminine

> More than this I will not ask,
> faced with mysteries dark and vast.
> ROBERT HUNTER

A large part of what feminist psychology has to offer the environmental movement is vision—a vision of what our human experience could encompass if liberated from the need to dominate and control. As our defensive walls of separation and domination start to disintegrate, we

7. Keller, *From a Broken Web*, p. 3.

become open to a world of increasing richness, complexity, and beauty. We are able to appreciate the diversity of life without reducing it to notions of "more important" or "less important." Feminist ecopsychology understands that in bonding with the natural world, ecstatic states of celebration and interconnection are unleashed—experiences that, in modern society, are repressed in ourselves and oppressed in others.

As we begin to gently dissolve the hard shells of our encapsulated egos, we open up to the realm that Jungian theorist Gareth Hill calls the dynamic feminine. The term "feminine" is best understood here not as referring to women as a sex, but to the set of qualities that are systematically devalued in a patriarchy. Hill's unique contribution lies in expanding the notion of "the feminine" beyond the usual nurturing and motherly images, which he calls the "static feminine." The dynamic feminine, in contrast, represents "undirected movement toward the new, the nonrational, the playful. It is the flow of experience, vital, spontaneous, open to the unexpected, yielding and responsive to being acted upon. . . . Its effects are the uplifting, ecstatic inspiration that comes from the experience of transformed awareness. . . . The dynamic feminine is perhaps most simply symbolized by a spiral, representing the disorienting and transforming experience of new awareness."[8] This is the realm of the wild imagination, of chaos erupting out of predictability.

The dynamic feminine has been expressed mythologically by such figures as Dionysus, Pan, and Coyote, and is often associated with untamed lands and forest groves. Charlene Spretnak conveys a sense of the dynamic feminine as embodied by the goddess Artemis, as she dances with her animal and human companions in the forests of Arcadia:

> The animals were drawn to the tree. They rolled over its roots and encircled the trunk. In a larger ring the dancers raised their arms, turning slowly, and felt currents of energy rising through their trunks, turning faster, through their arms, turning, out their fingers, turning, turning, to their heads, whirling, racing, flying. Sparks of energy flew from their fingertips, lacing the air with traces of clear blue light. They joined hands, joined arms, merged bodies into a circle of current that carried them effortlessly.
>
> Artemis appeared before them standing straight against the tree, Her spine its trunk, Her arms its boughs. Her body pulsed with life, its rhythms echoed

8. Gareth Hill, *Masculine and Feminine: The Natural Flow of Opposites in the Psyche* (Boston: Shambhala, 1992), pp. 17–20.

by the silvered tree, the animals at Her feet, the dancers, the grass, the plants, the grove. Every particle of the forest quivered with Her energy. . . . She began to merge with the sacred tree, while the circle of dancers spun around her. They threw back their heads and saw the shimmering boughs rush by. When Artemis was one with the moon tree, the circle broke. Dancers went whirling through the grove, fully exhausted on the mossy forest floor.[9]

The dynamic feminine, which stands in stark contrast to domination and control, is clearly a devalued quality in the industrial West. From the witch burnings of the Renaissance to the current hysteria over the use of psychedelic drugs, the dominant culture has sought to eradicate this mode of existence by any means necessary.

This aspect of the feminine relates to the environmental crisis in complex ways. It would be naive to expect that dancing naked in the moonlight is going to put an end to consumerism or curb population growth. But we believe that reawakening to the dynamic feminine is an important part of learning to live sustainably. In this mode, we are confronted with mystery, wildness, and danger. Facing nature on its own terms means becoming acquainted with its chaotic, strange, and frightening aspects as well as the familiar and comfortable. In many Earth-based cultures, the Earth is revered for its mystery as well as its beneficence. This is seen in the practice of designating certain powerful areas as "sacred places"— lands that are understood to stand outside of ordinary life. One does not approach a sacred site trivially, but prepares emotionally to partake of its wild and unpredictable qualities. These sites are tinged with mystery and darkness as well as the miraculous, and a visit evokes wonder, awe, and fear.

More recently, the influence of the dynamic feminine can be seen in the bioregional movement. Bioregionalism involves breaking down existing social structures and respecting nature's own creative contours. At the level of governments, this includes re-drawing political boundaries so that they are based on the integrity of natural systems. Culturally, bioregionalism seeks to replace the growing corporate monoculture with traditions and sensitivities that spring from the qualities of the land. On all levels, bioregionalism has challenged centralized, top-down, linear approaches to life, and has reclaimed the concept of anarchy. In the

9. Charlene Spretnak, *States of Grace: The Recovery of Meaning in the Postmodern Age* (San Francisco: HarperSanFrancisco, 1991), p. 142.

words of bioregionalist Jim Dodge, "Anarchy doesn't mean out of control; it means out of *their* control."[10]

Embracing the bioregional vision requires more than recycling, or driving less, or even minimizing our consumption, although all of these are important. It involves a change in our sense of identity, so that we allow our surroundings to grow *into* us, to let the land reclaim us like ivy growing over an old house, or wildflowers pushing up through cracks in the pavement. It means the death of the old industrial self and the birth of something new.

We now circle back to our beginning. The story of the well-maidens did not end with the loss of vitality in the land. Instead, it continued as the daughters and sons of the well-maidens, conceived in rape, were destined to wander through the dispirited land in seach of healing. These shadowy beings, offspring of both nature's guardians and its destroyers, have a great deal to say to those of us living in the present age—we whose destiny it is to bear the dual inheritance of the destructive aspects of our culture and the living soul that continues beneath it.[11]

10. Jim Dodge, "Living by Life: Some Bioregional Theory and Practice," in Van Andruss, Christopher Plant, Judith Plant, and Eleanor Wright, eds., *Home! A Bioregional Reader* (Philadelphia: New Society, 1990), p. 8.
11. We would like to thank Ellyn Kaschak, Karen Spangenberg, and Charlene Spretnak for comments on an earlier draft of this essay.

The Wilderness Effect and Ecopsychology

ROBERT GREENWAY

To ROBERT GREENWAY, ecopsychology is a search for language to describe the human–nature relationship. It is a tool for better understanding the relationship, for diagnosing what is wrong with that relationship, and for suggesting paths to healing. These are issues he has been exploring for more than thirty years. As a wilderness leader, he has seen the profound transformations that take place during extended stays in the wilderness and the equally dramatic changes that occur upon the return to everyday urban life. Based in part upon these experiences, he is creating a theoretical framework and an ecopsychological language that identifies the core of the environmental crisis as arising from a culturally created and maintained *mode of knowing* that dominates Western culture and that, in essence, creates a dualistic split between knower and known (and thus between humans and nature). To reverse our tragic and growing alienation from nature, he deems it essential that we free ourselves from "addiction to dualism" through extended forays into wilderness, meditation, and other awareness-expanding experiences.

When I first brought my interests in wilderness and ecopsychology to the innovative psychology department at Sonoma State University in 1969, they were quite separate activities. I had known from my own life and from incorporating wilderness experiences into Peace Corps training programs in the 1960s that the wilderness experience, if conducted as a retreat from cultural dominance, could have a profound impact on the psyche. And from adopting ecological and systems ideas in educational contexts in the 1960s, I believed that a marriage of the two fields was essential for an understanding, if not a healing, of the human nature relationship.

As the wilderness courses became in the 1970s a program for training wilderness leaders, and agencies and schools became interested in incorporating wilderness experiences, it became crucial to communicate what *happened* to people in the wilderness. Thus, the wilderness experience gave rise to a search for a language that could reveal the dynamics of the human–nature relationship; the growing public concern over environmental degradation became the motivation. (This reveals my central bias: both ecology and psychologies are, at base, *languages*, and thus the search for an "ecopsychology" is a search for a language as well.)

For me this search was much enhanced by the emergence of transpersonal psychology in the 1970s, in essence a psychological language about relationships. At that time, the issue of the dualistic and isolated "ego" or "self" was fully on the table, and a language of sorts emerged that applied not only to spiritual or psychedelic experiences (with which transpersonalists have from the beginning been enthralled) but to the human–nature relationship as well. This aroused my interests in Jung's theories of this relationship, focused on his concepts of archetype and synchronicity, as well as in Gregory Bateson's ecological (systemic) work on the roots of mental illness. Bateson was a doorway back into John Dewey's magnificent philosophical analysis of dualism, written sixty-five years ago. I also benefited from the psychological work informed by psychedelics (such as that of Stanislav Grof and Ralph Metzner) and by Buddhist practice (notably that of Ken Wilbur and Joanna Macy). Always underlying this quest for language has been the exquisite prose and poetry of the "nature writers" such as Gary Snyder, Annie Dillard, Barry Lopez, Aldo Leopold, Richard Nelson, and many others, who were indeed finding a voice to express our relationship to nature. Any "new" ecopsychological language would need to be cognizant of, and complementary to, the languages already flowing and flowering about humans and nature.

So what had been a wonderful but naive practice, the escape to wilderness, became a very self-conscious study of the dramatic changes people go through during extended (and carefully structured) stays there. "The wilderness experience" and "psychoecology" (as I have been calling ecopsychology over the years) became complementary, two sides of the same coin.

Most of the wilderness excursions were two weeks, although some were for three and even four. It was initially a full-semester course at Sonoma State; as the program developed, it eventually became part of a two-year curriculum (which included everything from intensive physical preparation to courses in psychoecology, transpersonal psychology, wilderness theory, and the like). Thus, participants in a wilderness excursion, drawn from the entire university community (including fellow professors, graduate students from other departments, local psychotherapists and psychiatrists, and various wilderness leaders from around the country) tended to form a tight-knit, cooperative community even before leaving.

The trip itself would be designed to encourage participants to leave behind the props of culture and enter fully into wilderness. Food would be carefully organized to be fully nutritious but "just enough." Only items essential to health and safety were allowed (no books! no cameras! not even writing paper).

As much as possible, everything prior to and during a trip would be ritualized—driving to the trailhead, dividing the food, weighing the packs, distributing community equipment, then later everyday activities such as ways of walking or cooking. Special attention would be paid to crossing the boundary into wilderness, often in the form of a river or stream. Within a few days, participants would speak of being "home," and I would know that we had crossed into wilderness psychologically as well as physically.

In the first few days on the trail there was much basic instruction as well—sanitation, walking and pack techniques, skills of fire building and shelter installation, very careful and detailed instruction in "no impact" camping.

The pace, direction, and many of the activities were decided by the group as a whole. Everything short of life-threatening situations was decided by consensus. A group might be athletic, energetic, full of ideas and plans, or quiet, contemplative, even lazy. The point was for the group to become as fully empowered and safe as possible. This reduced stress, but it also opened possibilities of relating to wilderness in unique ways—ways closed to groups of strangers, casual friends, or individuals.

Since the "wilderness course" was much talked about around the university, many of the same practices were repeated from year to year: an "alone time" lasting three or more days; all-night chanting rituals; climbs to peaks at sunrise or sunset or in silence in the moonlight; separate camps for several days for men and women, with ritualized ways of coming back together; and, more rarely, exploring the wilderness together. Occasionally a trip would be occupied with heavy weather, illness, or "something to work out in the group," although the trips were not advertised as therapy or healing but rather as opportunities to explore one's relationship with nature.

Participants often became ebullient to find that fears prior to the trip proved unfounded. Occasionally someone expressed boredom or tried to goad the group into conflict or various feats of derring-do. For the most part, though, just *being* in the wilderness, alone and together, and the simple acts of living and moving together, leaving no trace, cooking and sleeping, tuning in to fire and water and various celestial events, became the fully occupying agenda. Together we experienced the incredible drama of a genuine relationship between humans and nature unfolding.

The following was written after a trip some years ago. I hope it might convey a little of the flavor of my particular approach and the kinds of physical and psychological changes that the trips might elicit.

There were twelve of us on a warm June day along the upper reaches of the Middle Fork of the Eel River in Northern California—one of the few completely healthy, undammed rivers left in the state.

As it happened we were six men and six women, two of whom were sisters, one twenty-two and the other fourteen; their father was one of the men.

We were near the end of a two-week trip; we had gone as deep into the center of the wilderness as we could, and as deep into our hearts and minds. We had adopted games and structures we knew would open us beyond our familiar constraints. Now, in the fullness of our opening, our ability to feel and understand reached unexpected depths. We were astonished at the limitations of our precious assumptions about ourselves.

We had awakened our bodies by plunging daily in the still-frigid, snow-fed waters, awakened to the sun from the peaks at dawn, and chanted nonsense sounds alone and together. We had prayed, laughed, and cried, told our stories, shared long silences, and become children again when the sisters' father one warm evening taught us the "real way" to play kick the can.

We had gone out alone like heroes on grail quests in search of dramatic and important visions that would guide our lives and make our decisions for us. Instead, we found in tiny scale and modest simplicity perfection all around us: a column of ants dragging home the last remnants of may flies; sensuous manzanita trunks rising like red muscled limbs out of banks of chartreuse moss; small trout flashing in the pools; every brooklet a lovely series of miniature waterfalls, making chords with the pools as if tuned by a master musician intimate with our deepest emotions.

We had fasted, and with parched lips facing east all day had felt the sun moving over our heads from front to back, the north wind drying our tears as we waited and watched, released slow breath by slow breath into deepening surrender, into webs of meanings that seemed to reach into our cores and beyond.

And so, back together after such work on this particular day, our last before leaving, we scrambled downriver over rocks and through pools, splashing, noisy, pulled to something, some place, perhaps something beyond image; we weren't exactly sure.

We came upon a huge pool that seemed bottomless—shadings of blue-green darkening almost to black in the depths; sheer walls of blue-gray slate rising thirty feet above either bank; huge rounded boulders above and below the pool, over which the water poured in gushing falls. We knew without speaking that we had found "the place."

We fell silent at the sight, knowing somehow that this would be the turning point, "the most sacred," the place of deepest wilderness, for this day, for this trip, for this time in our lives, and perhaps in our entire lives.

We remained silent as, one by one, we entered the pool. Later someone would comment that for the first time on the trip the water did not shock us. We swam, crawled onto the hot rocks, warming our bodies on the smooth surfaces and contours we each found. Most of us slept for a time. Later some spoke of amazingly vivid dreams.

After a time we gravitated toward a large flat space on top of one of the rocks next to the pool and formed a circle, our habit over the past weeks. And then, without quite knowing how it happened, distance disappeared and there was an openness into ourselves that was an openness to each other, that embraced the pool, the river, and farther out into the wilderness, the "other world," the whole Earth, the universe.

We looked frankly at each other, enjoying our clear eyes, our health; smiling, weeping, we saw each other as if for the first time, as if there had never been any distance. Some quietly spoke from their hearts, simple things—sharing a memory, thanking someone for a favor.

We sang some of the songs that had been most helpful to us, drawing out our best voices and harmonies, blending in with the sound of the river.

Then a shadow passed over us, a rare golden eagle passing between us and the sun, and we saw that other shadows had lengthened along the canyon walls. With a wild cry someone jumped up and dived again into the pool. We all followed and the water once again was icy, shocking us, tightening our skin.

We walked slowly back to our camp, which now seemed a familiar home, and quietly cooked our meal. As the evening cooled, we were a little shy, and there were many deep looks into the fire.

The younger of the sisters said that night, in our last circle before leaving: "Now I'm ready to go back to the other world. I choose not to let a day like this become a common thing."

So, apart from our stories and poetry, what can be said about the wilderness experience using ecological and psychological language that does justice to the experience and accurately enhances our understanding of it? What is this now much-vaunted "wilderness effect"? Does our struggle to describe it didactically help us develop an "ecopsychology," let alone suggest paths of healing the human disjunction with nature that appears to be destroying possibilities for a human future on this planet?

As literally thousands of groups arise to lead people into various kinds of wilderness experiences, for a wide variety of goals, the resulting "wilderness effect" is increasingly accepted as a given. It is said that without intimacy with nature, humans become mad. It is also said that our culture is pathogenic with regard to natural processes. Thus, it seems healthy to attempt to retreat from "culture" and embrace "natural processes" in their fullest and most pristine forms.

The issue here is the extent to which we can leave culture behind. We leave the urban scene *physically* of course, although it is common among wilderness leaders to speak of the beginning of trips as "cleaning out" times, when the "poisons" presumed to be stored in tissues are released. But if we're "culture bound"—that is, locked into a voracious web of reinforcements that continually penetrate and are in turn supported by our collective mental processes, then how much change, actual psychological change, can happen in the wilderness?

When entering the wilderness psychologically as well as physically, participants most often speak of feelings of expansion or reconnection. We might interpret these as expansion of "self," or as reconnection with adaptations of our evolutionary past, still layered in our deeper psyches, or simply with complete and fully natural systems (systems which include death, fear, and violence, as well as beauty and elegance, in wondrous balance).

For many the wilderness experience means release of repression—release of the inevitable controls that exist in any culture. Particpants who speak of this benefit tend to see its source not so much in the external wilderness, but in the "internal wilderness" of physiology, instincts, archetypes, and the like.

It is obvious that we are dealing with an extremely diverse experience, which each person tends to remember and to interpret differently. It is also obvious, to me at least, that I am attempting to explore an experience of such depth and complexity that the terms "ineffable" or "spiritual" are appropriate. It appears to be an experience of exquisite beauty and clear impact for most people, and one that either dissolves upon return to the urban culture or places the individual in more or less severe conflict with that culture. Thus, as will all research on "learning" or "therapy" or "transformation," generalizations are always questionable, the research always a challenge.

After a few years mushing around with various approaches to wilderness classes, when things settled down a bit, I began conducting research on the process—for my own edification and to satisfy nervous deans and department heads. From the more than 1,380 persons passing through the program I have collected approximately 700 questionnaires, 700 interviews, 52 longitudinal studies, and more than 300 personal responses to trips (stories, myths, poems, and drawings).

Here are some preliminary descriptive statistics:

90 percent of respondents described an increased sense of aliveness, well-being, and energy;

90 percent stated that the experience allowed them break an addiction (defined very broadly—from nicotine to chocolate and other foods);

80 percent found the return initially very positive;

53 percent of those found that within two days the positive feelings had turned to depression;

77 percent described a major life change upon return (in personal relationships, employment, housing, or life-style);

38 percent of those changes "held true" after five years;

60 percent of the men and 20 percent of the women stated that a major goal of the trip was to conquer fear, challenge themselves, and expand limits;

57 percent of the women and 27 percent of the men stated that a major goal of the trip was to "come home" to nature;

60 percent of all respondents stated that they had adopted at least one ritual or contemplative practice learned on the trip; 17 percent of those studied longitudinally (nine out of fifty) stated that they were still doing the practice after five years;

92 percent cited "alone time" as the single most important experience of the trip; getting up before dawn and climbing a ridge or peak in order to greet the sun was cited by 73 percent of the respondents as the second most important experience of the trip. "Community" or the fellowship of the group was cited by 80 percent as the third most important experience.

Among my most vivid findings are changes in dream patterns: 76 percent of all respondents reported dramatic changes in quantity, vividness, and context of dreams after about seventy-two hours of entering into the wilderness; 82 percent of those expressed a change in content of dreams from "busy" or "urban" scenarios at the outset to dreams about the group or some aspect of the wilderness. It seems on the average to take three or four days for people's dreams to catch up with them! As I have said, not completely in jest, this pattern suggests that our culture is only four days deep.

On the whole, the differences in statements between men and women are so pervasive, matching my own in-field observations, that I have come to assume that men and women have remarkably different experiences of wilderness. It seems that the transition into wilderness is easier for women and the transition back into the urban world easier for men. This at least seems to be true given the rather "soft" approach I use, as opposed to more aggressive approaches geared toward "conquering fear" or "gaining power." But the degree to which these findings may reveal intrinsic physiological, cultural, or political differences is no more clear than in the myriads of other gender studies.

What might all this mean? Certainly, if "cultures" do in fact intertwine in some systemic manner with human mental processes, so do the processes of nature as found in the wilderness—whether the same processes or different ones we can only guess. But in general, we think we are seeing the wide divergence between Western culture and pristine wilderness writ vividly on the psyches of those experiencing extended stays "away from cultural reinforcement" and "vulnerable" to the natural dynamics of wilderness. We would infer from this that small, tribe-like communities, sitting around fires at night, intimacy with celestial events, and the like are indeed familiar to us, are experiences not that far "below" our cultural programming.

To talk about this with a psychological language conversant not only with our deepest "peak" or "spiritual" experiences but also with the field of ecology and the study of relationships and systems, does of course (alas) require, if not a new language, at least a redefining of existing ones.

For example, "Mind" is used by scientists of all kinds these days as a label for "psyche" or "mental processes." The clear bias is that Mind is at least a property of a separate individual, if not very specifically tied to the brain or individual neuropsychology. And yet Bateson, John Dewey before him, and Buddhist philosophy long, long before either, have defined Mind as the sum of all natural processes and the information that emanates from them. Mind is an immanent property of the universe. (The intuition, often expressed in poetry, that as we shine our little lights into the mystery of the cosmos we are exploring a vast intelligence, reflects this more systemic and Buddhist viewpoint.) Mind seen in this way is not limited to the human brain. It is more fundamental than consciousness, and encompasses all consciousness.

Consciousness would therefore be a property of Mind that allows for self-reflective experience. Consciousness arises *out* of Mind and thus can exist in various relationships to it. In urban-industrial Western culture, consciousness is often experienced as separate from Mind. Certainly the self-reflective consciousness that has emerged in humans has brought us incredible insights about ourselves and our universe and incredible tools meant to enhance our various capabilities. But just as certainly, this ability to make distinctions and "self-reflect" now appears as a beautiful capacity run amok, proceeding from distinction to disjunction, from reflection to alienation, and from alienation to the kind of full-blown split between subjects and objects (or between the poles of any disjunction) termed "dualism." Dualism summarizes our cultural "mode of knowing" or "information processing" and is perhaps the source of our pervasive sense of being disconnected. This in turn produces our obsession with needs and wants—the massive addictions that characterize our period in history.

"Ego" is another of those hoary psychological terms that begs for clarification if it is to be used in a psychological context. It of course refers to "executive" functions in the Freudian scheme, the summary of mental processes that manage relations between the more natural ("instinctive") id, and the more cultural, repressive, moralistic superego. But consider "Ego" as the collection of cognitive abilities that, simply, serve our various need-fulfilling activities. Making distinctions would be just one of many of these activities (categorizing, sequencing, and linking would be others). "Ego," therefore, would be the "home" of that capacity which, when overstimulated or used to excess would split us from natural processes. Or rather—and this is important—would *lead us to believe* that we're split from natural processes. Certainly our cultural experience, urbanized as it is, would reinforce this conviction.

Every culture tends to reinforce different patterns of egoic processing. Our culture seems to have inflated "distinction making" until it dominates not only Ego but our entire consciousness as well. Thus we could say that our consciousness is split from Mind and that the conscious *experience* of this phenomenon is one of separation, though in fact we continue to be immersed in nature! The experience of separation is an essential context for domination; domination is the root of exploitation. And thus we destroy our habitat, the very basis of our survival as a species.

Thus, with regard to the wilderness experience, using these terms to exemplify a psychoecological language (many additional terms are of course necessary), we can say about the psychological changes taking place in the wilderness that there is a shift from culturally reinforced, dualism-producing reality processing to a more nondualistic mode. In essence, consciousness remains, but the dominance of consciousness by the need-crazed egoic process (especially the making of distinctions) diminishes, leaving a simpler, "nonegoic" awareness in its wake. And as has been shown through studies of both the psychedelic and meditation experiences (both, in my opinion, closely parallel to the wilderness experience), such non–goal-oriented awareness seems to have the capacity to open consciousness to Mind—that is, to the more natural flows of information from nature. In this sense, we could say that when humans can open their consciousness to natural processes, they find "nature reinforcing itself" (and of course, when open to cultural processes, we experience "culture reinforcing itself").

From this perspective, the prevalence of depression or other severe problems upon a sudden return from the wilderness to the urban world can be explained as the contrast between widely divergent forms of egoic processing (and the accompanying different modes of consciousness). People often are quite explicit about how their minds feel "open" and "airy" in the wilderness, as contrasted with "turgid," "tight," and "crowded" in urban culture. People also talk very clearly about "entering into the Wilderness Mind" or "the Mind of the River," and this seems indeed to be a very comfortable and beautiful experience.

This kind of verbal exploration of the wilderness experience (here summarized only very partially) has been very useful in investigating such issues as just how psychologically different people enter into the wilderness. Obviously, many (if not most) wilderness excursions— those that attempt to reproduce cultural comforts if not basic cultural dynamics—cross the wilderness boundary physically but not psychologically, even though every wilderness trip will of course have some effect. I have found it useful to posit a gradient between the polarity of culture and wilderness—a gradient of the "wilderness effect"—ranging from "none" (no effect) to a complete blowout of one's usual programs for processing reality. Somewhere along this gradient is a transition point, where one's mode of information processing switches from culture-dominated (which in the case of our culture would be dualism-producing) to nature-dominated (which presumably would be something closer to what would be called a "systemic communion"). Thus, this change point along the gradient is the *psychological* wilderness boundary, and it is my perception that not many cross it. Many "empowerment" types of wilderness programs, for example, are not experiencing wilderness on its own terms but are using wilderness to develop skills dictated as "useful" or "empowering" by our culture. There is nothing wrong with empowerment or adjustment per se, but if the culture to which we are adjusting is destructive of nature, then we have a problem. This may be yet another example of exploiting wilderness to serve the voracious needs of a culture increasingly attempting to distance itself from nature.

As I've said, when consciousness opens fully to wilderness and immerses itself in natural processes, the return is almost always a painful experience. In returning to the culture, we plunge ourselves back into the forces that split consciousness from nature, or Mind, in the first place. In the painful "reentry" experience, we *feel* our newly open and connected beings congeal into hardened, separate, well-defended selves. Although unpleasant, this process is perhaps a unique opportunity to experience mindfully the cultural forces that normally operate outside our awareness.

A key issue becomes how to maintain, or integrate, wilderness-learned modes of knowing when living again within our culture. In the early years of the wilderness program, I attempted to "up the ante" by adding more "ego-dissolving processes" without adequate follow-up. Often the initial euphoria upon returning to the comforts of civilization would give way within hours, or a few days at most, to disruptive, dysfunctional behavior.

Interestingly, with yoga and meditation added to both the preparation and post-trip periods, as well as to the trips themselves, such dysfunctions almost completely ceased. Group support was essential, and I suspect this was part of the "protection." Practices such as meditation, when seriously undertaken, are explicitly designed to facilitate the arousal of nonegoic awareness. To be able to open to the same awareness that occurred in the wilderness through an ongoing practice could extend the transformations of consciousness into everyday life within the culture. I think this an important key to minimizing reentry problems.

I also suggest coming back as slowly as possible. A few days at a "halfway house" between wilderness and full cultural experience has been extremely helpful. I counsel wilderness participants to leave the wilderness without regret, without holding on, to find healing in the transition, and also to plan for continuing transitions between wilderness and culture on a regular basis. It is also helpful to establish political and cultural relationships with the wilderness visited. Since all wildernesses are at risk—all are being damaged in one way or another—there are plenty of opportunities for such relationships.

Of course, continuing with the wilderness group itself supports an ongoing healed relationship with nature. This can be a basis for future trips and continuing meditation practices—something like a twelve-step group for those "in recovery from civilization."

Humans have the idea, now centuries old, that we are above natural processes rather than immersed in them. We have thought, and continue to teach our children to think, that we can control nature, at least most of the time, and we have felt validated in this belief by the modest success of some of our inventions.

This is still a popular idea, but perhaps we're beginning to awaken to all the ways we cannot control nature and to all the damage we cause when we try. To some—an increasing number, I hope—there is a growing attitude that we have no choice but to find our appropriate role amid the infinite webs of natural processes.

Somewhere in there—assuming we're not a mutation that has failed—there's a contribution we can make to the whole, something unique, something comparable to the eagle's eyesight, the dolphin's hearing, the salmon's perfect motion when turning to dig the spawning bed in clean gravel.

Perhaps the wilderness experience can help us get there, help us to reconnect, help us open to the wisdom inherent in the infinite information systems of natural networks.

Or perhaps when we come to realize the rapidly degrading quality of all wilderness areas from overuse, the escalating threats to wilderness from resource-dependent industries, or the fact that in much of the world "wilderness" is seen in terms of desperate survival rather than recreation, we can come to see "the wilderness experience" as a vision or a model of modes of healing that don't require wilderness. Perhaps the clearest evidence of our recovery will be that we do not demand that wilderness heal us. We will have learned to let it be.

For a wilderness that must heal us is surely a commodity, just as when we can only look at wilderness as a source of endless wealth.

Let that which serves the culture—at this point in our history at least—be done in the culture. And if we do use wilderness, let us use it in ways that further its rehabilitation as well as our own. Let us use it for those healing processes that cannot take place anywhere else.

The Ecology of Grief

PHYLLIS WINDLE

A S A PROFESSIONAL environmentalist and a hospital chaplain
trained in grief counseling, Phyllis Windle uniquely embodies
the full interdisciplinary complexity of ecopsychology. In this essay
on the mourning she has experienced for environmental loss—and
the way in which she has been inhibited from openly expressing that
bereavement—she captures the sensibility required by a new ecological self. She reminds us that "for an environmental ethic to succeed,
nature needs to be meaningful to us on a variety of levels, including
the emotional." Her essay also asks challenging questions about the
degree to which professional science may be gender-biased. In suggesting that women scientists have a stronger sense of "our personal
attachments to the organisms and systems we study," she raises the
possibility that science itself, including ecology, may have to be psychologically transformed if our emotional bond with the Earth is to
be restored.

> For one species to mourn the death of another is a new thing un-
> der the sun.
> ALDO LEOPOLD

[One] who remains passive when overwhelmed with grief loses
[the] best chance of recovering elasticity of mind.

CHARLES DARWIN

Henry Mitchell's gardening column in the *Washington Post* for Sunday, April 8, 1990, was entitled "The Demise of the Dogwood." Mitchell wrote it shortly after the dogwood anthracnose (*Discula destructiva*) was first detected in the Washington area; it had been killing trees in New England and on the West Coast since the late 1970s and was already widespread in the Great Smoky Mountains. Mitchell interviewed Jay Stipes, a plant pathologist, who feared the disease could "annihilate the species."

Mitchell's column stunned me. Memories of dogwoods came flooding back. Nonbotanists think botanists identify trees in winter by magic, but distinctive flower buds are part of the secret. Surely many plant taxonomy students, facing their first test in winter botany, remember dogwoods' readily identifiable buds with a fondness like my own. Other University of Georgia graduates will remember Athens adrift in pink and white flowers in the spring. A fellow graduate student, a Californian, referred to "dogwood clouds," and I remember her image every year when the dogwoods bloom in Washington. I also remember my first wild dogwoods. Across a southern Illinois field, a few gloriously white-blooming trees stood against a background of dark pines. I was doing field work with the man I loved, and those wild trees blossomed in my heart, too.

I have now been following news of dogwood anthracnose for several years. Why, I wonder, did this bad news for the environment hit me so hard? Why do I want to commemorate the dying trees? I am an ecologist. Also, I am a trained hospital chaplain, an expert on death, dying, and grief. Finally, I realize: I am in mourning for these beautiful trees.

This realization was slow in coming because almost all of the literature on grief pertains to the death of humans. However, a significant number of professional veterinary societies and veterinary schools now research pet loss and counsel grief-stricken pet owners. Their work shows the similarity between grieving for the human members of our families and for the animals to which we are attached. Additional research indicates that other types of loss also cause grief: reactions to the loss of an arm or leg, of a home, or of a job show similarities to the loss of someone we love.

Generally, mourning has certain recognized (if disorderly and chaotic) phases: from the shock and numbness of the initial weeks of bereavement, through months in which yearning and then disorientation predominate, to the longest period, in which people reorganize their lives, internally and externally. At first, acceptance of death is only intellectual. Later steps, including emotional acceptance and the reshaping of oneself and the outer world to reflect the new reality, are often more difficult but just as critical to recovery. During this period, feelings of sadness, anger, depression, and despair are common. Dogwood anthracnose stirs all these feelings in me. This disease also reminds me that no one becomes an environmental biologist for money; this science is a labor of love.

The Love of Species and Places

Biologists often love their organisms. Ecologists often love their field sites. Does anyone really doubt it? Read E. O. Wilson's work and imagine how he feels toward ants. Watch Jane Goodall interact with chimpanzees and ask what she feels for them. Read some of George Woodwell's essays, or Rachel Carson's, and gauge the depth of their passion. Listen to graduate students when they return from the Organization for Tropical Studies' field sites in Costa Rica and hear their awe, delight, and tenderness for the land. Probably others feel the same about Hubbard Brook and Coweeta; the mountain research stations in Crested Butte and Nederland, Colorado; Warren Woods and the biological station at Douglas Lake in Michigan; and all the other beautiful places where we have done research, taught, and lived.

Personally, this attachment still embarrasses me sometimes. I was recently asked, in a television interview, how I felt about melaleuca (*Melaleuca quinquenervia*), the nonindigenous tree that is displacing native vegetation in and around Everglades National Park. Colleagues and I had been examining the problems caused by melaleuca, and I had already answered the predictable questions on the nature and severity of the trees' effects and possible responses. But how did I feel about the tree? I answered laughingly that, as a botanist, I had to admire a tree that was so successful. I could hear the enthusiasm in my voice. Later, I repented my candor and prayed the editor would not make me look like an insensitive fool.

This passion, this ability and willingness to admire and care about other species and places, may be among biologists' most admirable qualities. Our attachments may even be necessary and important. Nobel Prize–winning geneticist Barbara McClintock speaks about her "feeling for the organism," her intimate knowledge of the individual corn plants in her research projects, and her deep enjoyment of that knowledge. "Good science cannot proceed without a deep emotional investment on the part of a scientist," concludes McClintock's biographer, Evelyn Fox Keller.[1]

The factors that influence what work we choose and love are complex and psychological, as well as social, economic, and political. These factors make biologists' attachments to nature complicated and deep. For example, I learned to be competitive at the knees of much older siblings. Now, I laugh that my dissertation was on plant competition. Washington is filled with agricultural policy analysts who, like me, found a professional way to remain connected to our rural roots.

Sometimes attachment to nature fills needs unmet by other people. As a child, Sylvia Earle, the oceanographer, found among the plants and animals of the Gulf of Mexico consolation for an unhappy move in childhood. Not only did McClintock's "feeling for the organism" provide her with unusual insight, it also provided emotional sustenance during times without much friendship or professional support.

Certainly my love of plants and natural beauty is a gift from my father, a lifelong gardener. Like him, I am more proficient at loving plants than loving children. Illinois's woods and fields salved my childhood loneliness. As I grew up, wild and beautiful places quite naturally came to represent not just sanctuary from painful events, but also the deepest mysteries of life and that which transcends our individual experiences.

Although we rarely acknowledge the nature and depth of our biological and ecological loves, outsiders have a clear radar for them. Notice how quickly developers accuse us of caring more for spotted owls, snail darters, and wildflowers than for people. Our guilty backpeddling sug-

1. Evelyn Fox Keller, *A Feeling for the Organism* (San Francisco: W. H. Freeman, 1983), p. 198.

gests we know they are right; at least about our love for the organisms
and places in which we invest our life's work, if not about how people
rank in our affections. Certainly the reporter who asked me about melaleuca knew enough scientists to anticipate an interesting answer if he
asked how a plant ecologist felt about a tree.

The importance of our relationships to the natural world should surprise ecologists less than it does others. Ours is a science of relationships.
Usually, though, we do not consider our personal attachments to the
organisms and systems we study. Perhaps the ideal of the dispassionate
observer stands in our way. Or perhaps women scientists notice these
connections more readily. Maybe we needed more female peers before
we could speak of these matters openly.

I no longer doubt the importance or nature of my attachment to dogwoods. Nor do I feel alone in my grief for their loss.

The Grief of Ecologists

In all strict logic, the loss of a species of bird on some small remote island mat-
ters little to the future of the world. Even the irreversible loss of soil and vegeta-
tion from some eroded African hillside is a small thing. Yet people grieve. . . .
These feelings can not be embodied in the hard and brittle logic of science, but
they may have truth of another kind, for all that.   MARTIN HOLDGATE

David Norton writes about the loss of an endemic New Zealand mistle-
toe, subtitling his article "An Obituary for a Species." Aldo Leopold en-
titles an essay about a favorite place "Marshland Elegy." I ask a U.S.
Forest Service pathologist about his reaction to dogwood anthracnose,
and he speaks of his depression. "It's sad," *The Seattle Times* quotes Jim
Litchatowitch, a biologist, when officials declare the lower Columbia
coho salmon extinct.

Ecologists are both blessed and cursed in seeing natural systems
clearly. We see what is there and also know what is gone. I know that
dogwoods formerly bloomed along Skyline Drive in Virginia, and for me
the forest understory will never look the same. Similarly, the loss of a
forest system, not that of a single species, haunts Bill McKibben:

The end of nature probably also makes us reluctant to attach ourselves to its
remnants, for the same reason that we usually don't choose friends from

among the terminally ill. I love the mountain outside my back door. . . . But I know that some part of me resists getting to know it better—for fear, weak-kneed as it sounds, of getting hurt. If I knew as well as a forester what sick trees looked like, I fear I would see them everywhere. I find now that I like the woods best in winter, when it's harder to tell what might be dying. The winter woods might be perfectly healthy come spring, just as the sick friend, when she's sleeping peacefully, might wake up without the wheeze in her lungs.[2]

Likewise, Michael Soulé's anguish regards broad ecological losses: "As the number of exotics in most regions produces a cosmopolitanization of remnant wildlands, there will be an agonizing period of transition, especially for ecologists. . . . There are moments when the destruction of a favorite place, of entire biotas and ecosystems, seems unbearable and the future looks bleak indeed."[3]

Scientists and resource managers usually do not speak freely about this aspect of our feelings for the places and organisms that are part of our work any more than of our love for nature. "The sadness discernible in some marshes arises, perhaps, from their having once harbored cranes. Now they stand humbled, adrift in history."

I treasure the poetry of Aldo Leopold's expression here. I suspect, though, that it is on our faces, not the marsh's, that the sadness is discernible. Perhaps it is our discomfort with that sadness that sees a marsh in tears. Any chaplain would say that we do better by crying our own tears.

But mourning for ecological losses has no simple or predictable path. I suspect that ecologists, like other scientists, are prone to inhibiting the pain of grief. We are solidly attached to the life of the mind, and of the several steps experts consider essential to recovery, only the first is intellectual.

I speak from experience. I am tempted to dismiss my feelings for dog-woods as irrational, inappropriate, anthropomorphic. My arguments go like this: another tree will take the dogwood's place; death is part of the life-cycle, too; evolution removes as well as adds species. These arguments are all true. Timing is the key issue, though. Premature reassur-

2. Bill McKibben, *The End of Nature* (New York: Random House, 1989), p. 21.
3. Michael Soulé, "The Onslaught of Alien Species and Other Challenges in the Coming Decades," *Conservation Biology* 4 (1990), pp. 234, 238.

ance and pressure to accept a loss just short-circuit the grieving and recovery process.

Our external as well as our internal worlds may make environmental losses difficult to mourn. We have almost no social support for expressing this grief. When I sit beside a hospital bed as a chaplain, I expect people to cry about the unwelcome changes they are experiencing. I expect and accept patients' dark and intense feelings—rage at life's unfairness and guilt for doing too little, for example—and anticipate despairing questions about life's meaning. Their tears (and sometimes my own) are a sign of work well done. Honest conversations about grief that come quite naturally at a bedside are far more difficult at a lab bench or conference table. Thus it is harder for me to speak freely about my grief for dogwoods with ecological colleagues than with fellow chaplains.

Gaps in knowledge also make for a particularly difficult period of mourning. (This makes recovery from divorce so formidable.) Environmental problems often involve high doses of uncertainty. Where did dogwood anthracnose originate? Is acid rain partly responsible for its spread? Are some trees resistant or not? Now experts fear less for the total demise of the species but more for the loss of trees above, say, elevations of three thousand feet. Charles Fenyvesi, in the *Washington Post* (June 27, 1991), calls out: "Hope for the dogwood."

So do I grieve for my lovely dogwoods, or not? Reducing uncertainty and disbelief is important in getting grief off to a good start. For that reason, many hospitals and religious groups stress seeing the body. In fact, this step is considered so important to coping with grief that it is built into certain hospitals' sudden-death protocols. With the dogwoods, however, it is unclear whether I should look for bodies or cultivate hope. Even if I decided to grieve, how would I go about doing it?

The Usefulness of Ritual

People have always used rituals to help themselves mourn and recover from grief. For example, funerals usually reinforce the awareness of loss, sanction remembering, facilitate the expression of feelings, provide support, guide the needed reorganization of life, and affirm life's meaning. Funerals and memorial services serve as a rite of passage between initial shock and the longer, more private phases of grieving. Not all mourning customs are religious, though. We give gifts, eat together, show group solidarity, and protect mourners—all ways to help the grief-stricken.

The NAMES quilt—that collection of more than fourteen thousand fabric panels memorializing those dead of AIDS—is a particularly effective nonreligious ritual commemorating private and public loss. Making individual panels heals the makers; viewing the assemblage links those touched by tragedy. It has also become a powerful means to educate people and to call for political action.[4]

There are scientists among us who also think in terms of rituals, even funerals, for the species and places we are losing. The Wisconsin Society for Ornithology dedicated a monument to the passenger pigeon in a state park in 1947. Ecologists gathered on October, 12, 1992, where Columbus may have landed in the Bahamas to "conduct a funeral ceremony for the natural environment of the Western hemisphere. They will mourn the demise of the New World's natural heritage and the eradication of entire groups of indigenous Caribbean people."[5]

This is dramatic stuff, perhaps too outrageous for many ecologists' tastes. The importance of rituals in helping mourners cope is undisputed, however, and I see no reason why ecologists should not tap this resource in these difficult times. We could create a quilt of our own, with panels to celebrate the species we have loved and lost. We could hold a wake for a precious piece of land, gathering to tell stories of the field trips, research, and academic degrees that one particular place provided. We could create a family album, filled with the recollections of our professional grandparents, writing about the natural areas they have loved and lost in their lifetimes. We could create a fund for memorials to invest our losses with public meaning. Our mourning rituals could celebrate, too, and affirm our faith in the processes of ecology and evolution. We could note the remaining beauty of the earth, the birth of new species or subspecies, and the grand rhythms of the biogeochemical cycles.

4. NAMES Project, *The Quilt: Stories from the NAMES Project* (New York: Pocket Books, 1988).
5. See H. J. Viola and C. Margolis, eds., *Seeds of Change* (Washington, D.C.: Smithsonian Institution Press, 1991), p. 249.

Most of our contemporary mourning customs are important in the first weeks and months of the grieving process. I suspect that ecologists are more likely to need support in a longer, continuing way. Environmental losses are intermittent, chronic, cumulative, and without obvious beginnings and endings. Thus, we may have to devise our own unique customs. But they might be customs much needed by a society facing many kinds of transition.

The Benefits of Grieving Well

Experts urge us to grieve not only because successful grief is beneficial, but also because failure to grieve can have such far-reaching consequences. Generally, problems originate in two ways. Mourning can become excessive and prolonged, leading to chronic grief from which recovery never seems to come. Alternatively, we can inhibit the process. It becomes distorted, and grief emerges in different forms. The results are not trivial. Unresolved grief is the underlying cause of problems for as much as 20 percent of the people treated at some substance abuse centers.[6]

Grief is not pleasant, as anyone knows who has mourned a child, a parent, a close friend, or a spouse. At the same time, it has its own bittersweet richness and intensity. Charles Darwin concluded that grieving serves us well in the long term. Colin Murray Parkes's landmark study elaborates this idea:

> Willingness to look at the problems of grief and grieving instead of turning away from them is the key to successful grief work in the sufferer, the helper, the planner, and the research worker. . . . We may choose to deal with our fear by turning away from its source. . . . But each time we do this we only add to the fear, perpetuate the problems, and miss an opportunity to prepare ourselves for the changes that are inevitable in a changing world.
>
> Times of transition are times of opportunity and any confrontation with an unfamiliar world is both an opportunity for autonomous mastery and a threat to one's established adjustments to life. . . . But there are some life changes which, because of their magnitude or because of a particular characteristic, carry a special risk of producing, not maturation, but dislocation.[7]

6. G. W. Davidson, *Understanding Mourning* (Minneapolis: Augsburg Publications, 1984).
7. Colin Murray Parkes, *Bereavement* (New York: International Universities Press, 1974), pp. 194–95.

Perhaps the transition ahead for ecologists is just such a risky one. This makes it especially urgent that we do our grief work.

What might we get from tackling this seemingly unpleasant task? People emerge from grief with new insights about their relationship to the deceased and renewed energy for loving again. The benefits might extend far beyond our individual recovery. Aldo Leopold's work is a case study. Robert Finch describes Leopold's evolution, with the theme of environmental loss as a way station, as "a necessary, important sojourn in the wilderness of loss, ignorance, and self-education from which Leopold will finally wrest his holistic 'land ethic.' "

As ethicists and others explore the underpinnings necessary for our care-filled treatment of the Earth, they often return to this same idea: the importance of the nature and depth of our relationship to other organisms and to the Earth itself. Stephen Kellert suggests that, for an environmental ethic to succeed, nature would need to be meaningful to us on a variety of levels, including the emotional. Here again it is ecologists' deep attachment to organisms and systems that is our strength—a potential model for others to emulate.

What might we need to model this process? "Fortitude," says Soulé, "when the temptation to turn and walk away is almost overpowering." Also, we shall need passion, commitment, creativity, energy, and concentration. We shall have none of these if we fail to grieve (alone and with each other) for the magnificent trees, the lovely animals, and the beautiful places that we are losing.[8]

8. Much of my training in grief counseling was done on leave from the Office of Technology Assessment. I am grateful for that support. However, the views expressed here are my own and not those of OTA. Good Samaritan Regional Medical Center and Phoenix Childrens Hospital in Phoenix, Arizona, Alexandria Hospital, Alexandria, Virginia, the Pastoral Counseling and Consultation Centers of Greater Washington, and Westminster Presbyterian Church in Washington, D.C., also provided support for this work. My thanks go to Kathy Parker, David Wayland, Michael Soulé, and Daryl Chubin for critically reading a draft of this article. I appreciate their encouragement to develop these ideas further, along with that of Chris Elfring, Beth Chadsey, and Gilbert F. White.

PART TWO

ECOPSYCHOLOGY
IN PRACTICE

EVERY POLITICAL MOVEMENT seeks to change human behavior. Environmentalists, in their struggle to invent ecologically sustainable human institutions, confront some of our species's most deeply entrenched forms of dysfunctional behavior.

Many methods have been developed by ecopsychologists for reeducating our environmental conduct. They include Terrance O'Connor's aggressive ethical interventions, Sarah Conn's ecotherapy, Leslie Gray's shamanic counseling, Steven Harper's use of the deep wilderness, and Laura Sewall's techniques for ecological seeing. William Cahalan searches out the ecological potential of Gestalt techniques, Elan Shapiro makes use of environmental restoration as a therapy that saves both the psyche and the natural habitat, and Joanna Macy uses her workshops to help discover empowerment on the far side of despair.

Until we understand the motivations that make people do what they do, the changes we achieve are apt to be superficial and short-lived. The greatest contributions ecopsychology has to offer the environmental movement are new ways of healing and of educating.

Therapy for a Dying Planet

TERRANCE O'CONNOR

I N THE MID-EIGHTIES, during a lecture to an audience of divorced men and women, Terrance O'Connor suddenly experienced an "outburst" of environmental concern. His experience speaks to the impatience therapists were then beginning to feel with the restricted, often self-absorbed context of their profession. Just as Paul Shepard had come to see that environmentalists needed a deeper sense of the psychological dimensions, so O'Connor had begun to feel the need of broadening therapy to reach beyond the individual and the family. His expression of that need is blunt; the methods he found for meeting it are far from subtle, but his assertion of a new professional ethic is a clear wake-up call. He also neatly links the nonsustainability of person-to-person relationships with that of our human-to-planet relationship. In both cases, he contends, we settle for "petty relationships" in which "control, denial, and abuse are tolerated."

There is a story, perhaps apocryphal, about an incident that occurred in Frieda Fromm-Reichmann's practice shortly before she left Germany for the United States. A young woman with numerous irrational fears came to her for help. During the course of the psychoanalysis, the patient gradually overcame her fears, and after three years the therapy was successfully ended. A few weeks later the young woman, who was Jewish, was picked up by the Gestapo and sent to a concentration camp.

By helping people adapt to a destructive society, are we doing more harm than good? Today, as desert sands advance across Africa like conquering armies, and life is on the retreat in every continent, it occurs to me that the sad tale of Fromm-Reichmann's client is more relevant than ever.

We sit in our offices helping parents raise children, divorcees get their bearings, couples find ways to deepen their relationships, while outside the air gets fouler and the oceans' ecosystems break down. In a year's time, if we are successful, the parents and children are doing well, the divorcee is enjoying her independence, the couple has developed a more satisfying relationship. Meanwhile hundreds, perhaps thousands of species, have vanished forever from the Earth. Each hour, five square miles of rainforest are destroyed; by the end of a year, this area of destruction is the size of Pennsylvania.

We are facing an unparalleled global crisis, a disaster much greater than Hitler, Stalin, or the Khmer Rouge could ever create. What is the meaning of therapy, and what is the responsibility of the therapist in such a world?

A few years ago I was giving a talk titled "The Mature and Healthy Intimate Relationship" to a group of divorced people. Midway through the talk a woman asked, "Last week we had a speaker who said that some people are satisfied with very limited relationships. So why should we want this mature relationship? Why should we bother?" The question caught me off guard. "I don't know," I admitted. "I would think that the benefits would speak for themselves. But obviously everyone has a choice."

I went on with my presentation, but her question kept nagging me until eventually I lost all concentration and came to a halt. "I need to stop here and go back to the question I was just asked," I finally said. "Let me say something about the status quo. The status quo is that the hole in the ozone layer is as big as the United States. The status quo is that some scientists are predicting that by the middle of the next century global warming will result in most of the coastal cities in the United States being below sea level, and will make the grain belt a wasteland. The status quo is that acid rain, besides destroying the lakes and forests, is now considered to be the leading cause of lung cancer after cigarette smoke. The status quo is that thirty-five thousand people die of starvation every day. Also every day, two or more species become extinct, not due to natural selection but due to deforestation and pollution. By the year 2000 this is expected to accelerate to one hundred species a day. In other words, mass extinction. What does this say to you? To me it says that the status quo is that the planet is dying! The planet is dying because we are satisfied with our limited relationships in which control, denial, and abuse are tolerated. The status quo is that we have these petty relationships with each other, between nations, with ourselves and the natural world. Why should we bother? Because healthy relationships are not an esoteric goal. It is a matter of our very survival and the survival of most of the life upon this earth."

After this outburst I stood silently facing an apparently stunned audience staring back at me. I was trying to remember where I had been in my presentation when a man in the back stood up and began talking about the destruction of the rainforests. The whole feeling in the room had shifted. The greater part of the audience had come in concerned with their own loneliness. As we began to look at all of our personal concerns from a global perspective, we could see that the patterns of control, denial, and projection that sabotage intimate relationships are the very patterns that endanger the world. To change these patterns is to change not just our social lives but our relationship to the planet.

In *The Unheard Cry for Meaning*, Viktor Frankl says that in finding meaning we are "perceiving a possibility embedded in reality," and that, "unless we use the opportunity to fulfill the meaning inherent and dormant in a situation, it will pass and be gone forever." Citing his own experience as an inmate in Auschwitz and Dachau, and his work with POWs, he asserts that the will to meaning has survival value; that those most likely to survive were those who were oriented toward something outside themselves, a meaning to be fulfilled: "In a word, existence was dependent on 'self transcendence.'" And so it is today. A transcendence of sorts is necessary if we are to meet the challenge of the global crisis, a transcendence of who we are in relationship to the human community and to the planet. Another way of saying this is that it is time for a shift in context. As Paul Watzlawick says in *Pragmatics of Human Communication*, "A phenomenon remains unexplainable as long as the range of

observation is not wide enough to include the context in which the phenomenon occurs."

We took a powerful leap when we widened our view of the individual's problems to include the family system in which they occurred. Perhaps it is time for another leap. It is time to begin to go beyond our
individual families to attend to the human family.

Of the thirty-five thousand people who die of starvation each day, the
large majority are children. Whose children are these? If we are the human family, these are our children, pure and simple. Tens of thousands
of our children starve to death each day, not because there is not enough
food to feed them, but because we are a dysfunctional family. Look at
us! We are at once overcontrolling and dreadfully neglectful. Like the
alcoholic family, we ignore the bodies piling up in our living room, and
we ignore them at our growing peril.

As the problems become more evident, I am getting a more receptive
response when I talk or write about the global crisis. Still, avoidance reactions are common. Most boil down to "I don't want to hear about it,"
or "It's not my responsibility." Some people convince themselves that
"it's not happening" or that "it's not my planet." Some even mask their
despair in a quasi-spiritual facade of nonattachment: "What the hell, it's
only one planet. There are billions." More common are those who will
admit to feeling a bit guilty about not doing anything. The equation here
is: doing nothing plus feeling guilty about it equals doing something.

Action is called for, but action motivated by guilt may only compound
the problem. We are in disharmony with the world because we are in
disharmony with ourselves. Guilt is an indication of this. Guilt is a warning that there is an incongruity in our value system, a schism in our sense
of self that needs to be investigated. If we act without introspection, we
simply throw our weight to one side of the inner conflict, increasing the
disharmony. Our actions will be incomplete and fragmented. We will
make some token move and fall back into denial and minimization. To
heal is to make whole.

A few years ago I spent some time alone in an isolated cabin far from
a road, without water or electricity. I hiked in with a stack of books. For
a week I sat on the porch and watched a blacksnake lying in the rafters
and the chipmunks scurrying between rocks; I listened to the song of
the wind through the trees. I read about the state of the world. I cried.

It was like reading the minute details of one's mother's cancer. When I had enough of reading and crying I went for long hikes. I followed a magnificent stream. The woods were lovely. I saw deer and grouse and wild turkey and once, I think, a coyote. I came back to the porch and read some more, and sometimes I cried, and sometimes I raged, and sometimes I looked up at the ancient stones and beautiful trees and the abundance of life around me and I loved it so fiercely I thought my heart would burst.

If this is not my planet, whose is it? If this is not my family, whose is it? If not my responsibility, whose? I am both the victim and the victimizer. I am the cause and I am the cure. When I act out of this realization, I act not out of guilt but out of self-love, a love that includes my family, which includes my planet. When I look, I see. When I educate myself, I break through my denial and see that humankind is facing an absolutely unprecedented crisis. When I act from this knowledge, I act not out of obligation or idealism, but because I live in a straw house and I smell smoke. I realize the truth that, in Krishnamurti's words, "You are the world, and the world is on fire."

An awareness is dawning, and a shift is occurring. In the face of the darkening clouds there has been some very positive movement around the globe. The lessening of tensions between East and West is the absolutely necessary beginning to saving the world. We all know that if Mom and Dad can get together, the rest becomes workable. If the former Soviet Union and the United States can continue to build trust, we can liberate enormous energies in the forms of money, natural resources, technology, intelligence, and action to meet the common threat. And in our own backyards a revolution is taking place, a powerful grass-roots movement. I am referring to the astounding proliferation of twelve-step groups in the past few years.

While there are many healing aspects to the twelve-step groups, two interest me here. The first is the philosophy of giving up the attempt to control that over which one has no control. Ultimately this seems to me to be blowing the whistle on our hubris, our worship of the will that has allowed us to gain dominion over the world. This is the will with which spouses try to dominate each other, and that our clients struggle to control, rather than find harmony with themselves and the world. This will is a useful tool, but it is a jealous and petty god.

The second quality of these programs that gives me hope is their emphasis on responsibility for oneself and to each other. There is a recognition that we are all in this together. As therapists we have learned some unforgettable lessons about our limits, but we have also witnessed the wondrous unfolding of human potential. We know better than most that reality is dependent upon our perception of it, and that a simple change in our point of view can yield a host of new possibilities. So how does an awareness of the global crisis translate to specific behaviors in our offices? In my waiting room I have a shelf stacked with literature from environmental organizations. Above the shelf is a photograph of the Earth taken from space. Above the photograph is a sign that reads, "Mother Earth Needs You." Beside the photograph is a brief synopsis of the dangers and opportunities of the global crisis. Some of my clients are suffering from personal crises of such intensity that they are unable to focus on anything else. For them, my "opportunity corner" has little interest. But overshadowing many of my clients' genuine issues is the general malaise to which President Carter was so impolitic as to refer a decade ago, in a speech to a nation yearning to escape to the good old days. To these clients I mention the global crisis as I might tell an Ericksonian story or an incident from my own life. I bring it in intentionally when it is relevant and therapeutic.

Clients struggling with the purpose and meaning of their lives are often doing so in obsessive isolation from the movement of life around them. They are attempting to achieve a goal, such as marriage, without first being in relationship with themselves and the human community. Coming to grips with the global crisis offers both a deeper understanding of the human condition and a motivation to break down the psychological barriers that allow us to tolerate our starving children and ailing oceans. I have even, upon occasion, interrupted a client's obsessive, self-absorbed soliloquy with, "Are you aware that the planet is dying?" I might interrupt a professional debate on the best therapeutic modality with the same question.

I am not suggesting that we drop our therapeutic tools, but that we use them with awareness of a rapidly and profoundly changing planet. Perhaps Frieda Fromm-Reichmann should have simply advised her patient to flee. We do not have that option. When I speak of global consciousness, I am talking from a perspective in which the difference between client and therapist is only a difference of role. We are equally responsible for the state of the planet and equally affected by it. I must say that I do not see my colleagues being much more free of malaise and denial than are my clients. Isn't it strange that we supposed experts and healers of human relations give but passing notice to our extraordinarily unhealthy relationship to the planet as a whole, a relationship that will ultimately undermine our work completely?

We must become more aware. And contribute that awareness rather than our denial to the stream of human consciousness. An active membership in just one environmental group puts one in the pipeline to receive all the information and direction one needs. We must become part of the solution rather than part of the problem. What is the responsibility of a therapist on a dying planet?

Physician, heal thyself.

When the Earth Hurts, Who Responds?

SARAH A. CONN

SARAH CONN BEGAN experimenting with the "self–world" connection in psychology in the mid-1980s. She has since become a major practitioner and teacher of environmentally related therapeutic techniques. In individual and group work, her approach often involves unusual, imaginative forms of intervention that actively direct her clients' attention to the ecological context of their anxieties and distress. Her concept of "materialistic disorder" represents a clear challenge to the American consumer culture. Drawing upon the insights of Deep Ecologists like Arne Naess, she attempts to replace the isolated, atomistic personality that dominates psychotherapeutic theory with an ecological sense of the self. In this essay, she shows how the concept of the "relational self," first developed in feminist psychology, expanded in her work to take on environmental significance. She also recounts her ecological awakening and reviews the early history of ecopsychology at the Center for Psychology and Social Change in Cambridge, Massachusetts.

On a spring day several years ago, I stopped to buy strawberries by the side of the road in Cambridge, Massachusetts. They were beautiful, irresistible, and inexpensive. I bought a large box and put it on the front seat of my car. As I drove away, I was filled with sensual pleasure: the tender smell filling the car, the sweet taste, the anticipated delight of my family when I carried the large box into the house. The berries connected me to the sunshine, the rain, the soil, the farmer. Life in that moment seemed very good.

Then I noticed the writing on the box. The strawberries were from California. A dark feeling swept over me, as suddenly I was also connected to the truckers, the oil companies, and the farming conglomerates, to the ozone hole, monoculture, and soil depletion. I could see a fine, white substance on some of the berries. "I had better not eat any more before washing them," I thought. But what about the farm workers who planted, cultivated, and picked them? Were those workers suffering from pesticide poisoning? How much were they paid? What happens to the soil in which these strawberries are grown? How could this man sell these strawberries so inexpensively? What am I supporting in the larger world by buying these strawberries? What can I do in my everyday life to take into account the whole web represented by these strawberries with which I am now becoming so intimate?

Each of us has, with or without awareness, the ability to connect to the whole interdependent web of life on Earth at any moment and in any activity in our daily lives. Everything we touch comes from the natural world and can connect us to it in the way the strawberries connected me to the sun, rain, and soil. But most of us still seem to act as if the Earth and its nonhuman aspects were separate from us, something "out there" with no life of its own, and therefore unrelated to our "merely personal" concerns.

When I began my life as a psychotherapist, I could not have predicted how greatly ecological insights like these would one day affect my work. Certainly nothing in my professional training prepared me to take on environmental responsibility in my work. I arrived at ecopsychology by a long, circuitous route that leads through the peace and women's movements of the early 1970s and last to environmentalism. At each stage, I learned something that would later help define the self–world connection for me.

It was during and immediately after the Vietnam era that I decided to become a clinical psychologist, a wife, and a mother—in that order. All of these endeavors were centered "in-house," from my office on the third floor to the laundry in the basement.

My oldest child started elementary school and I went to register her. When I first entered the building, I felt huge, much too big for that space. The last time I had been in such a building, I realized, I had been small enough to fit under a desk during air-raid drills. As I sent my child into the wider world in 1979, all my fears from my own childhood in the 1950s returned. With them came anxiety, anger, and isolation, feelings that propelled me out of the house in search of a larger community. I found that community among people in my city who were addressing the nuclear threat in grass-roots peace organizations. They included the anti-nuclear activists Helen and Bill Caldicott, who were then neighbors of ours and who were involved in one of the major projects I joined.

For years after that I kept my peace activism and the spiritual awakening that accompanied it separate from my work as a clinical psychologist, until I realized that I needed to heal that disconnection. In 1985, I organized a conference for the Massachusetts Psychological Association on "The Psychology of Individual and Collective Survival," at which I presented my work on a model for the development of social responsibility. Through that conference, I met other psychologists who shared my concern. These connections eventually led to my first courses on the self–world connection, focusing first on nuclear war and peace, and in the late 1980s on other environmental issues.

I soon realized that working in groups was important in a number of ways. The issues I was confronting were enormous and attending to them was frightening and frustrating. A supportive, compatible group where one could face all aspects of living in an endangered world was essential. Joanna Macy's despair-and-empowerment model was influential in my beginning to work with others in organized, regular, and deep ways. I continue to belong to groups that range from personal activism to professional peer supervision. One example is the Boston Women's Peace Research Group, which I participated in founding in 1987. Here is a description of our process from a paper we wrote together four years later. It summarizes the power of the relational context to stimulate the creativity and effectiveness of the individual participants in the group, a conviction I would carry over into ecopsychology.

Our group of six began meeting in 1987 as the Boston Women's Peace Research Group to explore our common interests in peace and social change, and particularly our shared search for factors that enhance or impede individuals' and group's capacities for peacemaking. We each brought a history of social commitment, ebbing and flowing with the cycles of our lives; a curiosity about the sources of our own commitment and that of others; and a hunger for a creative process rooted in connections with like-minded women.

Our intention was that we would each present our work to the group and receive feedback and support from the others. Every meeting began with a check-in during which each of us shared her personal struggles with the issues and with her work. Each person had moments of feeling overwhelmed by the momentum of the arms race, and each person struggled continuously about ways to take effective action while holding on to some coherence in her life, relationships, and jobs. We found that time spent exploring these connections between "the personal and the political" had several benefits. It helped each of us to make better decisions and work more effectively as individuals. Our meetings went more smoothly after each woman had received some validation and support on the preoccupations she had brought with her. And the content of those meetings grew in richness and depth because they were grounded in our own experiences. Our meetings have often moved between tears and ideas, through empathic connection with the personal struggle of one of us, to a theoretical exploration of the forces for and against peacemaking in the wider culture. For each of us, in different ways, the BWPRG has enhanced our involvement and commitment to peace work.[1]

Out of this grew another group. Janet Surrey (one of the theorists at Wellesley College's Stone Center, a major center for the study of women's psychology and relational theory) and I invited three other psychotherapists to join us in exploring ways to integrate a larger social context into our clinical work. We called ourselves the "Global Therapy Group." In seeking to expand the boundaries of therapy, I again drew upon the work of Joanna Macy. Her living-systems perspective on our psychological responses both to the nuclear threat and to the degradation of the biosphere has informed my teaching from its beginning. Another major influence is the Vietnamese Buddhist teacher Thich Nhat Hanh, who taught the same message of interdependence from a different perspective. Studying with these teachers and practicing meditation for many years taught me to pay attention to multiple levels of connection and the

1. Sylvia Staub and Paula Green, eds., *Psychology and Social Responsibility: Facing Global Challenges* (New York University Press, 1992), p. 289. The other members of BWPRG were Susan Brooks, Priscilla Ellis, Sally Mack, Bianca Cody Murphy, and Janet Surrey.

many consequences of my actions. Teaching undergraduates who were
not psychologists, as I did for five years at Tufts, led me to *The Gaia Peace
Atlas* and the annual publications of Worldwatch Institute. From the students I learned a lot about economic and social-change issues. In fact, I
was on my way to a class at Tufts when I stopped to buy the strawberries
I mentioned at the outset. That moment was an epiphany: all these influences converged as I sat in my car with the strawberries beside me.

Fortunately, I was able to find a place where my concern for the wider
social context of therapy was welcome. Since 1983, when it was founded
by John Mack and others, the Center for Psychology and Social Change
at the Harvard Medical School has been laying the foundation for a new
psychology, one rooted in sustainable, mutually enhancing relationships
among humans and between humans and the more-than-human natural
world. The goal of the center is a transformation of consciousness in order to integrate body and mind, ecology and psychology, soul and spirit.
In 1988, the center arranged an appointment for me at the Harvard Medical School to teach a course for human-services providers, dealing with
the psychology of global awareness and social responsibility. Two years
later I participated at the center with Walter Christie, a psychiatrist, and
William Keepin, an environmental scientist, in organizing the first ecopsychology conference. Under the title "Psychology As If the Whole
Earth Mattered," we looked at the new conceptual models and practices
psychology needs if it is to help achieve sustainable, mutually enhancing
human–Earth relationships.

The center continues to work toward an ecopsychological transformation of theory and practice in psychotherapy. From my experience
teaching courses there, I believe that many psychotherapists are highly
concerned about the human–Earth connection and would bring it into
their work if they knew how. We have not been taught how to move out
of the office, in our theories or in our practice. Most of us are still operating out of old paradigms that constrict our professional movement.
Moreover, with the encroachment of the large insurance corporations
into health care, pychotherapy is in grave danger of becoming unrec-
ognizable as a healing profession; it is more and more driven by economics. "Managed care," for example (which can be a contradiction in
terms when we speak of psychotherapy), constricts our movements even
more. Healing requires openness, an exploration of ways to remember

our wholeness, to reconnect with other humans and with the natural world. The most obvious effect of the industrial age is that much of what we touch in our everyday lives is far removed from its roots in the Earth; its production, transportation, and disposal present major problems to the Earth. The plastic pen I hold, for example, is made from coal or petroleum or cellulose from cotton fiber, combined with salt, air, water, lime, and sulfur. Its production, transportation, and disposal depletes and pollutes the Earth. So when I reconnect with my roots in the Earth through this pen, I am confronted with painful information, just as I am when I observe the strawberries deeply.

I have raised the question, "When the Earth hurts, who responds?" The answer is, I believe, that each of us now experiences in some way— physically, psychologically, economically, or politically—the pain of the Earth. The news about environmental degradation is hard to avoid. Anyone who walks, breathes, looks, or listens knows that the air, the water, and the soil are being contaminated and that nonhuman species are disappearing at alarming rates. Yet the great majority of us, in this country and in much of the Western world, seem to be living our lives as if this were not so. Because we experience the self as separate from the Earth, we feel either overwhelmed by or removed from what we learn about environmental deterioration; we become helpless or indifferent in the face of it, and unable to respond except with numbness and denial.

The common Western belief has been that in order to respond to the "outside world," we have to get our individual psyches in order first. Almost as if we lived in a vacuum, we view the "self" as a bounded, masterful agent who is separate from and prior to the "outside" world, including the natural world. In psychotherapy, we have pathologized and individualized personal pain, viewing any "pain for the world" as a probably pathological experience that has been projected outward. When we act, we tend to address specific personal problems, or sometimes social, economic, or political issues, without much attention to how they are interrelated or affected by the larger context of the degradation of the biosphere. We have, in short, cut ourselves off from our connection to the Earth so thoroughly in our epistemology and our psychology that even though we are "bleeding at the roots," we neither understand the problem nor know what we can do about it.

This disconnection spans all three major "forces" in modern psychotherapy: the psychoanalytic, the behavioral, and the humanistic. All have tended to reflect uncritically the larger context of radical individualism that has become the cultural pathology in our time. In this context, modern psychology as a whole has viewed the individual as an independent, self-contained, separate self motivated by purely egoistic needs and drives to seek personal pleasure and avoid personal pain. This cultural emphasis on the self-contained individual has translated into psychological doctrines like "drive reduction," "reinforcement," and "exchange theories" that seem, in the words of M. Brewster Smith, "to give scientific authority to self-interestedness." They present "the pursuit of self-interest, of self-development, and self-actualization as the primary ends of existence."[2] It is no wonder, then, that none of the diagnostic categories in the *Diagnostic and Statistical Manual IV* addresses the human–Earth relationship in any dynamic way. The *DSM IV* is almost exclusively individualistic in its orientation, contributing to the tendency to pathologize personal pain rather than link it to the larger context.

As an ecopsychologist, I would like to see a revision of the *DSM* that looks at individual symptoms as "signals" of distress in our connection with the larger context or as a defect in the larger context itself. For example, I would interpret what I have called "materialistic disorder," the need to consume, as a serious signal of our culture's disconnection from the Earth. Because we are cut off from our roots, we have forgotten how to hunt for and gather up its treasures, either concretely or imaginatively. Our only current way of hunting and gathering seems to be shopping and accumulating merchandise.

One of my clients, who grew up in a poor, lower-class family, and who from very early in life focused a lot of her energy on making money, has long suffered from, among other things, a severe case of materialistic disorder. In her case, the need was for shoes, electronic equipment, and furniture. In this she is a microcosm of the culture. The inner emptiness that results from the breakdown of community and the rise of consumerism leads people toward addictive behavior as they attempt to fill that emptiness with products, substances, celebrities, and activities.[3] This

2. M. Brewster Smith, "Psychology in the Public Interest: What Have We Done? What Can We Do?" *American Psychologist* 45, no. 4 (1990), 530–36.
3. Philip Cushman, "Why the Self Is Empty," *American Psychologist* 45, no. 5 (1990), 599–611.

client both suffers with and perpetrates the pain of the Earth. Her ad-dictive consuming has improved gradually over the years as she heals from the abuse and deprivation she suffered as a child; she has gone from owning three hundred pairs of shoes to fifteen. This client eventually presented dramatic evidence of the growth of an ecological self. Her roommate had never believed in buying large electronic items or auto-mobiles unless in cooperation with others, nor in purchasing furniture new. She would instead buy old, used pieces and refinish them. My client has joined in this furniture-restoration work and has realized that there is something healing about restoring a table or chair. "You really get to know it intimately by restoring it," she said. "You come to love it." And now, in a major step for her, she is planning to give up her fast sports car to purchase, cooperatively, a more practical, ecologically sound ve-hicle. For this woman, self-healing and attention to the Earth go hand in hand, for in order to do restoration work, whether it be with a piece of furniture, a personal history, or an ecological system, one must enter into an intimate and loving relationship.

The focus on the self-contained individual is accompanied by a cul-tural overemphasis on rational thought to the exclusion of emotional re-sponsiveness, so that pain, or indeed emotional experience of any kind, also tends to be pathologized or truncated rather than validated, en-couraged, and fully felt. The tendency to pathologize deep emotions about the world may result in hurrying the client through the pain rather than encouraging her or him to enter fully into the experience. To do so deprives the person of the potential power that resides in what Miriam Greenspan calls the "dark emotions."[4] We then deprive the larger con-text of the feedback represented by the person's response.

In contrast, an ecologically responsible construction of the self will require what Arne Naess calls an "ecological self," which includes not only growth in human relationships with family and community, but a broadening of the self through identification with all beings, even with the biosphere as a whole. This broadened identification is the basis for the mutuality and passionate engagement, the direct experience of in-terconnectedness, called for by the ecological crisis of our time. When

4. Miriam Greenspan, "Healing Through the Dark Emotions," paper presented at the con-ference "Toward a New Model of Psychotherapy: Connecting the Personal and the Global," at the Massachusetts School of Professional Psychology, May 1991.

we are able to experience this interconnectedness, we need no moral exhortation to adjust our behaviors and our policies in the direction of ecological responsibility. As Naess points out, if we "broaden and deepen" our sense of self, then the Earth flows through us and we act naturally to care for it. In Immanuel Kant's terms, we then engage in "beautiful acts" rather than "moral acts," motivated not by our moral duty to do what is right but rather acting out of positive inclination and pleasure.[5]

An active self–world connection would provide a true "fourth force" in psychology, one that goes beyond the psychoanalytic, behavioral, and humanistic focus on human needs to emphasize the relational nature of the self and the transpersonal, transhuman aspects of reality. "Who I am," Edward E. Sampson observes, "is defined in and through my relations with others; I am completed through these relations and do not exist apart from them. Therefore, my work on behalf of others is simultaneously work on behalf of myself."[6]

While the basic challenge of an ecologically responsible psychotherapy is to develop ways in which clients can see their "merely personal" problems as microcosms of what is happening in the larger world, the sense of the uniqueness of the individual that has emerged over the past few centuries is not to be thrown away. It is to be taken with us as we awaken to our place in the whole. The individual self is, in Arthur Koestler's term, a "holon," simultaneously both a whole, with special qualities and experiences that need to be honored, and a part of a larger whole, whether it be a family, a community, a bioregion, or the living planetary ecosystem. There is danger in overemphasizing any one of these qualities. If we develop rigid boundaries around the self-as-whole, then we separate ourselves from the world and are unavailable to the nourishment essential to aliveness and growth; the capacity for mutuality and engagement is diminished. If, on the other hand, we develop diffuse boundaries and experience only the self-as-part, then we can be swept away by the larger whole, losing the ability to give feedback to the system

5. Arne Naess, "Self-Realization: An Ecological Approach to Being in the World," in John Seed, Joanna Macy, Patricia Fleming, Arne Naess, eds., *Thinking Like a Mountain* (Philadelphia: New Society, 1988), p. 28.
6. Edward E. Sampson, "The Debate on Individualism: Indigenous Psychologies of the Individual and Their Role in Personal and Societal Functioning," *American Psychologist* 43, no. 1 (1988), 20.

from our unique perspective. The capacity for mutuality and engagement is again diminished.

Ecology teaches us that a diverse, open system, when faced with environmental stress, has more ways to respond to challenge than a uniform, closed one. That response requires semipermeable boundaries that are neither too rigid nor too diffuse. In this view, the notion of "the survival of the fittest" finds a new meaning. No longer are the most fit those species or individuals capable of having power over others in a competitive struggle. "The survival of the fittest," as Lewis Thomas reminds us, "does not mean those fit to kill; it means those fitting in best with the rest of life."[7] "Fitting in" refers here to the ability to be open to and to contribute, from one's unique sense of self, to the well-being of the whole system.

A client of mine, after moving to a tropical country, returned for a session while visiting New England. She was having a recurrence of the anxiety episodes that had brought her to therapy many years before. She had returned to New England to sell her house and land, which she loved, and to say good-bye to her family, with whom she was very close. A family crisis was making the transition even more difficult. After exploring this seemingly "personal" level of experience for a while, I asked her how she was saying good-bye to her land here. I knew she had landscaped her house in New England in order to attract the birds, "her creatures," as she called them. She was worried that the new owners would not keep her creatures happy or that they would even sell some of the land for development. She had been born and raised in New England and felt the trees and birds were part of her. In her new country, on the other hand, the landscape was strange, the creatures different. She had worked on her new land, but the plants were so unfamiliar that she felt lost. Then one day while working, she saw an alligator, which terrified her. She was reassured by friends native to the local ecosystem that she would get used to alligators, but the terror was still there, and it was now connected to going out on the land. She was confined indoors more than she ever remembered.

As we explored her experience, what emerged was her sense of shrinkage as a person since she moved to the new country. When the

7. Lewis Thomas, "Are We Fit to Fit In?" *Amicus Journal* (Summer 1981).

family crisis occurred at the same time she was selling her New England house, she had no familiar landscape to provide a holding environment, and her anxiety attacks recurred. As we focused on her connection to the landscape, she decided to learn more about the habits of alligators, to see if she could include them among her "creatures."

I have recently reread Aldo Leopold and have begun to wonder what the therapeutic implications of his "land ethic" might be. I am developing ways to explore with clients their experience of "home," in terms of what they know or can find out about the place they inhabit. What do they know about the soil in their neighborhood? Or the formation of the bedrock? How much rain falls each year and where does it go? What watershed are they in? What kinds of trees are native to their neighborhood? Can they tell by looking? What trees are they drawn to?

In psychotherapy, asking questions is an essential part of the healing process. We can begin to ask ourselves, our clients, our friends and neighbors questions about our relationship with the larger world, including the natural world.

The model I use in the classroom, in the office, and in workshops is intended to create interventions that contribute to the development of an ecologically responsible focus on the self–world connection. This approach involves a greater degree of participation by the therapist than is usual in some models of psychotherapy. To enter into a more relational, ecological experience of self requires a softening of boundaries between therapist and client. All of us are, after all, faced with the same world, living on the same Earth. Although "boundary crossing" has been at the center of the abuse some clients have experienced in psychotherapy, and the whole arena of "intervention" in clients' lives is controversial, I do feel it is important to attend to clients' sufferings from the perspective of interdependence and interconnectedness within the larger context. Strategic questioning, often used in psychotherapy to enhance certain kinds of awareness, is a way to point to these aspects of experience. My questions about the connections clients have with other humans and with the natural world are one kind of intervention. I might also encourage people to actively seek out a connection with the natural world that will sustain them and inform them as they deal with their own and others' pain.

1. *Awareness* refers first to an awareness of the larger world, including

its problems. It would have been easy to focus exclusively on the family crisis of the woman already mentioned, giving no attention to her connection with the natural world. But in the process of both asking and answering questions, we can become aware of ourselves and of the world. What about the larger context comes to our attention? What is our response to environmental problems that have recently been on the news? With whom do we talk about these problems?

When these questions are asked—whether in psychotherapy, in the classroom, on the street, or in airplanes and buses—there is always a surprise in store for the questioner. People may not talk with others about these issues, but most people have something to say and are grateful to be asked. Even simple questions have the potential to wake up both the questioner and the person questioned and empower them both to act further.

Awareness refers not only to the remote and abstract problems of the larger world, but also to our experience of the beings and things closest to us in our everyday lives in all their "eachness" and "suchness." In my therapy groups, I often suggest practices such as looking, listening, meditating, writing, or drawing, that encourage clients to examine the quality of their awareness in everyday life, as well as their awareness of the larger world and the relationships between these levels.

2. *Emotional responsiveness* refers not only to the sensual awareness just described, but also to the ability to feel and engage rather than to become numb and dulled. In our tendency to pathologize and personalize emotional pain, the full energies of the emotions may be suppressed or dissipated. Furthermore, we may work at expressing them for the sole purpose of overcoming the suppression, "getting them out." One danger in "expression for its own sake" is that we "dump" emotions into our relationships and create "pollution" that we will eventually have to clean up. Another danger about "getting emotions out" is that we do not stay with them long enough to contact the information in them, or to find the emotional energy that moves us in relationship to another or to a particular problem. When expressed in ways that serve to connect us with others and with the larger world, these emotions can both inform and empower us.

In psychotherapy, I elicit and encourage attention to emotional responsiveness to the world in a number of ways. I inquire actively about my clients' reactions to the larger context, including the natural world, validating these reactions as important sources of energy. I also look at what they describe as personal, inner pain not only as an expression of their unique personal history or circumstances, but also as an expression of the Earth's pain. In listening, I try to tack back and forth between the personal level and the level of larger cultural, political, and more often now, ecological systems.

For example, when a client in both individual and group therapy began to have flashbacks of sexual abuse, I worked at accompanying her in individual sessions into the depths of her pain, while at the same time (and the timing is important) enlarging the context within which she experienced it. The larger context includes the amount of sexual abuse that is being addressed in the culture at present and that fills the media. I also include abuse that occurs in a still-larger context by looking at the abuse at all levels that we are confronting as a species: between men and women, between adults and children, between humans and animals, and between humans and the Earth.

Another way to enhance both awareness and emotional responsiveness is by focusing on the bodily sense of the emotion being expressed and doing visualization work with it. For example, a fifty-year-old man who had grown up as a poor child in Central America, and who had achieved financial success as an adult in the northeastern United States, came to therapy after a severe heart attack. He wanted to address some basic questions about where he belonged in the world and what he needed to do next. He felt that his life was not working and that drastic changes had to be made. We focused on the bodily sensations connected with a particularly intense emotional combination of sadness, anger, and disappointment that seemed to be associated with his current marital difficulties. When we did this, he visualized going deep into the Earth and coming out in a tropical forest near a spring from which a waterfall bubbled up. His tears began to flow as he imagined sitting under this waterfall experiencing the water as tears flowing through him. "This is so big," he said, "so much more than my own personal sadness." When I asked him if he could name it, he at first said it felt like the "collective unconscious." This label seemed to distance him from his own emotional responsiveness. He said he had been thinking that his next endeavor should address environmental issues, but that he was not aware of feeling so intensely about it. When we went back to the bodily sensations and an open visualization in a later session, a guide appeared who took him back to the waterfall and told him to sit in the water, to let it run through him, to feel the sadness of the world every day in order to learn how to love. He developed a vision of moving back to his Central American country, living in a compound with others, and setting up a think tank on ecology.

3. *Understanding* is the ability to integrate the information that comes into awareness with our emotional responsiveness, to see our own part in the whole picture. This refers back to the "holonic" nature of the ecological self, simultaneously a whole and a part, a system within larger systems. An important part of understanding is the ability to move back and forth between the individual in all her particularity and the Earth as a whole in all its systems and processes. Active imagination is required to make these connections.

In psychotherapy, besides asking the kinds of questions mentioned earlier about clients' experiences of the larger world, I also work with clients' family trees, looking at the relationship models they have in their family backgrounds. In the course of asking questions about their families, I can learn about their particular histories of relationship to the larger context, including the natural world. In teaching, I use a similar family-tree exercise, looking at the history of political, cultural, social, and environmental influences in students' backgrounds.

In the classroom or in workshops, I have used an exercise that demonstrates the interconnectedness of global problems. I ask students to brainstorm about problems facing the world today, to name them and call them out as they think of them. I write them on the blackboard in random order. When the blackboard is full (which does not take very long), I ask the students to look at the list in silence and then draw a picture demonstrating what feelings are evoked. Then I suggest that they name their drawing and show it to one other student. This exercise leads to lively, intimate conversations about their pain for the Earth. Focusing back on the board, I ask them to tell me which problems are connected to each other. They call out that Third World debt is connected to deforestation, for example, or that AIDS in Africa is connected to illiteracy, which is connected to poverty, and so on. Very soon, the board is full of connecting arrows. Finally, I ask each student to pick one problem that he or she feels drawn to work on and notice the arrows attached to it. They can see, by following the arrows around the board, that working on one problem will affect every other problem. The challenge is to find one's niche, one's particular way of contributing to the world.

4. *Action* refers to the willingness to work actively for the health of the Earth by engaging in behavior that addresses ecological problems. But action in our culture of individualism and liberal ideology is problematic. In therapy, I can assign homework that involves going into natural settings and observing and interacting with the natural world without violating any of the norms of neutrality that are important in the therapeutic setting. Often people can be encouraged to garden, or to become involved in restoration work, or to participate in rituals that include nature. But what is missing is any developed sense of engaging in collective action that confronts and ultimately changes the larger system whose destructive aspects are becoming part of what we attend to in therapy. I am beginning to explore this with clients. I ask if they have any avenues for joining with others in some productive action. Very little is available to them, either in their present lives or in their imaginations. They seem to be stuck in thinking individualistically. "I'll go on television and on talk shows to wake people up about our health system and the need for an alternative," they say; or "I'm thinking of writing a book to expose the environmentally destructive practices of my company." Their solutions are individual ones, rather than attempts to find their niches in cooperative, collective action. There is work to be done in looking at the role of collective action in mental health and psychotherapy.

These four aspects of the self–world connection are interrelated and interdependent. If we ignore the process involved in these interrelationships, then we diminish the effectiveness of psychotherapy, of teaching, or of engagement in the world. If one aspect is ignored, the quality of the others suffers, as does the quality of the person's or group's overall effectiveness in confronting a problem. If the process is working well, when one aspect grows, the others are enabled to work. If we know of a polluted water supply in our locality, if we let ourselves feel fully the fear and outrage stimulated by the image of poisoned water flowing into our homes, and if we engage in some local action to clean it up, it is likely that our understanding will grow. We will begin to see the connections between this local problem and larger problems of industrial waste, unsustainable development, and overconsumption that affect the hydrosphere, the Earth's water system, as a whole.

My husband, Lane Conn, speaks of the "canary in the mine shaft view of psychotherapy." The Earth hurts; it needs healing; it is speaking through us; and it speaks the loudest through the most sensitive of us. I believe that that pain wants to speak through a great many more of us. When people are unable to grieve personal losses openly and with others, they numb themselves, even constricting their muscles in order not to let the grief show. This can become chronic, leading them to see, hear, feel, and breathe less. The same process of numbing and constriction occurs with our loss of connection to a sense of place in a viable, thriving ecosystem. Many of us have learned to walk, breathe, look, and listen less, to numb our senses to both the pain and the beauty of the natural world, living so-called personal lives, suffering in what we feel are "merely personal" ways, keeping our grief even from ourselves. Feeling empty, we then project our feelings onto others, or engage in compulsive, unsatisfactory activities that neither nourish us nor contribute to the healing of the larger context. Perhaps the currently high incidence of depression is in part a signal of our bleeding at the roots, being cut off from the natural world, no longer as able to cry at its pain or to thrill at its beauty.

The challenge of an ecologically responsible psychotherapy is to develop ways to work with the "purely personal" problems brought by clients so that they can be seen not only as unique expressions but also as microcosms of the larger whole, of what is happening in the world. The goals of therapy then include not only the ability to find joy in the world, but also to hear the Earth speaking in one's own suffering, to participate in and contribute to the healing of the planet by finding one's niche in the Earth's living system and occupying it actively.

> A little too abstract, a little too wise,
> It is time for us to kiss the Earth again,
> It is time to let the leaves rain from the skies,
> And let the rich life run to the roots again.
> Robinson Jeffers

Shamanic Counseling and Ecopsychology

AN INTERVIEW WITH LESLIE GRAY

L ESLIE GRAY IS an ecopsychologist with unique qualifications—after completing her doctoral training in psychology she went on to study for ten years with native shamans, medicine people, and folk healers. Building upon this rich background, Gray has created a form of shamanism specifically tailored to modern urban settings, a practice she calls shamanic counseling. In this interview, conducted by journalist Pamela Sloane, Gray describes the shamanic worldview that guides her work and presents two fascinating case histories that illustrate several of the unusual techniques she employs. She also speaks to the promising but challenging issues that surround the cross-fertilization of ecopsychology and shamanism: Can ecopsychology legitimately trace its roots to shamanism? What alternatives to "talking cures" does shamanism offer ecopsychology? And finally, how can nonnative ecopsychologists approach native peoples to learn about shamanism without abusing this ancient wisdom tradition—or the people who have kept it alive and vibrant for thousands of years?

SLOANE: What is ecopsychology?

GRAY: Ecopsychology is an emerging field that recognizes that you cannot have sanity without sane relationships with your environment. Currently in the U.S., groups of cutting-edge thinkers have been participating in dialogues ultimately aimed at the creation of a new profession combining the sensitivity of the psychotherapist with the expertise of the environmentalist.

SLOANE: Is there a practice that accompanies ecopsychology, or is it a body of thought?

GRAY: Right now, it's mainly a body of thought, but fortunately, those who are forging this new field will not have to reinvent the wheel. We have only to look at the cross-cultural practices of perennial shamanism to find effective models of applied ecopsychology.

SLOANE: What do you mean by perennial shamanism?

GRAY: Shamanism is the oldest form of mind/body healing known to humankind. It involves the use of altered states of consciousness for the purpose of restoring well-being to those who are experiencing ill health or helplessness. Shamanism is estimated by archeologists to be at least forty thousand years old. It's been practiced perennially   or continuously—by virtually all indigenous peoples up to today. Only in the West were its practices essentially eradicated, because of the so-called Enlightenment.

SLOANE: How does shamanism relate to ecopsychology?

GRAY: The worldview of shamanism is that health equals balanced relationships with all living things. When someone is ill, shamanism attempts to restore power to them by putting them back in harmony with life. This idea that all things are connected, while a very ancient concept, is also a concept for the future. At the dawn of the twenty-first century, as we teeter on the brink of global catastrophe, it is precisely a shamanistic worldview that is our greatest hope.

SLOANE: So ecopsychology has its roots in shamanism?

GRAY: Definitely.

SLOANE: And this means that shamanistic techniques can be brought from traditional practice to contemporary application?

GRAY: Yes, exactly so. These practices have been used continuously, and are still in use today, by indigenous peoples all over the world. Shamanism provides a great inheritance for ecopsychology in terms of practical application. Emerging ecotherapies can look to shamanism for techniques to use clinically with individuals and with groups.

SLOANE: How does shamanistic healing contrast with Western psychotherapy?

GRAY: Western psychotherapy relies on analysis, interpretation, and understanding. As opposed to the "talking cure," shamanism seeks to change human behavior through techniques of personal empowerment.

SLOANE: You describe your work as "shamanic counseling," a term you are credited with originating. What is shamanic counseling?

GRAY: After I got my Ph.D. in clinical psychology, I spent ten years studying with native shamans, medicine people, and folk healers. I then created "shamanic counseling," which was my attempt to blend the best of my education in Euro-American psychology with what I had learned from my elders. In large measure, it has amounted to using an urban clinical setting to encase the techniques of shamanism. In other words, I meet with people in an office, we meet by appointment, and I don't get paid in chickens. Most of the focus of the work is on the use of sonic driving—drumming, rattling, and chanting—to enable the client to solve problems with more than their ordinary thinking.

SLOANE: What traditional techniques do you use in shamanic counseling?

GRAY: I apply various techniques, when fitting. Not everything from shamanism is appropriate to contemporary situations. For instance, a lot of traditional shamanism really is done with your extended family—maybe even the whole village—involved, and that's neither practical nor efficacious in urban-industrial society. But there are certain things, especially the quintessential undertaking of a "journey" to consult with spirits, that are highly adaptable to nontraditional settings. Making allies with the things in the natural world around us; talking to the stone people; acquiring an animal as a guardian spirit; soul retrievals—these are just some of the core shamanic practices that *can* be done with an individual client in an office in an urban environment. Also, shamanic counseling tends to motivate people to get out into nature more and away from an exclusively urban environment. City and suburban people get into ruts. It isn't that they don't have access to wilderness areas; right here in the San Francisco Bay Area, for example, it's easy to get to some spectacular beaches, some nature preserves, and some huge urban parks. Yet people get into a kind of urban rut, where they don't ever get out of the city. Shamanic counseling inspires them to explore their environment. They even start seeing the connection between the city and the nature that's around them.

SLOANE: Your training is strongly in the Western tradition, and we can all appreciate the work required to earn a Ph.D. in psychology. What caused you to break from that rigorous formal schooling and devote your practice to shamanic counseling?

GRAY: Ironically, the break, as you call it, started at the very beginning of my training in Euro-American psychology. My very first semester I read a book called *The Discovery of the Unconscious: The Origins of Dynamic Psychiatry,* by Henri F. Ellenberger, which purported to trace psychiatry from shamanism to mesmerism to hypnotism to Freud. As I was reading Ellenberger, it struck me that we had gone in the wrong direction, that what was being depicted as "progress" was deevolution rather than evolution. That's when my interest in shamanism began. In that same first semester, in my research methodology class, when they asked what people wanted to do, I said I wanted to give Rorschachs to Eskimo shamans. It was immediately made clear to me that this was not an appropriate project for a graduate student in clinical psychology. So I submerged it; I went underground. I really began going to two schools at the same time. I studied everything about shamanism I could get my hands on. I spent a lot of time in the anthropology library; I rented anthropological films on shamans; I talked to everyone I knew who could tell me about shamans. While all this was going on, I was also doing my program in clinical psychology. In my last couple of years of graduate school I ventured out to meet some shamans for the first time and learn from them directly. So, I was really living a double life throughout my Eurocentric training. Ultimately, what occurred was not a break but a synthesis. What changed was my bringing these two approaches together in a way that worked for me, indeed, in a way that *embodied* my personal experience. In all honesty, I didn't start out with the intent to practice shamanism myself; I simply was fascinated by it. After I had spent a good deal of time with several Native American shamans, I came to admire them. It seemed to me that their primal therapeutics were more powerful and effective than what I was learning in graduate school. But it still hadn't occurred to me to practice these methods myself.

But it wasn't until a life-changing vision turned me around that I first felt what could be described as a *call* to do shamanism. In this vision, I was sitting on a rock in a body of water. I looked down at the water and realized that there were roiling snakes everywhere. One huge dragon-like snake rose up and crunched my bones and chewed me up and spat me onto the rock in the shape of the four directions. As this happened, I felt myself rising. I looked around and saw vivid magenta and orange colors, like a sunset or sunrise. I realized that I was seeing a sky above and a sky below, and it was the Great Spirit. All of a sudden, inexplicably, I changed my mind and decided to come back down. When I did, I found myself sitting on the rock looking back out into the magenta and orange, only now I was dressed in buckskin and I had a snake necklace around my neck and a snake belt around my waist. I felt peaceful. I got up and walked back down the mountain in perfect balance, step by step by step. The minute I had that vision I knew that I was supposed to practice shamanism.

SLOANE: What influence did your own heritage as a Native American have on your development of shamanic counseling?

GRAY: My heritage is one of the reasons that I so instantaneously saw the power of the shamans described in *The Discovery of the Unconscious*. I think many people of nonnative background may have looked upon Ellenberger's reports of shamanic healings as "primitive." Also, many readers of the book may have carried with them the stereotype of Indians as a "vanishing race." That perspective can blind one to the contemporary relevance of Native American psychology, and also blind one to opportunities to encounter Indian shamans.

SLOANE: Can you give us a case history from your shamanic healing practice?

GRAY: Sure. I'll change the name of the client and any revealing details for the sake of privacy. "Roy" came to me for "vocational counseling plus," as he called it. He had recently quit a well-paying job because it was not fulfilling. Over the past ten years he had developed a pattern in which he would work in business or government for a year or two, get fed up with the superficiality, quit, and then enroll in an alternative educational institution to study eastern religion, new psychotherapies, or body work—studies that he regarded as having "relevance and depth." However, after only six months or a year he would decide that school was not hard-nosed or practical enough, and he would leave and return to business. Consequently, after ten years he had neither earned a degree nor stayed with a job long enough to achieve "success."

When I saw him he complained of feeling "stuck" or "paralyzed." He felt that there was nothing for him either in business or in school. I asked him if he would be willing to try a traditional method of "rock-seeing" in order to resolve his dilemma. He agreed, and I instructed him to go out into nature and to let a rock find him. I told him to remember exactly where the rock was located, because he would return it to that spot and thank it for its help after we had used it. When he brought the rock to our next session, we asked it if Roy should enroll in school or if he should return to the business world. I told Roy to pose his question to each of the four sides of the rock. He was to gaze at each side and see as many images as he could on its surface. He was then to ask himself what the rock could be telling him with these particular images about the answer to the question. In the end, we pooled all the images from all four sides of the rock to get the answer. As a result of the rock divination, Roy decided to become a property manager by day and to go to school at night, and he no longer felt pulled in irreconcilable directions.

SLOANE: In terms of contemporary Western psychology, would you say Roy was projecting aspects of his inner life onto the rock and then allowing himself to "see" what he was actually projecting?

GRAY: That's one theory. There are many theories, and one can entertain them all simultaneously. An indigenous person might see this rock divination as one of the stone people coming as an ally to a person seeking help. The language of the rock is its ability to show the seeker images; that's how rocks can talk to you. Rocks don't use ordinary human speech, but if we can pay attention to *their* language, they can actually help us solve problems by giving us gifts of information. The imagery Roy got out of his interaction with the rock fused apparently disparate things. For example, he saw fiery water, solid air, soundless thunder. These gifts of information shifted his capacity to problem-solve into a unified realm where he overcame what he was experiencing as paradox, that is, the tugging in opposite directions, one toward business and the other toward healing. The key point here is that we native people experience such healing images as a gift from the rock, and we express gratitude. What Western psychology has done with the so-called projective principle is to diagnose and categorize people—not to *directly* heal people. I personally prefer to talk about the stone people caring about human beings and being willing to sacrifice their energy to help us live here on Earth, and I am grateful that they are willing to do that.

SLOANE: Do you have another example?

GRAY: Okay. "Andrew" was a young man who had recently become an aide in the psychiatric unit of a large hospital. He was feeling overwhelmed, less by his work, he said, than by his relationships with other staff. In several months he had made no friends on staff. He felt his lack of training was glaring in their eyes, and he feared that some wanted to expose him as incompetent. He described the problem, nonetheless, as primarily due to his own lack of self-confidence. He complained that his exaggerated deference to superiors, his stammering, excuse-making manner, as well as his interpersonal withdrawal from others, were the main contributors to this problem, yet he felt helpless to stop these behaviors.

I informed him that the shamanic diagnosis of his situation would be one of power loss and that the remedy was the restoration of a guardian spirit, in the form of a power animal that I would retrieve from the other world and blow into him. The next time I saw Andrew, he had performed a simple purification procedure of fanning himself with sage smoke and fasting lightly for twenty-four hours. When he arrived at my office, I put us both into an altered state of consciousness via a tape of drumming. I came back from my "journey" and blew the spirit of a mountain lion into Andrew. He in turn reported that on his journey he had felt like a cat, and he was surprised at the coincidence. I then instructed him to go out into nature and dance his animal.

Two weeks later I saw him, and he reported a remarkable change at work. People seemed to be acting friendly toward him, and he had joined a staff support group. Most important, he no longer felt afraid of his co-workers and was confident enough to express his thoughts and feelings to them. After our last meeting, he had gone to a local nature preserve to dance his newly acquired mountain lion spirit. He had just begun to dance; shaking his rattle, he had leapt upon a rock. At the moment he landed he found himself staring into the yellow eyes of a mountain lion that inhabited the preserve. He was astonished and froze on the spot. The lion locked eyes with him for several minutes. Andrew said he knew at once that this was a profound affirmation from his guardian, and following that experience he felt a surge of well-being that positively affected every area of his life, especially his work.

SLOANE: Would you compare Andrew's experience with the "creative visualization" technique used by contemporary psychotherapists?

GRAY: Andrew did not "create" a mountain lion guardian. I journeyed for him to another realm and looked for a power animal that would be willing to come back and be of assistance to him in the form of a guardian or ally or helper. I altered my state of consciousness, and I brought that willing spirit animal back for him. It is often said of shamanism that "the doctor takes the medicine to cure the patient."

SLOANE: Is a shamanic journey a guided visualization?

GRAY: Absolutely not. A minimal framework is provided for the journey. Then the drum is in charge of transporting the journeyer to another realm, where the visionary experience occurs. The *content* of the experience is neither described nor suggested by me. It comes entirely as an interaction of that person with spirit.

SLOANE: A lot of people will be looking to make equivalents between shamanic counseling and current practices.

GRAY: Well, they're not the same. One of the biggest things missing from mainstream psychology is *spirit*. For example, "guided imagery" is not about spirit. It's a psychological technique employing visualization, and it's essentially practiced *upon* a patient by a psychotherapist. Shamanic journeys are an interaction, a direct link, between the patient and spirit. So the real shamanic counselor is the power animal.

SLOANE: Is there a central theme in the case histories you just gave us?

GRAY: I'd say that synchronicity is a consistent theme. In shamanism, synchronous experience is considered a sign of health and the lack of synchronicity a sign of deterioration. Notice that it is after "meaningful coincidences"—Roy's resolved paradoxical images and Andrew's encounter with the mountain lion—that these clients began to feel congruent. In shamanism, when you feel congruent with your life, you've been restored to personal power. This stands in contrast to conventional Eurocentric psychotherapy in which, when you *understand* your life, your are cured of a mental disorder.

SLOANE: From the case histories, it appears shamanic and contemporary practices *can* effectively be merged.

GRAY: That is precisely what the new ecotherapy (applied ecopsychology) will be—that very merging. It may not involve incorporation of all the specific techniques of shamanism. It may be primarily the inclusion of the worldview of shamanism—that health is defined as a balanced relationship with your habitat, your ecosystem. This kind of relating empowers you as well as the ecosystem, so that both remain sustainable by generating aliveness in each other. There's an old Chuckchee shaman saying: "Everything that is, is alive." Indigenous peoples believe that you have to do your part to keep the earth alive, i.e., you must have reciprocal relations with the environment. You tend the natural world, and it in turn empowers you and gives you energy and health.

SLOANE: How can nonindigenous ecopsychologists approach indigenous peoples in order to learn more about their healing connection with the earth?

GRAY: Well, I think a little humility is in order. There is a tendency for people in the overculture to presume a lack of sophistication among those who don't rely heavily on industrial methods. So if ecopsychologists honor the fact that they have a great deal to learn from primal people, they will be getting off to a good start. First show respect, and then really listen. I don't recommend running around Indian reservations looking for enlightenment. Pitch in first and ask how you can serve their needs as *they* define them.

SLOANE: As ecopsychology emerges, in what ways can practitioners give back to indigenous peoples for their significant contributions to our working knowledge of healing?

GRAY: Those who would seek to learn might first roll up their sleeves and ask how they can help. There is so much work that needs to be done. Native communities are plagued by high rates of teenage suicide, infant mortality, and unemployment, by environmental assault by business and government, and on and on. When business wants to dump toxic waste on reservations, or when the government decides to use the airspace over reservations for fighter pilot practice, ecopsychologists should support the struggles for native survival and native sovereignty. The truth is that we are all in this together, that none of us will survive unless the industrialized, militarized societies control their appetites and begin to *identify* with *all* the peoples on this Earth.

SLOANE: What pitfalls do you see in the development of ecopsychology?

GRAY: I think there is a danger that ecopsychology might lapse into trying merely to combine environmentalism with academic psychology. If that happens, it will recreate the very problems it is trying to solve. It will end up, for example, with a tacit Newtonian dualism between that which is alive and that which is not, between living beings and *its*. I would posit that the primary reason indigenous cultures have been able to have sustainable relationships with the Earth is that they do not turn the Earth into an *it* from which they are separate. Also, unlike perennial shamanism—which in this regard fits hand in glove with the understanding of contemporary physics—ecopsychology might fail to acknowledge that we are inextricably intertwined with that which we study. In other words, mainstream psychology itself must change if it is to make a contribution to ecopsychology. It must free itself from its own outdated model.

SLOANE: What is your parting thought regarding the relation of our shamanic heritage and ecopsychology?

GRAY: We've had more than forty thousand years of shamanic experimentation about how to live healthily on this earth. There are many models of sustainable indigenous societies. There are no models of sustainable industrial societies. It would be tragic to waste this accumulated knowledge, and it would be redundant for ecopsychology to generate models of a sustainable future without learning from the way of life of the more than 300 million indigenous people living in the world today.

The Way of Wilderness

STEVEN HARPER

MODERN PSYCHOTHERAPY IS almost universally practiced during a fifty-minute hour in an office, in a building, in a city or suburb. The pattern is all but automatic; opening a "practice" means opening an "office" that must usually be reached by driving a car along a congested freeway through a threatening city. Ecopsychology poses a powerful challenge to such therapeutic business as usual. It reminds us that the original environment in which teachers and healers sought to save people's souls was the natural environment, and the farther from "civilization," the better. Is it possible that certain unconscious assumptions about the world are built into the city? Do those assumptions prevent both therapist and client from finding the most effective kind of healing? Is urban culture itself concealing repressed contents that need to be reclaimed and returned to consciousness for analysis?

Wilderness therapy—or "practice," as Steven Harper prefers to call it, by way of making a vital distinction—is the boldest ecopsychological method so far developed for raising questions like these. It abandons the office, the city, the clock in favor of a setting that more closely corresponds to the natural habitat that has always been used by traditional cultures for healing the troubled soul. As Harper suggests, the authentic experience of wilderness undercuts all our suppositions about the "civilized" and the "primitive" in ways that can deliver a "reality shock." If we approach nature as he proposes, we may find ourselves asking where the "wilderness" really is. Is it perhaps within us, still waiting to be explored?

———————

A culture that alienates itself from the very ground of its own being—from wilderness outside (that is to say, wild nature, the wild, self-contained, self-informing ecosystems) and from that other wilderness within—is doomed to a very destructive behavior, ultimately perhaps self-destructive behavior.   GARY SNYDER

Our hike had started the night before, when my friend had said, "The moon is out, let's walk." We met at three o'clock that morning and began hiking up through the redwood-covered canyon to the coast ridge of Big Sur. My young heart was hurting from the breakup of a long-term relationship. Even though I had spent a good amount of time working with the pain, I felt shut down and separate from everything in my life.

We struck a leisurely pace, following whatever seemed to arise in the moment. Sometimes I found myself in tears, other times stopping to drink water from the creek or investigate a new plant, sometimes talking, other times quiet. We followed exactly what was before us, and as the day wore on I found myself softening to and accepting whatever emerged inside. My heart and belly felt expansive, and gradually I was overcome by the strangest sensation of webs connecting me with all that was around. I could sense webs of light extending out of me to every living thing and from them to me. I was sustained by all that surrounded me. The experience slowly dissipated as we climbed to the summit of the ridge, where I stood smiling, sweat in my eyes. And although I still had more grieving to do, the experience stands out as a clear turning point in my healing process, as well as in my life.

People have always turned to wilderness to become whole again. We need only think of the many primary cultures that use intensified wilderness experience as a rite of passage to see these healing qualities at work. The "civilized" person, however, has approached wilderness from a very different place. Our society is unique in the degree to which we have tried to split ourselves off from nature. We have lost touch with many basic, yet quite mature, ways of knowing nature that were commonplace to our ancestors. But we may also be unique in our potential for accessing far more modes of being and knowing than our ancestors could. These include a wider understanding of scientific and natural phenomena, and the shared wisdom of a worldwide array of psychological, cultural, and spiritual practices. When we embrace that which is most wholesome of both "old" and "new," we may find that wilderness holds the potential for transformative experiences that were perhaps never possible before.

Since the 1960s there has been a growing interest in using the wilderness as an environment for many of the new humanistic and existential therapies. There are numerous programs that use wilderness as a setting for their specific tradition or technique. I am more interested in those transformations offered by wilderness directly. Wilderness is a way and a tradition in its own right. If we are willing to be still and open enough to listen, wilderness itself will teach us.

Though I approach wilderness as a psychologist seeking to bring wholeness to the lives of those I lead out, I do not consider what I do "therapy"; I prefer the word "practice." Nature itself has shown me this crucial difference. Therapy, as it is commonly used, implies illness; it implies that there is a beginning and an end to treatment. Above all, it requires a "therapist," someone who is the "expert" in dealing with somebody else's life, and who gives analysis, interpretation, and advice. Therapy, in this sense, has been coopted by the mental-health industry, which I regard with some suspicion as perhaps having a vested interest in illness, in control of when and where therapy starts and stops, and in a hierarchical relationship between therapist and client. On the other hand, practice implies process; there is no beginning or end, but a lifetime of engagement and discovery. When we are truly willing to step into the looking glass of nature and contact wilderness, we uncover a wisdom much larger than our small everyday selves. Uninterrupted and undisturbed nature takes care of itself. One of my favorite guidelines for facilitators comes from Esalen Institute's cofounder Richard Price, who used to make the same distinction I am making here between therapy and practice with respect to Gestalt. Price liked to say, "Trust process, support process, and get out of the way." He frequently added, "If in doubt, do less." Personal evolution then becomes like nature; instead of being a struggle, our process, uninterrupted and undisturbed, becomes unfolding growth. Wilderness is a leaderless teacher; there is no one preaching change to us. The only personal transformations that occur arise from within ourselves.

My hope is that ecopsychology will opt for seeing the split between nature and human nature as needing a healing process rather than therapy as I have described it, recognizing that we are, in a sense, prefigured by nature. Our relationship with nature is more one of *being* than *having*. We *are* nature; we do not *have* nature. As Alan Watts once expressed it: "You didn't come *into* this world. You came *out* of it, like a wave from the ocean. You are not a stranger here."

Wilderness experience has many variables. How long should the work take? How many people should there be in the group? What combination of age and gender works best?

I have led wilderness experiences as brief and simple as a three-hour walking trip with one inexperienced person; I have also led three-month excursions into rugged terrain that involved several experienced mountaineers. There is a common misconception that the path of wilderness is only for those who have experience and expertise. I have found that experienced hikers and campers can be jaded and no longer willing to be students of nature, while people with less experience out of doors are often hungrier to learn and therefore more open to possibilities. Whether experienced or not, I most enjoy those who have the openness that Suzuki Roshi called "beginner's mind," perhaps because they help me experience wilderness anew. I prefer a group that is balanced in gender and race and that has a wide range of ages; but I have discovered that if the ranges are too great, the group will spend most of its time socializing and working to find common ground rather than experiencing wilderness. In my early years, I worked with many younger people, mainly of high school and college age; as the years go by, I find myself dealing with groups of older participants, some as old as seventy-five, with an average age of about forty.

How rugged should the work be? And how expert should the participants be? If a wilderness experience is too rugged for an individual or the group, people almost without exception retreat to habitual ways of coping with stress, even if these are highly dysfunctional. If the trip is not rugged enough, groups stay with habitual styles of relating to self, others, and nature. I try to find the creatively rugged edge for each group and for each individual within the group. Some trips demand exceptional physical ability, while others are specifically designed for physically challenged people. Most programs require only average physical ability, but above-average psychological motivation.

The groups I lead now are between ten to sixteen in size, though respect for the selected wilderness ecosystem has a lot to do with determining numbers. Deserts, for example, generally require smaller groups and more low-impact camping skills than most temperate forests. The trips range between one and two weeks, though with high school and college students, five-week trips are best. The optimum length of the stay is that which allows people to achieve a certain feeling of belonging where we have come—a sense that we are not strangers here. For this to happen, there should be enough time for individuals to undergo the "midcourse blues," a period of boredom and depression in which our romanticized idea of being in nature is worn down. Once the group has gone through this transition, interesting things begin to happen. We find that we no longer feel like outsiders or visitors; we feel at *home* in wild nature.

This feeling has a lot to do with breaking down the emphasis on the Disneyland sense of "beauty." The *look* of the land often determines that response. Many tourists, for example, confronted by a scene that is "pretty as a picture," react to natural beauty by rushing for their cameras. But sight is only one of our senses. I try to encourage letting the wilderness in through all the senses: touch, hearing, smell, and taste. Above all, I try to make the experience whole and honest. It must include what happens and what you feel when night falls, when the weather turns hot or cold or rainy, when the bugs come out, or when the cute little rabbit you have been watching screams a death-call as it is whisked away in the talons of an eagle.

Wilderness is not always a carpet of flowers. Wilderness also includes gray rainy days, animal-fouled water, dark, perilous forests, and deathly dangers. For example, our culture constantly avoids mud and rain; vacation ads depict white, clean beaches and sunny skies. When it rains, everyone scampers about crouched over as though water will dissolve them like Oz's Wicked Witch of the West. Metaphorically, our willingness to be in the mud and rain can reflect our willingness to be in our internal mud and rain. To put oneself in mud and rain is more than a matter of tolerance; it is active participation in our own "raininess" or "muddiness." True contact with wilderness requires more than resignation to muddy times; it requires nothing less than attentiveness to *all* there is around us if we desire to know its secrets. This is not to advocate taking vacations in rainy places, although at times that may not be a bad idea. I do advocate a willingness to be *with* and at times to *become* our dark, sometimes muddy, sometimes painful wild nature.

Wilderness begins teaching as soon as we plan the adventure. We must decide what to take with us and what to leave behind. A critical aspect of experiencing wilderness is the willingness to simplify. But, paradoxically, simplicity is not as easy as it sounds. The tools and techniques we choose to take into wilderness can dilute and drastically alter our direct experience with nature. So, we begin by questioning each tool we bring. Wilderness work starts with a basic ecological question: what do we really need?

A computer programmer I once worked with came to the first-night meeting of a seven-day trip with a pack full of the latest technical camping gadgets. He looked as if he had stepped out of a camping-equipment catalog. After a long talk about simplicity I convinced Dan to leave behind a good number of things. Even though the rest of the group were carrying simple tarps, he clung steadfastly to his new high-tech, cocoonlike tent. As the trip progressed, most of our group took to sleeping under the stars and the expansive night sky. Dan, on the other hand, put up his tent first thing at each camp and crawled into its protective walls, to emerge only when necessary. Finally one full-moon night, the group gently urged him to try a night outside exposed to the elements. We slept that night in a circle with our heads to the center. Upon awakening the next morning, Dan proceeded to share his delight in watching the moon travel the night sky. He continued to tell us about his life at work, insulated from human contact by an array of the latest computer equipment. He saw that his life had become void of living things, to the point where he was afraid of almost any human contact. From that morning on not only did he engage with other group members more, but he took it upon himself to see what in his pack he could do without. On the last night he stayed up much of the time feeding the fire and occasionally dozing off lying on the bare ground. Dan woke the group that morning with a howl of childish excitement. He talked the whole group into an early morning dip in the nearby ice-cold stream. We walked to the trail-head that day energized and feeling fully alive. Even though Dan clearly had the heaviest pack, he definitely had the lightest load.

Upon entering wilderness, one of the first things almost everyone experiences is an enlivening of the five senses. Suddenly, we are bathed in (and sometimes overloaded with) new sounds, awesome sights, interesting textures, different smells and tastes. This awakening of our senses, or perhaps better stated, "coming to our senses," is a subtly powerful and underrated experience. People learn how greatly some of our basic modes of perception have been dulled in order to survive in the urban world; many have been deadened unnecessarily. As long as we remain unaware of the richness of our senses, we have little choice about what we sense, and thus our perception is censored. I have seen this rebirth of sensory aliveness and keen alertness happen time and again in myself and others. Once this occurs, we can consciously choose, as well as expand, our modes of perception. When these fundamental senses are cultivated with practice and time they can be honed to a fine edge. They can be integrated into our everyday lives.

With practice and patience, sensory awareness can be cultivated to a more focused awareness I call "attentiveness." In wilderness, we begin to develop a sustained continuum of mindfulness. We are not necessarily focused on a single object, but rather on the stream of awareness itself. A journey through wilderness is in itself an awareness continuum. We are invited to observe with attentiveness what emerges around each bend of the trail, what unfolds before us over each hill. This does not mean that we have forgotten or lost the past (we can remember the trail out) or that we do not creatively drift into the future (we can speculate about the easiest, safest path to follow). We are instead attentively aware of wherever our awareness flows: the past, present, or future. In a sense, the means becomes the end, and our journey becomes an unfolding process to which we become attentive.

Once, while visiting Kenya for four months, I had the opportunity to spend two weeks walking through the back country along the west rim of the Rift Valley. Previously, I had traveled in parts of the United States where grizzly bear are a mild threat. This, however, was the first time I had traveled in an environment where I was potentially threatened by numerous animals. We encountered deadly poisonous snakes, came upon hippos near a river, and saw lion prints outside our tents in the morning. These, however, were not the major threat. The cape buffalo, which will charge unpredictably when startled, is more fearsome. We spent days walking through thick brush clapping loudly, then quietly listening, to let any unsuspecting buffalo know we were approaching. On a few occasions we saw the brush in front of us shake as we heard the thrashing and heavy rumble of hooves. At first, we were all on edge. Eventually the fearfulness caused by danger dropped away, replaced by a relaxed but keen alertness that seemed to permeate the entire group. While much of this aliveness stayed with me, I have rarely since experienced such a quality of awareness.

Wilderness, precisely because it is inevitably physical, raises deep questions about matters of gender in ways that, in the office, therapy may easily avoid. Gender considerations are there from the very outset of the expedition. For example, early in a trip I frankly address women's menstrual cycle. I discuss how to deal with used sanitary napkins in an environmentally sound way. I note that a woman may, much to her surprise, find that her cycle changes in wilderness; on extended trips, women in the group, like women in tribal societies, may find their periods synchronizing. I am amazed at how often adults blush or make nervous jokes about this most basic and obvious biological difference between women and men. Typically, the tendency is to deal with this topic in a secretive way. The women whisper about it among themeselves or it is ignored completely.

Whenever the subject of gender comes up, I remember Mark. During college he had played football. The rigors of medical school and the demands of being a doctor had taken the youthful health he had known.

When an older woman in our group caught up with and then passed Mark on a steep section of the trail, he grew angry. Even though I had cautioned everyone to find their own pace, Mark was used to being stronger than women. In a classic tortoise-and-hare way, he charged ahead and then rested, while her pace was slow and steady. Mark ate a big slice of humble pie later that day when my female coleader took some of the weight from his pack. It was especially difficult because he had boasted our first night that he was willing to help any of the weaker hikers in our group, not so subtly implying it might be the women. Mark went to bed early that night with hardly a word. The next morning as we went around the circle for check-in, Mark brought up his attitude about the roles of men and women and was clearly reevaluating them. Two of the women expressed their anger at Mark's behavior our first night. While we discovered no great solutions to the issues facing men and women, there was by the end of the trip a mutual appreciation of the differences between us.

Differences of physical size and stamina show up immediately and raise gender issues. If the women in the group are smaller and less physically fit than men, or if the men are smaller and less physically fit than the women, this brings up any number of age-old questions about the division of labor. For example, if I carry more weight, will you set up the tent and cook? Frequently wilderness evokes the unacknowledged feminine or masculine side of a woman or man. Then, discussions that compare masculine and feminine values and ways of being arise, as well as speculation about whether these are genetic or socially learned. I attempt to set a tone that acknowledges gender differences and at the same time challenges gender-bound roles. Because these differences between men and women show up so unavoidably in wilderness, I prefer to work with a woman coleader who can balance any gender biases I bring to the group.

In all the trips I lead, I see wilderness as our primary teacher. For this reason I consciously acknowledge the transitions of entering and leaving the wilderness with rituals. Over the years I have experimented with many forms borrowed from other traditions and cultures. For example, at the trailhead I have asked group members to make offerings, or kneel and touch the ground, or to bathe in the water (a washing away of the old to be new again), or simply take a moment of silence together. On many trips I ask participants to drop their given names and find a "trail name" that comes from a dream or an aspiration or that better describes who they feel they really are. From that time on, I often discourage talk about our professions and the "outside" world. The ritual I most often use is borrowed from Shinto. Shinto offers a balance to the typical western view; it recognizes rocks, trees, mountains, streams, and other things of nature as having life or spirit. We do two big claps and one bow with palms together in front of our faces. I think of the claps as a simple announcement—first to nature, then to myself and the group—that I am here to be aware, to be alive, and to practice. The act of bowing is potent and speaks for itself. We do this again at the end of each trip to acknowledge and thank nature, ourselves, and our companions. I encourage people to find traditions or rituals that have meaning to them and then to find a way to incorporate this practice into their daily lives.

The moment we step across the threshold and outside our usual cultural environment, our boundaries, blinders, and bonds begin to loosen. It is called "culture shock" among travelers, although it is perhaps better termed "expanding-reality shock." It is the shock that reverberates through the whole body–mind system when we suddenly realize that reality may be larger than our familiar scope—and very different. This shift is made every time we enter an internal or external wilderness. Personally, I experience it as a feeling of strangeness: a dizzying nausea may cloud my head and stomach, and sometimes anxiety, fear, and restlessness run through my body–mind. Doubts may arise and I might find myself asking, "Why?"

Outside familiar cultural boundaries and within wilderness, there are noticeable and sometimes radical shifts in the perception of time and space. The technologically induced fast pace of life is slowed down to a more natural tempo. People commonly report a sense of "timelessness" when they are immersed in nature. Time becomes less linear and more cyclic. We experience simple things such as day and night, the seasons, and the tides as a spiraling cycle rather than a linear progression. Space, instead of being measured in linear distance, is measured in experienced distance. Our culture-bound perception of these basic categories is so fundamental that it is difficult to move away from them and to trust our own immediate experience. Yet, when we are able to transcend our culturally defined experience of time and space, a new and different world opens up.

In wilderness practice, there can be moments of serious emotional stress. I do not seek to elicit strong emotions, but if they emerge I work with them. Marcie, a mother of three, offers a vivid example. Marcie was in transition after her last child had "left the nest," as she put it. After years of taking care of her family, she had come on this trip to do something for herself. Not long after we started up the trail I noticed that Marcie was not with us. I told the group to take a rest and walked back down, where I found her standing on a mildly steep section of the trail. She was shaking uncontrollably, gasping for shallow breaths, frozen in place. Overwhelmed with fear of falling off the trail, she was what rock climbers call "gripped." While the hillside we stood on was steep, it was far from dangerous.

Earlier in my career I would have tried to talk Marcie out of her fear logically—as if fear is ever logical—or I might have challenged her to be strong and overcome it. Instead I supported her state, saying simply, "You're OK, let this happen." She burst into tears and began to shake even more. I encouraged her to allow herself to feel the fear rather than push it away. After some minutes of deep sobbing, she began to relate to her larger fear of feeling as though she was falling from the trail of the life she had known for so many years. Who was she, if not a mother with children to take care of? Once again, I encouraged her to enter into those feelings. After some time and more tears, Marcie began to feel the ground beneath her feet. She realized that indeed she was being supported by the trail, that gravity was holding her to the Earth. Slowly she shifted to seeing and feeling what was there rather than what was not there. Gradually Marcie began hiking up the trail to join our well-rested group with a feeling of ease and trust in her body.

In the process of growth and transformation we must begin to reclaim and own the rejected parts of ourselves. The essence of wilderness practice is to *be* wilderness. The very idea that wilderness exists as something separate lets us know how much we have disowned of our internal as well as our external wildness. In wilderness, because of our close experiential contact with nature, we gradually begin to reclaim whatever it is we have projected onto the natural world.

Primary cultures have always had ways for people to become "things" outside of themselves. In their rituals and rites of passage, people become the Other: the animals, the plants, or the rocks. They use dance, visualization, masks, and costumes to help them fully embody the Other. Some primary peoples were so fully immersed in wilderness that apparently wilderness did not exist as a separate entity. Jeannette Armstrong, an Okanagan Indian I met at a workshop, told me that in her language there is no word for "wilderness." She thought one root of our alienation lay in the very fact that we believed there was such a split in reality between the human world and wilderness. Thus, to step out of our limited definition of self, to *become* these wild, natural things and experience them, is to give life not only to them but to those parts of ourselves.

Wilderness, through the history of civilized society and possibly before, has been the object of projection for many a dark shadow. "The word wilderness," as René Dubos notes, "occurs approximately three hundred times in the Bible, and all its meanings are derogatory." Deeply seeded in the psyche is the image of evil darkness in wilderness.

Much of today's destructive behavior comes from having projected our disowned darkness onto wilderness. As every psychotherapist since Freud has noted, it requires a vast amount of energy to repress and/or project the shadow. To go into wilderness is to face the shadow of wild nature at its source. When we identify with our wilderness shadow, consume it, and assimilate it, we thereby reown this vital and powerful energy.

Jan, an urban business executive, came to a wilderness trip I was leading that entailed three days and nights out alone. Although Jan had little experience in the outer wilderness, she was quite skilled at working on inner exploration. On the final night out, just before dark, a king snake slithered through her lone camp. She had always been afraid of snakes and was not sure what to do, since this was the only snake she had encountered outside of a zoo. As night moved in around her, she found herself looking over her shoulder wondering if the snake might come back to get her. For the first time in her peaceful solitude, she was beset by anxiety and fear. She tried to calm herself and think of other things; then she realized she was trying to push away the idea and feeling of the snake and possibly some part of herself.

"I decided I must become the snake," she told me later. "I fashioned a snake mask from bark and grass. I began, self-consciously at first, moving and making sounds as a snake. I spent what felt like hours lying on the ground undulating and hissing. I shifted from thought to raw feeling and felt alive, sensuous, and on fire, all at once. I spoke as the snake to Jan. I told her she had deadened herself to her passion, to her ability to move with strength and sensuality."

Jan returned to our group on the morning of the fourth day sleepy yet full of vitality. She recounted the story of her experience, and to the amazement of the group, she performed another snake dance for everyone to witness. When she finished, she jokingly promised to do a repeat performance on the table at her next board meeting. To this day the image brings a smile to my face.

The instinctual self, which has its roots deep in the history of evolution, is our culture's shadow. It was perhaps necessary to leave much of our instinctual self behind as we evolved further. Yet we did not need to deaden ourselves in giving up our instinctual self. It is crucial that we reclaim our wildness, because this is where vitality lives. Jung wrote of the need for elements of instinctive animal nature in the whole and healthy person. Calvin Hall and Vernon Nordby, in their *Primer of Jungian Psychology*, best summarize this:

> The person who suppresses the animal side of his nature may become civilized, but he does so at the expense of decreasing the motive power for spontaneity, creativity, strong emotions, and deep insights. He cuts himself off from the wisdom of his instinctual nature, a wisdom that may be more profound than any learning or culture can provide.

There is, however, a vast difference between analyzing the instinctual self and experiencing it. Few psychologists, Jungians included, have been willing to step across this chasm into the realms of experiential becoming.

Wilderness calls forth the instinctive animal self. Using one's instinctual sense more, living closer to the basic survival needs of food and shelter, sitting gazing into the coals of a fire late at night: all these experiences allow the repressed instinctual self to emerge. As this "wild" uncultured self emerges in its many shapes and forms, we have the opportunity to explore its realms. We can begin to discover where civilization and wildness intermesh and integrate. Fritz Perls once said, "One of the most important responsibilities—this is a very important transition—is to take responsibility for our projections, re-identify with these projections, and become what we project." In an environment close to the one in which we evolved, we can recollect a time when we stalked others and were ourselves stalked and hunted. We can, like Jan when she became the snake, at least in part relive and regain the knowledge of our stages of evolution: as simple organisms in the ancient seas, as fish, as reptiles, as amphibians, as mammals, as primates, as prehistoric humans. As we reexperience our forgotten primordial self, we have the opportunity to catch experiential glimpses of the origin of the primordial images, the archetypes. The awareness of ourselves, our environment, and the relationship between them, or simply the awareness of our expanded self, is the experience of wholeness. We must even reown our *incompleteness* if we are to become whole again. The experience of wholeness, however brief, is perhaps the most healing experience available to us.

On a two-month canoe trip across the Northwest Territories of Canada, I was blessed with such an experience. Near the end of a long day of paddling the sun was low in the sky and my mind had long ceased its normal chatter. I had the sensation of becoming my paddling and all that was around me. Stroke after stroke I was called to merge with my experience until "I" was no more. Only perception existed, a perception that was more complete, more whole than any I have known in a usual state of consciousness.

Yet no matter how fully we experience the primordial self while in the wild, the real work begins when we return. Even the most potent wilderness journey can be lost in a few moment or days, brushed off by saying "I've got to go back to the *real* world now." The experience is suddenly discounted as though the untamed natural world were not real. Wilderness becomes objectified, a thrilling adventure vacation that is kept in photos in a shoe box and stored in a closet. For those who work with wilderness, whether as therapy or as practice, the greatest challenge is bringing it all back home.

How can we find this same sense of sacredness in everyday life? Like any powerful personal transformation, the awesome (and many times overwhelming) experience of wilderness can be difficult to incorporate successfully into our daily life. We emerge from wilderness changed. At some core level we feel deeply touched. Still, in the peacefulness we so often feel, there is also confusion or profound sadness. For we have seen dynamic balance. We have felt the meaning of wholeness and holiness. We have experienced parts of ourselves and parts of the universe that have been long forgotten. Upon emergence from wilderness we are confronted with our inconsistencies and notice more than ever before how drastically out of balance we live. Many return to a great sense of loss or pain, realizing how cruelly we have divided our lives. This schism is felt deeply and can make living our "regular" life very difficult. We can feel as though we have fallen from grace.

Frequently people make changes in life-style to achieve more balance. Some engage in environmental activism in the political sense; others are inspired to engage with the whole environment they live in (relationship to self, others, and the world). Whenever possible I like to have a series of follow-up meetings, in which members of the group come together to support each other and tell their stories of joy and despair, of struggle and success in incorporating wild nature into who we are and how we live.

As we begin to practice what we have learned, we see that nature is everywhere and that we really may not need to go to physical wilderness to experience wild nature. There are many paths, both ancient and new. There are as many ways to reenter the experience as there are people. I recommend almost any practice that includes the body, that encourages awareness, that can be done out-of-doors occasionally. Among those I favor are some movement arts (aikido, ta'i chi, dance, yoga), many meditation styles (vipassana, Zen), some psychological practices, and many practices that come to us from traditional cultures (ceremony, chanting, drumming).

We must be willing to bring back from wilderness more than ideas and philosophies. It is in practice and in the embodiment of what we discover that we find integration. The *example* of nature is that life is to be lived, to be experienced. Otherwise, if we are not able to incorporate what we have learned in a real and practical way, wilderness work becomes another faddish thrill. The poet and farmer Wendell Berry tells us it is not enough to ask, "What can I do with what I know?" without at the same time asking, "How can I be responsible for what I know?"

Over the years I have found myself, more often than not, recommending gardening to workshop participants who seek ways of staying connected outside of the wilderness environment. When practiced in a sustainable way, gardening and farming are activities in which people and wild nature intermesh and begin to coevolve. Gardening yields deep insights into how we can physically, mentally, and spiritually find creative balance between wild nature and human nature. Gardening immerses us in a basic natural cycle that directly sustains our life. We get our hands dirty and our bodies sweaty. Gardening can be the physical embodiment of symbiosis and coevolution, the "ground" in which we practice what we have learned in wilderness. We give to the Earth as well as receiving.

True giving arises naturally and without effort, not from a feeling of guilt or from environmental correctness. When we care for the Earth in this way we can begin to reinhabit the land on which we live; and we can reinhabit ourselves only when we have learned to reinhabit the Earth. We are part of a circular, spiraling dance in which every part feeds the others and the whole.

Like the tightrope walker who is never still but always in movement, we must find our stability in the balance of constant adaptive movements. We have learned that stable organisms are those able to adapt to the changing environment and still maintain enough consistency to benefit from their form. There is a balance between too much change and too little change. Individually and collectively, we also need to balance between rational and nonrational modes of knowing, between "technological" and "natural" modes of human life support, between simplicity and complexity. As we move toward this elusive balance and wholeness, sometimes gracefully but most times not, I find myself filled with hope, touched by the beauty of life. I remember the words of Charles Darwin, who first taught us our evolutionary continuity with the natural world. "From so simple a beginning endless forms most beautiful and most wonderful have been, and are being evolved." Perhaps through direct experience of nature we will continue this "most beautiful and most wonderful" evolution consciously, as nature aware of itself.

Notes on Wilderness Work

To explore the path of wilderness, first consider whether you can get started or continue on your own or within the context of a group of friends. There is a good chance you may not need "professionals." The primary issue is safety, in two respects: (1) Do you or your group have enough wilderness skills to be physically and emotionally safe? (2) Do you have the necessary low-impact wilderness living skills to be safe to wilderness?

In undertaking an organized wilderness trip, you are probably seeking one or more of the following: physical wilderness travel and living skills; the support of a group of like-minded people; the facilitation of a leader experienced in the "inner" spectrum of wilderness. Regardless of whether you are doing your own trip or participating in an organized group, I recommend staying close to home and within your local bioregion. Establish an inner wilderness practice that can be done before and after the trip.

A growing number of groups and people now leading high-quality wilderness work are interested in ecopsychology. Many of the best groups are small and more difficult to find than the larger organizations that advertise. Word of mouth is one of the best ways to find a group that will reflect your interests.

Be clear about your own expectations and concerns. Ask questions before signing up. What is the organization's basic intentions? What do the leaders hope you will come away with? Is there a clear intention to connect with nature? Describe your personal intentions and ask leaders whether it is realistic to expect them to be met. What type of support do they offer after a trip? Do they teach and practice low-impact wilderness living skills? How long have they been leading trips, and how long have they led trips in the area to which they are going? What type of medical training and support is available? What structures and forms are used (rituals, practices, style of leadership)? Are you able to talk to the actual leaders of the trip you are planning?

The following groups and individuals have been long established and have made significant, unique connections between wilderness work and ecopsychology:

The School of Lost Borders
Stephen Foster and Meredith Little
Box 55
Big Pine, CA 93513

Northstar Wilderness
Robert Greenway
Box 1407
Port Townsend, WA 98368

Breaking Through Adventures
Rick Medrick (in particular the trip he leads with Dolores LaChapelle)
Box 20281
Denver, CO 80220

Earthways
Steven Harper
Box 303
Big Sur, CA 93920

The Skill of Ecological Perception

LAURA SEWALL

PSYCHOLOGY IS A RICH and varied field, encompassing diverse viewpoints and perspectives. While clinical psychologists struggle with the complexities of human pain and healing, research psychologists pursue insights into the human condition gleaned from laboratory experimentation and scientific analysis. This essay illustrates how the knowledge gained through one area of psychological research—perceptual psychology—can contribute to ecological awareness. Perceptual psychologist Laura Sewall points out that our sensory capacities—taste, smell, sight, hearing, and touch—are the fundamental avenues of connection between self and world. She argues that the deadening of our senses is at the heart of the environmental crisis and that reawakening them is an integral step toward renewing our bond with the Earth. Specifically focusing on vision, she offers five perceptual practices that can help us to "come to our senses."

Set aside the learned ways of perceiving the world as dead matter for your use and see if you can recover again your actual perception of the world as a community of beings to whom you are meaningfully related.   ERAZIM KOHÁK

The ecological crisis may be the result of a recent and collective
perceptual disorder in our species, a unique form of myopia which
it now forces us to correct.   DAVID ABRAM

I take David Abram's statement quite literally. Our "collective myopia"
is one manifestation of psychic numbing—a psychological defense
against witnessing the world's pain. It is a form of denial that shields us
from fully experiencing the latest reports on ozone depletion, increasing
pollution, toxicity, poverty, illness, and the death of species. Full awareness hurts. In response we build defenses, twist ourselves into something we collectively label as variations on the themes of madness or
depression, or we choose between a variety of convenient distractions.
And, in a culture with the luxury to do so, we turn down the volume.
We become numbed to our feelings, to what we might hear and see; in
part, we suffer from collective myopia. Unfortunately, it doesn't stop
there. Our myopic defense blinds us to the urgency and severity of current Earth conditions. Consequently, we continue our destructive and
habitual behavior. We deny the need to change, and the need for radical
reevaluation of ourselves. In the midst of collective denial, we further
perpetuate the destruction of the biosphere. Our collective myopia thus
becomes both cause and effect of the environmental crisis.

Nonetheless, we are beginning to recognize the human dimensions
of our ecological and social crises. Many of us are searching for explanations of our misbehavior toward one another and the Earth and asking
how we might have brought this upon ourselves. These explanations are
numerous and provocative, including the advent of agriculture or industrialization, a dichotomous Judeo-Christian paradigm of good and
evil, and the legacy of a Cartesian interpretation of reality.

In *The Voice of the Earth,* Theodore Roszak presents a provocative theory that the roots of our collective misbehavior can be found in the historic and conceptual split between "in-here" and "out-there." This
dichotomy manifests as the large and despairing gap we feel between
ourselves and nonhuman nature. In response, Deep Ecology and progressive psychology have begun to flesh out a conception of an ecological
self, in which the division between inner and outer worlds becomes an

arbitrary and historical distinction. In contradiction to an identity in which the mature self is culturally defined as fully individuated and possessing intact, absolute, decisive, and divisive boundaries, the ecological self experiences a permeability and fluidity of boundaries. This manifests as an empathy and identity with family, friend, lover, community, humanity, and similarly, with the whole of the nonhuman world. An empathy and identity with all that is ideally translates into a radical awareness of interdependence—a recognition that to tread heavily on the Earth is to tread heavily upon one's self.

My hope for a sophisticated response to contemporary ecological and psychological conditions calls for a return to our essential, animal selves, the selves that evolved in relation to the nonhuman natural world. In particular, our sensory systems are exquisitely evolved channels for translating between "in-here" and "out-there." Fifty percent of the cortex of the brain is thought to be devoted to processing visual information, indicating a profound, evolutionary commitment to vision as a means of joining inner and outer conditions. From a pragmatic perspective, this means that perceptual practice can ameliorate cultural conditioning and psychic numbing by reawakening our senses and intentionally honoring subjective experience.

This notion is consistent with James Hillman's prescription for preservation. He suggests that we are aesthetically or sensually numb, and that the soul longs for a reawakening of pleasure and beauty. In Hillman's view, it is a contemporary moral imperative to refine our aesthetic sense, and in so doing, we begin to feel a deepened sensuality and a relinquishing of boundaries that separate. We begin to care for that which we see, and ideally, we find ourselves loving the material world, our Earth. Because love alters behavior, honoring sensory and sensual experience may be fundamental to the preservation of the Earth.

There is another major rationale for developing a perceptual practice. Perception, consciousness, and behavior are as radically interdependent as the rest of our biosphere. Thus, perceptual shifts alter consciousness, consciousness alters behavior, and even unconscious leanings alter perception. Given our blatant need for ecologically conscious and consistent behavior, the development of skillful ways of seeing offers a direct path for consciousness intervention and behavioral change.

Skillful perception is a devotional practice. It is essentially learning to see, and thus consists of cultivating those aspects of the visual process that are modifiable, or that can be developed by a kind of mindfulness. In relation to developing an ecological consciousness, skillful perception necessarily includes emphasizing perceptual practices that help us to extend our narrow experience of self and to experience sensuality, intimacy, and identification with the external world. Skillful perception is the practice of intentionally sensing with our eyes, pores, and hearts wide open. It requires receptivity and the participation of our whole selves, despite the potential pain. It means fully witnessing both the magnificence and destruction of our Earth. It is allowing one's identity and boundaries to be permeable and flexible. I refer to this way of perceiving as ecological perception. Mindfulness and practice brought to the entirety of our sensory experience clearly serve to alter consciousness and behavior. Ecological perception is most essentially the perception of dynamic relationships.

There are five perceptual practices that I have identified as both modifiable by experience and directly relevant for perceiving our ecological conditions. These practices include (1) learning to attend, or to be mindful, within the visual domain; (2) learning to perceive relationships, context, and interfaces; (3) developing perceptual flexibility across spatial and temporal scales; (4) learning to reperceive depth; and (5) the intentional use of imagination.

1. Learning to Attend

Learning to attend is the first step in developing an ecological way of seeing. Attending is the flip side of psychic numbing; it is the enhancement of selected sensory information. Focused attention produces a richness of color, a depth of sensory experience, and often means the difference between seeing and not seeing. The ability to fully use our attentional capacity is a learned skill, requiring the practice of mindfulness and awareness. Attention is currently defined as both "endogenous" and "exogenous." Endogenous attention refers to a kind of perceptual readiness. It is the largely unconscious placement of one's focus on internal desires, needs, and priorities. It acts as a filter or gate, selecting particular information from the visual field. This process serves to affirm our expectations and help us to identify what we are looking for; when I am hungry, restaurant signs "pop out" of any long row of commercial buildings. Endogenous attention also refers to a focus on the familiar or exciting. For example, when I begin to see the difference between two species of cholla cactus, and am excited by my discovery, the vast garden of cacti suddenly shifts and becomes richly differentiated; full, round, fuzzy cactus arms are suddenly in distinctive contrast to long, lanky cactus bodies. And with my attention oriented toward newfound distinctions, I am no longer able to see the desert landscape as populated by a single species of cholla. This form of attention works in reverse as well; my first two weeks of working in a Tanzanian game park were most notable for what I couldn't see. My experienced companions readily saw eland, giraffe, and gazelle among acacia and tamarind trees. Having no familiarity with African wildlife, I looked and looked, to no avail. Slowly however, with growing familiarity, my ability to spot animals became equally refined. Thus endogenous or internally oriented attention serves to select or filter incoming information in accordance with familiarity and expectations, and with forms of mental arousal: excitement, desire, and need.

By filtering the visual world consistent with previous experience or mental states, endogenous attention builds and perpetuates one's view of reality. This is both problematic and useful. By selecting information to be consistent with expectations and familiarity, endogenous attention may reinforce habitual judgment, dislike, and denial. Alternatively, if we attend to intentionally chosen and unabashedly value-laden priorities, we alter the ways in which we filter information, and consequently, interpret the visual world. Thus, if we wish to "see as if the Earth matters," or tease and stimulate our aesthetic sensibilities, we must be prepared to see beauty. This requires nurturing one's aesthetic desire and taking a moment to observe texture, curvature, form, color, or the soft slope of a grassy, golden hillside cast against an enormous blue sky. It takes a moment, and initially requires conscious participation and recognition. It requires noticing what one notices, and choosing to honor that which appeals and provokes, and is felt within one's body and soul. With practice, that which was noticed and given aesthetic value soon "pops out" of a landscape. Our intention becomes a new habit, a new way of seeing, and one becomes easily drawn to beauty, and thus to loving the landscape.

Exogenous attention, on the other hand, refers to the way in which our gaze is drawn to novelty or change within the visual field. From an evolutionary perspective, it is essentially a focusing of energy for the purpose of locating potential opportunities or threats. It is locating the bear in split seconds, or for the skilled tracker, it is noticing any change in the landscape, even across considerable distance or among a chaotic background of scattered, fallen leaves. It is spotting the osprey resting among a coastline of tall pines. To develop this ability, one must nurture a receptive stance and a sensitivity to spatial and temporal changes within the landscape. This particular form of attention seems to be most susceptible to psychic numbing; when numb, we notice as little as possible. Thus, intentionally nurturing this form of awareness requires getting out of one's head; it is opening one's self.

Attention, focused both internally and externally, is an exceptionally dynamic, fluid, and flexible process. Because some degree of attentional focusing is automatic, we take our ability to attend for granted. But research in perceptual psychology has demonstrated that (1) one's ability to visually attend is a learned skill, requiring effort; (2) attending has facilitory, or beneficial, effects for processing visual information; and (3) the placement of our attentional focus may fully determine our subjective reality. This research obviously implies that learning to attend has profound implications for receiving and interpreting the tremendous variety and magnificence of the visual world.

Further, there is evidence suggesting that attentional patterns may physically alter the neural pathways in the brain. This research was initiated by David Hubel and Torsten Wiesel's Nobel Prize–winning work identifying the structure, development, and modification of the visual cortex.[1] More recently, research has indicated that the activation of attentional mechanisms is necessary for structural change to occur within the visual cortex. Structural changes are essentially alterations in the strength of the synaptic connections between neurons, causing the formation of new neural associations and pathways. The synaptic connections are strengthened as a function of activity and, most significant, in conjunction with the presence of neurotransmitters subserving attentional mechanisms. Once strengthened, a synapse requires a lower threshold of input to fire, or to pass a signal down its neural pathway.

1. David H. Hubel and Torsten N. Wiesel, "Functional Architecture of Macaque Monkey Visual Cortex," *Proceedings of the Royal Society of London,* series B, 198 (1977), 1–59.

This strengthening facilitates the activation of entire neural networks. Because each neuron has many hundreds of synaptic connections to other neurons, the strengthening of a particular connection may alter the routing of a signal, thus forming or activating a new neural pathway. Theoretically, neural networks constitute our schemata, which deter-. mine the ready categorization of visual input. In practical terms, this process suggests that visual system structure, or neural networks, determine our perceptual tendencies. Thus, by strengthening particular synapses, and consequently particular neural pathways, our attentional choices not only select and enhance specific information, but also influence the ways we categorize visual input. It is therefore important to become conscious of where and how we direct our attention.

In sum, our attentional focus, both internally and externally, influences and creates subjective reality by facilitating the perception of some objects, relations, and events to the exclusion of others. Despite the highly subjective nature of perception (due to attentional processes), we make behavioral choices based on what we see. In the context of the role consciousness and behavior play in perpetuating our ecological crisis, the research clearly suggests that we would be wise to become mindful of where we place our attention. Learning to attend is, in essence, a spiritual practice. It is mindfulness in the visual domain. According to Buddhist monk Thich Nhat Hanh, the first step in a spiritual practice is the cultivation of a "wakeful presence." If this is mindfulness, then attention may, in addition, bring us spiritually closer to the visible world. Any deity knows we need it.

2. Perceiving the Relations

We have a materialistic culture. We are interested in identifying, naming, and obtaining objects. In addition, our intellectual tradition supports objectification or the separation between "in-here" and "out-there." This dichotomization extends far into the conceptual realm: the spiritual is cleaved from the material, and the sensual is antithetical and problematic for the rational. The reduction of wholes and systems into component parts lies at the heart of many of our intellectual traditions. As a consequence, we readily perceive *things* and are relatively insensitive to the relationships between them. We are not particularly adept at perceiving the interface between media and forces, context, or processes, and we rarely "read the signs," or perceive the potential depth of our own relationship with the world "out-there." Rather, our identity is conceptually independent of the biosphere upon which we depend, and our perceptual tendency is to see objects.

Alternatives to object identification exist. One example is how Barry Lopez describes the Inuit way of perceiving a wolf. We might say, "a male wolf does this." An Inuit is likely to say, "a male wolf, on a mid-summer's day in which the clouds were particularly billowy and white, when the sun was nearly overhead, and when a caribou grazed within a half mile, does this." Inuits perceive context and refer to it continually. As identifiers of objects, those of us who are subject to Western, culturally determined perceptual behavior rarely consider context. Context adds a dimension of complexity out of keeping with our desire for fact, or "absolute truth."

One way to make this shift from perceiving objects to perceiving context or relations is to observe the interface between water and land. Water flows all over rocks and sand. We can see water flow over, under, and around. We see water deflect, merge, lick, crash, and softly lap up against. We see water reflect like giant mirrors. We see it take away and give back, and we see all of this in relation to land. And we may notice that flow *is* the relationship. It is the dynamic property of what may be the most essential and contrasted material relationship within our experience. It is the interface between elemental forces; ocean and land, river and mountain. It is where erosion meets resistance, hard meets soft, still meets fluid, and where tawny-colored sand meets deep blue water.

Visual contrast identifies where everything meets everything else. It catches our attention and points to the interface, the place where merging and interdependence happen. Among other things, contrast depicts change and influence. If one is sensitive, visual contrast also feels good. For example, it feels good when one enters Skull Valley and first glimpses the old cottonwoods. They form a long curving line, winding in slow arcs along the creek. In contrast to the high desert, spreading for many miles in all directions, they are big, billowy, beautiful things. They are brilliant green against bone-dry, sun-drenched desert. They indicate the presence of water and quench a visual thirst.

Contrast represents the most fundamental of relations within the visual world. Contrast effects demonstrate that perception changes as a function of relatedness within the visual world; in other words, perception differs when objects are seen in relationship, rather than within a kind of perceptual isolation. Therefore, an inclusive, relational view of the world differs in appearance from one consisting of quantified, utilitarian objects. If we legitimize and practice a relational view, we act in response to a world that reveals forces and vibrancy, one that appears dynamic, and by extension, alive. This practice allows for our own engagement. We may find ourselves being "part of," or "in relationship with." It follows that subjective reality matters.

Giving full credence to subjective reality means valuing our participation with the world. Participation implies inserting one's consciousness into the space between ourselves and the Other. The insertion of consciousness makes meaning and metaphor; it allows frogs to become princes, ravens to become messengers, and gnarly old oaks to be grandfathers. As we attribute meaning and dynamism to water and rock, and as we allow animism and vitalism to exist in the field of our consciousness, we might also perceive ourselves as part of an exchange, the human dimension of which is observation, story, and "reading the signs." "Reading the signs" is the attentive observation of the landscape, and refers to both the meaning we attribute to the landscape and to believing the message. Although this process may challenge our culturally constructed reality, it represents a highly prized ability among the Yoruba people of Nigeria; it guides the tracker and the shaman, and may be the essence of creating a mutually respectful relationship between ourselves and the nonhuman world. By reading the signs, we bring conscious participation to the moment of observation, making visible the previously unseen. Thus, conscious participation is essentially the creation of meaning and, by definition, value, unimpeded by material concerns.

When fueled by beauty and sensuality, our relationship with the visible world may move our hearts. As the visible world becomes meaningful and vital, we feel it in our bodies. The sensory world thus becomes directly embodied in us; the relationship is visceral, and subjective experience becomes sensuality. We fall in love. Participation in this way is essential if we are to care enough for Earth; we need to view her through "love eyes." Under romantic influence, her appearance will undoubtedly change. No matter. We must value our subjective and sensual response as if all our lives depend on it.

Relationships in the visible world are indicative of processes, systems, and the ways in which forces interact, influence, support, and degrade. It is important that we learn to see them, for they signify both the ways in which the elements and forces of nature come together and our own undeniable relatedness. Learning to see the relations requires time to observe and attention to contrast, to the interface between things. Visible relationships are signified by qualities, such as color and curvature, texture, and the juxtaposition of forms. For example, in northern California, the Mendocino hills on late-summer afternoons are golden, gentle, and overlapping. They dive into and rise from one another, and capture the potency of form. Our own relationship with the visible world is enhanced by metaphor and meaning, and again, by taking time to look. Participation is felt by sensations in our bodies and shifts in our hearts— by a sweet and unmistakable resonance.

3. Perceptual Flexibility

The third step to an ecological way of seeing is the development of perceptual flexibility. It requires a fluidity of mind in which the magic of the visible world is revealed by relinquishing one's expectations and nurturing a freshness of vision. It is seeing familiar patterns within apparent chaos, rearranging the pieces and allowing a new image to emerge. For example, the symmetry between a rocky shoreline and its reflection may suddenly become both pattern and metaphor, revealing statues, Buddhas, and arrows pointing upriver.

Perceptual flexibility requires very little training. Visual illusions are especially useful for encouraging flexibility because they provide instantaneous feedback. A Necker cube is a classic visual illusion that demonstrates the fluidity, almost fickleness, of perception. A Necker cube is a simple line drawing, showing all twelve edges of a cube. With a mere leaning of thought, a Necker cube typically bounces between two distinct appearances. The illusion is a perceptual reversal in which four edges, initially depicting the nearest face of the cube, perceptually shift such that the same four edges suddenly depict the back side of the cube. For some observers, the Necker cube may stubbornly linger as a solid, unchanging box. With a few moments of perseverance, however, most observers are able to shift perspectives with ease. The flexibility required for larger shifts in perspective feels very similar. Given a bit of willfulness and a stretch of one's imagination, a rock wall may suddenly become a familiar person's profile, or the reflection at the water's edge may depict arrows or signs to be followed. The perspective shifts, and if one chooses to listen, the landscape speaks.

Seeing a face in a vast rock wall is an easy perceptual leap; we have a natural tendency to look for the familiar, or to make meaning out of the visible world. Looking for the face as an intentional practice prepares one for larger, and perhaps more relevant, stretches of perception and imagination. Perceptual flexibility includes what I refer to as fractal consciousness, or the perceptual ability to make comprehensible leaps across spatial scale. It is the ability to perceive self-similar patterns at a variety of spatial scales. With the addition of curiosity and knowledge, fractal consciousness may serve as a doorway. For example, a pencil-thin runoff from a single rainstorm may spill, twist, and turn like the nearby creek, or mirror a river; with imagination, this may translate into the recognition of a massive drainage system. This stretch of perception is easily followed by the recognition that the Colorado River, for example, drains much of Colorado west of the Continental Divide, as well as large sections of Utah and parts of other states, but never empties into the Gulf of California. One might ask what happens to the river water, and learn that it is taken for irrigation or beef production, for water shares, and for human consumption, all of which drain the river dry. Thus, fractal consciousness may serve to extend awareness to more inclusive dimensions, such as that of the Colorado drainage, or of the biosphere. With practice, the perception of interrelatedness may become increasingly accessible, and perhaps, unavoidable.

As a further extension, fractal consciousness may similarly be built into the perception of time, thus encouraging the ability to perceive a temporal reality beyond the scheduled, urban, closeted self. This frees time from our imposition of form, which makes it into "stuff" whose value is quantified, subdivided, and billed by the hour. We can begin to stretch our imaginations to encompass time scales far beyond that of a human lifetime: what are the implications of perceiving, truly perceiving, forest time? Fractal consciousness in relation to time may be used to develop foresight, or the ability to shift between a time scale based in minutes to one in which the lifetime of a redwood becomes the unit of measurement or point of reference. Foresight capability thus provides a relative perspective of time; the lifetime of a redwood depends on numerous environmental conditions, including temperature and soil composition, rainfall, and logging. Perceptual flexibility across time and events provides an opportunity to predict the ways in which human-scaled time interacts with the pace of Earth processes, for example, the way erosion and the deposition of nutrients interact with the depletion of topsoil due to contemporary forestry and farming techniques. Foresight provides the opportunity to "view" and consider the world we will leave to our grandchildren.

4. Reperceiving Depth

The fourth element of an ecological way of seeing concerns the way we perceive depth. Reperceiving depth is most concerned with a change in worldview and associated proprioceptive responses, rather than a literal change in visual habits. It involves talking to ourselves and allowing a sensual response that comes from a recognition of being within, held by, and always touched by Earth and air.

In "Merleau-Ponty and the Voice of the Earth," David Abram suggests that depth is the primordial dimension, because we are entirely *in* depth. If we adopt a Gaian interpretation, we are *within* the biosphere as opposed to *on* a planet. Conventional reductionistic science defines depth egocentrically, or as that which is out in front of us: it is the narrow part of the visual field in which signals from both eyes overlap. This conception of depth perpetuates a worldview in which separation is enhanced; like any worldview, this influences the ways in which we actually perceive. In contrast, Abram defines depth with a biocentric emphasis, and with reference to the implications of viewing one's self as *within* the biosphere: "For many who have regained a genuine depth perception, recognizing their own embodiment as entirely internal to, and thus wholly dependent upon, the vaster body of the Earth, the only possible course of action is to begin planning and working on behalf of the ecological world which they now discern."[2]

Abram suggests consciously choosing a way of seeing in which our

2. David Abram, "Merleau-Ponty and the Voice of the Earth," *Environmental Ethics* (Summer 1988), 101–120.

organic embeddedness is deeply recognized. The recognition of *being within* carries with it a number of psychological repercussions. Quite noticeably, a sense of being within produces a distinct vulnerability; it is a recognition of one's psychological permeability and lack of control. But there is also a kind of ecstatic liberation, a freeing from the need to control. One feels a relinquishing of defenses and separation, and with it a mysterious sensuality. Conceptually, being within and "wholly dependent upon" the body of the Earth requires a kind of communication or exchange not unlike that shared with a lover.

If we are part of a communication system within the Gaian organism, then perception is our best channel for listening, and for communication. But Abram points out that our notions of communication, as an activity, are limited by twentieth-century frenzy and techno-habits. He suggests that true perception is more akin to communion, a kind of nonverbal, spirited form of communication. Perception then becomes a vehicle for communion with the nonhuman natural world and may be experienced as a spiritual practice. We experience reverence, simply by looking.

Altering one's sense of living *on* a planet is perhaps best practiced by hiking into a canyon. Within a deep canyon, one experiences verticality. Verticality is a visual dimension that becomes less familiar as it increases. Thus the deeper one goes, the greater potential for transcending perceptual habits. Verticality conveys being among, or within. The Grand Canyon is vertical and red, cast against a bright blue background. It is a provocative landscape, hard to define and easy to feel. Within the Grand Canyon, I feel my whole body in relationship with Earth; she is laid open and inviting. As I work hard to go deeper, my defenses dissolve, and I am vulnerable and receptive. Receptivity facilitates identification; I often find myself spontaneously identifying with much that I see, and much that I see is absolutely gorgeous. It is powerful medicine, particularly in an age of disembodiment and disenchantment. Sensing our embeddedness within the biosphere may also be practiced with imagination: imagine being seen by trees, boulders, and stones, by rivers and animals. Imagine that they are watching. It produces a notable, sensual experience of being "part of," within something magnificent and much vaster than ourselves.

5. *The Imaginal Self*

The fifth element of an ecological way of seeing is imagination, the practice of visual imagery. Learning to work with visual imagery shows us the power of our worldview to determine perception and, ultimately, reality. Among other benefits, imagination provides the opportunity to invent our worldview.

The images we carry, or the visions we create, are significant determinants of subjective reality and choice, and consequently, of our world's future. Images serve as guides, or templates for the myriad unconscious decisions we make; they inform us of our own previously determined desires and priorities, and we act accordingly.

Unfortunately, we have lost, or nearly lost, the power of our active imaginations. The ubiquity of television, canned and capitalized media imagery, psychic numbing, and widespread disempowerment have served to replace images spontaneously generated from one's vast imaginal self. We have unconsciously, and perhaps irresponsibly, relinquished our ability to imagine. As an antidote, we simply need to practice. Rekindling this ability requires the active engagement of one's imagination and includes taking time to lie on a soft floor, on a bed of moss, or covered in silky sand. With practice, one's ability to imagine becomes colorful, vivid, creative, and emotionally provocative, thus enriching and influencing our psychological experience. With practice, we can develop clear visions, images for our children, for the future, to which we will be devoted. These visions are the images to nurture and feed with psychological energy. They are the images that may guide our daily, unconscious choices. They are the images that will serve to create the world in which we wish to live.

A Message from Gaia

The Earth speaks to us through our bodies and psyches. She often cries, and many of us feel her tears and see her pain. Recognizing her voice is perception. I experience it as a force of nature entering me, like light. In other moments, I feel as if Mercury has delivered a handwritten message from Gaia, signed by all the relations. Their signatures are patterns in snow, or squawks and screeches, or abstract forms shifting into patterns and symbols, and a sense of the sacred. In those moments, it feels as if the Earth is calling for me to awaken.

The Earth calls continually. She calls us with beauty, sometimes truly breathtaking, sometimes heart wrenching, and always provocative and visceral. We are embedded in a multidimensional web of beauty. It is where we are, *now*. We are also at the interface between an objectified world and postmodern relativism, between a kind of cultural arrogance and unified traditions. Matthew Fox calls it an "age of weddings." Martha Heyneman refers to this era as a "moment of grace," in which great transformations may occur. The moment calls for the reperceiving of our Earth, for perceiving the myriad and magical relations that may inform an ecological ethic. If we are receptive to the ways in which the landscape speaks to us, or the ways in which perception serves as a channel for communion, we may reawaken and preserve a sense of human integrity within the family of all relations.

Ecological Groundedness in Gestalt Therapy

WILLIAM CAHALAN

G ESTALT THERAPY, in contrast to most schools of psychotherapy, is inherently ecological in its personality theory, worldview, and methodology. The person is seen as fully embedded in the world, and the world is seen as more like a living organism than like a nonliving mechanism of separate interacting parts. Despite this underlying connection with the natural environment, Gestalt therapists are just beginning to pay specific attention in their work to the client's engagement with the natural world beyond the interpersonal sphere. In this essay, William Cahalan presents some of the techniques he has borrowed and elaborated from Gestalt to achieve a deepened sense of the full therapeutic environment.

I want to offer an ideal of healthy functioning, which I call "ecological groundedness," which represents an expansion of the traditional Gestalt emphasis on living and acting "in-the-world." Introspection and self-reflection are seen as part of gathering oneself after contact with the "environment," preparing for further contact or engagement.

Groundedness is a dynamic state of the person that includes the sense of confidence, pleasure, and wonder resulting from progressively deepening contact with the wild and domesticated natural community of the person's neighborhood and larger land region: with unpaved ground, soil, or landscape; with weather and the diversity of native plants and animals; and with human family, neighbors, and local cultural activities. The person has a growing sense of the ways in which these aspects of home or place are intimately connected with his or her self and household as well as with each other.

A more literal aspect of groundedness within this broader, more inclusive state is the development of the bodily confidence and grace that occur while regularly experiencing on foot one's actual home ground or landscape.

Growing food and cultivating the soil can be central to this experience. Being grounded is enhanced and renewed by periods of extended, sensuous, empathic engagement with the world, balanced by restorative moments of inward reflectiveness. This rhythm involves an intuitive cycling between the individual's more contracted, contained sense of self, on the one hand, and a more expanded, relational, or extended sense of self on the other, including the ability to lose oneself at times in union with the world. When we experience this self-extended state, the Earth tends to be sensed as the all-embracing, enduring Self of which the individual is one unique but temporary expression.

As the individual cultivates this intimate sense of belonging, she or he may discover, in the seasonal turning of her or his own life within this larger life, the deep urge to grow and mature, to ripen and "leave seed" to the wider community— and to anticipate death as the final resigning or giving back of self to the elements and beings of the land community that have birthed and sustained the self.

There seems to be a deep, genetically based need in all people for such rootedness or sense of place, in which our very nervous system requires this face to face, balanced giving and taking, a self-corrective interchange within the human and nonhuman life community. This inborn set of needs evolved especially during our species' evolution for millennia within a village-centered, hunter-gatherer way of life. Many of the values and practices developed in such cultures need to be drawn upon by people in our time, since our industrial society constantly produces our disconnectedness.

On an individual level there are various personality styles that foster disconnectedness, a sense of emptiness, or a lack of groundedness. One of the most basic patterns involves clinging to core images of self as owner (of traits, things, land "resources," and people), rather than primarily sensing oneself as a *process of relating*. The "self as owner" identity is partially a defense against the urban-industrial "dislocation" from a basic sense of rootedness or place.

Rhythms of Engagement

In working to cultivate the client's ecological groundedness, as in my past more-traditional practice, I emphasize the following kinds of things: I follow my own and the client's rhythm of engagement with, and withdrawal from, each other, now also in relation with the natural world in which we are both immersed. I work toward inclusion of the whole person in his or her activity, including attention to supportive breathing and mobility, presence of varied qualities of self, and a full range of available emotion, as he or she moves into contactful looking, listening, moving, and touching. I also explore the ways in which the client is blocking or interrupting fulfilling engagement and withdrawal. I invite graded experimenting to increase awareness of present activity and of how new, unfamiliar activity feels.

I give special attention to the following:

1. Aspects of my personal manner and office setting naturally communicate my interests and values to clients, and influence them to be intrigued, repelled, indifferent, or maybe some combination of these. These aspects might include my comfortable, usually casual manner of dress, my tendency to notice and savor the weather, the presence of lots of potted plants, or my recycling containers for paper and aluminum cans. From the beginning, then, there is grist for the therapeutic mill in the client's reactions to me.

2. I often tell clients in an early session that besides the expected focus on their ways of relating to themselves and other people, I also tend to include a focus on how they relate to other aspects of nature. I explore any hesitations, much as I would if the reluctance were about family

relationships or other more traditional areas. Although most of this section refers to work with adults, I have found that adolescents and children often enjoy my inclusion of nature.

3. Just as the client is not only telling me about interactions with people who are not present but is also interacting in the session with me, she or he is at each moment during the session relating with other aspects of nature. I begin attending to this as well as to the interpersonal dimension in the simple, obvious ways that we Gestalt therapists might call grounding or support work. In doing this I often talk about these activities in more explicitly ecological language than I used in the past. For example, I invite clients, as they let their breathing regulate itself, to know that they, I, and all the rest of the animal kingdom are now taking in oxygen produced by the plant kingdom, and are releasing carbon dioxide back to the plants. Also, as I explore with the client the movement and blocking of emotion, I may call this an aspect of the "life force" in her, which is also in the grass and trees. I may say that this energy came to her from the sun through her food, and is being released in her with each breath of oxygen and beat of her heart. We may at times savor the light in the room or outside the window as a wonderful, usually taken-for-granted emanation from the sun, and another form of the excitement or emotion in us.

4. In the same way that I might, in more traditional ways, share little pieces of information about such things as how the client's lower-back tightness may be connected to ways of breathing, or to ways of thinking about and expressing anger or sexual feelings, I keep the didactics brief. I try to honor the client's particular readiness, or lack of it, to consider such knowledge or beliefs of mine, and I encourage an experimental attitude and freedom to directly disagree.

5. I assume that no matter how cut off clients are from direct, healthy interchange with wider nature in their lives, they are also now and in their childhood emotionally nourished by it in some half-aware ways. These can be recognized and possibly expanded. Clients often become more open to this when I ask about early memories of pleasure, awe, or fascination with the nonhuman, natural aspects of their world. Often clients, especially fairly fragmented ones, tell emotional stories of pets, their yard of grass, garden, and trees, rainfall and sunlight, and so on—

and of the role that their love of these played in their own survival of disconnected or abusive relationships with their parents. During this kind of remembering, the client often becomes aware of sadness from losses such as the bulldozing of old, familiar tree groves, or the sacrificing of grassy hillsides and secret ravines to housing developments and shopping malls. It can be suggested to clients that such emotion is a form of our natural excitement, of the life force in them. Such sadness is expressive of natural human compassion (passion with), our basic empathy and connectedness with all life. As such, these awarenesses have the potential to move the person into meaningful involvement that is more likely to be personally empowering.

6. In attending to my own and the client's interaction with nature, I may begin suggesting that we walk or sit outside for part or all of the session. We might separate and then meet back at the same spot. I may suggest as an experiment that we walk together or sit without talking, but signal nonverbally to each other about things we notice, if we want to. We may describe to each other what we notice from time to time, and I often actively work with the client then, inviting him to actively engage with and imaginatively extend himself into that tree, stream, or rock, discovering what he can take away from that encounter. What often becomes apparent is the connection between the interpersonal relating and the relating with wider nature. The weather, trees, birds, sidewalk, landscape, and car exhaust may become the predominant focus, but often our collaborative, supportive presence to each other is a strong contributing background context, which may then be brought into the foreground and explored for a while, too. Even when our dialogue does not focus on nonhuman nature, the quality and energy of such exploration is often enhanced by the immediate multisensory presence of the natural community.

7. In preparation for going outdoors, or after we are out, I work with the client's support and grounding while she is seated, standing, or walking, encouraging her to adjust to and savor her interaction with gravity. I may also invite her to enjoy the pulsing of blood, breathing, and energy development as aspects of her membership in Earth's body. I introduce, for the client's consideration, the image of the Earth as a living, abiding, self-regulating body within which we and all species are

temporary forms. We have come from and will return to the Earth. We are in constant, often unconscious communion with Earth, participating in her self-regulation and development.

Membership in the Earth's Body

Here is one version of a guided experience that I might ask a client to try as an experiment in sensing their membership in Earth's body:

> Let yourself settle into the floor or ground, allowing yourself to comfortably adjust to the Earth's gravitational embrace. Close your eyes. Maybe you can faintly feel your blood pulsing in your neck and fingertips. Enjoy this automatic cycling, knowing that it is actually part of the larger water and mineral cycles of your region. Just as our blood nourishes us, water is the blood of Earth. . . . Now notice your breathing, and gently follow its rhythm for a few minutes. Like blood pulsing, breathing is mostly automatic, an enjoyable and natural, taken-for-granted life process. Know that all the oxygen you and all animals are taking in at this moment is a gift of green plants, given off by them as they breathe in the carbon dioxide that we and other animals have exhaled. Open your eyes and see some of the plants that are breathing with you. As water is Earth's blood, so air is the breath of our larger Earth body. Now close your eyes again, and feel your own energy, which may be rising as your breathing has deepened: notice your muscle tone, slight movement, or felt readiness to move. Know and appreciate the source of this energy, which is the sun. Open your eyes now and take in the sunlight. This sunlight energy in you is released with each heartbeat and each breath, having come to you from plants through the food chain. Now use your energy to slowly stand up. Begin to walk slowly around the room, feeling the ground, savoring each step. See the sunlight in the room, which is present even if the day is cloudy. Let your breathing regulate its own pace and depth. Look at the green plants again and whatever else you can see. Know that the plants, this building, and everything else came from and will return to the Earth, as will you and I.

I often work to enhance pleasurable interaction with the ground as the client stands and walks, releasing tensions that may be blocking free movement. This can lead to a silent walk outdoors, after which we explore the client's (and my own) wide variety of responses. For example, there is often either resistance to or pleasure in the experience of merging or being confluent with an aspect of the world, or with the world as a whole, as encountered at a given point on the walk.

There is a tendency in our culture for people to "retroflect" or armor themselves, maintaining the sense of being a spectator who relates to nature as static scenery that is "out there." I help clients notice and eventually experiment with moving out of such a spectator stance.

Another experiment I suggest is that the client explore his neighborhood on foot in some of the previously described ways. I also suggest that before going out he research where his tap water, food, light, and heat come from in nature, and what the effects of producing these commodities are. I tell him to anticipate a gradual deepening of sensitivity, knowledge, and rootedness over time as he gets to know the sources of his household economy (which are often at great distances), and then the nearby and more compelling houses and yards, neighbors who are also on foot, particularly inviting trees, ravines, wooded areas, blackberry thickets, migrating and nesting birds, woodchuck holes, and other aspects of his local natural community.

I suggest that the person continue this researching and walking regularly and leisurely throughout at least one cycle of four seasons. I often contribute by sharing my excitement around the time of the solstices, planting and harvest times, full moons, and so on as we mark our movement through the reassuring cycles of Earth time.

As a result of regular faithful attention to "finding oneself" within the home region, it is possible to grow into the kind of groundedness that I described earlier.

The Case of Rhonda

Rhonda, in her mid-thirties, had a distracted look about her, only fleetingly interrupted by a bright half smile as she would whimsically make an ironic remark. She was an intelligent but fairly fragile person. She came to therapy wanting help with agoraphobia and with intense anxiety generally. In our sessions she was only tenuously able to see some possible link between her passivity and her sense of vulnerability in the face of neglect or nastiness from others, her self-effacing way of thinking, and her anxiety and agoraphobia. After about three months of weekly meetings, I asked her what animal she was most like. She looked surprised and then intrigued, and said "a lion." She described her strength and her ability to fend off attack, which freed her to roam at will. She then paused for a while and said she guessed that she was actually now, in contrast to childhood, more like a deer in her flightiness and vulnerability. I helped her explore the possible strengths of being a deer, in addition to the costs, and of how she still might draw on the lion's qualities in herself. This began further work with her animal aspects, as well as with domestic and wild animals that she encountered near her house and in the woods nearby. This process drew her out of her bound-up, self-effacing style to some extent, and she gained some inspiration and energy from it. The animals became powerful metaphors for stretching beyond her passive position, and for drawing on outer and inner "wild nature" as a source of personal power.

We wove the work with human relationships and relations with the nonhuman world together in a number of ways. She gained strength from intentionally cultivating groundedness within the nonhuman world. This helped her in her effort to be more self-possessed and assertive with relatives and others with whom she had previously felt very susceptible to being pushed around.

Ultimate Ground

Such work with the nonhuman dimension tends to bring up the client's relationship to ultimate reality, to all that exists, to what some would call the spiritual. I think that all people have the urge to connect meaningfully (the word "religion" comes from *re-ligio*, meaning "reconnecting") with something larger than the human race and our own creations. While I personally think of "spirit" as just the sentience and creative activity of all matter and energy, not as anything separate from matter, I try to be open to various formed and unformed beliefs that my clients hold about ultimate reality.

The client may believe in a transcendent God, in the whole of nature as constituting the ultimate intelligence or ground of all being, in some variation of these, or may embrace agnosticism. In any case, the kind of approach that I describe here can contribute to the client's life a more palpable sense of being part of a meaningful reality beyond the merely human world severed from its context and source.

The sense of thankfulness that is involved often naturally leads to a desire to give back, to live less as a consumer and more in balance with the Earth, which in a sense is our true body, our real self.

Restoring Habitats, Communities, and Souls

ELAN SHAPIRO

CRUCIAL TO LIVING in harmony with the natural world is the idea of reciprocity, of giving back to the Earth for all that it has provided. Reciprocity is integral to the rituals and customs of all native peoples, but it runs directly counter to notions of private ownership of the land and natural resources. In the highly urbanized contexts in which most of us live, how is it possible to give back? How can this gesture become part of our own healing? In his highly creative program, ecopsychology educator and consultant Elan Shapiro integrates the much-needed work of habitat restoration with group meetings that encompass ritual, psychological insight, and community building. The result is a full and lasting connection to the land being restored.

━━━━━━━

Inner-city children collect native grass seed in Chicago vacant lots for prairie restoration. Tireless tree planters turn wastelands into woodlands in desertified regions of Tunisia and Kenya. Churches and businesses "adopt" streams and beaches as aspects of their community-participation programs. Ranchers, loggers, and back-to-the-land bioregionalists in Northern California discover that their economic and community well-being depends on how well they can work together to restore the health of a watershed. Children in hundreds of Japanese schools cry "Come back salmon!" as they release salmon fry they have raised into depleted rivers. Central American farmers rediscover and plant a rich mix of forgotten precolonial crops, restoring a measure of species diversity in their localities.

These glimpses reveal aspects of a blossoming, grass-roots movement for environmental restoration. Restoration projects may be urban or rural, professional or volunteer, on wildlands or agricultural lands, in strip-mined areas or in backyards. By mimicking the life-sustaining patterns inherent in a place, they aim to bring back the vitality and diversity that the community living there needs in order to thrive. Through environmental restoration, people are coming back to Earth with their bodies: cleaning up and decontaminating; clearing out and planting; building erosion-control structures and sapling protectors; and weeding, mulching, and monitoring. They are learning, through their hands and their hearts, to identify with the pain and the healing of the ecosystems that sustain them.

Environmental restoration work can spontaneously engender deep and lasting changes in people, including a sense of dignity and belonging, a tolerance for diversity, and a sustainable ecological sensibility. This art and science of helping the web of life in a particular place heal and renew itself can serve as a mirror and an impetus for individual and community renewal. Because of this inherent power, environmental restoration has become one of the key activities through which I practice ecopsychology.

The emerging field of ecopsychology explores the basic shifts in our patterns of identity and relationship that occur when we include our connection to the web of life around us as essential to human well-being. When I work with people—whether through outdoor activites such as gathering edible plants or as an institutional recycling consultant—I help them mend their ties to the other species and cultures that share the web with them, particularly in the place they call home. At the same time, I interweave this practice with the psychospiritual work of reclaiming the disowned parts of their inner world. Each process requires and enhances the other.

Restoration and Spontaneous Personal Change

A number of forces operate to link individual human and community healing with the process of habitat restoration. People experience deep pleasure and release from sweating together—feeling the elements of soil and water, rock and plant, while doing a common task with a visible positive outcome. The usually suppressed vision of living as part of an earthy, purposeful community becomes intensely tangible. Many people who usually work in isolation form spontaneous little teams. Activists who generally relate to "the environment" with tension and worry become giddy and exhilarated and invent songs to accompany the process. During site visits spread over the course of a year or two, the songs and the teamwork and the giddiness continue, but with an extra measure of dignity, confidence, and groundedness, as participants begin to notice signs of healing in the habitat they are restoring. How rare an experience of wholeness and accomplishment for those of us in the automated, "developed" world!

When doing restoration, people become involved with a place in a very active and embodied manner. As a result, they often "fall in love" with it with an intensity I have seen matched only on extended wilderness journeys. By thinking through and taking the steps that will help remove the destructive influences, stabilize the system, and support the forces of regeneration already present, they become imprinted by and identified with the place's different species and elements, and by their web of relationships.

Since the tasks involved in restoration work engage both mind and body in understanding and, to some extent, in mimicking the complex patterns of relationship in a healthy and diverse community, people naturally absorb the vitality and wisdom inherent in a place. We often start out with a single focus—an endangered species or a trashed creek—but may soon find ourselves inextricably linked to the trees and the loggers upslope, the chemical company and the air quality in the valley, or the families down the street. In attempting to help an ecosystem, we learn to think like that system and to reclaim our own biological wisdom.

Wilderness journeys, nature walks, and adventure sports, when sensitively undertaken, can catalyze an intense bonding with the Earth as a nurturing parent. Although this bonding serves as a powerful source of healing and transformation, participants are often left with a deep sense of powerlessness and depression upon returning to "normal" life.[1] Adopting the bold stance involved in restoration work can catalyze a different kind of transformation. By becoming active partners in regenerating the health of their localities—and, in a less dramatic way, of the Earth as a whole—people start to reverse the soul-numbing patterns of exploiting and abusing the source of so many life-sustaining gifts. They also begin to release the often-repressed, but nonetheless crippling, emotions—guilt and shame, grief and despair, loneliness and powerlessness—associated with going along with the relentless machinery of corporate consumer culture.

Once we have bonded with the Earth, we cannot escape growing up and learning to treat this primal parent as partner, friend, and ally as well. Restoration work involves people as partners in a mature, collaborative relationship with the natural world. In such a relationship we naturally ask, "How can I give back as well as receive?" and, if we have been insensitive and hurtful, "How can I make amends?" In this process of cleaning up our mess with our first parent, with the very foundations of our existence, we set in motion a pattern of reciprocity, of sacred exchange. This pattern can reverberate through the ways we treat other humans and other cultures and the way we treat ourselves, promoting a "partnership way" of life.[2]

Restoration and Cultural Transformation

Not only individuals change—cultures can change as well. The Mattole River valley of Northern California, once a beautifully forested region, was stripped of 90 percent of its old-growth trees in forty years. The near extinction of the salmon in the river led a group of concerned people to

1. Robert Greenway, "Mapping the Wilderness Experience: Ideas and Questions Gleaned from a Twenty-two-year Study of a University Wilderness Program," paper presented at Fifth World Congress-Symposium on International Wilderness Allocation, Management, and Research, September26–October 2, 1992, Tromsø, Norway.
2. Riane Eisler and David Loye, *The Partnership Way* (San Francisco: HarperSanFrancisco, 1990).

attempt to bring back its habitat.[3] After learning how to catch some of
the remaining salmon, extract eggs and sperm, release them, and hatch
thousands of native fingerlings to restock the river, they discovered that
this wasn't enough. The clear-cut and overgrazed slopes upstream were
sliding into the river and filling the salmon's gravelly spawning areas
with silt. To restore the salmon runs meant to restore the watershed—
the whole area that drained into the river.

To restore the watershed, they first had to *know* it, not as a series of
properties and abstract political boundaries, but as a living organism
with its own integrity, however wounded. Teams were trained to walk
the land and to survey and map its many patterns, including salmon
habitat, old-growth distribution, and logging history. Doing this work
required cultivating community consensus on goals and priorities. Years
were spent building a working alliance of back-to-the-land bioregionalists, loggers, cattle ranchers, fishing people, and many other groups
with widely varying agendas. As the alliance and its efforts have become
more successful, community members have acted as consultants for
other watershed alliances, developed a watershed-based school curriculum, and taken local players on the road to share their saga via a mu-
sical comedy. The challenges of coming to realize the boundaries of
home together—initiated by the mysterious pull of one endangered
species—helped to spawn a culture of restoration whose impact keeps
spreading through the global network.

Restoration Work

Working on a restoration project as an ecopsychology educator/consul-
tant involves me with students, clients, and volunteer groups in many
different contexts. I may be leading an afternoon program at a conference, helping a school or business develop a positive long-term relationship with its natural surroundings, or teaching in a graduate program.
Whatever the context, I begin with experiential exercises that enhance
and integrate each person's awareness of her inner worlds, of the group,
and of the place. But, most important, I let the place and the task be the
primary teachers.

3. Freeman House, "To Learn the Things We Need to Know," in Richard Nilson (ed.),
Helping Nature Heal (Berkeley, Calif.: Whole Earth/Ten Speed Press, 1991).

I invite people to walk unhurriedly and unintrusively through the place and to sit or lie down attentively, sensing its flavors and its presence. In this way, they begin to encounter the area—its contours, treasures, wounds, and mysteries—in an immediate way. As Malcolm Margolin suggests, one of the best ways to learn about erosion is to get out on a slope during a heavy rain, lie down on your belly, and simply watch what happens.[4] You then can experience firsthand the profound contrast between raindrops hitting blades of grass and sliding gently to the ground, versus hitting bare earth and sending it splattering.

While providing a biological, cultural, and historical overview of the site, I describe the potential dangers of human intervention. If we intervene in hasty and overly manipulative ways, rather than patiently attending to the needs and rhythms of a particular place, we often find that we have created more problems than we have solved. Even the most thoughtful restoration project can have unintended consequences. By acknowledging the shadow side of restoration work at the outset, I create a space in which people can reflect on parallels to other forms of change work, both personal and social, where speediness and intrusiveness can undermine the healing process.

To clarify the ecological context, I demonstrate how climate, vegetation, wildlife, water, soil, geologic formations, and human cultures and structures work together at the site. Once this framework is established, the situation itself often helps participants discover the web of connections. An elementary-school science project in Northern California offers a good example of this kind of contextual learning.[5]

In attempting to restore the habitat of an endangered shrimp species, children eagerly planted willows to help stabilize the eroded banks of a creek. Along the way, they encountered a rancher who, while having little interest in the life cycle of freshwater shrimp, acknowledged that the willows might help quail—which he had loved to hunt—return to the area. As the project continued, however, the youthful enthusiasm of the students drew the rancher into involvement not only with the shrimp, but also with the health of the watershed. His involvement eventually ignited the interest of other ranchers, who are also beginning to

4. Malcolm Margolin, *The Earth Manual: How to Work on Wild Land Without Taming It*, 2d edition (Berkeley, Calif.: Heyday, 1985).
5. Laurette Rogers, Brookside School, San Anselmo, California, personal communication.

work with the students on this project, seeing that the health of their individual properties depends on the health of the whole system.

I often convey this kind of ecological context through dramatic storytelling, sometimes with the help of other naturalists, restorationists, and involved community members. As we learn about a place as an ever-changing entity with a long history of human involvement—some of it respectful and sustainable, some of it short-sighted and abusive—we feel more grounded, humble, and receptive about the task we face, able to go beyond the superficial impulse simply to "fix it" by doing a great deal of planting.

Taking the dramatic mode a step further, I may encourage participants to enact, with movement, gesture, and vocalization, the roles of the animals, plants, elements, and people present in the place. In an urban creek restoration project, for example, some thirty of us played at being the whole watershed, evolving over time from its earlier, wilder phase, through its current degraded condition, to its future self-sustaining state. Among the roles people chose to enact were: baby plants on a stripped slope struggling to take root; soil particles either protected under the seedlings or washing into the creek; raindrops trickling or rushing through plants and soil and converging into the muddied creek; and humans altering the place over time in various benign or destructive ways. Together, through this environmental-education game, we playfully began to embody the contours, relationships, and patterns of transformation in a natural watershed community.

Paralleling the more "objective" natural and cultural orientation just described, I work "subjectively," facilitating the psychological changes that enable a more spacious and inclusive sense of self. Drawing upon Depth Psychology, particularly the Jungian tradition, I explore, for example, the mysterious process by which our many layers of interrelatedness actually enhance the work of individuation. I also have adapted Winnicott's concept of the "holding environment" as a way of working with situations that encourage a primal bonding with the natural world.[6]

My practice derives, as well, from traditions such as Gestalt therapy, sensory awareness, somatic psychology, martial arts, and Buddhist meditation. Aspects of each of these traditions invite people to focus moment

6. D. W. Winnicott, *Playing and Reality* (London: Tavistock, 1971).

to moment on being as present as possible to both inner experience and the situation or "other" they are contacting. In this way, they attempt to reawaken our inherent wisdom and self-healing abilities.

Many of the concepts and methods I use come from Gestalt therapy, since its initial assumptions (if not its contemporary practices) are among the most ecological and relational in Western psychology.[7] Gestalt puts great trust in the biological wisdom of our organism and assumes that the organism and its environment form an inseparable unity. According to this tradition, a healthy person makes good contact and has complete and satisfying interactions with whatever emerges in the foreground of his awareness, without shutting out the surrounding field. By implication, a healthy self requires a healthy environment in which to function.

Much of Gestalt work focuses on how we split off and polarize both inner parts *and* self and world. It sees this fragmentation as both a cause and a symptom of contemporary pathology. Gestalt practitioners may suggest behavioral and awareness experiments to clients that help them discover, through focusing on the way they make contact in the present, their patterns of blocking and fragmenting. These discoveries may be augmented by creative and somatically based methods that help clients reintegrate disowned parts of themselves and that renew their capacity for unitary functioning with their environment.

Balance of Attention

Perhaps the simplest and most basic experiential method I use involves drawing attention to breathing as a process of continuous rhythmic contact and exchange with trees, birds, and other people, since air is the nurturing ocean within which we all live. Whether walking, sitting, stretching, or weeding, we attend both to the quality of our breathing and inner sensing and to the unique presences in our surroundings. We also focus on the boundaries through which these worlds come into contact and on the quality of the connection and exchange that is occurring. In this way, we embrace the entire continuum of inner and outer experience.

7. Frederick Perls, Ralph Hefferline, and Paul Goodman, *Gestalt Therapy: Excitement and Growth in the Human Personality* (New York: Dell, 1951).

In helping people experiment with this shifting balance of attention, I may suggest that we move back and forth between having open and closed eyes during a period of perhaps fifteen or twenty minutes. Many people discover an unforced kind of meditation in this way, as a natural sense of concentration and engagement gradually emerges. Experiences with balance of attention can also provoke some combination of a "close encounter" with another species or element, a fresh opening to previously unconscious feelings or images, and a sense of more fluid and permeable boundaries through which a different quality of contact can occur.

The inclusive quality of perception encouraged by balance of attention can increase our tolerance for diversity, both within and outside ourselves. Certain aspects of restoration projects—such as removing large clusters of exotic plants that crowd out native species and reduce wildlife diversity—favor this process. In the San Francisco Bay Area, for example, we are often faced with weeding entire slopes covered with an invasive shrub, Scotch broom. Either at the outset of this kind of work, or partway through it, I have people hold one tall broom plant and breathe and sense and move with it. This offers them an opportunity to experience and honor the plant's uniqueness and beauty, as well as their relationship with it, before uprooting it. For people who have prior experience in habitat restoration, this experiment may be either unsettling or refreshing. They generally have become accustomed to viewing broom plants in only one way—as the enemy, the immigrant dominators of the gentler, more noble native plants.

Later, in the context of a process group, as I reflect on this experiment with the participants, some may uncover the roots of their need to categorize and distance from the other. For example, during an ongoing project, one person found himself grappling with his growing discomfort in feeling righteous and pure about his environmentalism. Another recognized how easy it is to hate and distance herself from the part of her that eats uncontrollably. Gradually, as we worked with the feelings and insights that were surfacing, we came to understand ecological awareness as more than just facts about ecosystems, but also as an inclusive *sensibility*, an embracing of both the diversity around us and the many selves within us, even if they are not all as noble and beautiful as we would like them to be. We all continued to pull out the broom plants with gusto when we returned to the slope, but with a balance of attention that increased our empathy and our sensitivity to the experience of taking their lives. In doing so, we were ever so gradually uprooting the mental patterns of polarizing and putting down that keep us split off from the deeper currents of restoration.

Metaphor and Mirroring

The metaphors that the restoration process suggests often resonate deeply with participants' self-healing work. They can also can bring up unexpected issues, for example, death and transformation. The concrete task of the situation, together with skillful facilitation, can also provide the medium for working through these issues. Julia, a participant in one of my projects on an Oakland college campus, hated cutting down the acacia and eucalyptus saplings that choked out native plant and animal diversity in a trashed and neglected ravine. Her feelings began to shift when we read aloud, from a book about native peoples' lives in this area, descriptions of the varied vegetation and abundant wildlife that once shared this place with a more sustainable human culture. We also took the time to create a brief ritual honoring Julia's identification and empathy with the life of these young, robust creatures. What helped her most of all was being in charge of one of the next phases of the project: using the cut saplings to make steps along a trail in a particularly steep area of the ravine. She proudly returned to finish the trail and committed herself to maintaining it.

Reflecting with me later, Julia said that uprooting the saplings enabled her to experience her fear of loss and death more fully. Being creatively involved in recycling these problematic parts of the ravine then helped her to trust more in the natural flow of her own life. The trail became a living symbol of a relatively nonintrusive way of navigating life's unpredictable qualities. It also became a pathway to a lively partnership between her more culture-bound and her wilder parts.

Both cultural and personal issues can be brought up by the metaphorical aspects of working with native and immigrant species. Ramona, a participant in a project built into a weeklong conference, initially expressed misgivings about the value of pulling out a huge patch of Scotch broom. She suspected that the process merely served a privileged conservationist preoccupation with pristine environments. I didn't dispute the validity of her concerns. But as we talked it became clear, in addition, that her own repetitive experiences of rejection and abuse, as a woman, a lesbian, and a Chicana, had left her without much of a sense of hope, empowerment, or, for that matter, excitement about wiping out "problem" immigrants.

Once she became involved, however, Ramona acknowledged the strange pleasure she took in exterminating these rugged creatures, pulling them up by their deep roots. She also began discovering little native plants, often bent over or spindly, but still alive, under the slowly retreating horde of broom: live oak, tan oak, toyon, wild strawberry, honeysuckle, milkmaids. In less than an hour, we discovered twelve native species, some of them even flowering, basking in the light after their sudden release from the shroud of weeds.

Now glowing with excitement, Ramona asked me how long it would take before the hillside would be filled with this glorious diversity. I told her it could take years of follow-up weeding, seed gathering, and planting to ensure that the gentle, bent-over plants she had revealed would be strong enough to resist the persistent broom culture and evolve into a thriving community. Undaunted, she returned to the site with some of her teammates several times to clear more space and find even more varieties of rugged survivors.

Months later, Ramona wrote to tell me that working with those few hundred square feet of earth had given her the inspiration and courage to deal much more proactively with the sense of isolation caused by differences of race and sexual preference at her workplace. It had rekindled her vision of the very real, yet smothered, possibility of living in a rich, diverse, natural community.

A skilled facilitator can increase metaphorical learning through weaving relevant scientific information into stories. This method can be used, for example, when rehabilitating slopes stripped down by heavy logging or overgrazing. We usually need to put temporary physical barriers (such as brush mats) in place, in addition to planting appropriate vegetation, to prevent topsoil from eroding during heavy rains. If I can't find a rainstorm in which to immerse people (as in Malcolm Margolin's example), I might tell them about engineering studies showing that doubling the speed of water flow exponentially increases its erosional impact on topsoil. Raindrops that hit blades of grass first are dramatically slowed by the time they reach the earth. As we come back over time to monitor the project, we can sense how both the spreading roots and the canopy of leaves have begun to protect the thin film of soil that supports the life community on our slope. Eventually, the slope no longer requires the temporary barriers.

Processes such as these can naturally mirror the contemporary experience of being bombarded with the relentless overload of information, technology, and pollution, or of the repeated abuses suffered by victims of oppression. In order to have a respite from the destructive influences of society, we find we have to put short-term support systems in place to stabilize our situation. Staying isolated in our pain perpetuates the downhill slide. Gradually, though, for our soul's deep mending to occur, we need the more complex healing process like that of the diverse plant community, with its spreading roots and shoots. A healthy watershed needs a multistoried plant community to help it gently absorb heavy rains, so that the waters can be a source of vitality rather than ruin. So, too, our souls cry out for a rich inner life and for a grounded, diverse community to slow up the bruising pace of our lives, to create a holding environment in which we can turn our trials into sources of strength and integration.

Cultivating the Connected Self

Whenever I introduce a conscious psychospiritual dimension to restoration work, I acquaint people, implicitly or explicitly, with the ecopsychological concept of an "ecological" or "connected" self. Such a self expands beyond our human-centered conditioning and sense of being split off and separate, in order to engage intimately with other species, cultures, and people, as well as with places. To live in a relational way requires a gradual opening to broader, more permeable boundaries. The boundaries need to be clear enough that we can hold our own as creative, responsible partners, yet pliable enough that we can bond and identify not only with our immediate family and ethnic heritage, but also with the whole spectrum of beings around us. In my work, I attempt to facilitate this transition from the isolated individualistic self that our culture reinforces to one whose boundaries are fluid enough to allow for both creative individuation and intimate connection. As many people's experience will attest, this fluidity actually enhances, rather than diminishes, an individual's sense of her particularity and unique gifts.

Just as monocropping in agriculture destroys the rich diversity that healthy communities need, so does the splitting off of people by race and class. Any work dealing with the shift from a fragmented to a more inclusive self needs to focus on the complex interrelationship between our crippling isolation from nature and from the different parts of the human community. Restoration offers a potent opportunity to join the issues of biological and cultural diversity with the work of creating a safe holding environment for our own abused and exploited parts. On a field trip with my students in a holistically oriented graduate program, we helped restore an eroded watershed burned in the 1991 Oakland firestorm. The East Bay Conservation Corps, a major force in local restoration work, has helped to implement this project to train young people, mostly inner-city African Americans and Hispanics, in restoration and leadership skills. Each of the trainees worked closely with a small group of my nearly all-white, relatively privileged students, for two hours, instructing and supervising them, sharing their skill in working with seedlings in a damaged watershed. The camaraderie and bonding that emerged were so strong that the two groups could hardly separate from each other when the corps members had to leave.

The rest of us then walked up the creek above the burned area to a spot in a small valley that felt relatively undisturbed and also very round and embracing. We sat quietly, listening to the creek and the birds, reflecting on both our immediate experience and the ideas we had discussed in an earlier class. We noticed how rooted we felt here after working with trees and how our sense of self felt wider and more porous, our boundaries more fluid. We had just, without even noticing, eased through layers of agonizing racial and class isolation. I drew people's attention to the softer boundaries of this watershed as well, with its creek crossing through both Oakland and Berkeley and flowing through wealthy highlands and poverty-stricken flatlands alike. We also noticed how the holding environment created by this safe, round little basin nurtured us, enabling us to open ourselves to the feelings of fragility aroused by planting tender seedlings in this fire-swept place.

Pitfalls and Promises

Those who would like to integrate restoration into their psychological or educational work—perhaps by prescribing it for themselves or their clients or by using it to ground an elementary-school science curriculum—need to be aware of certain pitfalls and limitations within the field. The projects that I have described are at one end of a continuum that ranges from those designed with the well-being of an entire region as their guiding vision to those designed purely for mitigation purposes. Environmental restoration is all too often the outcome of agreements made between developers and government agencies to rehabilitate an isolated and degraded habitat while they proceed to destroy a mature, existing one. Just as focusing solely on specific stress-related symptoms doesn't heal the fragmentation of our psychic life, creating a patchwork of little restoration sites fails to deal with the fragmentation of habitats. Without spacious and interconnected habitats, wildlife extinction accelerates.

Environmental restoration, inspiring as it is for occasional volunteers, can be exhausting and low-paying work for those who labor regularly in this field. Ensuring people's and institutions' ongoing commitment to this slow, long-term process is not easy in a rootless society. The profound psychological and cultural issues this work brings up are rarely explored in the course of most projects. Finally, some projects, reflecting our deep-seated conditioning to control and to go for the quick fix, undermine the inherently regenerative powers of the places they are supposed to be helping.

These concerns are serious enough. We could also ask whether a few thousand restoration projects around the globe can make much of a difference in the face of the loss or paving over of tens of billions of tons of topsoil every year. In fact, however, environmental restoration, though only a small part of the movement to create a just and sustainable world, provides both a positive vision of a healthier world for all and a felt *experience* of working together with the immense regenerative powers of the natural world. Restoration can also generate meaningful work, as well as personal and community renewal, in areas suffering from unemployment and social breakdown. And an idea or movement whose time has come can shift rapidly from the edges of society's attention to a position of much greater impact.

The Psychology of Sustainability

There are broader ways to think of environmental restoration that are equally relevant to a contemporary understanding of psychological health. In the sustainable-agriculture movement, including commu-

nity and backyard organic gardening, people turn monoculturally exploited farmland or trashed city lots back into complex plant communities, involving humans and places in cycles of mutual long-term
benefit. This helps people experience, at the primal level of feeding,
that meeting our basic needs can be done in caring rather than depleting ways. Psychologist Cathy Sneed's Garden Project, for example, has
helped hardened criminals from the San Bruno, California, jails find
a sense of dignity and worth as nurturers of life who can come back
to their inner-city communities with vital survival and entrepreneurial
skills.[8]

In fact, any activity that helps realign our lives from more exploitative
to more collaborative ways of interacting with our world can be seen as
restorative of our "environment," both inner and outer. Walking or bicycling instead of driving gets us sensuously circulating in the world
while it also eases the burden on the atmosphere needed by owls, oaks,
and people alike. Teaming up with neighbors to stop toxic emissions in
our neighborhoods builds a sense of belonging and community while
protecting soil, water, and air. Reusing or recycling scrap materials in
our homes and workplaces helps bring a sense of coherence and wholeness to our fragmented and wasteful ways of being, while slowing the
pace at which we deplete Earth's treasures. Educational work that encourages children to hold snakes and hug trees, and community-healing
work that helps people embrace their common struggles while honoring
their differences, are equally significant restoration activities that also
cultivate the connected self.

Each time we settle into our breathing, feeling our biological presence, sensing the changes in the weather and the wildflowers, we experience in our bones the immense creativity of the web of life.

Each time we embrace our fragments *and* our integrity, letting our
boundaries soften, we are helping to reweave the tattered fabric of our
souls.

Each time we open to the quality of our present connection, we become bridges between cultures and between species, between a root-

8. Jane Gross, "A Jail Garden's Harvest: Hope and Redemption," *New York Times,* September 3, 1992. For more information, contact the Garden Project, 35 South Park, San Francisco, CA 94107, (415) 243-8558.

less, reckless society and one that lives by cycles that nurture and abide.

Each time we learn how to join together and mend our ties with our own little place called home, we link our souls with the soils that sustain us, and nurture the network that is healing the Earth.[9]

9. I wish to thank my editor and collaborator, Lisa Orlando, for her invaluable contribution to the development of this piece. If not for her reluctance, I would list her as co-author. I am also indebted to my colleagues Robin Freeman, Ed Grumbine, Stephanie Kaza, and John Thelen-Steere, whose frank and detailed feedback midway through the writing process made it a truly collaborative effort.

Working Through Environmental Despair

JOANNA MACY

JOANNA MACY HAS been active as a teacher, scholar, and activist in the civil rights and peace movements since the 1960s. Her approach to political issues has always emphasized the emotional and psychological dimensions of experience. In the mid-1980s she developed a set of introspective techniques that help people find a sense of empowerment through an honest confrontation with such paralyzing negative emotions as rage, guilt, and despair. The issue she invited her audiences to address was the threat of thermonuclear annihilation. For the past several years she has been drawing upon the same methods to conduct workshops on equally menacing environmental conditions. With John Seed, the Australian environmental activist, she has created the Council of All Beings, a collective mourning ritual that allows participants to work through their deeply repressed emotional responses to ecological disaster. In this paper, she explains how she created her workshop methods. She also analyzes the emotional obstacles that inhibit people from taking action on environmental problems and suggests ways to overcome them.

Until the late twentieth century, every generation throughout history lived with the tacit certainty that there would be generations to follow. Each assumed, without questioning, that its children and children's children would walk the same Earth, under the same sky. Hardships, failures, and personal death were encompassed in that vaster assurance of continuity. That certainty is now lost to us, whatever our politics. That loss, unmeasured and immeasurable, is the pivotal psychological reality of our time.

The responses that arise from that reality are compounded by many feelings. There is terror at the thought of the suffering in store for our loved ones and others. There is rage that we live our lives under the threat of so avoidable and meaningless an end to the human enterprise. There is guilt; for as members of society we feel implicated in this catastrophe and haunted by the thought that we should be able to avert it. Above all, there is sorrow. Confronting so vast and final a loss as this brings sadness beyond the telling.

Even these terms, however—anger, fear, sorrow—are inadequate to convey the feelings we experience in this context. They connote emotions long familiar to our species as it has faced the inevitability of personal death. But the feelings that assail us now cannot be equated with dread of our own individual demise. Their source lies less in concerns for the personal self than in apprehensions of collective suffering—of what happens to others, to human life and fellow species, to the heritage we share, to the unborn generations to come, and to our blue-green planet itself, wheeling in space.

What we are really dealing with here is akin to the original meaning of compassion: "suffering with." It is the distress we feel in connection with the larger whole of which we are a part. It is our pain for the world.

No one is exempt from that pain, any more than one could exist alone and self-existent in empty space. It is inseparable from the currents of matter, energy, and information that flow through us and sustain us as interconnected open systems. We are not closed off from the world, but rather are integral components of it, like cells in a larger body. When part of that body is traumatized—in the sufferings of fellow beings, in the pillage of our planet, and even in the violation of future generations—we sense that trauma too. When the larger system sickens, as is happening in our present age of exploitation and nuclear technology, the disturbance we feel at a semiconscious level is acute. Like the impulses of pain in any ailing organism, they serve a positive purpose; these impulses of pain are warning signals.

Yet we tend to repress that pain. We block it out because it hurts, because it is frightening, and most of all because we do not understand it and consider it to be a dysfunction, an aberration, a sign of personal weakness. As a society we are caught between a sense of impending apocalypse and the fear of acknowledging it. In this "caught" place, our responses are blocked and confused. The result is three widespread psychological strategies: disbelief, denial, and double life.

Disbelief

Although much of my life is taken up with the environmental movement, I often find it difficult to grasp the reality of the dangers facing us. The toxins in the air, food, and water are hard to taste or smell. The spreading acreage of clear-cuts and landfills are mostly screened from public view. The depletion of the great Ogallala Aquifer and the destruction of the protective ozone layer are matters of concern, but are maddeningly abstract. The things that disappear—the frogs or topsoil or bird song—are not as likely to catch my attention as what remains for me to perceive. And the more perceptible changes, like the smog layer over my city or the oil globs on the beach, accrue so gradually they seem to become a normal part of life. Although ubiquitous, these changes are subtle, making it hard to believe the gravity and immediacy of the crisis we are in.

Denial

Such difficulties of perception tend to make the ecological crisis a matter of conjecture and debate; and this in turn renders it easy to slip into denial. We may then take refuge in rejection, dismissing the notion that things are as bad as the reports and rhetoric of the environmental movement suggest. We may choose to see the more radical environmentalists as "special interests," their prophecies of doom to be ridiculed and their motives impugned. Denial is facilitated, furthermore, by the sheer multiplicity of factors at play in the planetary crisis. Conditions worsen in many dimensions simultaneously: water shortages, toxic dumping, loss of wetlands, deforestation, the greenhouse effect, and so forth. Although each issue is critical in its own right, it is their interplay that most threatens our biosphere, for they compound each other systemically. However, it is precisely these systemic interactions that are hard to see, especially for a culture untutored in the perception of relationships.

Double Life

And so we tend to live our lives as if nothing has changed, while knowing that everything has changed. This is what Robert Lifton has called leading a "double life." On one level we maintain a more or less upbeat capacity to carry on as usual, getting up in the morning and remembering which shoe goes on which foot, getting the kids off to school, meeting our appointments, cheering up our friends. All the while, there is an unformed awareness in the background that our world could be extensively damaged at any moment. Awesome and unprecedented in the history of humanity, the awareness lurks there, with an anguish beyond naming. Until we find ways of acknowledging and integrating that level of anguished awareness, we repress it; and with that repression we are drained of the energy we need for action and clear thinking.

Many of us have had the experience of responding to emergency. We may have rushed to douse a fire, or pulled a friend away from a moving truck, or raced to a child who fell into deep water. Each of us has the capacity to drop everything and act. That power to act is ours in the present situation of peril, all the more so since we are not alone. No outside authority is silencing us; no external force is keeping us from responding with all our might and courage to the present danger to life on Earth. It is something inside us that stifles our responses.

What is it that leads us to repress our awareness of danger, miring so many of us in disbelief, denial, and a double life? I believe finding an answer to that question is an essential part of environmental political action. Uncovering the deep roots of repression is part of what psychology can offer environmentalists in pursuing their work.

That will happen only if psychologists wake up to the importance of the environmental crisis in the lives of their clients. But because of the individualistic bias of mainstream psychotherapy, we have been conditioned to assume that we are essentially separate selves, driven by aggressive impulses, competing for a place in the sun. In the light of these assumptions, psychotherapists tend to view our affective responses to the plight of our world as dysfunctional and give them short shrift. As a result, we have trouble crediting the notion that concerns for the general welfare might be genuine enough and acute enough to cause distress. Assuming that all our drives are ego-generated, therapists tend to regard feelings of despair for our planet as manifestations of some private neurosis. Once, when I told a psychotherapist of my outrage over the destruction of old-growth forests, she informed me that the bulldozers represented my libido and that my distress sprang from fear of my own sexuality. A teacher has written to me, saying, "Even in my therapy group, I stopped mentioning my fears of contamination from the toxic dump near our town. Others kept saying, 'What are you running from in your life by creating these worries for yourself?'"

Many people, conditioned to take seriously only those feelings that pertain to our immediate welfare, find it strange to think that we can suffer on behalf of the larger society—and on behalf of our planet—and that such suffering is real, valid, and healthy.

The Fears That Hold Us Captive

For the past several years, in leading workshops that seek to bring empowerment out of despair, I have found it useful to begin by enumerating the fears that hold us captive and inhibit action. Here are some of them:

Fear of Pain

Our culture conditions us to view pain as dysfunctional. There are pills for headaches, backaches, neuralgia, and premenstrual tension—but no pills, capsules, or tablets for this pain for our world. Not even a stiff drink helps much. As Kevin McVeigh says in his despair-and-empowerment workshops: "Instead of survival being the issue, it is the feelings aroused by possible destruction that loom as most fearful. And as they are judged to be too unpleasant to endure, they are turned off completely. This is the state of psychic numbing."

To permit ourselves to entertain dread for the world is not only painful but frightening; it appears to threaten our capacity to cope. We are afraid that if we were to let ourselves fully experience our dread, we might fall apart, lose control, or be mired in it permanently.

Fear of Appearing Morbid

A sanguine confidence in the future has been a hallmark of the American character and a source of national pride. To judge by commercials and by the nation's political campaigns, the successful person brims with optimism. In such a cultural setting, feelings of anguish and despair for our world can appear to be a failure to maintain stamina or even competence.

Fear of Appearing Stupid

Our culture values competence. It conditions us to expect instant solutions. "Don't bring me a problem unless you have the answer," Lyndon Johnson used to say during the Vietnam War. Similarly today, many feel that we should not complain about a situation unless we have already devised a "solution" to it. It is hard to express dread of radioactive emissions from a nearby nuclear reactor, for example, without getting enmeshed in an argument over our society's needs for electricity and challenged to produce an alternative energy strategy. If we cannot then proceed to display an impressive command of facts and figures about the biological effects of low-level radiation, and about the immediate economic feasibility of nonpolluting energy paths, we can feel stupid and frustrated, as if our concerns were without grounds.

People are inhibited from expressing their anxieties because they feel that in order to do so they need to be walking data banks and skillful debaters. Taking action on behalf of our common world has unfortunately become confused with winning an argument.

Fear of Guilt

To acknowledge distress for our world opens us also to a sense of guilt. Few of us are exempt from the suspicion that as a society—through expedience, life-style, and dreams of power—we are accomplices to catastrophe. How can we become informed about the spread of hunger, homelessness, or pollution without feeling somehow implicated?

Each morning's fat and informative *New York Times* is produced by decimating acres of forest, as are the piles of paper I devote to my teaching, writing, and research. I suspect that both the shirt I am wearing and the word processor I am using were assembled in overseas factories by underpaid young Asian women, drawn from their village families to labor long hours without safety regulations or environmental protection.

Even the most "necessary" car trip I make adds pounds of carbon dioxide and heavy metals to the already saturated atmosphere.

It is hard to function in our society without reinforcing the very conditions we decry, and the sense of guilt that ensues makes those conditions—and our outrage over them—harder to face.

Fear of Causing Distress

Pain for the world is repressed not only out of embarrassment and guilt, but out of compassion as well. We are often reluctant to express the depths of our concerns because we don't want to burden or alarm our loved ones. We try to protect them from the distress we feel, and even from the knowledge that we feel it. We don't want them to worry, either on their own account or on ours. And so, partly out of concern for them, we keep up the pretense of "life as usual."

For parents, the psychological burden of living in a threatened world is especially poignant. Given the scenarios environmental scientists present to us, it is not surprising that, when we let ourselves think of what the future may hold for our children, the images that arise are of wastelands, deprivation, disease. Yet we usually bury those images, sealing them off behind walls of silence, so that our children can be carefree in the present moment. This burden is all the weightier for those of us who believe that a parent should be all-wise, all-protective, and in control.

The same kind of self-censorship occurs in children who often see quite clearly what is happening to our world. Aware of what their parents find too painful to confront, they learn not to voice their own dread. They play along with the fantasy that our present way of life can continue indefinitely.

Fear of Provoking Disaster

There is also the superstition that negative thoughts are self-fulfilling. This is of a piece with the notion, popular in New Age circles, that we create our own reality. I have had people tell me that "to speak of catastrophe will just make it more likely to happen."

Actually, the contrary is nearer to the truth. Psychoanalytic theory and personal experience show us that it is precisely what we repress that eludes our conscious control and tends to erupt into behavior. As Carl

Jung observed, "When an inner situation is not made conscious, it happens outside as fate." But ironically, in our current situation, the person who gives warning of a likely ecological holocaust is often made to feel guilty of contributing to that very fate.

Fear of Appearing Unpatriotic

Deep in many of us, deeper than our criticisms and disappointments about national policies, lies a love of country. It is woven of pride in our history and heroes, of gratitude for what they won for us. Particularly in America, built as it was on utopian expectations, this love of country seems to require of us a profound and almost religious sense of hope—a belief in our manifest destiny as a fulfillment of human dreams.

To entertain feelings of despair over our country's present condition and future prospects seems un-American. If I allow these feelings to surface, am I lacking in allegiance? If I express them, an I peddling doom? Am I weakening our national will? In a time of crisis, some would have us silence our fears and doubts, lest they erode belief in the American dream.

Fear of Religious Doubt

When images of a dying Earth do manage to break through our defenses, many religious people insist that "God won't let this happen." Simply entertaining these images seems to challenge our belief in a loving and omnipotent deity, and in the goodness of creation itself. Are feelings of despair over the growing possibilities of disaster a sign of inadequate faith?

Throughout history, human suffering has always tested our belief in a divine order. The issue is known as theodicy: how to square the existence of evil with the existence of a benign and powerful God. That question has brought us back again and again to a core truth in each major religious heritage: the deep, sacred power within each of us to open to the needs and suffering of humanity. That power—a wellspring of love, compassion, and service—is proclaimed in the psalms and prophets of Judaism, in the cross of Christ, in the path of the Buddhist bodhisattva, and in the brotherhood at the heart of Islam. Yet we tend to forget that those traditions summon us to take the travail of our world within ourselves. Assuming, perhaps, that our God is too fragile or too limited to encompass that pain, unsure whether God will meet us in the midst of such darkness, we hesitate to let ourselves experience it, lest our faith be shattered or revealed as inadequate.

Fear of Appearing Too Emotional

Many of us refrain from expressing our deep concerns for the world in order to avoid creating the impression that we are prey to our feelings.

For centuries the dominant Western white-male culture has erected a dichotomy between reason and emotion. Assuming that reality can be apprehended in an "objective" fashion, it has accorded higher value to the analytical operations of intellect than to the "subjective" realm of feelings, sensations, and intuitions. Many of us, schooled in the separation of reason from feeling, discount our deepest responses to the condition of our world. Grief for expiring species? Horror for the millions in hunger? Fear of spreading nuclear contamination? Those are "only" feelings, frequently dismissed in ourselves and in others as self-indulgent.

Given the different ways the sexes are socialized in our culture, men suffer more than women from the fear of appearing emotional. Displays of feeling can cause men to be considered unstable, especially in work situations. Yet women experience this fear too. They often withhold their expressions of concern and anguish for the world lest these be treated condescendingly, as "just like a woman."

Fear of Feeling Powerless

A frequent response that people make to the mention of acid rain, world hunger, or other ominous developments is, "I don't think about that, because there is nothing I can do about it."

Logically, this is a non sequitur: it confuses what can be thought with what can be done. When forces are seen as so vast that they cannot be consciously contemplated or seriously discussed, we are doubly victimized; we are impeded in thought as well as action.

Resistance to painful information on the grounds that we cannot "do anything about it" springs less from actual powerlessness—as a measure of our capacity to effect change—than from the fear of *experiencing* powerlessness. The model of the self that predominates in Western culture is, "I am the master of my fate and the captain of my soul." It makes us reluctant to engage in issues that remind us that we do not exert ultimate control over our lives. We feel somehow that we ought to be in charge of our existence and emotions, to have all the answers. And so we tend to shrink the sphere of our attention to those areas in which we feel we can be in charge.

The forms of repression I present here take a mammoth toll of our energies. A marked loss of feeling results, as if a nerve had been cut. As Barry Childers has said, "We immunize ourselves against the demands of the situation by narrowing our awareness." This anesthetization affects other aspects of our life as well—loves and losses are less intense, the sky is less vivid—for if we are not going to let ourselves feel pain, we will not feel much else either. "The mind pays for its deadening to the state of our world," observes Robert Murphy, "by giving up its capacity for joy and flexibility."

This state of absence, or at best this dulled human response to our world, is called "psychic numbing," a term coined by Robert Lifton in his noted study of Hiroshima survivors. After originally using the term to describe the psychological effect of witnessing massive annihilation, Lifton then later concluded that the phenomenon extends to all of us now, as we are confronted with vast forces laying waste to our world.

Breaking Through Despair

We urgently need to find better ways of dealing with this fear and repression. Can we sustain our gaze upon the prospects of ecological holocaust without becoming paralyzed with fear or grief? Can we acknowledge and live with our pain for the world in ways that affirm our existence and release our power to act?

Such questions arose for me when I worked years ago in citizen efforts to stop radioactive contamination from nuclear reactors. The more I learned about the scope of the problem and its biological consequences, the greater grew my despair—a despair very difficult to express to my family and community. I felt like the sole victim of a unique and nameless disease. Later I learned that I was far from alone, and that others carried in their different ways sorrow for our planet and its people.

In August 1978, at Notre Dame University, I chaired a week-long seminar on planetary survival issues. College professors and administrators had prepared papers to deliver on themes ranging from the water crisis to environmental effects of nuclear technology. As we convened, I took time to acknowledge that the topic we were addressing was different from any other, that it touched each of us in a profoundly personal way. I suggested that we introduce ourselves by sharing an incident or image of how it had touched us. The brief introductions that followed were potent, as those present dropped their professional manner and spoke simply and poignantly of what they saw and felt happening to their world; of their children; of their fears and discouragement. That brief sharing transformed the seminar. It changed the way we related to each other and to the material, and it unleashed energy and mutual caring. Sessions went overtime, laced with hilarity and punctuated with plans for future projects. Some kind of magic had happened. Late one night as a group of us talked, a name for that magic emerged: "despair work."

Just as grief work is a process by which bereaved persons unblock their numbed energies by acknowledging and grieving the loss of a loved one, so do we all need to unblock our feelings about our threatened planet and the possible demise of our species. Until we do, our power of creative response will be crippled.

In striking upon "despair work," we were not being rhetorical; we were groping for an explanation of what had just happened. We knew that it had to do with a willingness to acknowledge and experience pain, and that this pain for our world, like pain for the loss of a loved one, is a measure of caring. We also knew that the joint journey into the dark had changed us, bonding us in a special way, relieving us of pretense and competition. Something akin to love had occurred, an alchemy that caused us to feel less alone and bolder to face the challenges ahead.

This occasion led to the further development of despair work in groups, and to the spread in many countries of what we originally called "despair and empowerment workshops." In the course of the 1980s they became known as "Deep Ecology workshops," because they help people perceive more clearly not only the ecological crises confronting us, but also the dynamic web of life in which we all are held. Arne Naess, the Norwegian philosopher who coined the term Deep Ecology, called for the development of forms of community therapy in order to heal our society's relationship with the Earth. These workshops can be seen as "community therapy."

Despair work has proliferated under a variety of names and forms, including popular rituals like the Council of All Beings, in which collective mourning plays a key role. Overcoming avoidance and numbing, this psychological and spiritual work sharpens awareness of our collective plight. At the same time, it brings us home to a sense of mutual belonging to the living body of Earth, as this work uses our very pain for the world to revitalize our connections and our capacities.

In designing these workshops with a growing number of colleagues, I drew on years of exploring the interface between spiritual growth and social change, years of adapting meditative practices to empower people as agents for peace and justice. Yet the workshops themselves taught me more than I could have imagined. The thousands of people with whom I have worked in church basements, community centers, and classrooms have revealed to me, in ways I had not foreseen, the power, size, and beauty of the human heart. They have demonstrated that pain for our world touches each of us, and that this pain is rooted in caring. They have demonstrated that our apparent public apathy is but a fear of experiencing and expressing this pain, and that once it is acknowledged and shared it opens the way to our power.

Five Principles of Empowerment

As I meditated on the lessons I learned from these workshops, and on the connections between pain and power, five principles emerged to illumine the nature of despair work and encapsulate its assumptions.

Feelings of pain for our world are natural and healthy

Confronted with widespread suffering and threats of global disaster, responses of anguish—of fear, anger, grief, and even guilt—are normal. They are a measure of our humanity. And these feelings are probably what we have most in common. Just by virtue of sharing this planet at this time, we know these feelings more than our own grandparents or any earlier generation could have known them. We are in grief together. And this grief for our world cannot be reduced to private pathology. We experience it in addition to whatever personal griefs, frustrations, and neuroses we bear. Not to experience it would be a sign of moral atrophy, but that is academic, for I have met no one who is immune to this pain.

Pain is morbid only if denied

It is when we disown our pain for the world that it becomes dysfunctional. We know now what it costs us to repress it, how that cost is measured in numbness and in feelings of isolation and impotence. It is measured as well in the hatreds and suspicions that divide us. For repressed despair seeks scapegoats and turns, in anger, against other members of society. It also turns inward in depression and self-destruction, through drug abuse and suicide. We tend to fear that if we consciously acknowledge our despair we may get mired in it, incapacitated. But despair, like any emotion, is dynamic—once experienced, it flows through us. It is only our refusal to acknowledge and feel it that keeps it in place.

Information alone is not enough

To deal with the distress we feel for our world, we need more than additional data about its plight. Terrifying information about the effects of nuclear pollution or environmental destruction can drive us deeper into denial and feelings of futility, unless we can deal with the responses it arouses in us. We need to process this information on the psychological and emotional level in order to fully respond on the cognitive level. We already know we are in danger. The essential question is: can we free ourselves to respond?

Unblocking repressed feelings releases energy and clears the mind

This is known as catharsis. Repression is physically, mentally, and emotionally expensive; it drains the body, dulls the mind, and muffles emotional responses. When repressed material is brought to the surface and released, energy is released as well; life comes into clearer focus. Art, ritual, and play have always played a cathartic role in our history—just as, in our time, psychotherapy does. By this process the cognitive system appropriates elements of its experience, and by integrating them gains a measure of both control and freedom.

Unblocking our pain for the world reconnects us with the larger web of life

When the repressed material that we unblock is distress for our world, catharsis occurs, and also something more than catharsis. That is because this distress reflects concerns that extend beyond our separate selves, beyond our individual needs and wants. It is a testimony to our interconnectedness. Therefore, as we let ourselves experience and move through this pain, we move through to its source and reach the underlying matrix of our lives. What occurs, then, is beyond catharsis.

The distinction here is important. To present despair work as just a matter of catharsis would suggest that, after owning and sharing our responses to mass suffering and danger, we could walk away purged of pain for our world. But that is neither possible nor adequate to our needs, since each day's news brings fresh cause for grief. By recognizing our capacity to suffer with our world, we dawn to wider dimensions of being. In those dimensions there is still pain, but also a lot more. There is wonder, even joy, as we come home to our mutual belonging—and there is a new kind of power.

To understand why this should be so, and what this kind of power is, we need to look at the theoretical foundations of the work. The principles just listed derive from some of the oldest and newest insights into the nature of reality and are rooted in a worldview that is essential to the understanding of despair work.

The Living Web of Natural Systems

What is it that allows us to feel pain for our world? And what do we discover as we move through that pain? To both these questions there is one answer: *interconnectedness with life and all other beings.* It is the living web out of which our individual, separate existences have risen, and in which we are interwoven. Our lives extend beyond our skins, in radical interdependence with the rest of the world.

Contemporary science, in what may be its greatest achievement, has broken through to a fresh discovery of this interrelatedness of all living phenomena. Until our century, classical Western science had proceeded on the assumption that the world could be understood and controlled by dissecting it. Breaking the world down into ever-smaller pieces, classical Western science divided mind from matter, organs from bodies, and plants from ecosystems, then analyzed each separate part. This mechanistic approach left some questions unanswered—such as, how do these separate parts interact to sustain life and evolve?

As a result of such questions, scientists in our century, starting with the biologists, have shifted their perspective. They began to look at wholes instead of parts, at processes instead of substances. What they discovered was that these wholes—be they cells, bodies, ecosystems, or the planet itself—are not just a heap of disjunct parts, but dynamic, intricately organized and balanced systems, interrelated and interdependent in every movement, function, and exchange of energy. They saw that each element is part of a vaster pattern, a pattern that connects and evolves by discernible principles. The discernment of these principles is what is known as "general-systems theory."

Ludwig von Bertalanffy, the father of general-systems theory, called it a "way of seeing." And while it has spawned many derivative theories relating to particular fields and phenomena, the systems perspective has remained just that—a way of seeing, one recognized by many thinkers as the greatest and farthest-reaching cognitive revolution of our time. Anthropologist Gregory Bateson called it "the biggest bite out of the Tree of Knowledge in two thousand years." For, as the systems view has spread into every domain of science from physics to psychology, it has turned the lens through which we see reality. Instead of beholding random separate entities, we become aware of interconnecting flows—of energy, matter, information—and see life forms as patterns in these flows.

Sustained by these currents, open systems evolve in complexity and responsiveness to their environment. Interacting, they weave relationships that shape the environment itself. Every system, be it a cell, a tree, or a mind, is like a transformer, changing the very stuff that flows through it. Flows of matter and energy create physical bodies; flows of information make minds. Both kinds of flow generate interdependencies weaving each being into the larger ecology, the web of life.

The old mechanistic view of reality erected dichotomies, separating substance from process, self from other, and thought from feeling. But given the interweaving interactions of open systems, these dichotomies no longer hold. What had appeared to be separate self-existent entities are now seen to be so interdependent that their boundaries can be drawn only arbitrarily. What had appeared to be "other" can be equally construed as an extension of the same organism, like a fellow cell in a larger body. What we had been taught to dismiss as "only" feelings are responses to input from our environment that are no less valid that rational constructs. Feelings and concepts condition "other"; both are ways of knowing our world.

As open systems we weave our world, though each individual consciousness illumines but a small section of it, a short arc in vaster loops of feeling and knowing. As our awareness grows, so does that of the web. It would seem that we are part of a larger coming to consciousness. The web of life both cradles us and calls us to weave it further.

Positive Disintegration

How, if we let ourselves feel despair, can we remember our collective body? How can our pain for the world make us whole again?

Processes of growth and transformation are never pain free. They require a letting go of outmoded ways of being, of old assumptions and old defenses. As both science and religion confirm, this letting go can be a passage through darkness.

The living system learns, adapts, and evolves by reorganizing itself. This usually occurs when its previous ways of responding to the environment are no longer functional. To survive, it must then relinquish the codes and constructs by which it formerly interpreted experience. Systems philosopher Ervin Laszlo explains this as the exploratory self-organization of open systems; and psychiatrist Kazimierz Dabrowski, thinking along the same lines, calls it "positive disintegration."

This process can be highly uncomfortable. As we open like a wound to the travail of the world, we are susceptible to new sensations and confusions. Bereft of self-confidence and hopefulness, we can feel as though we and our world are "falling apart." It can make some of us frantic; some of us, in desperation, become mean. That is because the system (i.e., each of us) is registering anomalies, new signals from the environment that don't match previously programmed codes and constructs. To survive, then, the system must change.

To experience pain as we register what is happening to our world is a measure of our evolution as open systems. This is true not only from the perspective of systems science but from that of religion as well. How many mystics in their spiritual journey have spoken of the "dark night of the soul"? Brave enough to let go of accustomed assurances, they let their old convictions and conformities dissolve into nothingness, and stood naked to the terror of the unknown. They let processes, which their minds could not encompass, work through them. It is in that darkness that birth takes place.

As our pain for the world is rooted in our interconnectedness with all life, so surely is our power. But the kind of power at work in the web, in and through open systems, is quite different from our customary notions of power.

The old concept of power, in which most of us have been socialized, originated in a particular worldview. This view saw reality as composed of discrete and separate entities: rocks, plants, atoms, people. Power came to be seen as a property of these separate entities, reflected in the way they could appear to push each other around. Power became identified with domination. Look it up in the dictionary; more often than not it is still defined as exerting your will upon other people: "power" means "power over." In such a view, power is a zero-sum game: "The more you have, the less I have," or "If you win, I lose." It fosters the notion, furthermore, that power involves invulnerability. To be strong, to keep from being pushed around, defenses, armor, and rigidity are needed in order not to let oneself be influenced or changed.

From the systems perspective, this patriarchal notion of power is both inaccurate and dysfunctional. That is because life processes are intrinsically self-organizing. Power, then, which is the ability to effect change, works from the bottom up more reliably and organically than from the top down. It is not power over, but power with; this is what systems scientists call "synergy."

Life systems evolve flexibility and intelligence, not by closing off from the environment and erecting walls of defense, but by opening ever wider to the currents of matter-energy and information. It is in this interaction that life systems grow, integrating and differentiating. Here power, far from being identified with invulnerability, requires just the opposite—openness, vulnerability, and readiness to change. This indeed is the direction of evolution. As life-forms evolve in intelligence, they shed their armor and reach outward to an ever-wider interplay with the environment. They grow sensitive, vulnerable protuberances—ears, noses, eyeballs, lips, tongues, fingertips—the better to feel and respond, the better to connect in the web and weave it further.

We may well wonder why the old kind of power, as we see it enacted around us and indeed above us, seems so effective. Many who wield it seem to get what they want: money, fame, control over others' lives; but they achieve this at a substantial cost both to themselves and to the larger system. Domination requires strong defenses and, like a suit of armor, restricts our vision and movement. Reducing flexibility and responsiveness, it cuts us off from fuller and freer participation in life. "Power over" is dysfunctional to the larger system because it inhibits diversity and feedback; it obstructs systemic self-organization, fostering uniformity and entropy.

Power as Process

As open systems dependent upon larger, evolving systems, we must stay open to the wider flows of information, even when certain information seems inimical to our self-interest, where the needs of the whole, and other beings within that whole, are seen as commensurate with our own. Only then can we begin to think and act together. For this we need a "boundless heart." This I believe we have within us by virtue of our nature as open systems. If we can grieve with the griefs of others, so, by the same token, by the same openness, can we find strength in their strengths, bolstering our own individual supplies of courage, commitment, and endurance.

How does power as process—"power with" rather than "power over"—operate in our lives? We don't own it. We don't use it like a gun. We can't measure its quantity or size. We can't increase it at our neighbor's expense. Power is like a verb; it happens through us.

We experience it when we engage in interactions that produce value. We have such interactions with loved ones and fellow citizens; with God; with music, art and literature; with seeds we plant; or with materials we shape. Such synergistic exchanges generate something that was not there before and that enhances the capacities and well-being of all who are involved. "Power with" involves attentive openness to the surrounding physical or mental environment and alertness to our own and others' responses. It is the capacity to act in ways that increase the sum total of one's conscious participation in life.

This kind of power may be most familiar in relationship to a partner, spouse, or child. As you help them develop their strengths and skills, your own sense of well-being increases. This power, which enhances the power of others, does not originate in you, but you have been party to its unfolding. You are its channel, its midwife, its gardener.

We can recognize this power by the extent to which it promotes conscious participation in life. To deprive someone of his or her rights is an exercise of force, not power. It diminishes the vitality not just of that person, but of the larger system of which we all are a part, which is now deprived of their participation and resources. Therefore the exercise of power as process demands that we unmask and reject all exercises of force that obstruct our and others' participation in life.

The concept of synergistic power summons us to develop our capacities for nurturance and empathy, important lessons for those who have been socialized to be competitive, especially the men in our society. But it is equally true that this notion of power presents a challenge to those who have been conditioned to please, and who have been assigned by society the more passive and nurturing roles. I am referring, of course, to women. For them, "power with" can mean being assertive, taking responsibility to give feedback, and participating more fully in the body politic.

Through our pain for the world we can open ourselves to power. This power is not just our own, but belongs to others as well. It relates to the very evolution of our species. It is part of a general awakening or shift toward a new level of social consciousness.

We can see that our planetary crises are impelling us toward a shift in consciousness. Confronting us with our mortality as a species, they reveal the suicidal tendency inherent in our conception of ourselves as separate and competitive beings. Given the fragility and limited resources of our planet, given our needs for flexibility and sharing, we have to think together in an integrated, synergistic fashion, rather than in the old fragmented and competitive ways—and we are beginning to do that. Once we tune into our interconnectedness, responsibility toward self and other become indistinguishable, because each thought and act affects the doer as much as the one done to.

Where, then, does despair fit in? Why is our pain for the world so important? Because these responses manifest our interconnectedness. Our feelings of social and planetary distress serve as a doorway to systemic social consciousness. To use another metaphor, they are like a "shadow limb." Just as an amputee continues to feel twinges in the severed limb, so in a sense do we experience, in anguish for homeless people or hunted whales, pain that belongs to a separated part of our body—a larger body than we thought we had, unbounded by our skin.

Through the systemic currents of knowing that interweave our world, each of us can be the catalyst or "tipping point" by which new forms of behavior can spread. There are as many different ways of being responsive as there are different gifts we possess. For some of us it can be through study or conversation, for others theater or public office, for still others civil disobedience and imprisonment. But the diversities of our gifts interweave richly when we recognize the larger web within which we act. We begin in this web and, at the same time, journey toward it. We are making it conscious.

PART THREE

CULTURAL
DIVERSITY AND
POLITICAL
ENGAGEMENT

THIS COLLECTION CLOSES with an exploration of diversity that could be provided only by writers willing to challenge the reality principle of urban-industrial culture. Carl Anthony, a leading figure in the environmental justice movement, proposes that the core of the environmental crisis lies in the festering, planet-devouring cities of a society that has neglected its closest and most precious form of diversity: that of our fellow human beings, each of whom has a story to tell that measures the true size of the psyche. John Mack reminds us of the hard political facts that ecopsychology must face in its effort to redefine the meaning of "sanity." In the convergence of ecofeminism and ecopsychology, Betty Roszak finds the beginning of a "symposium of the whole" that may broaden the resources of sanity. The Deep Ecologist David Abram pays homage to the wisdom of a magical vision of nature that has all but vanished from the modern world. Finally, Jeannette Armstrong, drawing upon the insights of Okanagan culture, reminds us that not all human beings drifted into a state of alienation from their habitat; many were driven from the land by a dominant culture in the grip of forces that now look madder than any form of "superstition" that colonizers or missionaries may once have attributed to indigenous people.

Freud defined the goal of psychotherapy as the "return of the repressed." He never realized how political that goal might be. For that matter, even the revolutionary spirits of modern society never foresaw that the repressed might include the nonhuman world as well as our fellow humans.

Ecopsychology and the Deconstruction of Whiteness

AN INTERVIEW WITH CARL ANTHONY

C ARL ANTHONY HAS come to play a special role in the environmental movement. As president of Earth Island Institute and director of the Urban Habitat Program, he has insisted on keeping the
political issues surrounding race at the center of the environmental
crisis. As an architect and town planner, he has emphasized the ecological role of the city, not simply in terms of economic impact but as
the moral barometer of our society. He reminds us that without justice
in the cities, there will be no solution to problems of wilderness and
open space, endangered species and natural beauty. In this interview
with Theodore Roszak, he offers an astute ecopsychological insight
into the mystique of "whiteness," showing how the delusionary pursuit of "purity" has distorted the relationship of the dominant culture
with both people and the planet. Moreover, he offers a way forward
based upon a respect for the many stories that make up our human
diversity.

━━━━━━━━━

ROSZAK: Carl, your interest in ecopsychology comes as a great gift to the
movement. You bring a special perspective to both ecology and psy-

chology, one that places the troubled cities of our planet at the very center of the world environmental crisis. It's encouraging to know that you
feel ecopsychology can make a contribution to your work. At the same
time, your view of ecopsychology is a challenging one. For a moment,
let's try to imagine that you are speaking to an aspiring ecopsychologist
who is seeking, in some sense, to hear the "voice of the Earth." You have
said that the "success of ecopsychology will depend not only upon its
ability to help us hear the voice of the Earth, but to construct a genuinely
multicultural self and a global civil society without racism." Will you
expand on that remark?

ANTHONY: Ecopsychology tells us that the healing of the self and the
healing of the planet go together. The environmental justice movement
could benefit from that insight; it needs a greater understanding of the
psychological dimensions of environmental racism. But a framework for
such an understanding hasn't yet been established. There is a blind spot
in ecopsychology because the field is limited by its Eurocentric perspective, in the same way that the environmental movement as a whole has
been blind to environmental racism. There are a lot of people who would
like to hear the voice of the Earth who are not currently being reached
by the movement for Deep Ecology, which, I believe, can be seen as the
basis for ecopsychology. That's partly because these people are confronted with a series of traumatic losses that don't show up on the radar
screen of those who are approaching ecological issues from an aesthetic
point of view and whose concern is for preserving the beauties of wilderness. The people I have in mind could include small farmers who
really love what they were doing but who have been evicted from the
land. But, in particular, I am thinking of the sense of loss suffered by
many people who live in the city, who are traumatized by the fact that
they don't have a functional relationship with nature. It is not just a
question of being able to walk along the beach and enjoy the ocean
or the sky.

I think of my next-door neighbor, a woman seventy years old: her
parents were sharecroppers who were driven off the soil in the South by
a combination of mechanization and the boll weevil. They were also
driven away by the Ku Klux Klan and the inability to go the polls to vote.
If you search the pages of ecological literature, you don't find anything

about that kind of pain. People in that situation are generally not the people who are being reached by the Deep Ecologists. Deep Ecology is in touch with something, but the desire of a tiny fraction of middle- and upper-middle-class Europeans to hear the voice of the Earth could be in part a strategy by people in these social classes to amplify their *own* inner voice at a time when they feel threatened, not only by the destruction of the planet, but also by the legitimate claims of multicultural human communities clamoring to be heard.

I agree that, as point of departure, we need to acknowledge that, no matter what the noise level, each person is entitled to hear his or her own inner voice. That's an important first step to hearing the voices of others as well as the cry of the Earth. But the ability to respond intelligently, creatively, and compassionately to the claims of human communities is undermined by the false sense of privilege that comes from the propensity to think of oneself as white. Wanting to hear the voice of the Earth, the notion that nature is crying out in pain, has a limited potential for reaching and touching a lot of people who are living much more prosaic life-styles than those who think about these matters in a more intellectual and philosophical way. People of color often view alarmist threats about the collapse of the ecosystem as the latest stratagem by the elite to maintain control of political and economic discourse.

ROSZAK: How would the "multicultural self" help Deep Ecology get through to these people?

ANTHONY: In order for the themes of Deep Ecology to have resonance for the people I'm imagining, we have to know *who they are*. People who believe, as I do, that the ecological threat is real, believe we have to construct a self that's capable of harboring the voices of many different people and cultures, not just so-called white people. This is what I mean by a genuinely multicultural self. The truth of the matter is: we have an official story about who we are as a people, who's really important, who's in the mainstream and who isn't. This story is like refined sugar. It's not a real story about real people. It's been packaged and processed beyond recognition. I don't believe it includes the stories of most people in this country; but in particular it's very deficient for dealing with the reality of people of color.

ROSZAK: I agree that for many people, mainly middle-class whites, the environmental movement seems to pole-vault over a whole range of problems that really cannot be ignored. For example, there's a cliché that runs through the environmental movement—and this includes ecopsychology. It has to do with people being "alienated" from nature. But the alienation is usually treated as a subtle, long-term, psychological process. This overlooks the fact that simple coercion has been very effective in divorcing some people from nature.

ANTHONY: Exactly. Talk about the long-term process: a lot of people reach back into mythical times to find a story that can make the connection with the land. One of the reasons people do that is because it makes divorce from nature more socially acceptable and less painful because it has a mythical quality. There is a story I came across recently in the book *Black Rage* by William Grier and Price Cobbs that touched me deeply. This was about a man eighty years old who describes a time when he was twelve. He saw his friend placed in a cage and taken off to be lynched because he was accused of raping a white woman. When he experienced that, he knew that he had to get out of town. For almost seventy years, he found it impossible to settle down. He became an itinerant preacher who never stopped being tortured by memories of violence. Sometimes in the middle of a sermon he would cry out: "How could they do that to a little boy?" Now there's an example of being uprooted simply because the level of hostility is so great that you have to keep moving.

There's something else that comes to mind when we talk about having a sense of place: the way violence can blight our experience of place, even our home. There's a character in Toni Morrison's novel *Beloved*, her name is Sethe. She can't let herself remember the beauty of the plantation she escaped from because it is drenched in memories of slavery. She wakes up from nightmares wondering if hell might not also be a pretty place.

ROSZAK: Or there's another assumption that is frequently made: that we have lost our sense of place in the modern world almost voluntarily, because of career opportunities or the generally footloose character of industrial society. Once again, this overlooks the fact that some people have lost their place in the world for much more obvious and brutal reasons.

ANTHONY: Yes, because of direct political or economic force. I think this is a theme that runs throughout American history. Many people have experienced this sense of being driven away from a place that was once their home. If they haven't had that experience personally, then their very-near ancestors, their parents or grandparents have. And they never talk about it. Instead, we reach back into prehistory, back to the time when the hunting and gathering people decided to settle down and become agriculturalists. Of course, that history is also real, but it doesn't capture the experience of people who were driven out by the Enclosure Acts of Britain, or the people who were subjected to pogroms in Russia and Eastern Europe, or the black people who were captured and put in the holds of ships and then forced to work on plantations. There is a tendency to romanticize the Native American struggle; but even "the trail of tears," the uprooting of the Cherokee people who were forced to march a thousand miles across the South to settle in Oklahoma—things like this are not dealt with directly. The sense of alienation and loss is either dealt with mythically or in some sanitized version.

ROSZAK: I've had the feeling that often the Native American experience, which is such a clear act of conquest, is used to concentrate the whole sense of violation in one ethnic group without realizing that this is far from being the exclusive experience of one group. The Native American experience comes to serve as a way of packaging all the shame in one convenient parcel.

ANTHONY: I think that's right. And there's another aspect to this. For the national community, it is less threatening to deal with the Native American population because, first of all, they are a relatively small group; and, second, they generally are far away from the places where most Americans live out their daily lives. So most people don't have to confront the reality of what the Bureau of Indian Affairs has done directly. They can be concerned about these things when they choose and can turn the concern off when they choose.

ROSZAK: There's a strange irony surrounding the role of blacks in America, isn't there? Here are a people who were forcibly brought to this continent primarily to work on the land; they were bonded to the soil by violence as the society's most basic farming population. Now in the late twentieth century we think of blacks almost exclusively as people of the city, of the inner city. Our cities are becoming more and more a black community produced by white flight into suburban areas. Could you reflect on the environmental implications of that?

ANTHONY: It's incredibly ironic. And it's never talked about in the environmental literature. There's simply no acknowledgment of that experience. I see it as central to the ecological issue that when blacks were forced to work the land, the process of human domination and the exploitation of nature occurred at exactly the same time. Murray Bookchin has discussed this in a general way in *The Ecology of Freedom*. You could see it happening in places like Virginia when the opportunity arose for people to exploit the land by moving away from subsistence agriculture to the cash crop of tobacco. Some people were so crazy about this crop that they weren't even raising enough food to eat; they would rather sell tobacco for cash and buy food. At the point they realized that this one crop was a source of great potential wealth, they looked around for a labor force to cultivate the land. That's when slavery began to develop and harden. So you can see this pattern of lack of caring, a pattern of ruthless exploitation of the land coming precisely at the time of the institution of slavery.

In this connection, I find the whole question of "whiteness" so interesting. About the time that slavery was introduced, the first English settlers called themselves "Christians," and they called the populations that they encountered "pagan," or sometimes "savage." As more Europeans arrived, they called themselves "English" or "Dutch" or "French." But then came Bacon's Rebellion in 1676. A group of indentured servants and African slaves organized a rebellion in order to kick the aristocratic elements out; this was a precursor of the American Revolution. And the colonists realized that if the indentured servants ever got together with the black people and the native people, they wouldn't have a future. That's when the word "white" was invented as we use it. What "whiteness" did was to unify all the Europeans who were coming here, people who, in Europe, would not at all be unified. Many of them spoke different languages, and many had been at war with each other for centuries. "Whiteness" was very effective in creating a sense of solidarity, especially among those who had suffered hardship. Now they could see a real opportunity for them to get some action. They could say, "I've had my problems back there in the old country, but now I have a good shot at being an aristocrat or living high on the hog." The result was this cultivated contempt for black people and for indigenous people. The important environmental aspect of this social polarization was that people had to visualize the wilderness as being "empty."

ROSZAK: Meaning belonging to nobody, available to be occupied, and having no rights of its own to be honored.

ANTHONY· Exactly. They couldn't say, "We've arrived at this place and here are these other people and why don't we talk to them in a neighborly way and find something that everybody can live with." Ruth Frankenberg refers to the "social construction of whiteness." She speaks of whiteness as being "intrinsically linked to unfolding relations of domination." I see it as an unmarked, unnamed status, a structured invisibility that lends itself to false, universalizing claims that reduce other people to marginality simply by naming them as different races.

But now here's the complication. For two hundred years, very few white women came over for the European settlers. So the settlers intermarried with Native Americans. Our stories never say anything about how the trappers and the pioneers ended up in relationships with Indian women—whether it was rape or whether it was love or whatever. We have a whole set of populations that actually represent the coming together of indigenous people and Europeans. Their story never gets mentioned. We don't talk about them. That's why the construction of a multicultural self means the deconstruction of the idea of whiteness, and the corresponding ability to meet others as equals.

What I find really curious is: there doesn't seem to be any interest in finding out what those people experienced, what the traumas were, what the confusions were. Why not? I think the insistence on "purity" blocks that out. You see, there is enormous power that comes from abstraction and purity. The minute you start getting involved with people, taking their stories seriously, you don't know where your loyalties are, you're not sure who you represent, or what your basic mission is. Things start getting confused. If basically these white people are pure, and if their destiny is to dominate this continent, and if other people don't exist, the domination can't be seen as transgression. You don't need to embrace the truth; you can maintain this thrust across the land without coming to terms with the human or ecological consequences. But the minute you recognize that there is *a human being* there who might happen to be *your child*—you see? Which is the story of most African Americans in this country; they have European-American roots.

We take our definition of race to be a real hard line; we take it to represent some real division among the people in the world. Actually it is not that at all. It's an ideological and equivocal concept that has very little biological basis. So then you have to ask yourself, if that's true, *what is really going on here?* And I would argue that this separation within the human community is deeply reflected in the separation between people and nature. Nature is also defined as "other," in the same way as these "other" people.

ROSZAK: I've noticed in your writing that you sometimes use the words "abstraction" and "purity" interchangeably. Are you in fact using them synonymously? Purity strikes me immediately as having a positive value, whereas abstraction has the sense of being emptiness, nothingness.

ANTHONY: The fact that you think that "purity" is positive really troubles me.

ROSZAK: Well, the word is usually used that way. If something is "pure," you think . . .

ANTHONY: . . . that it's one hundred percent pure. Like pure granulated sugar, pure white bread. Meaning unsoiled, unsullied, undamaged, unconnected with dirt. So white people are "pure" and clean. And black people are "dirt." If you want to get into the psychoanalysis of this, I think there is a very rich and interesting set of connections here dealing with anality and excrement. These associations echo in a frightening way in our cities. Some parts of cities are considered attractive and other parts are waste. It's a bodily metaphor: you eat one part and you shit the other part. It's not an accident, for example, that the environmental justice movement is focused on both toxic waste *and* race. If you throw people away and you throw material away, it is no accident that they are not separated: you just throw them away together. When I talk about purity, what I'm really saying is that there's been an obsession with this question of white people not getting soiled.

ROSZAK: In every society where working the land has involved class distinction, getting your hands dirty has been low status. After generations of that, it's no wonder a society develops an environmental crisis. The people who have the power to make a difference are people who no longer want to get their hands dirty. But getting your hands dirty is an integral part of having a healthy environmental movement—for example, when it comes down to recycling your own garbage.

ANTHONY: And all this gets magnified by racism because then certain kinds of work are considered "nigger work." Only the lowest sort of people did that in the Old South. Even the poor whites said, "Well, at least I don't do nigger work." That is what replaces a caring set of relationships to the land. If you're white, you're part of that group of people who are getting the benefit of manifest destiny; you get the whole package. You get to dominate the land and everybody on it. Other people are marginalized. White people benefit from a whole series of relationships that have an enormous confluence. One is obviously the perfection of the market as a device for making decisions about everything. Then there's science, which extends your mechanical power. And then, in a curious way, even in art, we find this preoccupation from the Renaissance on with perspective as a way of scientifically controlling things in the distance. You can now check out what's happening miles away, and you can place it all on this grid that goes off to the vanishing point. With the coming of the European expansion there has been a whole series of inventions that have increased the potential power for domination by abstraction. Abstraction means distance from immediate experience, from annoyingly concrete particulars, the substitution of a remote symbol for a given sensuous reality. But that's what ecology is all about: *the real complexity*. You have to deal with the fact that there is a river here, or deal with the fact that bugs come. In contrast, the whole idea of "perfection" leads to monoculture: flatten the land, have only one crop, come along with an airplane and spray. You don't have to deal with the fact that this is an organic process. That's one of the reasons why racism is so hard to deal with. It brings up a much richer tapestry of human emotions, a much greater sense of either humor or tragedy, than most Americans are willing to deal with. A friend of mine, Margot Adair, calls this monocultural ideal the "Wonder Breading of America." This is where the ecology of the matter has to come in. We are coming to the end of the monoculture. Manifest destiny is over; now we start seeing the diversity. My feeling is that the ecological metaphor gives us the opportunity to be able to be comfortable with a more diverse sense of ourselves as well as other people. But I think we have to learn the stories.

ROSZAK: I notice that you use the word "story" a lot. The more stories, the better. But some of the stories are cover stories. A people can have a collective cover story.

ANTHONY: That's true. Partly we have stories that are lies. But what may be worse, we only have a limited range of stories, when we ought to have a much fuller range of stories. I've been studying my way through the American story, especially black culture, black history. I've gotten to the point where I grew up in Philadelphia. What did we learn? We learned about Peter Stuyvesant, we learned about William Penn, we learned about the Mennonites, we learned about the Vikings. But we didn't learn a thing about the Italians. A third of the people at my school were Italians, but I don't know why they came over here. We didn't learn anything about the Poles, nothing. A lot of the kids were from Poland: Polish Catholics or Polish Jews. And God knows we didn't learn anything about black people.

So here I am, growing up in this place, surrounded by these people. I have no idea who I am, I have no idea who they are. But I knew who William Penn was. Now what does that do to my ability to function with the people around me? I'm dealing with a blank deck here. Think of all the problems that came up during the late sixties in Boston or Cicero. The whites in Cicero, near Chicago, didn't want black people moving into their neighborhoods; they were trying to defend their ethnic identity. But if we had known all the stories, it would have been a lot easier to say, "I see, I understand, I know what happened to those people and why they came here." If we really know everybody's story in a rich way, you are not dealing with a mystery.

ROSZAK: I'd like to come at this point from an ecopsychological perspective. You and I were at a conference together where the Council of All Beings ritual was performed. The Council of All Beings is a way of working through environmental despair; it involves imaginative exercises, some theater, some forms of grieving. It was invented by Deep Ecologists John Seed and Joanna Macy. Among ecopsychologists, the council is becoming a well-known gesture of emotional and sympathetic solidarity with the planet. The catch phrase for the ritual is a quotation from the ecologist Aldo Leopold, who suggested that we have to learn to "think like a mountain." I know you have some reservations about the council that have to do with what you refer to as the importance of "stories."

ANTHONY: Well, it was funny to me. I've been saying to my friends for a long time, "Why is it so easy for these people to think like mountains and not be able to think like people of color?" That always struck me as being curious. But the reason for that has nothing to do with color; it has to do with stories. Let's take your book, for example, *The Voice of the Earth.* I don't believe you told any stories about any people of color in your book; you probably don't even know them.

ROSZAK: That's true.

ANTHONY: You see, if you have stories about Crazy Horse or Chief Seattle, then you can say, "This reminds me of what Crazy Horse said." But then you might also say, "This reminds me of what Nat Turner said or did, or Frederick Douglass or Zora Neale Hurston."

ROSZAK: Let's stay with the Council of All Beings for a moment longer. Maybe the reason people prefer to take on the guise of a mountain or a wolf is because mountains and wolves can't talk back and tell you how wrong you are. On the other hand, suppose you were in a group where you said you were going to tell the story of someone of a different race or ethnicity. They might tell you that you don't know what you're talking about.

ANTHONY: I think that's one of the reasons. But this needn't be a big problem, because if you are actually in dialogue with people, and somebody tells you you don't have it right, then you say, "Well, tell me what is right." And then you say, "Okay, I'll remember that." And the next time, you tell it differently. Not being right is only a problem when you have a very tenuous, fearful relationship with somebody. But if you are in substantial dialogue with another person, then you learn through trial and error. Fear is really the problem.

ROSZAK: I'd like to bring something up that has to do with stories. There is one wing of the environmental movement that plays a special role in ecopsychology. I'm referring to the ecofeminists, many of whom feel that women have a special role to play in speaking for the imperiled Earth. They feel that in many ways the treatment of the Earth and the treatment of women are parallel. And then too, Native Americans have been readily identified as people close to the land, whose fate and the fate of the land are sympathetically recognized. Now there are a whole set of references that the dominant white society has with blacks and these include nature references. But in the case of blacks, the psychological associations don't come out favorably. They come out as references to jungles, savages, and wildness, and they take on a threatening aspect. Has it ever occurred to you that this is a strange reversal of the way in which nature metaphors and associations work?

ANTHONY: It's interesting to me that you used the word "jungle," because now we call it "rainforest."

ROSZAK: Rainforest, right. More benign. "Jungle" is the more menacing word.

ANTHONY: And when I was growing up we always talked about "swamps." Now we talk about "wetlands." Do you know what a "wetland" is? It's a swamp that white people care about.

In the thirties, there was a huge amount of effusive romantic description of black people; some of it sounds really weird now when you read it. It had a lot of the same qualities that people talk about these days with respect to Native Americans: beat the drum, take me back to the Earth. And people fed into it. Then at some point it began to become incongruous with the reality of how people were living, so it stopped.

I think the problem is projection: white people want to be able to project on the world the images that have allowed them to control the world. *Why is there so much energy put into that?* I mean, it's not natural, is it, this need to control? You have to ask yourself what is really going on here. What I see from a psychological point of view is a whole series of lies and denials that white people have built up about the world and they can't let go of them.

ROSZAK: You're saying that there is an ecology of human diversity that has not been comprehended by the environmental movement. We know more about the ecology of nonhuman species than about ourselves in our diversity. The ecology of human stories, especially as they appear in an urban civilization, has not been taken into account. It is not normally understood to be an environmental or ecological matter; it's shelved in another category, as sociology or politics. But in fact, it's an integral part of what's got to be dealt with. Because the *city* has to be dealt with.

ANTHONY: That's right.

ROSZAK: Then let's talk about the city and all that it has come to represent in environmental philosophy, policy, and ecopsychology. Tell me about the role of the city in solving what we call the environmental crisis.

ANTHONY: Well, most obviously, many of our environmental problems are directly related to the way we live in cities. Fifty percent of the world's population now live in cities, and seventy percent of the people in the United States live in cities. One of the more dramatic illustrations of this is a report that was prepared by the South Coast Air Quality Man-

agement District about the Los Angeles air basin. It pointed out that one
percent of global warming comes from Los Angeles alone. What more
dramatic illustration do you need than this? That this one tiny place on
the map produces one percent of global warming. Seventy percent of the
city is paved over; people ride around in single-occupancy automobiles,
pushing out exhaust. Fifteen to twenty thousand people a year die in Los
Angeles from respiratory conditions directly related to air quality. Most
of them are people of color and poor people. This was supposed to be a
garden city; people went there because they thought it was going to be
Utopia. That, by and large, is the story of our cities: most of them are
now unlivable.

We make our cities more miserable than they need to be. You could
probably get rid of eighty percent of the paving in Los Angeles and make
it infinitely more habitable. If you had mass transportation, and if you
had places that people could walk, if you had neighborhoods that were
more self-reliant, you'd have more space, it could be made livable. If we
really want to solve our environmental problems, instead of running
from the city we have to rebuild it.

ROSZAK: If the city is at the heart of every environmental issue we might
want to talk about, and if the cities are becoming ungovernable, then the
issue of justice is at the core of the environmental crisis.

ANTHONY: I think that's true, but I also think the issue of beauty is at
the core. If you are incapable of seeing the beauty that's around you and
the beauty of the people around you, if you are constantly running from
them, then you can never make your peace, you're always trying to escape to somewhere else. But if we appreciated living in a multicultural
neighborhood, appreciated something beautiful there, the beauty of
people from different places who have different stories, then instead of
running from it you'd be drawn to it.

ROSZAK: You are talking about the human and social beauty that you
can find in cities if you look for it. But of course the word "beauty" in
the environmental movement is almost entirely reserved for natural,
nonhuman beautiful things.

ANTHONY: I've read stories about people traveling across the desert and not finding any beauty in it. "This is a wasteland, there's no water, it's dead. Let's get the hell out of here." But now, of course, people look at deserts and marvel at them, at all the rich life and the diversity of beings that are there. In order to do that you have to be willing to slow down and be there a little bit. Of course, the other problem has to do with the fact that our manufactured environment is so hideous. If you go to any poor country that has any kind of indigenous traditions—Portugal, Africa. . . . I mean look at this photograph I took of this house in a West African village. The people make these homes out of grass; it's woven with incredible care. It's just grass but it's like a symphony. The fact that we have increased our power over nature can take a lot away from us. We drive around at eighty miles an hour rather than having to walk. That means you make a place like San Pablo Avenue, here in my neighborhood, a street where it's impossible to walk. *That's* like being in a wasteland.

ROSZAK: I want to ask you one final question. Suppose we wanted to frame a curriculum in ecopsychology. What is the one thing you feel would be a necessary part of it that you don't see there now?

ANTHONY: I think of two things. What I believe is most urgent has to do with the idea of "whiteness." The monolithic human identity that has been built around the mythology of pure whiteness is destructive. We have to find a way to build a multicultural self that is in harmony with an ecological self. We need to embrace human diversity in the way we deal with each other—as opposed to the notion that white people are the mainstream and everybody else is "other." An ecopsychology that has no place for people of color, that doesn't deliberately set out to correct the distortions of racism, is an oxymoron.

Second, and related to this, is the importance of the urban issue. I am obviously trying to put these two concerns together. That's what my work is about in the Urban Habitat Program. Respect for cultural diversity, for social justice, and for multicultural leadership must be at the heart of restructuring our cities to protect and restore natural resources by meeting basic human needs. That's the framework we need to rebuild our cities and become balanced with nature in order to protect the planet. But the only way we can do that is also to respect human diversity and social justice so they can be incorporated into doing what we have to. There is a lot of work that has to be done among the people of color. This is really difficult for me. Among the people of color, among the black people, particularly, we have to learn a whole new attitude toward ourselves and the people around us. When I talk about multicultural leadership, I mean that black people need to move away from a mode in which we simply identify with our victim selves. I'm not saying we should deny the victim part; but I'm saying that we lose part of our humanity if we don't also accept our capacity to provide leadership for the whole community. We have to learn how to *own* that part of our experience, spiritually and psychologically. We have to be willing to take responsibility for the outcome, not only for our own communities but for everybody. There is no other way.

The Politics of Species Arrogance

JOHN E. MACK

F OR JOHN E. MACK, professor of psychiatry at Cambridge Hospital
in Massachusetts, inventing a psychology that comprehends our
relationship to the Earth is far more than an intellectual or therapeutic
project. It entails a call for political commitment. Through his Center
for Psychology and Social Change (formerly the Center for Psychological Studies in the Nuclear Age), Mack has long been one of the
strongest advocates in his profession for making psychology socially
relevant. Here, turning to the issue of environmental degradation, he
issues a call for "new forms of personal empowerment for ourselves
and our clients that integrate exploration and activism."

━━━━━━━

In April 1990 I was in Japan for a United Nations conference held in the
industrial city of Sendai on the relationship of science and technology to
international peace and security. On the night before returning to the
United States (which happened to be Earth Day, April 22), while sleeping in a typical old-style Japanese inn in Kyoto, I had a dream that reflected my experience of coming back to a country that had been
changed drastically from the place I had once known. Thirty years ago
my wife, infant son, and I had lived for two years near Tokyo, in an old
house with shoji screens and tatami mats, in a country of exquisite

beauty. When I came to the conference, I returned to a polluted land desecrated by the mindless excesses of industrialization. On every small hill was a tower for power lines that draped themselves ungracefully across the countryside, dominating the landscape of miniature rises and subtle contours.

In my dream I am on a hillside just across the Hudson River, perhaps in New Jersey, through which I often drove with my parents on the way to the seashore in my childhood. Someone is lecturing to a group of us, as if we were at the conference for which I have come to Kyoto, telling us that there is still much beauty in the New York City environs. Then, with others from the conference, I take a kind of quick aerial and ground tour of these hills but see no beauty, for on each field of straw-colored New Jersey swamp grass there is at least one rectangular industrial or commercial building. Furthermore, there is an unmistakable chemical stench that pervades the scene, which is only partially acknowledged by the group.

The scene shifts to a meeting around a conference table where people are sharing their experiences and discussing what is bothering them. I say that it troubles me most, beyond what we have witnessed, when someone, or a policy, or some enterprise, pretends that reality is different from what my own perceptions tell me it is—that is, when someone or something invalidates my direct experience. Then a man sitting across the table from me reacts intensely and positively to my sentiment, and I feel very much supported.

I will return shortly to certain of the dream's meanings.

We now sense a need for a new psychology of the environment in order to understand what we have done, and continue to do, individually and collectively, to the Earth that is our home, so that we may change our behavior, locally and globally, in order to save its life. But how is this to be done? How do we invent a new psychology of our relationship to the Earth? I use the word "invent," because of its implication of creating something new, an entity or a combination of things that has not been put together before.

Without a human problem there is no psychology, or at least not a clinical or dynamic one, so we start by identifying the problem, one that might have existed before, but that has gained preeminence as a result of new historical and cultural circumstances. Freud and his followers to a degree invented psychoanalysis in response to the fact that the extreme, deceitful ordering of men's and women's sexual lives by a rigidified bourgeois society was becoming emotionally intolerable and producing behavioral and physiological manifestations that could not be understood or treated by the medicine or neuropsychiatry of the day. We confront now a new kind of problem, global in scope, namely, the agonizing murder of the life systems of the Earth, the home on which we depend for everything, and that affects each of us in profound, personal ways, no matter how intensely we may deny it.

This new psychology must include not only the development of a body of theory that would understand or interpret our relationship to the environment, but also ways of working with clients and patients that will bring forth direct or disguised thoughts and feelings in relation to the environment, and empower constructive initiatives. At the very least, this must mean that when we hear expressions of distress about pollution or other forms of environmental destruction in dreams and other forms of communication, we not hear or interpret these simply as displacements from some other, inner source. For example, a young woman in a human growth workshop that I co-led in Manhattan complained that she could not do all of the work, which involved exercises using rapid deep breathing, because the air was too foul. "I can't breathe," she said repeatedly. "It's just too toxic. Are there chemicals stored here?" (There were not. The room we used was a dance hall on the lower West Side.) Others in the workshop resonated with this woman's complaint and acknowledged the foulness of the city's air. But they were able to complete this part of the workshop. Although her complaints could have been connected to early childhood experiences of disgust or intrauterine distress ("toxic placentary influences or insufficient nourishment," as Stanislav Grof has called it),[1] there was no opportunity to explore this possibility. Yet the acknowledgment of the validity of her complaint enhanced positively her further participation and experience in the workshop.

But what kind of psychology is relevant to a problem of this scope? What would a psychology of the Earth be like? It would need to be comprehensive, holistic, and systemic; indeed, I am not sure what the correct

1. Stanislav Grof, *The Adventures of Self-Discovery: Dimensions of Consciousness and New Perspectives in Psychotherapy and Inner Exploration* (Albany, N.Y.: SUNY Press, 1988).

terms would be, except that they must convey the fact of wholeness, connection, interrelatedness, and complexity. It would have to be dynamic psychology—in the sense that it would need to explore profound, largely ignored conscious and unconscious feelings, impulses, and desires in relation to the physical world—rather than one of the variations on neurophysiology or biochemistry that now dominate the American psychiatric establishment. In addition to recognizing the systemic nature of the problem, the practitioners of this dynamic psychology of the environment would need to tell unpleasant or unwelcome truths about ourselves—here is one of the meanings of my dream—as we have learned to do from psychoanalysis, but now in an altogether new arena. We would need to explore our relationship with the Earth and understand how and why we have created institutions so destructive to it. Even in Freud's time, dynamic psychology was relational, initially describing the forces connecting the agencies of the psyche (id, ego, superego), and between and among individuals in dyadic relationships, families, and small groups. But a relational psychology of the Earth would be much broader, including our connectedness to peoples and other creatures all over the planet and with the Earth itself as a living entity.

Actually we (by "we" I mean, by and large, citizens of Western and other industrialized nations, for many native cultures experience and avow a very different relationship to their environment) do have a psychology, or at least a prevailing attitude, conscious and unconscious, toward the Earth. We regard it as a thing, a big thing, an object to be owned, mined, fenced, guarded, stripped, built upon, dammed, plowed, burned, blasted, bulldozed, and melted to serve the material needs and desires of the human species at the expense, if necessary, of all other species, which we feel at liberty to kill, paralyze, or domesticate for our own use. Among the many forms of egoism that have come to be the focus of psychodynamically oriented psychologists in an age of self-criticism about our narcissism, this form of species arrogance has received little scrutiny. This attitude contrasts dramatically with the pragmatic, live-and-let-live, and reverential relationship with nature that is reflected in the words of Native American leaders, who recognize our complete interdependence with the Earth and the need to live in balance and harmony with nature. The Sioux medicine man John (Fire) Lame

Deer wrote, "To come to nature, feel its power, let it help you, one needs time and patience for that. Time to think, to figure it all out. You have so little time for contemplation; it's always rush, rush, rush with you. It lessens a person's life, all that grind, that hurrying and scurrying about." The seemingly mindless destruction of the natural landscape by the Japanese, a people who have been known for their delicate appreciation of nature, attests to the degree to which disciplined industrialization and accretion of wealth can overwhelm such sensitivities and separate us from the Earth itself. This cutting off of consciousness from a connection with nature, and the spirit that most peoples throughout human history have experienced as inherent in it (and in us, of course, as part of nature), is one of the supreme negative achievements of modern, industrially developed humankind. This separation is painfully demonstrated in modern Japan and is reflected in my dream. One must wonder how or why we have done it, how we have so overdeveloped the use of reason at the expense of feeling, in the service of a fear-driven need to conquer other peoples and the material world on a planet with a growing population that is perceived as yielding finite, diminishing resources.

So a psychology of the environment would be an expanded psychology of relationship, a conversation or experiencing in the deepest parts of our being, of our connection with the Earth as sacred. I say sacred because I do not believe that a mere threat to survival will be sufficient to create this new relationship without a fundamental shift in the nature of our being, as Czech president Vaclav Havel so eloquently told the U.S. Congress in 1990: "Without a global revolution in the sphere of human consciousness, nothing will change for the better in the sphere of our being as humans, and the catastrophe toward which this world is headed be unavoidable." Havel surely must have been personally revolted to discover the environmental catastrophe that his Communist predecessors left him, and which I witnessed from a train traveling from Prague to Berlin.

But here we encounter a problem in developing the new psychology, for it must, by virtue of the very nature of the task, include a powerful spiritual element. This will mean, for example, a reanimation of the forests and of nature, which we have so systematically and proudly denuded of their spiritual meaning. As pointed out in a recent article in the newsletter of the International Research Center for Japanese Studies

(Nichibunken), entitled "Animism Renaissance," which acknowledges Japan's "responsibility for a great deal of destruction of tropical rain forests," "severe natural destruction started at a point parallel with that of the disappearance of animism."

Here, then, is the problem. By and large, we in the West have rejected the language and experience of the sacred, the divine, and the animation of nature. Our psychology is predominantly one of mechanisms, parts, and linear relationships. We have grown suspicious of experiences, no matter how powerful, that cannot be quantified, and we distrust the language of reverence, spirit, and mystical connection, recalling perhaps with fear the superstitions and holy wars of earlier periods. Academic psychology, embodying now a reverence of numbers, tight reasoning, and linear thinking as opposed to intuition, direct knowing, and subjective experience, is likely to look askance at efforts to reinfuse its body with the imprecise notions of spirituality and philosophy, from which it has so vigorously and proudly struggled to free itself in an effort to be granted scientific status in our universities, laboratories, and consulting rooms.

But this cannot be helped. For the route to a new psychology of the environment, which might contribute to our protecting it, probably cannot be achieved by measuring our reactions or talking about the problem. Only experiences that profoundly alter our view of nature and reconnect us with the divinity in ourselves and in the environment can empower people to commit themselves to the prodigious task before them. The therapeutic methods must be powerful enough to shift the ground of our being so that we experience the Earth in its living reality. This is why people like Walter and Ellen Christie, Joanna Macy, and Stanislav and Christina Grof, who have been pioneers in creating methods of reconnecting us with the Earth and with ourselves in nature, rely on experiential, imaginal, and consciousness-altering or opening approaches.[2] People who open themselves to this connection, discovering their "ecological selves," often seem to encounter disturbing images, bad smells, and other psychological experiences suggesting the Earth's desecration in their dreams, fantasies, and deeper consciousness. This imaging can become intolerably painful but also seems to empower people,

2. See Walter Christie, "Human Ecology," a series of six articles in *Habitat: Journal of the Maine Audubon Society* (1984–85).

impelling them to take action on behalf of the deteriorating environment.

What I have described so far is, in a sense, the easy part of the problem. Deepening our conscious awareness, reanimating our connection with the Earth, is important and can lead to responsible initiatives by individuals. But the stench of my condensed Japanese–New Jersey dream landscape, the pollution of our world, and the destruction of its resources by the Earth's expanding population are the problems of humankind as a whole, acting collectively through institutions, especially corporations, often with direct or indirect governmental support. For a psychology of the environment to be meaningful, it must address these powerful institutional, structural, and systemic realities. Social institutions are, in a sense, the expressions of our collective psyches. But we come to take their existence and modes of operating so much for granted that to consider openly that we have the power to modify, transform, and dismantle them will, inevitably, encounter intense resistance because of the political, economic, and psychological vested interests with which they are associated. To bring about structural changes of this kind, psychologists will need to work closely with policy makers, corporate leaders, economists, and many people representing other related disciplines and groups committed to social change.

The political and personal resistance to environmental transformation can be flagrant. When I was in Japan, for example, I read that industrial pollution in Korea had become so severe that the water in the public water system in Seoul was condemned as unsafe. A professor at Seoul University who documented the severity of the industrial pollution problem was fired, and people who supported environmental change were accused by the government of being communist sympathizers. I had a similar experience in Paris in 1988 upon returning from a conference in Findhorn, Scotland, titled "Politics as If the Whole Earth Mattered." Fresh from hearing moving talks about the pollution problem and the Green movement in Britain and elsewhere in Europe, I shared my experience and concern with a French psychologist, who dismissed these environmental concerns as communist propaganda, despite the fact that her own senses would confirm their truth.

Resistance to facing the costs of environmental transformation may extend beyond top management to the shareholders themselves. Initiatives proposed by shareholders from various environmental groups were overwhelmingly rejected by the vastly greater numbers of the company's supporters at Exxon's annual shareholders' meeting in April 1990. Pleas about wildlife destruction, poisoning of children by toxic chemicals, and other dangers from hazardous waste were ignored, presumably because reparative or healing actions might reduce shareholders' profit margins and dividends. One Exxon spokesperson told the environmentalists: "Store your car, stop flying airplanes, and walk or ride a horse in the winter snow or summer heat." Over and above the speaker's insensitivity, the remark is interesting for its implication, which is not so far off the mark—that what is at stake is the way we live in a developed society and the fact or extent of industrialization itself.

It is not realistic to expect that the environmental crisis will be solved simply by deindustrialization. But the unwelcome news the new psychology for the environment will need to communicate is that the unbridled license given in the West to free-market forces, and the irresponsible overbuilding of heavy industries in the socialist systems, have both led to the same disastrous result—a planet dying in the excesses of human waste. As my barber put it, "Johnny, we are drowning in our industrial feces."

The greatest challenge we now face in this rapidly changing world is to create political institutions that use the resources of power and responsibility in conjunction with economic structures accountable to future generations of human beings, to other species, and to the Earth itself. Psychologists of the environment, while enabling increasing numbers of people to connect with the Earth and its transcendent meaning, must also participate with committed citizens, as well as community and corporate groups, in a broad-based movement aimed at nothing less than the transformation of our political and economic institutions. Ultimately this means joining with others in a search for alternatives to the material values that now dominate the spirit in the United States and much of the world.

An environmental movement on the scale necessary to bring about the changes essential to protect the Earth, a process to which psychology has a useful contribution to make, must be authentically international and cross-cultural in two senses.

First, we in the developed countries must be aware what powerful precedents are set by our example. When we destroy our own forests, pollute our air, and poison our streams with our industrial and personal garbage, it avails us little to admonish developing countries for unhygienic industrialization. Often-heard arguments, such as the fact that we cut down our timber in a more orderly manner than the developing countries that are destroying their rainforests, become trivial in relation to the psychological and economic forces involved.

Second, we need to be aware of the economic priorities and vital needs of the peoples of developing countries. Campaigns to save natural resources such as trees and animals—upon which impoverished peoples depend for their livelihoods—cannot be effective without addressing the material needs of those societies.

In sum, a psychology of the environment, to be comprehensive, must include at least the following elements:

1. *An appreciation that we do, in fact, have a relationship with the Earth itself,* and the degree to which that relationship has become inimicable to the sustaining of human lives and those of countless other species.

2. *An analysis of traditional attitudes toward the Earth in our own and in other cultures that may facilitate or interfere with the maintenance of life.* The dominant attitude toward the Earth in the industrially developed countries has been one of unchecked exploitation.

3. *The application of methods of exploring and changing our relationship to the Earth's environment that can reanimate our connection with it.* These approaches must be emotionally powerful, experiential, and consciousness expanding, opening us to ourselves in relation to nature.

4. *An examination of politics and economics from an ecopsychological perspective.* Political and economic systems, institutions, and forces embody collective attitudes toward the Earth and its living forms, but have a compelling life of their own. Psychologists committed to environmental change must, therefore, work with professional environmentalists, policy makers, population experts, corporate leaders, economists, and others to make these structures compatible with an environment that can support the continuation of human life and well-being.

5. This will mean, even more than in the case of the nuclear threat, that, to be effective, *psychologists will need to become professionally and personally committed and involved outside their offices and laboratories.* We must discover new forms of personal empowerment for ourselves and our clients that integrate exploration and activism, becoming—men and women together—archetypal warriors in the battle to protect our planet.

The Spirit of the Goddess

BETTY ROSZAK

B ECAUSE IT QUESTIONS the gender stereotypes that underlie our society's "manhandling" of women and of nature, ecofeminism has always been an inherently psychological approach to environmental issues. Carried forward into the field of ecology, the feminist contention that "the personal is the political" has discovered some of the richest insights available to ecopsychology. Deep Ecologists can be credited with challenging the "anthropocentrism" that has distorted Western society's encounter with the nonhuman world. But ecofeminists have gone further. Identifying Deep Ecology as a male-dominated movement, they contend that it is specifically *androcentrism*—our compulsively masculine science and technology—that lies at the root of our environmental disconnection. As long as assigned gender roles go unexamined, especially in Third World nations where women are often limited to domestic subservience and childbearing, such basic environmental issues as population growth will be much harder to solve. In this essay, based upon a lecture presented to the 1990 summer conference of the Green Party of Sweden, Betty Roszak asks if some ecofeminists—especially those in the Goddess movement—may not be creating a new sexual dichotomy that burdens women with the role of "saving the world" and denies men the sensitivity they will need to renew their emotional bond with the Earth.

Some years ago, when the American dancer and choreographer Martha Graham was touring with her company, she introduced her dance dramas with a brief introductory lecture to her audience. Speaking of *Seraphic Dialogue*, her dance based on the life of Joan of Arc, she said, "The ancestors are always with us. They speak through our blood." Later in her talk she remarked: "The phoenix is born anew every morning."

These two seemingly antithetical statements have stayed in my mind ever since. When I recognized the phenomenon of the return of the Goddess in contemporary feminist thought, I saw that if we are to take the spirit of the Goddess seriously we must come to terms with both the phoenix and the ancestors. But first I should like to mention an event in my life that will have some bearing on these questions.

When my daughter was an infant, I was living on the Stanford University campus in California, very much immersed in the everyday, often tedious and fragmenting activities of raising a child. This was in the early 1960s, when women were still expected to engage in housekeeping and childrearing as their chief source of validation. One day I took some time off to attend a lecture being given by one of my college culture heroes, Lewis Mumford, whose writings I had admired in my youth. The lecture, entitled "Apology to Henry Adams," was an eloquently argued plea for reviving the bold historical interpretations put forth by Adams at the beginning of the twentieth century. Adams had warned prophetically of the disastrous paths science and technology were to take in the new century, and of the inevitable estrangement from nature and the organic that would ensue from the coming development of megamachine culture.

At the end of his lecture, Mumford quoted from Adams's "The Dynamo and the Virgin," the poetic work in which Adams invokes the Virgin as a "counterpoise to chaos." Mumford saw Adams's thought as a corrective to the life-denying forces that even then were threatening humanity.

> Adams saw that we needed more feeling, feeling and gentling, such as infants first get at their mothers' breasts; such feeling as woman symbolically projected from the paleolithic Venus of Willendorf to the Venus of Milo, from Egyptian Isis to the Virgin of the thirteenth century; feeling that has poured into a thousand benign cultural forms . . . and expressed itself in every sus-

taining mode of embrace and envelopment and tender expression, from the kiss of greeting to the hot tears with which we take our leave from the dead. . . . To restore a human balance upset by our pathologically dehumanized technology, we must foster human feeling, feeling as disciplined and as refined, by constant application and correction, as our highest intellectual processes. To overcome the widespread sterilization of mind, we must unite a higher capacity for feeling with our higher capacity for thought, to produce acts that will be worthy progeny of both parents. This perhaps, at the end, was the lesson Henry Adams taught in his apostrophe to the Virgin.[1]

Hearing these moving words and pondering these ideas for the first time, I found in them a plea from a renowned male thinker for the elevation and use of all those feminine virtues my education had taught me to despise (and my husband had been taught to suppress and hide). I heard a plea for the restoration of those very traits considered trivial and inferior by the male-dominated academic world that was our environment at the time. Moreover, Mumford said, it was these very virtues that could save us all from the runaway dehumanization of life and the desacralization of nature. Far from being irrelevant to the real business of the world, the feelings I had for my child were so important that they could and must save the world. I took heart from Mumford's words, and from this seed began to grow the feminism of my later years. In the passage quoted, there are embedded a good many of the ideas and ambiguities of the uses of the Goddess in feminism. Not too many years later I found I had moved so far in my thinking that I could openly criticize Mumford and others for indulging in a kind of idolatry of "woman" as a symbol at the expense of women as individuals.

In an article in the American journal *Liberation*, I wrote:

Even Shaw, Mumford and Ashley Montagu have helped contribute to female acquiescence [to male domination] by investing "woman" with some kind of magical "life force" which will bring rationalistic, mechanistic-crazed men back to their senses. Writers like these invest the concept "woman" with all those ideals opposite to the masculine characteristics now in the process of ravaging the Earth. It is Henry Adams' opposition of the Virgin to the Dynamo: the mystic, forgiving maternal principle as savior and preserver of life, in the face of cold, rational male dominance.

1. Lewis Mumford, "Apology to Henry Adams," *Interpretations and Forecasts: 1922–1972* (New York: Harcourt Brace Jovanovich, 1973), p. 364.

I went on to say that though there is a great deal of truth in this formulation, the use of it could be distorted, corrupted and coopted by men for their own purposes. I said, "The effect of idealizing 'woman' is often the same as subjugating her." Whether caged or idolized, we are still kept from entering the world of men, which by consensus is the real world.

When I found women idealizing "woman" and exalting the feminine, I felt compelled to consider that with the same critical eye. Since then, the women's movement in America has developed in the direction of a new form of spirituality often termed "feminist spirituality." The first all-female conference on spiritual matters took place in Boston in April 1976. "Through the Looking Glass: A Gynergenetic Experience," as it was called, was a week-long expression of female energy, a magic cauldron into which many ingredients were stirred. There were incantations, music, dreams, moon meditations, exhibits and films on blood mysteries, workshops on feminist interpretations of the Tarot, women's hidden history, goddess worship, Amazons, the matriarchy, the martyrdom of the witches, discussions of the relationship between spirituality and politics, between women and ecology. In short, it was the kind of dazzling, dazing richly supersaturated mélange one had come to expect from the new-consciousness fairs we have seen in the United States, filled with variety, surge, dynamism, excitement, and the accompanying confusion that results from such mixtures.

When I spoke to the women who participated, and who later taught and wrote on the subject, they helped me define these amorphous components of a specifically feminist spirituality: they are group oriented and nonhierarchical, and have a strong emphasis on the body, on healing, on the uses of Third World and indigenous spiritual practices, and on the development of practical, personal knowledge for everyday use. Some groups have been practicing witchcraft as a revival of ancient folk religion. Covens of women meet regularly for their own form of nature worship, which often includes learning the medicinal uses of herbs and plants.

There are many women deeply concerned with recovering their lost history, so studiously ignored and neglected by patriarchal historians and anthropologists. They search the ancient past for myths of the mother goddess and the possibilities of a prehistoric matriarchal or, more accurately, matricentric culture. They study the witch trials of the

early modern period, looking for traces of women's wisdom, traces that
have been difficult or impossible to find because they have been suppressed by often-hostile or prejudiced male historians. The archaeolog-
ical reconstructions of Marija Gimbutas in her book *Goddesses and Gods
of Old Europe, 6500–3500* B.C., and the speculative prehistory of Riane
Eisler, whose *Chalice and the Blade* is an attempt to understand prepa-
triarchal cultures, have provided more scholarly underpinnings to the
idea of peaceful matricentric societies.

There are women who come together to dream, to meditate, to create
rituals. They pay attention once again to natural cycles, to the moon in
all its aspects, to menstruation and childbirth as physical and symbolic
events in women's lives. They learn to use nonaggressive healing powers
as alternatives to conventional medicine; they use their own newly discovered psychic powers to create rituals of healing and wholeness.

For example, several years ago one of the largest public rituals of this
kind took place in San Francisco as part of a conference on violence
against women. At the end of an arduous series of meetings and talks
devoted to voicing women's outrage at the violence done against us, the
ritualists prepared a beautifully jeweled sword to symbolize the seductive power of violence in our society. Hung high above the conference
hall, the sword was to receive a litany of chanted violent acts, all the
women of the conference directing their hostility and rage against it. After the chant of anger, there came the chant of affirmation and strength
against the forces of violence, and hope for what had been achieved at
the conference. Then there was a collective meditation on a peaceful
world, where the sword was transformed into an instrument of benev-
olence. With the end of the ritual came a great surge of exhilaration; after
a draining, exhausting weekend, the participants left with a sense of renewed possibilities.

Another ritual chant devised by a modern priestess brings out many
of the motifs of feminist spirituality:

> In the olden times the Goddess had many groves and wimmin served her
> freely and lived in dignity. The Goddess' presence was everywhere, and her
> wimmin knew her as the eternal sister. The patriarchal powers burned down
> her sacred groves, raped and killed her priestesses, and enslaved wimmin.
> Her name was stricken from books and the great darkness of ignorance de-
> scended upon womankind. Today there is a new dawn. . . . We, the wim-

min, are the grove, through us the return of the Goddess is evident. Let us give birth to each other spiritually as the Goddess brought forth the light of the world! Behold the Great Goddess of the ten thousand names!

In this chant we have the notions of the hidden history destroyed by patriarchy, the original peaceful times, the relation to nature in the sacred groves, and the return of feminine spiritual strength in a new form. The chant evinces a belief in the transforming power of word and image.

But why must the Goddess return? Where has she been and why are these images recurring at this juncture in history? Two powerful streams of dissent and protest, the women's movement and the ecology movement, come together here. Both have been struggling against the same form of oppression: patriarchal domination and exploitation. Nature, implicitly seen as female, has been subject to parallel forms of degradation.

We are all familiar with the terms of sexual aggression in common usage: the "rape of the Earth," "conquest of matter," and "domination of nature." Historically, this identification of nature with the female and the female as nature, and thus an inferior being, became dramatically emphasized with the development of modern science in the sixteenth and seventeenth centuries. Francis Bacon was formulating the new scientific method at the height of the witch craze in Europe, and was almost certainly influenced by the prevailing notions about women. Church authorities of the fifteenth century had used a popular handbook on the identification and treatment of witches, the *Malleus Maleficarum*, in searching out evil. "What else is woman," says this manual, "but a foe to friendship, an unescapable punishment, a necessary evil, a natural temptation, a desirable calamity, a domestic danger, a delectable detriment, an evil of nature painted with fair colors?" For Bacon and his followers, women symbolized the chaotic and untamed in nature. Both had to be tamed and mastered. But beyond this, nature as female had to be "interrogated," her secrets "wrested" from her. In his *New Atlantis,* Bacon advises that men need not have any scruples in "entering and penetrating into these holes and corners" because "the inquisition of truth" is the scientist's purpose. He must put nature "on the rack" in a "relentless interrogation."

Such blatant images of sexual aggression appear as a matter of course in the writings of many contemporary philosophers as well. In *Being and Nothingness*, Jean-Paul Sartre, writing on knowledge, says:

> The idea of discovery, of revelation, includes an idea of appropriative enjoyment. What is seen is possessed; to see is to *deflower*. If we examine the comparisons ordinarily used to express the relation between the knower and the known, we see that many of them are represented as being a kind of *violation by sight*. The unknown object is given as immaculate, as virgin, comparable to a *whiteness*. It has not yet "delivered up" its secret; man has not yet "snatched" its secret away from it.[2]

In this respect Sartre is a true heir of Bacon.

The degradation of nature in the pursuit of science has been well documented by scholars like Carolyn Merchant and Evelyn Fox Keller. Because science since its modern inception has been considered "male," women in science have at best been accepted as curious anomalies within the profession. In order to succeed in the masculine world of science, women have had to impersonate men. The astronomer Edwin Hubble gave his highest compliment to his female colleague, astrophysicist Cecilia Payne Gaposchkin, when he called her "the best man at Harvard." There are strong penalties for deviating from the masculine norm. No less a scientific hero than Max Planck warned early in this century that "nature herself prescribed to the woman her function as mother and housewife and . . . the laws of nature cannot be ignored under any circumstances without grave damage." Under such a threat is it any wonder that women were discouraged from entering the field?

The familiar metaphor of nature as female allows the masculine scientist to treat nature as inert, passive substance, infinitely manipulatable. In contrast, Evelyn Fox Keller gives us the example of the noted plant geneticist Barbara McClintock, who in studying plant chromosomes found that "the more I worked with them . . . when I was really working with them I wasn't outside, I was down there. I was part of the system." McClintock developed a relationship with plants for which Keller dares to use the word "love." She writes, "I use the word love neither loosely

2. Jean-Paul Sartre, *Being and Nothingness*, trans. Hazel Barnes (New York: Washington Square Press, 1966), p. 708.

nor sentimentally, but out of fidelity to the language McClintock herself uses to describe a form of attention."

The dominant masculinist mode of doing science wants nothing to do with getting "down there" or with the kind of engaged attention that could be called love, because then one cannot easily separate oneself from what is being studied; one becomes "part of the system." This makes it hard to impose upon, to conquer the substance with brute force. Such a form of attention requires an entirely different attitude, one that brings with it a new ecological awareness.

In this way of thinking, nature and the Earth are being revalued, not as inferior inert substance that exists only to serve human needs and be exploited for human uses, but as the very ground of our being, reinfused with the vital force that the masculine genius of modern science extracted from it.

The new ecological awareness calls for a renewed positive image of the feminine. Ecofeminism rejects the outmoded dualism of the scientific mode in favor of a sense of unity with all living things, for a worldview that emphasizes process, dynamic change, and the interrelatedness of all beings. Ecofeminism and ecopsychology both point the way beyond dualism and its either/or reductionisms. An ecological consciousness sees nature as alive, active, and capable of communicating with us. This insight carries us further to a sense of the sacred within nature. In a feminist spirituality, women are seeking to revive an age-old animist vision: not *mere* matter, but matter imbued with spirit.

This spirituality reclaims the body from the despised realm to which it has been relegated by centuries of dualistic thought. If woman equals nature and if nature equals woman, then ecofeminists celebrate the analogies and make them the central meaning of the Goddess. All the bodily functions, including sexuality and childbearing, are sacred. The biological cycles of life and death, of change and renewal, are seen as inherently spiritual events. Body and nature need not be transcended, but are to be *lived* in, experienced, and honored as integral parts of our spiritual understanding.

In its celebration of the cycles of nature and the fecundity and variety of life, this becomes a religion that goes beyond churches and temples, a religion of all times and places. There is an emphasis on the importance of place, rootedness, and growing things. Living in one's place becomes an element in a religion of ecological wholeness. Earth's body and our bodies are intimately connected, and the restoration of health to the one is intimately connected to the restoration of health in the other.

The Goddess becomes the great metaphor for the source of life. Union with the Goddess is not a union with something outside oneself. One practice in this new/old religion is the use of a mirror in a home shrine. The object of attention in this meditation is not an idol, icon, or photo of a saint or guru, but is a mirror in which one can see an aspect of the Goddess in oneself. The mirror is a reminder for a woman to attend to her own life cycles, to attend to her imagination, dreams, fantasy.

The Goddess is also important in promoting a sense of a specifically female power, and in rejecting the male notion of female power as inferior and dangerous (remember, an orthodox rabbi cannot touch a menstruating woman). The images of females as dolls, sexual toys, or destructive natural forces are replaced with the strong nurturing presence of the mother, not necessarily in a literal sense, but as a creator of arts, healing, agriculture, crafts, pottery, weaving, and so forth. Many of the group rituals have sought to concentrate group energy by a deliberate use of the will to alter the course of events. Women who have generally felt powerless find this a liberating experience that allows them to overcome a fear of their own directed will. The emphasis is on healing and cooperation rather than on the assertion of individualistic will as practiced in traditional magic.

A traditional women's literature is being rediscovered as well: the telling of stories, "old wives' tales" or grandmother stories in a new education of heart and spirit. What stories do we all have to tell? We ponder our ancestors; the themes played out in our heritage and our heredity become the serious meaning in the old stories. If we listen to the generations of spirit, we become firmly grounded. We know who we are and where we come from.

But this is not all. You are certainly more than your past history or your genetic material. Each morning the phoenix is born again and something fresh arises from the past. The physical world is filled with messages and each person listens and interprets these messages, through her own personal experience.

The ancestors and the phoenix cannot exist without each other. The ancestors can speak through the phoenix, making new words for each generation. As Robin Morgan says, "We *are* the myths. We *are* the Amazons, the Furies, the witches. We have never *not* been here, this exact sliver of time, this precise place. There is something utterly familiar about us. We have been ourselves before."

All this is by way of explaining why the Goddess has returned, why the figure of Gaia as presiding spirit of the Earth has spoken to so many women in the feminist movement. But the crucial question has to be raised. Are women once more to be identified with the archetypal mother, or Mother Nature? Do women have a special calling to save humanity and the Earth through a superior compassion and wisdom? Or is this just another repetition of the old stereotyping we have tried so hard to break? Are we not being used again subtly in the service of male power? By acknowledging a special relationship between women and nature, do we not reinforce the projection of male responsibility onto women as saviors of the world?

To put it another way: is the Goddess image of advantage to men only, so that they may have the muse of inspiration, the helpmeet at their side inflated to titanic dimensions, but still subordinate? Or is the Goddess for women only, as Robin Morgan envisions in these lines addressed to men? "And I will speak less and less to you, and more and more in crazy gibberish you cannot understand: witch's incantations, poetry, old women's mutterings."

Do we turn away from men, do we define ourselves by sex, revel in "the feminine"? The danger is that once more we may become self-separated, ghettoized, our culture relegated to "women's subjects" or "women's studies" so easily dismissed by the male hierarchies, so easily ignored. Moreover, there is danger in thinking that women as legislators in male-dominated politics can save the world. Even if all the politicians were women, as long as the institutions and thinking remain patriarchal, there can be no essential change. Experience has taught us that there is unfortunately nothing magical about women in power.

I suggest we cannot accept identity as symbolic: we are not "woman"; we are—every one of us—a human being with personal characteristics that may or may not approximate some statistical norm or some mystical notion of what "woman" is. As feminists we need to guard as much against a new sentimentalized interpretation of women as against the romanticization of nature. We must learn to mistrust a sentimentalized view of women, motherhood, the home. In many cultures and religions throughout the world, where the mother is venerated, women are suppressed.

When gender differences in personality and development are considered "inherent," even though such differences may seem to be advantageous to women, the patriarchal perspective is being perpetuated. Any biological or "natural" differences among groups can eventually be skewed to favor the group in power. Thus the new field of ecopsychology needs from the start to avoid such assumptions that women are in some sense "closer" to nature than men and therefore more intuitive, caring, and specially called to "save the Earth." Until every man accepts and expresses what has been called "the feminine" in his nature, and every woman is allowed to express what has been called "the masculine" in hers, we must be wary of setting ourselves apart as women in some new version of the noble savage, who bears all wisdom and will redress the wrongs and injustices of the world.

Ecofeminists and ecopsychologists together can move past such dubious dualistic notions, can go beyond the questionable cultural overvaluation of dominance, competition, and separation into a new vision of human identity. What we seek is wholeness and the creation of a new kind of knowing that cultivates rationality, self-confidence, intellect, and power alongside the nurturing, healing, compassionate, intuitive components of personality. Both ecofeminism and ecopsychology want to break free of the bonds of patriarchal inheritance, to become grounded in a new reality, aware of the sacred nature of each person and each being on the Earth. There is no Goddess in the sky; we are all the Goddess. Our saints and heroines are not dead; they live within us and, like the phoenix, are renewed each day.

Today the old exclusivities are disappearing; boundaries are breaking down; what has been ignored, neglected, or suppressed reappears with new strength. Beyond the citadel of the dominant rationality we move into a new ecological sensibility, the realm of the aesthetic imagination.

Let us imagine a postrational, postmechanistic, postdualistic philosophy where the place and experience of humans in the world will change qualitatively from the uniform reactions of lonely, indifferent individuals to patience, receptivity, and the multifarious; from aggression, isolation, and alienation to equality, cooperation, and involvement with the processes of nature; from grandiosity, closure, and control to celebration of the ordinary; from domination and hierarchy to a holistic communion of compassionate persons. Both the psychological and ecological implications of such a change are profound. As the ecofeminist and physicist Vandana Shiva reminds us, "The marginalization of women and the destruction of biodiversity go hand in hand. Loss of diversity is the price paid in the patriarchal model of progress which pushes inexorably toward monocultures, uniformity and homogeneity." Precisely because industrial "progress" has inflicted the same subjugation upon women that it has inflicted on nature, "an ecofeminist perspective propounds the need for a new cosmology and a new anthropology which recognizes that life in nature (which includes human beings) is maintained by means of cooperation, and mutual care and love." "Diversity," as Shiva puts it, is "the basis of women's politics and the politics of ecology."[3]

Beyond the dualism of scientific objectivism we can extend into forms of knowing other than the strictly rational and linear, a thinking "through the body," as Adrienne Rich calls it. What ecofeminism has to teach is a use of knowing as an encounter, a participation. No knowledge can be strictly detached or objective; this has been the valuable insight from quantum physics.

From the frontiers of science itself we can perceive a way beyond dualism. What is this new ecological sensibility? It is a flowing continuum of all the varying modes of perception, inclusive of and receptive to the teachings of the nonhuman world. The feminist ethic is also the ecological ethic of relationship and interrelationship, a philosophy of dialogue with multiple voices. This new feminism goes beyond gender into a politics of inclusion, of empathic connectedness. We understand now that our symbols are as important as our technologies, and our metaphors as important as our machines. There are other forms of power than "power over" or domination, for instance, the power of creativity implicit in nature. There are forms of growth other than the gross national product cited by the economists; there is psychological and spiritual growth waiting to be explored and developed. The dramatic political reversals of recent years have brought us to a pivotal point in the history of the Earth.

3. Maria Mies and Vandana Shiva, *Ecofeminism* (London: Zed Books, 1993), pp. 6, 164–65.

But change does not necessarily come from heroic or grandiose efforts. After long years of preparation, inner change may occur swiftly and suddenly. Great change can come from small, seemingly insignificant things—simple, ordinary things of everyday life that can radically alter our perceptions. There is no prescribed way for proceeding. The rituals and critiques of the ecofeminists and the theories and practice of the ecopsychologists may help us to explore and chart the territory, refining and perfecting our perception and intuition. Intuition itself, so misunderstood and ridiculed, can be viewed as an inherent aspect of our enlarged sense of knowing. Our intuitions are the fruit of meditation, contemplation, patience, and receptivity—in short, a close attention to both our outer and inner worlds. "Nature," as Goethe put it, "has neither core nor skin: she's both at once outside and in." What ecofeminism and ecopsychology have to offer is just this promise of connection: the inner with the outer, the self with the Other, the ordinary with the sacred, the person with the planet.

The Ecology of Magic

DAVID ABRAM

MAGIC SURVIVES IN the modern world primarily as carnival tricks or children's literature. But as David Abram discovered, in traditional societies magicians function as ecologists. An amateur sleight-of-hand artist as well as an ecological philosopher, Abram found that his research among the shamans of Bali radically changed his relations with the "more than human" world—until, that is, he returned to "civilization." His essay reminds us how much ecopsychology can learn from the ancient animistic sensibility, if we approach with patience and respect.

———————————

Late one evening, I stepped out of my little hut in the rice paddies of eastern Bali and found myself falling through space. Over my head the black sky was rippling with stars, densely clustered in some regions, almost blocking out the darkness between them, and loosely scattered in other areas, pulsing and beckoning to each other. Behind them all streamed the great river of light, with its several tributaries. But the Milky Way churned beneath me as well, for my hut was set in the middle of a large patchwork of rice paddies, separated from each other by narrow, two-foot-high dikes, and these paddies were all filled with water. By day, the surface of these pools reflected perfectly the blue sky, a re-

flection broken only by the thin, bright-green tips of new rice. But by
night, the stars themselves glimmered from the surface of the paddies,
and the river of light whirled through the darkness underfoot as well as
above; there seemed no ground in front of my feet, only the abyss of star-
studded space falling away forever.

I was no longer simply beneath the night sky, but also above it; the
immediate impression was of weightlessness. I might perhaps have been
able to reorient myself, to regain some sense of ground and gravity, were
it not for a fact that confounded my senses entirely: between the galaxies
below and the constellations above drifted countless fireflies, their lights
flickering like the stars, some drifting up to join the constellations overhead, others, like graceful meteors, slipping down from above to join
the constellations underfoot, and all these paths of light upward and
downward were mirrored, as well, in the still surface of the paddies. I
felt myself at times falling through space, at other moments floating and
drifting. I simply could not dispel the profound vertigo and giddiness;
the paths of the fireflies, and their reflections in the water's surface, held
me in a sustained trance. Even after I crawled back to my hut and shut
the door on this whirling world, the little room in which I lay seemed
itself to be floating free of the Earth.

Fireflies! It was in Indonesia, you see, that I was first introduced to
the world of insects, and there that I first learned of the great influence
that insects—such diminutive entities—could have upon the human
senses. I had traveled to Indonesia on a research grant to study magic—
more precisely, to study the relation between magic and medicine, first
among the traditional sorcerers, or *dukuns*, of the Indonesian archipelago, and later among the *djankris*, the traditional shamans of Nepal. The
grant had one unique aspect: I was to journey into rural Asia not out-
wardly as an anthropologist or academic researcher, but as an itinerant
magician in my own right, in hopes of gaining a more direct access to
the local sorcerers. I had been a professional sleight-of-hand magician
for five years, helping to put myself through college by performing in
clubs and restaurants throughout New England. I had, as well, taken a
year off from my studies in the psychology of perception to travel as a
street magician through Europe and, toward the end of that journey, had
spent some months in London, working with R. D. Laing and his associates, exploring the potential of using sleight-of-hand magic in psycho-

therapy as a means of engendering communication with distressed individuals largely unapproachable by clinical healers. As a result of this work I became interested in the relation, largely forgotten in the West, between folk medicine and magic.

This interest eventually led to the aforementioned grant, and to my sojourn as a magician in rural Asia. There, my sleight-of-hand skills proved invaluable as a means of stirring the curiosity of the local shamans. Magicians, whether modern entertainers or indigenous, tribal sorcerers, work with the malleable texture of perception. When the local sorcerers gleaned that I had at least some rudimentary skill in altering the common field of perception, I was invited into their homes, asked to share secrets with them, and eventually encouraged, even urged, to participate in various rituals and ceremonies.

But the focus of my research gradually shifted from a concern with the application of magical techniques in medicine and ritual curing, toward a deeper pondering of the traditional relation between magic and the natural world. This broader concern seemed to hold the keys to the earlier one. For none of the several island sorcerers whom I came to know in Indonesia, nor any of the *djankris* with whom I lived in Nepal, considered their work as ritual healers to be their major role or function within their communities. Most of them, to be sure, *were* the primary healers or "doctors" for the villages in their vicinity, and they were often spoken of as such by the inhabitants of those villages. But the villagers also sometimes spoke of them, in low voices and in very private conversations, as witches (*lejaks* in Bali)—dark magicians who at night might well be practicing their healing spells backward in order to afflict people with the very diseases that they would later cure by day. I myself never consciously saw any of the magicians or shamans with whom I became acquainted engage in magic for harmful purposes, nor any convincing evidence that they had ever done so. Yet I was struck by the fact that none of them ever did or said anything to counter such disturbing rumors and speculations, which circulated quietly through the regions where they lived. Slowly I came to recognize that it was through the agency of such rumors, and the ambiguous fears that such rumors engendered, that the sorcerers were able to maintain a basic level of privacy. By allowing the inevitable suspicions and fears to circulate unhindered in the region, the sorcerers ensured that only those who were in real and profound need of their skills would dare to approach them for help. This privacy, in turn, left the magicians free to their primary craft and function.

A clue to this function may be found in the circumstance that such magicians rarely dwell at the heart of their village; rather, their dwellings are commonly at the spatial periphery of the community amid the surrounding rice fields, at the edge of the forest, or among a cluster of boulders. For the magician's intelligence is not circumscribed *within* the society—its place is at the edge, mediating *between* the human community and the larger community of beings upon which the village depends for its nourishment and sustenance. This larger community includes, along with the humans, the multiple nonhuman entities that constitute the local landscape, from the myriad plants and animals that inhabit or move through the region, to the particular winds and weather patterns that inform the local geography, as well as the various landforms—forests, rivers, caves, mountains—that lend their specific character to the surrounding Earth.

The traditional magician, I came to discern, commonly acts as an intermediary between the human collective and the larger ecological field, ensuring that there is an appropriate flow of nourishment, not just from the landscape to the human inhabitants but from the human community back to the local Earth. By their rituals, trances, ecstasies, and "journeys," magicians ensure that the relation between human society and the larger society of beings is balanced and reciprocal, and that the village never takes more from the living land than it returns to it—not just materially, but with prayers, propitiations, and praise. The scale of a harvest or the size of a hunt is always negotiated between the tribal community and the natural world it inhabits. To some extent every adult in the community is engaged in this process of listening and attuning to the other presences that surround and influence daily life. But the shaman or sorcerer is the exemplary voyager in the intermediate realm between the human and the more-than-human worlds, the primary strategist and negotiator in any dealings with the Others.

And it is only as a result of his ongoing engagement with the animate powers that dwell beyond the strictly human community that the traditional magician is able to alleviate many individual illnesses that arise *within* that community. Disease, in most such cultures, is conceptualized as a disequilibrium within the sick person, or as the intrusion of a demonic or malevolent presence into his body. There are, at times, malevolent influences within the village that disrupt the health and emotional well-being of susceptible individuals within the community. Yet such destructive influences within the human group are commonly traceable to an imbalance between the human collective and the larger field of forces in which it is embedded. Only those persons who, by their everyday practice, are involved in monitoring and modulating the relations *between* the human village and the larger animate environment, are able to appropriately diagnose, treat, and ultimately relieve personal ailments and illnesses arising *within* the village. Any healer who was not simultaneously attending to the complex relations between the human community and the larger more-than-human field will likely dispel an illness from one person only to have the same problem arise (perhaps in a new guise) somewhere else in the village. Hence, the traditional magician or "medicine person" functions primarily as an intermediary between human and nonhuman worlds, and only secondarily as a healer. Without a continually adjusted awareness of the relative balance or imbalance between the local culture and its nonhuman environment, along with the skills necessary to modulate that primary relation, any "healer" is worthless—indeed, not a healer at all. The medicine person's primary allegiance, then, is not to the human community, but to the earthly web of relations in which that community is embedded—it is from this that her or his power to alleviate human illness derives.

The primacy of nonhuman nature for magicians, and the centrality of their relation to other species and to the Earth, is not always evident to Western researchers. Countless anthropologists have managed to overlook the ecological dimension of the shaman's craft, while writing at great length of the shaman's rapport with "supernatural" entities. We can attribute much of this oversight to the modern, civilized assumption that the natural world is largely determinate and mechanical, and that what is experienced as mysterious, powerful, and beyond human ken must therefore be of some other, nonphysical realm above nature—"supernatural." Nevertheless, that which is viewed with the greatest awe and wonder by indigenous, oral cultures is, I suggest, none other than what we would call *nature* itself. The deeply mysterious powers and entities with whom the shaman enters into a rapport are the same forces—

plants, animals, forests, and winds—that to literate, "civilized" Europeans are just so much scenery, the pleasant backdrop of our more pressing human concerns.

To be sure, the shaman's ecological function, his or her role as intermediary between human society and the land, is not always obvious at first blush, even to a sensitive observer. We see the shaman being called upon to cure an ailing tribe member of his or her sleeplessness, or perhaps simply to locate some missing goods; we witness him entering into trance and sending his awareness into other dimensions in search of insight and aid. Yet we should not be so ready to interpret these dimensions as "supernatural," nor as realms entirely "internal" to the personal psyche of the practitioner. For it is likely that the "inner world" of our Western psychological experience, like the supernatural heaven of Christian belief, originated in the loss of our ancestral reciprocity with the living landscape. When the animate presences with whom we have evolved over several million years are suddenly construed as having less significance than ourselves, when the generative earth that gave birth to us is defined as a soulless or determinate object devoid of sensitivity and sentience, then that wild otherness with which human life had always been entwined must migrate, either into a supersensory heaven beyond the natural world, or else into the human skull itself—the only allowable refuge, in *this* world, for what is ineffable and unfathomable.

But in genuinely oral, tribal cultures, the sensuous world itself remains the dwelling place of the gods, the numinous powers that can either sustain or extinguish human life. It is not by sending his awareness out *beyond* the natural world that the shaman makes contact with the purveyors of life and health, nor by journeying into his personal psyche; rather it is by propelling his awareness *laterally*, outward into the depths of a landscape *at once sensuous and psychological,* this living dream that we share with the soaring hawk, the spider, and the stone silently sprouting lichens on its coarse surface.

In keeping with the popular view of shamanism as a tool for personal transcendence, the most sophisticated definition of "magic" that now circulates through the American counterculture is "the ability or power to alter one's consciousness at will." There is no mention made of any *reason* for altering one's state of consciousness. Yet in tribal cultures that which we call "magic" takes all of its meaning from the fact that, in an indigenous and oral context, humans experience their own intelligence as simply *one* form of awareness among many others. The traditional magician cultivates an ability to shift out of his or her common state of consciousness *precisely in order to make contact with other species on their own terms.* Only by temporarily shedding the accepted perceptual logic of his or her culture can the shaman hope to enter into a rapport with the multiple nonhuman sensibilities that animate the local landscape. It is this, we might say, that defines a shaman: the ability to readily slip out of the perceptual boundaries that demarcate his or her particular culture—boundaries reinforced by social customs, taboos, and, most important, the common speech or language—in order to make contact with, and learn from, the other powers in the land. Shamanic magic is precisely this heightened receptivity to the meaningful solicitations—songs, cries, and gestures—of the larger, more-than-human field.

The magician's relation to nonhuman nature was not at all my intended focus when I embarked on my research into the medical uses of magic and medicine in Indonesia, and it was only gradually that I became aware of this more subtle dimension of the native magician's craft. The first shift in my preconceptions came when I was staying for some days in the home of a young *balian,* or magic practitioner, in the interior of Bali. I had been provided with a simple bed in a separate, one-room building in the *balian*'s family compound (most homes in Bali comprise several separate small buildings set on a single enclosed plot of land). Early each morning the *balian*'s wife came by to bring me a small plate of delicious fruit, which I ate by myself, sitting on the ground outside, leaning against my hut and watching the sun slowly climb through the rustling palm leaves.

I noticed, when she delivered the plate of fruit, that my hostess was also balancing a tray containing many little green bowls—small, boat-shaped platters, each of them woven neatly from a freshly cut section of palm frond. The platters were two or three inches long, and within each was a small mound of white rice. After handing me my breakfast, the woman and the tray disappeared from view behind the other buildings, and when she came by some minutes later to pick up my empty plate, the tray was empty as well.

On the second morning, when I saw the array of tiny rice platters, I asked my hostess what they were for. Patiently, she explained to me that they were offerings for the household spirits. When I inquired about the Balinese term that she used for "spirit," she repeated the explanation in Indonesian, saying that these were gifts for the spirits of the family compound, and I saw that I had understood her correctly. She handed me a bowl of sliced papaya and mango and slipped around the corner of the building. I pondered for a minute, then set down the bowl, stepped to the side of my hut, and peered through the trees. I caught sight of her crouched low beside the corner of one of the other buildings, carefully setting what I presumed was one of the offerings on the ground. Then she stood up with the tray, walked back to the other corner, and set down another offering. I returned to my bowl of fruit and finished my breakfast.

That afternoon, when the rest of the household was busy, I walked back behind the building where I had seen her set down two of the offerings. There were the green platters resting neatly at the two rear corners of the hut. But the little mounds of rice within them were gone.

The next morning I finished the sliced fruit, waited for my hostess to come by and take the empty bowl, then quietly headed back behind the buildings. Two fresh palm-leaf offerings sat at the same spots where the others had been the day before. These were filled with rice. Yet as I gazed at one of them I suddenly noticed, with a shudder, that one of the kernels of rice was moving. Only when I knelt down to look more closely did I see a tiny line of black ants winding through the dirt to the palm leaf. Peering still closer, I saw that two ants had already climbed onto the offering and were struggling with the uppermost kernel of rice; as I watched, one of them dragged the kernel down and off the leaf, then set off with it back along the advancing line of ants. The second ant took another kernel and climbed down the mound of rice, dragging and pushing, and fell over the edge of the leaf; then a third climbed onto the offering. The column of ants emerged from a thick clump of grass around a nearby palm tree. I walked over to the other offering and discovered another column of tiny ants dragging away the rice kernels. There was an offering on the ground behind my building as well, and a nearly identical line of ants. I walked back to my room chuckling to myself. The *balian* and his wife had gone to so much trouble to daily placate the household spirits with gifts—only to have them stolen by little six-legged thieves. What a waste! But then a strange thought dawned within me. What if the ants themselves were the "household spirits" to whom the offerings were being made?

The idea became less strange as I pondered the matter. The family compound, like most on this tropical island, had been constructed in the vicinity of several ant colonies. Since a great deal of household cooking took place in the compound, and also the preparation of elaborate offerings of foodstuffs for various rituals and festivals, the grounds and the buildings were vulnerable to infestations by the ant population. Such invasions could range from rare nuisances to a periodic or even constant siege. It became apparent that the daily palm-frond offerings served to preclude such an attack by the natural forces that surrounded (and underlay) the family's land. The daily gifts of rice kept the ant colonies occupied—and, presumably, satisfied. Placed in regular, repeated locations at the corners of various structures around the compound, the offerings seemed to establish certain boundaries between the human and ant communities; by honoring this boundary with gifts, the humans apparently hoped to persuade the insects to respect the boundary and not enter the buildings.

Yet I remained puzzled by my hostess's assertion that these were gifts "for the spirits." To be sure there has always been some confusion between our Western notion of "spirit" (which so often is defined in contrast to matter or "flesh"), and the mysterious presences to which tribal and indigenous cultures pay so much respect. Many of the earliest Western students of these other languages and customs were Christian missionaries all too ready to see occult ghosts and immaterial spirits where the tribespeople were simply offering their respect to the local winds. While the notion of "spirit" has come to have, for us in the West, a primarily anthropomorphic or human association, my encounter with the ants was the first of many experiences suggesting to me that the "spirits" of an indigenous culture are primarily those modes of intelligence or awareness that do not possess a human form.

As humans we are well acquainted with the needs and capacities of the human body—we *live* our own bodies and so know, from within, the possibilities of our form. We cannot know, with the same familiarity and intimacy, the lived experience of a grass snake or a snapping turtle, nor can we readily experience the precise sensations of a hummingbird sipping nectar from a flower, or a rubber tree soaking up sunlight. Our experience may well be a variant of these other modes of sensitivity; nevertheless we cannot, as humans, experience entirely the living sensations of another form. We do not know, with full clarity, their desires or motivations—we cannot know, or can never be *sure* that we know, what they know. That the deer experiences sensations, that it carries knowledge of how to orient in the land, of where to find food and how to protect its young, that it knows well how to survive in the forest without the tools upon which we depend, is readily evident to our human senses. That the mango tree has the ability to create or bear fruit, or the yarrow plant the power to reduce a child's fever, is also evident. To humankind, these Others are purveyors of secrets, carriers of intelligence that we ourselves often need: it is these Others who can inform us of unseasonable changes in the weather, or warn us of imminent eruptions and earthquakes—who show us, when we are foraging, where we may find the best food or the best route back home. We receive from them countless gifts of food, fuel, shelter, and clothing. Yet still they remain Other to us, inhabiting their own cultures and enacting their own rituals, never wholly fathomable. Finally, it is not only those entities acknowledged by Western civilization as "alive," not only the other animals or the plants that speak, as spirits, to the senses of an oral culture, but also the meandering river from which those animals drink, and the torrential monsoon rains, and the stone that fits neatly into the palm of the hand.

Bali, of course, is hardly an aboriginal culture; the complexity of its temple architecture, the intricacy of its irrigation systems, the resplendence of its colorful festivals and crafts all bespeak the influence of various civilizations—most notably the Hindu complex of India. In Bali, nevertheless, these influences are thoroughly intertwined with the indigenous animism of the Indonesian archipelago; the Hindu gods and goddesses have been appropriated, as it were, by the more volcanic spirits of the local terrain.

Yet the underlying animistic cultures of Indonesia, like those of many islands in the Pacific, are steeped as well in beliefs often referred to by anthropologists as "ancestor worship." Some may argue that the ritual reverence paid to one's long-dead human ancestors, and the assumption of their influence in present life, easily invalidates my contention that the various "powers" or "spirits" that move throughout the discourse of indigenous, oral peoples are ultimately tied to *non*human (but nonetheless sentient) forces in the enveloping terrain.

This objection trades upon certain notions implicit in Christian civilization, such as the assumption that the "spirits" of dead persons necessarily retain their human form, or that they reside in a domain entirely beyond the material world to which our senses give us access. However, many indigenous, tribal peoples have no such ready recourse to an immaterial realm outside earthly nature. For most oral cultures, the enveloping and sensuous Earth remains the dwelling place of both the living *and* the dead. The "body"—human or otherwise—is not yet a mechanical object. It is a magical entity, the mind's own sensuous aspect, and at death the body's decomposition into soil, worms, and dust can only signify the gradual reintegration of one's elders and ancestors into the living landscape, from which all, too, are born.

Each indigenous culture elaborates this recognition of metamorphosis in its own fashion, taking its clues from the particular terrain in which it is embedded. Often the invisible atmosphere that animates the visible world—the subtle presence that circulates both within us and around all things—retains within itself the spirit or breath of the dead person until the time when that breath will enter and animate another visible body—a bird, or a deer, or a field of wild grain. Some cultures may cremate the body in order to more completely return the person, as smoke, to the swirling air, while that which departs as flame is offered to the sun and stars, and what lingers as ash is fed to the dense earth. Still other cultures, like some in the Himalayas, may dismember the body, leaving certain parts where they will likely be found by condors or consumed by leopards or wolves, thus hastening the reincarnation of that person into a particular animal realm within the landscape. Such examples illustrate simply that death, in tribal cultures, initiates a metamorphosis wherein the person's presence does not "vanish" from the sensible world (where would it go?) but rather remains as an animating force within the vastness of the landscape—whether subtly, in the wind; more visibly, in animal form; or even as the eruptive, ever-to-be-appeased wrath of the volcano. "Ancestor worship" in its myriad forms, then, is ultimately another mode of attentiveness to nonhuman nature; it signifies not so much an awe or reverence of human powers, but rather a reverence for those forms that awareness takes when it is *not* in human form, when the familiar human embodiment dies and decays to become part of the encompassing cosmos.

This cycling of the human back into the larger world ensures that the other forms of experience we encounter, whether ants, or willow trees, or clouds, are never absolutely alien to ourselves. Despite the very obvious differences in shape, ability, and style of being, they remain at least distantly familiar, even familial. It is, paradoxically, this perceived kinship or consanguinity that renders the difference, or otherness, so eerily potent.[1]

My exposure to traditional magicians and seers was gradually shifting my senses; I became increasingly susceptible to the solicitations of non-human things. When a magician spoke of a power or "presence" lingering in the corner of his house, I learned to notice the ray of sunlight that was then pouring through a chink in the wall, illuminating a column of drifting dust, and to realize that that column of light was indeed a power, influencing the air currents by its warmth, and indeed influencing the whole mood of the room; although I had not consciously seen it before, it had already been structuring my experience. My ears began to attend, in a new way, to the songs of birds—no longer just a melodic background to human speech, but meaningful speech in its own right, responding to and commenting on events in the surrounding Earth. I became a student of subtle differences: the way a breeze might flutter a single leaf on a tree, leaving the others silent and unmoved (had not that leaf, then, been brushed by a magic?); or how the intensity of the sun's heat expresses itself in the precise rhythm of the crickets. Walking along the dirt paths, I learned to slow my pace in order to *feel* the difference between one nearby hill and the next, or to taste the presence of a particular field at a certain time of day when, as I had been told by a local *dukun*, the place had a special power and proffered unique gifts. It was a power communicated to my senses by the way the shadows of the trees

1. The similarity between such a worldview and the emerging perspective of contemporary ecology is not trivial. Atmospheric geochemist James Lovelock, elucidating the Gaia hypothesis, insists that the geologic environment is itself constituted by organic life and by the products of organic metabolism. In his words, we inhabit "a world that is the breath and bones of our ancestors." "Gaia: The World as Living Organism," *New Scientist* (December 18, 1986), 25–28.

fell at that hour, by smells that only then lingered in the tops of the grasses without being wafted away by the wind, by other elements I could only isolate after many days of stopping and listening.

Gradually, then, other animals began to intercept me in my wanderings, as if some quality in my posture or the rhythm of my breathing had disarmed their wariness; I would find myself face to face with monkeys, and with large lizards that did not slither away when I spoke, but leaned forward in apparent curiosity. In rural Java I often noticed monkeys accompanying me in the branches overhead, and ravens walked toward me on the road, croaking. While at Pangandaran, a nature preserve on a peninsula jutting out from the south coast of Java ("a place of many spirits," I was told by nearby fishermen), I stepped out from a clutch of trees and found myself looking into the face of one of the rare and beautiful bison that exist only on that island. Our eyes locked. When it snorted, I snorted back; when it shifted its shoulders, I shifted my stance; when I tossed my head, it tossed *its* head in reply. I found myself caught in a nonverbal conversation with this Other, a gestural duet with which my reflective awareness had very little to do. It was as if my body were suddenly being motivated by a wisdom older than my thinking mind, as though it was held and moved by a logos, deeper than words, spoken by the Other's body, the trees, the air, and the stony ground on which we stood.

I returned to North America excited by the new sensibilities that had stirred in me—my newfound awareness of a more-than-human world, of the great potency of the land, and particularly of the keen intelligence of other animals, large and small, whose lives and cultures interpenetrate our own. I startled neighbors by chattering with squirrels, who swiftly climbed down the trunks of trees to banter with me, or by gazing for hours on end at a heron fishing in a nearby estuary, or at gulls dropping clams on the rocks along the beach.

Yet very gradually, I began to lose my sense of the animals' own awareness. The gulls' technique for breaking open the clams began to appear as a largely automatic behavior, and I could not easily feel the attention they must bring to each new shell. Perhaps each shell was entirely the same as the last, and *no* spontaneous attention was necessary.

I found myself now observing the heron from outside its world, noting with interest its careful high-stepping walk, and the sudden dart of its beak into the water, but no longer feeling its tensed yet poised alertness with my own muscles. And, strangely, the suburban squirrels no longer responded to my chittering calls. Although I wished to, I could no longer engage in their world as I had so easily done a few weeks earlier, for my attention was quickly deflected by internal verbal deliberations of one sort or another, by a conversation I now seemed to carry on entirely within myself. The squirrels had no part in this conversation.

It became increasingly apparent, from books and articles and discussions with various people, that other animals were *not* as awake and aware as I had assumed, that they lacked any real language and hence the possibility of thought, and that even their seemingly spontaneous responses to the world around them were largely "programmed" behaviors, "coded" in the genetic material now being mapped by our scientists. Increasingly, I came to discern that there was no common ground between the unlimited human intellect and the limited sentience of other animals, no medium through which we and they might communicate and reciprocate one another.

But as the expressive and sentient landscape slowly faded behind my more exclusively human concerns, threatening to become little more than an illusion or fantasy, I began to feel—particularly in my chest and my abdomen—as though I were being cut off from vital sources of nourishment.

Today, in the "developed world," many persons in search of spiritual self-understanding are enrolling for workshops and courses in "shamanic" methods of personal discovery and revelation. Meanwhile psychotherapists and some physicians have begun to specialize in "shamanic healing techniques." "Shamanism" has come, thus, to denote an alternative form of therapy; the emphasis, among these new practitioners of popular shamanism, is on personal insight and curing. These are noble aims, to be sure, yet they are, I believe, secondary to *and derivative from* the primary role of the indigenous shaman, a role that cannot be fulfilled without long and sustained exposure to wild nature, its patterns and vicissitudes. Mimicking the indigenous shaman's curative methods without knowledge of his or her relation to the wider natural community cannot, if I am correct, do anything more than trade certain symptoms for others, or shift the locus of dis-ease from place to place within the human community. For the source of stress lies in the relation between the human community and the living land that sustains it.

Sadly, our culture's relation to the animate Earth can in no way be considered a reciprocal or balanced one: with thousands of acres of non-regenerating forest disappearing every hour, and hundreds of our fellow species becoming extinct each month as a result of our civilization's excesses, we can hardly be surprised by the amount of epidemic illness in our culture, from increasingly severe immune dysfunctions and cancers, to widespread psychological distress, depression, and ever-more-frequent suicides, to the growing number of murders committed for no apparent reason by otherwise coherent individuals.

From an animistic perspective, the clearest source of all this distress, both physical and psychological, lies in the violence uselessly perpetrated by our civilization on the ecology of the planet; only by alleviating the latter will we be able to heal the former. This may sound at first like a simple statement of faith, yet it makes eminent and obvious sense as soon as we acknowledge our thorough dependence upon the countless other organisms with whom we have evolved. Caught up in a mass of abstractions, our attention hypnotized by a host of human-made technologies that only reflect us back upon ourselves, it is all too easy for us to forget our carnal inherence in a more-than-human matrix of sensations and sensibilities. Our bodies have formed themselves in delicate reciprocity with the manifold textures, sounds, and shapes of an animate Earth; our eyes have evolved in subtle interaction with *other* eyes, as our ears are attuned by their very structure to the howling of wolves and the honking of geese. To shut ourselves off from these other voices, to continue by our life-styles to condemn these other sensibilities to the oblivion of extinction, is to rob our own senses of their integrity, and to rob our minds of their coherence. We are human only in contact and conviviality with what is not human. Only in reciprocity with what is Other do we begin to heal ourselves.

Keepers of the Earth

JEANNETTE ARMSTRONG

FOR THE LAST word in this anthology, we turn to the greater tradition of spiritual healing that predates and surrounds the psychology of modern industrial society. Jeannette Armstrong's essay might be read as an exercise in psychological and linguistic archaeology. She leads us through a searching analysis of sanity and madness as they are understood in her culture. Like many of the world's endangered indigenous languages, Okanagan compounds its vocabulary from a multiplicity of meanings; each syllable contains the insight of generations. Words are the history book of the people. Over the generations, "madness," as the Okanagans use the term, has accumulated a rich store of sociological, metaphysical, and environmental meanings. In the Okanagan fourfold vision of the self we can discern elements that anticipate the insights of Jungian, humanistic, Gestalt, and transpersonal psychology. Ecopsychology can be found there too, in Armstrong's conviction that "our most essential responsibility is to learn to bond our whole individual selves and our communal selves to the land."

—————

Scattered and Wild

As a child of ten, I once sat on a hillside on the reservation with my father and his mother as they looked down into the town in the valley floor. It was blackcap berry season and the sun was very warm, but there in the high country, a cool breeze moved through the overshading pines. Blue-birds and canaries darted and chirped in nearby bushes while a mead-owlark sang for rain from the hillside above. Sage and wild roses sent their messages out to the humming bees and pale yellow butterflies.

Down in the valley the heat waves danced, and dry dust rose in clouds from the dirt roads near the town. Shafts of searing glitter reflected off hundreds of windows, while smoke and grayish haze hung over the town itself. The angry sounds of cars honking in a slow crawl along the shimmering black highway and the grind of large machinery from the sawmill next to the town rose in a steady buzzing overtone to the quiet of our hillside.

My grandmother said (translated from Okanagan), "The people down there are dangerous, they are all insane." My father agreed, commenting, "It's because they are wild and scatter anywhere."

I remember looking down into the town and being afraid.

The words my grandmother and my father used to describe the new-comers in the valley offer a way into the perspective I wish to share with you.

Since that day with my grandmother and my father, I have heard the Okanagan terms for "insane" and "wild" used many times by many of my people to describe deeds of the newcomers that make no sense to us. I have come to discern the meanings in those terms as they are applied by an Okanagan person whose approach to life is other than that of the mainstream culture.

I have always felt that my Okanagan view is perhaps closer in expe-rience to that of an eyewitness and refugee surrounded by holocaust. I draw on this experience of witness to frame my own comments on a social crisis that has been interpreted in various fields of study as critical. As a Native American, I have felt that crisis as a personal struggle against an utterly pervasive phenomenon. My conflict has been to unremittingly resist its entrapment, while knowing that it affects every breath I draw. Through the lens of that perspective, I view the disorder that is displayed in our city streets, felt in our communities, endured in our homes, and carried inside as personal pain. I have come to the same conclusion as my grandmother and father that day long ago when we watched the new-comers enter the valley: "The people down there are dangerous, they are all insane."

My view could be thought of as a way to differentiate from the new-comers' experience of the world. I do not wish to draw conclusions about the newcomers, culture or psychology; however, I do wish to assist in seeking junctures in philosophy at which a transformative potential may be implicit.

Okanagan: A Language That Connects

Although I will do my best to share the way I, as an Okanagan born into this maelstrom, perceive the situation, I can do this only within the limited capacity permitted by a language that does not contain the words I require. My dilemma is to use the English language in a way that brings my meaning into clarity. I find that I must do this by deconstructing meanings in English that seem to me to affirm a cloistered view of things and by constructing new meanings.

I offer a way to look at the Okanagan parallel of the word "insane" and its meaning in order to illustrate some fundamental ways in which the Okanagan language differs in process from English.

I have no trouble remembering Okanagan words uttered a considerable time ago; this is because of the way the Okanagan language replays images in the mind. Okanagan is exclusively vocally rooted; it was never a written language, never transformed into visual symbols that could be translated back into sounds. It was always spoken.

I believe it may be wise to question the idea that language is a system of sound symbols, that is, that the word, as a sound, represents something definable. My thinking is that symbols, seen as compact surrogates of things, seem to take on a concreteness in and of themselves that supplants reality. Words in that sense define the reality rather than letting the reality define itself. Language sounds would be better regarded as patterns that call forth realities, as a sort of directional signal to a time and place.

Very loosely, I describe the Okanagan language as a system of sounds through which meaning is called forth by combining a variety of syllables that describe moving pieces of an ongoing reality that stretches away from the speaker. The active reality could be thought of as a sphere sliced into many circles. A circle could be thought of as a physical plane surrounding the speaker; this could be called "the present." Moving above and below the speaker, the surrounding sphere may be thought of as the "past" or the "future," with everything always connected to the present reality of the speaker. The Okanagan language creates links by connecting active pieces of reality rather than isolating them.

Although the present tense in the English language seems all-pervasive, "now" is actually an insubstantial thing that is tied to place in a very untenable way. "Now" just continues, as does all else; therefore we might perceive my meaning better if we leave the designations for "past," "present," and "future" aside and think instead of a vast thing that is continuing, in which we are immersed, and that we can call by making certain sounds.

If we put aside designations like nouns and verbs and think simply of sounds that revive components of reality from that in which we are continuously immersed, then we can think of a language that remakes little parts of a larger ongoing activity. This creates a system in which syllables are animated describers of pieces of activity and can be combined to develop meanings that then give a more complete picture, and could end up close to what might constitute a noun or a verb in English—though they are quite different to me when experienced in the mind.

Talking Talking Inside the Head

The Okanagan word for "insane" is a good example of this. The four syllables in the word, which are used to form the meaning, are each minidescriptions of an active reality. When put together they form a whole picture, which then becomes an action image describing "in a state of talking talking inside the head." Doubling the description "in the act of talking" forms a minipicture of *opposing* voices rather than simply *many* voices. The meaning of the word relies on further connection for coherence in context. It requires a larger active picture. The meaning can then become quite specific.

If I were to interpret/transliterate the Okanagan meaning of my grandmother's words, it might be this: "The ones below who are not of us [as place], may be a chaotic threat in action; they are all self-absorbed [arguing] inside each of their heads." My father's words might be something like this: "Their actions have a source, they have displacement panic, they have been pulled apart from themselves as family [generational sense] and place [as land/us/survival]."

In examining the meanings in this brief dialogue, the differences become clearer between self, community, surroundings, and time sense as understood in the mainstream culture from the Okanagan view of a healthy, whole person. I comment on my view of each only as I perceive them. I do not speak for the Okanagan people; rather I speak of my knowledge as an Okanagan.

By describing these differences, I wish to make clear why my grandmother and my father spoke those words that day long ago when we watched the newcomers enter the valley, words with which I know I agree: "The people down there are dangerous; they are all insane."

The Four Selves

The first difference I want to explore has to do with the idea of what we are as an individual life force within our skins, and how we might think that in relation to the unseen terrain we traverse as we walk the land. I speak of how we perceive that, and in consequence how we perceive the effect on the world around us.

When we, as Okanagans, speak of ourselves as individual beings within our bodies, we think of our whole being as made up of various capacities. We identify the whole person as having four main capacities that operate together: the physical self, the emotional self, the thinking, intellectual self, and the spiritual self. The four selves can be described as having equal importance in the way we function within and experience all things. The capacities can loosely be described as what joins us with the rest of creation in a healthy way. Each, including the body, is an internal capacity parallel to what is thought of as "mind."

The physical self, which is body as one part of the whole self, is dependent entirely on everything that sustains it and keeps it alive in an interface with the parts of us that continue outside the skin. We survive within our skin inside the rest of our vast selves. We survive by how our body interacts with everything around us continuously. Only in part are we aware in our intellect, through our senses, of that interaction. Okanagans teach that the body is the Earth itself. They say that our flesh, blood, and bones are Earth-body; in all cycles in which the Earth moves, so does our body. We are everything that surrounds us, including the vast forces we only glimpse. If we cannot maintain and stay in balance with the outer self, then we cannot continue as an individual life-form, and we dissipate back into the larger self. Our body-mind is extremely knowledgeable in that way. As Okanagans we say our body is sacred; it is the core of our being, which permits the rest of self to be. It is the great gift of our existence. Our word for body literally means "the land-dreaming capacity."

The emotional self is differentiated from the body-self, the thinking, intellectual self, and the spiritual self. In our language, the emotional self is thought of as the part with which we link to other parts of our larger selves around us. We use a term that translates as "heart." It is a capacity to bond and form attachment with particular parts and aspects of our surroundings. We say that we as people stay connected to each other, our land, and all things by our hearts.

As Okanagans we teach that this is an essential element of being whole, human, and Okanagan. We never ask a person, "What do you think?" Instead we ask, "What is your heart on this matter?" The Okanagan teaches that emotion or feeling is the capacity whereby community and land intersect in our beings and become part of us. By this capacity we are one with others and all our surroundings. This bond or link is a priority for our individual wholeness and well-being. The strength with which we bond in the widest of circles gives us our criterion for leadership. It is the source from which the arts spring in celebration and affirmation of our connectedness.

The thinking, intellectual self has another name in Okanagan. Our word for "thinking/logic" and "storage of information" (memory) is difficult to translate into English because it does not have a full parallel. The words that come closest in my interpretation have the meaning "the spark that ignites." We think of this capacity as simply a beginning point from which other things occur. We use a term that translates as "directed by the ignited spark" to refer to analytical thought. In the Okanagan language we translate this to mean that the other capacities we engage in when we take action are only directed by the spark of memory once it is ignited. We know in our traditional Okanagan methods of education that this self must be disciplined to work in concert with the other selves in order to engage its abilities far beyond its automatic-response capacity. We know, too, that unless we always join this capacity to the heart-self, its power can be a destructive force both with respect to ourselves and to the larger selves that surround us. A fire that is not controlled can destroy.

The spirit-self is hardest to translate. It is also referred to by the Okanagan as a part of the individual being, while at the same time being the larger self of which all things are part. We translate the word used for our spirit-self as "without substance while moving continuously outward." The Okanagan language teaches that this self requires a great quietness before our other parts can become conscious of it, and that the other capacities fuse together and subside in order to activate something else—which is this capacity. Okanagans describe this capacity as the place where all things are. It teaches that this old part of us can "hear/interpret" all knowledge being spoken by all things that surround us, including our own bodies, in order to bring new knowledge into existence. The Okanagan says that this is the true self; it has great power. It is a source for all things and affects all things if we engage it within the rest of our life-force activity. The Okanagan refers to it as the living source of our life.

Community: Our One Skin

The second difference I wish to discuss is our relationship as social beings to human social constructs. I want to outline how the Okanagan perceives this and how it might affect people around us.

A teaching of the Okanagan is that each person is born into a family and a community. No person is born isolated from those two things. You are born into a way of interacting with one another. As an Okanagan you are automatically a part of the rest of the community. You belong. You are them. You are within family and community. You are that which is family and community; within that you cannot be separate. You are not separate unless you totally leave people and live alone in the land.

All are affected by the actions of any one individual within family and community, and so all must know this in their individual selves. This capacity to bond is absolutely critical to individual wellness. Without it the person is said to be "crippled/incapacitated" and "lifeless." To not have community or family is to be scattered or falling apart.

The Okanagan refers to relationship to others by a word that means "our one skin." This means that we share more than a place; we share a physical tie that is uniquely human. It also means that the bond of community and family is a history of many before us and many ahead of us who share our flesh. We are tied together by those who brought us here and gave us blood and gave us place. Our most serious teaching is that community comes first in our choices, then family, and then ourselves as individuals, because without community and family we are truly not human.

The Language of the Land

The third difference between the Okanagan perception of the self and that of the dominant culture has to do with the "us" that is place: the capacity to know we are everything that surrounds us; to experience our humanness in relation to all else and in consequence to know how we affect the world around us.

The Okanagan word for "our place on the land" and "our language" is the same. The Okanagan language is thought of as the "language of the land." This means that the land has taught us our language. The way we survived is to speak the language that the land offered us as its teachings. To know all the plants, animals, seasons, and geography is to construct language for them.

We also refer to the land and our bodies with the same root syllable. This means that the flesh which is our body is pieces of the land come to us through the things which the land is. The soil, the water, the air, and all other life-forms contributed parts to be our flesh. *We are our land/ place*. Not to know and to celebrate this is to be without language and without land. It is to be *dis-placed*.

The Okanagan teaches that anything displaced from all that it requires to survive in health will eventually perish. Unless place can be relearned, it compels all other life forms to displacement and then ruin. This is what is referred to as "wildness": a thing that cannot survive without special protective measures and that requires other life forms to change behavior in its vicinity.

As Okanagans, our most essential responsibility is to learn to bond our whole individual selves and our communal selves to the land. Many of our ceremonies have been constructed for this. We join with the larger self, outward to the land, and rejoice in all that we are. We are this one part of Earth. Without this self we are not human: we yearn; we are incomplete; we are wild, needing to learn our place as land pieces. We cannot find joy because we need place in this sense to nurture and protect our family/community/self. The thing Okanagans fear worst of all is to be removed from the land that is their life and their spirit.

Hands of the Spirit

The fourth difference between the Okanagan conception of the self and that of the dominant culture has to do with the idea that, as Earth pieces, we are an old life-form. As an old life-form, we each travel a short journey through time, in which we briefly occupy a space as a part of an old human presence on the land.

The Okanagan word for "Earth" uses the same root syllable as the word for our spirit-self. It is also the word for referring to all life forces as one spirit in the same way as the human spirit capacity. The Okanagan points out that all things are the same in this way. In that capacity everything we see is a spirit. Spirit is not something that is invisible, in the mind, or subjective. It exists. We are part of that existence in a microscopic way. The Okanagan teaches that we are tiny and unknowledgeable in our individual selves; it is the whole-Earth part of us that contains immense knowledge. Over the generations of human life, we have come to discern small parts of that knowledge, and humans house this internally. The way we act in our human capacity has significant effects on the Earth because it is said that we are the hands of the spirit, in that we can fashion Earth pieces with that knowledge and therefore transform the Earth. It is our most powerful potential, and so we are told that we are responsible for the Earth. We are keepers of the Earth because we are Earth. We are old Earth.

Suggested Readings

DAVID ABRAM

Duerr, Hans Peter. *Dreamtime: Concerning the Boundary Between Wilderness and Civilization*. Translated by Felicitas Goodman. New York: Basil Blackwell, 1985.

Merleau-Ponty, Maurice. *Phenomenology of Perception*. Translated by Colin Smith. London: Routledge and Kegan Paul, 1962.

———. *The Visible and the Invisible*. Translated by Alphonso Lingis. Evanston, Ill.: Northwestern University Press, 1968.

Thomas, Elizabeth Marshall. *Reindeer Moon*. Boston: Houghton Mifflin, 1987.

STEPHEN AIZENSTAT

Hillman, James. *A Blue Fire*. New York: Harper & Row, 1989.

Meier, Carl A. *A Testament to the Wilderness*. Santa Monica, Calif.: The Lapis Press, 1985.

Romanyshyn, Robert. *Technology as Symptom and Dream*. New York: Routledge, 1989.

Samuels, Andrew. *The Political Psyche*. New York: Routledge, 1993.

Sardello, Robert. *Facing the World with Soul*. Hudson, N.Y.: Lindisfarne, 1992.

Watkins, Mary. *Waking Dreams*. Dallas, Tex.: Spring Publications, 1984.

CARL ANTHONY

Anthony, Carl. "The Big House and the Slave Quarter." Parts 1 and 2. *Landscape,* Summer 1976; Autumn 1976.

———. "Why African Americans Should Be Environmentalists." In Brad Erickson (ed.), *A Call to Action*. San Francisco: Sierra Club Books, 1990.

Anthony, Carl, and Luke Cole. *Race, Poverty & the Environment: A Newsletter for Social and Environmental Justice.* San Francisco: Earth Island Institute.

Berry, Wendell. *The Hidden Wound.* San Francisco: North Point Press, 1989.

Bookchin, Murray. *The Ecology of Freedom.* Palo Alto, Calif.: Cheshire Books, 1982.

Bullard, Robert. *Confronting Environmental Racism.* Boston: South End Press, 1993.

Ehle, John. *Trail of Tears: The Rise and Fall of the Cherokee Nation.* New York: Anchor, 1988.

Frankenberg, Ruth. *White Women, Race Matters: The Social Construction of Whiteness.* Minneapolis: University of Minnesota Press, 1993.

Grier, William H., and Price Cobbs. *Black Rage.* New York: Bantam, 1968.

Huggins, Nathan Irvin. *Black Odyssey: The African American Ordeal in Slavery.* New York: Random House, 1990.

Kovel, Joel. *White Racism: A Psychohistory.* New York: Columbia University Press, 1984.

Morrison, Toni. *Playing in the Dark, Whiteness and the Literary Imagination.* Cambridge, Mass.: Harvard University Press, 1990.

Sliker, Gretchen. *Multiple Mind: Healing the Split in Psyche and World.* Boston: Shambhala, 1992.

WILLIAM CAHALAN

Berry, Wendell. *The Unsettling of America: Culture and Agriculture.* New York: Avon, 1977.

Cahalan, William. *The Earth Is Our Real Body: Cultivating Ecological Groundedness in Gestalt Therapy.* Available from the author: 603 Enright Ave., Cincinnati, OH 45205.

Fillipi, Linda. "Place, Feminism, and Healing: An Ecology of Pastoral Counseling." *Journal of Pastoral Care* (Fall 1991), 231–42.

Leopold, Aldo. *A Sand County Almanac and Sketches Here and There.* New York: Oxford University Press, 1987.

Lovelock, James. *Gaia: A New Look at Life on Earth.* New York: Oxford University Press, 1979.

Perls, Frederick, Ralph Hefferline, and Paul Goodman. *Gestalt Therapy: Excitement and Growth in the Human Personality.* New York: Dell, 1951.

Roszak, Theodore. *The Voice of the Earth: An Exploration of Ecopsychology.* New York: Touchstone, 1993.

Sale, Kirkpatrick. *Dwellers in the Land: The Bioregional Vision.* San Francisco: Sierra Club Books, 1985.

Searles, Harold. *The Nonhuman Environment in Normal Development and in Schizophrenia*. New York: International Universities Press, 1960.

Snyder, Gary. *The Practice of the Wild*. San Francisco: North Point Press, 1990.

SARAH CONN

Bellah, Robert N., Robert Madsen, William M. Sullivan, Ann Swidler, Steven M. Tipton. *Habits of the Heart: Individualism and Commitment in American Life*. New York: Harper & Row, 1985.

Berry, Thomas. *The Dream of the Earth*. San Francisco: Sierra Club Books, 1988.

Conn, Sarah A. "Protest and Thrive: The Relationship between Personal Responsibility and Global Empowerment." *New England Journal of Public Policy* 6, no. 1 (Spring/Summer 1990), 163–77.

———. "The Self-world Connection: Implications for Mental Health and Psychotherapy." *Woman of Power* 20 (Spring 1991), 71–77.

Jordan, Judith V., Alexandra Kaplan, Jean Baker Miller, Irene P. Stiver, Janet L. Surrey. *Women's Growth in Connection: Writings from the Stone Center*. New York: Guilford, 1991.

Miller, Jean Baker. *Toward a New Psychology of Women*. Boston: Beacon Press, 1976.

Miller, Jean Baker, and Janet Surrey. *Revisioning Women's Anger: The Personal and the Global*. Work in Progress, no. 43. Wellesley, Mass.: Stone Center Working Paper Series, Wellesley College, 1990.

Sampson, Edward E. "The Challenge of Social Change for Psychology: Globalization and Psychology's Theory of the Person." *American Psychologist* 44, no. 6 (1989), 914–21.

Seed, John, Joanna Macy, Patricia Fleming, Arne Naess (eds.). *Thinking Like a Mountain: Towards a Council of All Beings*. Philadelphia: New Society, 1988.

Wallach, Michael A., and Lise Wallach. *Psychology's Sanction for Selfishness: The Error of Egoism in Theory and Therapy*. San Francisco: Freeman, 1983.

Watkins, Mary. "From Individualism to the Interdependent Self: Changing the Paradigm of the Self in Psychotherapy." *Psychological Perspectives* 27 (1992), 52–69.

CHELLIS GLENDINNING

Berman, Morris. *The Re-enchantment of the World*. New York: Bantam, 1981.

Glendinning, Chellis. *When Technology Wounds*. New York: Morrow, 1990.

———. *My Name Is Chellis and I'm in Recovery from Western Civilization*. Boston: Shambhala, 1994.

Mander, Jerry. *In the Absence of the Sacred: The Failure of Technology and the Survival of the Indian Nations*. San Francisco: Sierra Club Books, 1991.

Mumford, Lewis. *The Myth of the Machine: Technics and Human Development*. New York: Harcourt, Brace, 1967.

Sahlins, Marshall. *Stone Age Economics*. New York: Aldine de Gruyter, 1972.

Shepard, Paul. *Nature and Madness*. San Francisco: Sierra Club Books, 1982.

Winner, Langdon. *Autonomous Technology*. Cambridge, Mass.: MIT Press, 1977.

MARY E. GOMES AND ALLEN D. KANNER

Chodorow, Nancy. *The Reproduction of Mothering: Psychoanalysis and the Sociology of Gender*. Berkeley and Los Angeles: University of California Press, 1978.

Dodge, Jim. "Living by Life: Some Bioregional Theory and Practice." In Van Andruss, Christopher Plant, Judith Plant, and Eleanor Wright (eds.), *Home! A Bioregional Reader*. Philadelphia: New Society, 1990.

Frye, Marilyn. *The Politics of Reality: Essays in Feminist Theory*. Freedom, Calif.: Crossing Press, 1983.

Hill, Gareth S. *Masculine and Feminine: The Natural Flow of Opposites in the Psyche*. Boston: Shambhala, 1992.

Kaschak, Ellyn. *Engendered Lives: A New Psychology of Women's Experience*. New York: HarperCollins, 1992.

Keller, Catherine. *From a Broken Web: Separation, Sexism, and Self*. Boston: Beacon Press, 1986.

Miller, Jean Baker. *Toward a New Psychology of Women*. Boston: Beacon Press, 1976.

Roszak, Theodore. *The Voice of the Earth: An Exploration of Ecopsychology*. New York: Touchstone, 1993.

Spretnak, Charlene. *States of Grace: The Recovery of Meaning in the Postmodern Age*. San Francisco: HarperSanFrancisco, 1991.

Surrey, Janet. "Relationship and Empowerment." In Judith Jordan, Alexandra Kaplan, Jean Baker Miller, Irene P. Stiver, Janet L. Surrey (eds.), *Women's Growth in Connection: Writings from the Stone Center*. New York: Guilford, 1991.

ROBERT GREENWAY

Bateson, Gregory. *Mind and Nature: A Necessary Unity*. New York: Bantam, 1988.

Berry, Thomas. *The Dream of the Earth*. San Francisco: Sierra Club Books, 1988.

Bohm, David, and B. J. Hiley. *The Undivided Universe: An Ontological Interpretation of Quantum Theory*. New York: Routledge, 1993.

Dewey, John. *Experience and Nature*. New York: Norton, 1929.

Duerr, Hans Peter. *Dreamtime: Concerning the Boundary between Wilderness and*

Civilization. Translated by Felicitas Goodman. New York: Basil Blackwell, 1985.

Goldsmith, Edward. *The Way: An Ecological World View*. Boston: Shambhala, 1993.

Griffin, Susan. *Woman and Nature: The Roaring Inside Her*. New York: Harper Colophon, 1978.

Halifax, Joan. *The Fruitful Darkness: Reconnecting with the Body of the Earth*. San Francisco: HarperSanFrancisco, 1993.

Hendee, John C., and Vance G. Martin (eds.). *International Wilderness Allocation, Management, and Research: A Symposium of the Fifth World Wilderness Congress*. Moscow, Idaho: Wilderness Research Center, University of Idaho, 1994.

LaChapelle, Dolores. *Sacred Land, Sacred Sex, Rapture of the Deep: Concerning Deep Ecology and Celebrating Life*. Silverton, Colo.: Finn Hill Arts, 1988.

MacCormack, Carol, and Marilyn Strathern (eds.). *Nature, Culture, and Gender*. New York: Cambridge University Press, 1986.

Macy, Joanna. *World as Lover, World as Self*. Berkeley, Calif.: Parallax Press, 1991.

Mindell, Arnold. *The Shaman's Body: A New Shamanism for Transforming Health, Relationships, and the Community*. San Francisco: HarperSanFranciso, 1993.

Oelschlaeger, Max. *The Idea of Wilderness: From Prehistory to the Age of Ecology*. New Haven: Yale University Press, 1991.

Snyder, Gary. *Turtle Island*. New York: New Directions, 1974.

Swimme, Brian, and Thomas Berry. *The Universe Story: From the Primordial Flaring Forth to the Ecozoic Era*. San Francisco: HarperSanFrancisco, 1992.

Tarthang Tulku. *Knowledge of Freedom*. Berkeley, Calif.: Dharma Publishing, 1984.

Wilber, Ken. *Up From Eden: A Transpersonal View of Human Evolution*. Boston: Shambhala, 1986.

Woodman, Marion. *The Pregnant Virgin: A Process of Psychological Transformation*. Toronto: Inner City Books, 1985.

ALLEN D. KANNER AND MARY E. GOMES

Cushman, Philip. "Why the Self Is Empty: Toward a Historically Situated Psychology." *American Psychologist* 45 (1990), 599–611.

Durning, Alan. *How Much Is Enough? The Consumer Society and the Future of the Earth*. New York: Norton, 1992.

Johnson, Stephen M. *Humanizing the Narcissistic Style*. New York: Norton, 1987.

Larsen, Erik. *The Naked Consumer: How Our Private Lives Become Public Commodities*. London: Penguin, 1992.

Lee, Martin A., and Norman Solomon. *Unreliable Sources: A Guide to Detecting Bias in News Media.* New York: Lyle Stuart, 1990.

Mander, Jerry. *In the Absence of the Sacred: The Failure of Technology and the Survival of the Indian Nations.* San Francisco: Sierra Club Books, 1991.

Norberg-Hodge, Helena. *Ancient Futures: Learning from Ladakh.* San Francisco: Sierra Club Books, 1991.

Wachtel, Paul. *The Poverty of Affluence.* Philadelphia: New Society, 1989.

RALPH METZNER

American Psychiatric Association. *Diagnostic and Statistical Manual of Mental Disorders,* 4th ed. *(DSM-IV).* Washington, D.C.: American Psychiatric Association, 1994.

Berry, Thomas. "The Ecozoic Era." *Eleventh Annual E. F. Schumacher Lectures.* Great Barrington, Mass.: E. F. Schumacher Society.

Bratton, Susan Power. "Sleeping with Lions: The Wild and the Holy." *Orion* (Summer 1991).

deMause, Lloyd. *The Foundations of Psychohistory.* New York: Creative Roots, 1982.

Devereux, Paul, John Steele, and David Kubrin. *Earthmind.* New York: Harper & Row, 1989.

Hilgard, Ernest. *Divided Consciousness.* New York: John Wiley & Sons, 1986.

Liedloff, Jean. *The Continuum Concept.* Reading, Mass.: Addison-Wesley, 1975.

Metzner, Ralph. "The Split between Spirit and Nature in European Consciousness." *The Trumpeter.* (vol. 10, no. 1, Winter 1993).

Roszak, Theodore. *The Voice of the Earth: An Exploration of Ecopsychology.* New York: Touchstone, 1993.

Shepard, Paul. *Nature and Madness.* San Francisco: Sierra Club Books, 1982.

———. "A Post-Historic Primitivism." In Max Oelschlaeger (ed.), *The Wilderness Condition.* San Francisco: Sierra Club Books, 1992.

Snyder, Gary. *The Practice of the Wild.* San Francisco: North Point Press, 1990.

Velikovsky, Immanuel. *Mankind in Amnesia.* Garden City, N.Y.: Doubleday, 1982.

BETTY ROSZAK

Diamond, Irene. *Fertile Ground: Women, Earth and the Limits of Control.* Boston: Beacon Press, 1994.

Diamond, Irene, and Gloria Orenstein (eds.). *Reweaving the World: The Emergence of Ecofeminism.* San Francisco: Sierra Club Books, 1990.

Eisler, Riane. *The Chalice and the Blade.* San Francisco: Harper & Row, 1987.

Gimbutas, Marija. *Goddesses and Gods of Old Europe, 6500–3500* B.C. Berkeley and Los Angeles: University of California Press, 1974.

———. *The Civilization of the Goddess: Neolithic Europe Before the Patriarchy.* San Francisco: HarperCollins, 1991.

Keller, Evelyn Fox. *Reflections on Gender and Science.* New Haven: Yale University Press, 1985.

Merchant, Carolyn. *The Death of Nature.* New York: Harper & Row, 1980.

———. *Radical Ecology: The Search for a Livable World.* New York: Routledge, 1992.

Mies, Maria, and Vandana Shiva. *Ecofeminism.* London: Zed Books, 1993.

Noble, David. *A World Without Women: The Christian Clerical Culture of Western Science.* New York: Knopf, 1992.

Plant, Judith (ed.). *Healing the Wounds: The Promise of Ecofeminism.* Philadelphia: New Society, 1989.

Shiva, Vandana. *Staying Alive: Women, Ecology and Development.* London: Zed Books, 1988.

Spretnak, Charlene (ed.). *The Politics of Women's Spirituality.* Garden City, N.Y.: Doubleday, 1982.

THEODORE ROSZAK

Fox, Warwick. *Toward a Transpersonal Ecology: Developing New Foundations for Environmentalism.* Boston: Shambhala, 1990.

Hillman, James. *The Thought of the Heart and the Soul of the World.* Dallas, Tex.: Spring Publications, 1992.

Kakar, Sudhir. *Shamans, Mystics, and Doctors.* New York: Knopf, 1982.

Kauffmann, Stuart. *The Origins of Order: Self-Organization and Selection in Evolution.* New York: Oxford University Press, 1993.

Lovelock, James. *The Ages of Gaia.* New York: Norton, 1988.

Reeves, Hubert. *The Hour of Our Delight.* New York: Freeman, 1993.

Roszak, Theodore. *Person/Planet: The Creative Disintegration of Industrial Society.* Garden City, N.Y.: Doubleday, 1979.

———. *Where The Wasteland Ends: Politics and Transcendence in Postindustrial Society.* Berkeley, Calif.: Celestial Arts, 1990.

Stoehr, Taylor (ed.). *Nature Heals: The Psychological Essays of Paul Goodman.* New York: Dutton, 1977.

Suzuki, David, and Peter Knudtson. *Wisdom of the Elders: Honoring Sacred Native Visions of Nature.* New York: Bantam, 1992.

Torrey, E. Fuller. *Witchdoctors and Psychiatrists: The Common Roots of Psychotherapy and Its Future.* New York: Harper & Row, 1986.

Wilson, E. O., and Stephen R. Kellert (eds.). *The Biophilia Hypothesis.* Washington, D.C.: Island Press/Shearwater Books, 1993.

LAURA SEWALL

Abram, David. "The Perceptual Implications of Gaia." In Allan Hunt Badiner (ed.), *Dharma Gaia: A Harvest of Essays in Buddhism and Ecology.* Berkeley, Calif.: Parallax Press, 1990.

Conn, Sarah. "Protest and Thrive: The Relationship between Personal Responsibility and Global Empowerment." *New England Journal of Public Policy* 6, no. 1 (Spring/Summer 1990), 163–77.

Hillman, James, and Michael Ventura. *We've Had a Hundred Years of Psychotherapy and the World's Getting Worse.* San Francisco: HarperSanFrancisco, 1992.

Macy, Joanna. "The Greening of the Self." In Allan Hunt Badiner (ed.), *Dharma Gaia: A Harvest of Essays in Buddhism and Ecology.* Berkeley, Calif.: Parallax Press, 1990.

Naess, Arne. "Self Realization: An Ecological Approach to Being in the World." In John Seed, Joanna Macy, Patricia Fleming, and Arne Naess (eds.), *Thinking Like a Mountain: Towards a Council of All Beings.* Philadelphia: New Society, 1988.

Roszak, Theodore. *The Voice of the Earth: An Exploration of Ecopsychology.* New York: Touchstone, 1993.

ELAN SHAPIRO

Andruss, Van, Christopher Plant, Judith Plant, and Eleanor Wright (eds.). *Home! A Bioregional Reader.* Philadelphia: New Society, 1990.

Nilson, Richard (ed.). *Helping Nature Heal.* Berkeley, Calif.: Whole Earth/Ten Speed, 1991.

Shapiro, Elan. *Boundaries That Connect: Softening and Inter-relatedness in the Theory and Practice of an Emerging Ecopsychology.* 1989. Available from Elan Shapiro & Associates, 2135 Roosevelt Avenue, Berkeley, CA 94703.

Snyder, Gary. *The Practice of the Wild.* San Francisco: North Point Press, 1990.

PHYLLIS WINDLE

Davidson, Glen W. *Understanding Mourning.* Minneapolis, Minn.: Augsburg Publications, 1984.

Holdgate, Martin. "Postscript." In B. L. Turner II, W. C. Clarke, R. W. Kates, J. F. Richards, J. T. Matthews, and W. B. Meyer (eds.), *The Earth as Transformed by Human Action.* New York: Cambridge University Press, 1990.

Keller, Evelyn Fox. *A Feeling for the Organism.* San Francisco: Freeman, 1983.

Kellert, Stephen R. "Social and Psychological Dimensions of an Environmental

Ethic." *Proceedings of the International Conference on Outdoor Ethics*. Lake Ozark, Miss.: Izaak Walton League of America, 1987.

Leopold, Aldo. *A Sand County Almanac and Sketches Here and There*. New York: Oxford University Press, 1987.

McKibben, Bill. *The End of Nature*. New York: Random House, 1989.

Parkes, Colin Murray. *Bereavement*. New York: International Universities Press, 1974.

The Contributors

DAVID ABRAM is an ecologist, philosopher, and essayist whose writings have appeared in *The Ecologist, Orion, Parabola, Wild Earth, Environmental Ethics, Utne Reader,* and numerous anthologies. An accomplished sleight-of-hand magician, he has traded magic with indigenous sorcerers in Indonesia, Nepal, and North America. He is the author of *The Eclipse of the Earth: Animism, Language, and the Ecology of Sensory Experience.*

STEPHEN AIZENSTAT is the founding president of Pacifica Graduate Institute in Carpinteria, California, a core faculty member of Pacifica, and a clinical psychologist. His research centers on a psychodynamic process of "tending the living image," particularly in the context of dream work. He has conducted dream-work seminars for more than twenty years throughout the United States, Europe, and Asia.

CARL ANTHONY was an architect and city planner before he turned to environmental activism. He is president of Earth Island Institute and director of the Urban Habitat program in San Francisco. He is one of the leading voices of the environmental justice movement and a leading figure in the military–civilian conversion program for the San Francisco Bay Area.

JEANNETTE ARMSTRONG is director of the En'owkin International School of Writing in Penticton, British Columbia. She is a leading figure in the international indigenous people's political movement. In 1994 she was delegated by the Canadian government to visit and report on the uprising of the native people in Chiapas province in Mexico.

ANITA BARROWS is a poet, translator, and clinical psychologist practicing in Berkeley, California. Her book of poetry, *The Road Past the View,* won the *Quarterly Review of Literature* Contemporary Poetry Series Award for 1991.

LESTER R. BROWN is a MacArthur Fellow and founder and president of Worldwatch Institute in Washington, D.C. He is coauthor of *Saving the Planet, Full House,* and the *State of the World* annual reports. He has received The United Nations Environment Prize and The Blue Planet Prize.

WILLIAM CAHALAN is a Cincinnati-based psychologist, who has worked in a variety of inpatient and outpatient, public and private settings. In recent years he has been participating in the bioregional movement, working to integrate perspectives he has found in Gestalt therapy, evolutionary biology, ecology, and the environmental wisdom of primary cultures.

SARAH A. CONN is a clinical psychologist in private practice in Newton, Massachusetts, as well as a Lecturer in Psychology at Harvard Medical School and at the Center for Psychology and Social Change at Cambridge Hospital, where she teaches "Ecopsychology: Towards New Models of Mental Health and Psychotherapy" with her husband, psychotherapist Lane Conn.

ALAN THEIN DURNING, formerly a senior researcher at the Worldwatch Institute, now heads Northwest Watch in Seattle. He is the author of *How Much Is Enough?: The Consumer Society and the Future of the Earth.*

CHELLIS GLENDINNING is a psychologist, lecturer, and author. Her books include *My Name Is Chellis and I'm in Recovery from Western Civilization* and the Pulitzer Prize–nominated *When Technology Wounds: The Human Consequences of Progress.* Glendinning serves on the advisory board of Earth Island Institute and works with members of the Acoma and Laguna pueblos and the Navajo nation on uranium mining issues in the southwest. She lives in the village of Chimayo, New Mexico.

MARY E. GOMES is Assistant Professor of Psychology at Sonoma State University in northern California, where she teaches ecopsychology. She founded the Bay Area Ecopsychology Group in the San Francisco Bay Area, is associate director of the Ecopsychology Institute, and serves on the editorial board of the *Ecopsychology Newsletter.*

LESLIE GRAY is an Oneida/Seminole clinical psychologist, who has studied and trained with medicine people and elders from various tribal backgrounds. She has taught Native American medicine at UC Berkeley and cross-cultural shamanism at the California Institute of Integral Studies. Dr. Gray has a private practice in shamanic counseling in San Francisco.

ROBERT GREENWAY has been exploring the landscape of ecopsychology for more than thirty years. In the 1970s and 1980s he was Professor of Psychology at Sonoma State University, where he developed transpersonal, wilderness, and ecopsychology courses, as well as a graduate training program for wilderness leaders.

ALLEN D. KANNER is a clinical psychologist in private practice in Berkeley and Menlo Park, California, teaches ecopsychology at the Wright Institute in Berkeley, and is on the clinical faculty in the Department of Psychiatry and Behavioral Sciences, Stanford University Medical School. He is also a founding member of the Bay Area Ecopsychology Group in the San Francisco Bay Area, associate director of the Ecopsychology Institute, and serves on the editorial board of the *Ecopsychology Newsletter*.

STEVEN HARPER is director of Earthways Wilderness Journeys. He coordinates wilderness programs at Esalen Institute and teaches for Colorado Outward Bound and the National Outdoor Leadership School.

JAMES HILLMAN is one of America's leading Jungian analysts and one of the most creative forces in contemporary psychology theory and practice. His many works include *A Blue Fire, Revisioning Psychology,* and, with Michael Ventura, *We've Had a Hundred Years of Psychotherapy and the World's Getting Worse.*

JOHN E. MACK is Professor of Psychiatry at Cambridge Hospital, Harvard Medical School, and is founder of the Center for Psychology and Social Change, a leading force for the political and environmental application of psychology. He is the author of *The Alchemy of Survival: One Woman's Journey, A Prince of Our Disorder,* a Pulitzer Prize–winning biography of T. E. Lawrence, and *Abduction,* a provocative study of alien abductees.

JOANNA MACY is author of *Despair and Personal Power in the Nuclear Age, World as Lover and World as Self,* and *Mutual Causality: The Dharma of Natural Systems.* She is a scholar of Buddhism, general systems theory, and Deep Ecology, and is a well-known leader of despair and empowerment workshops in the United States and Europe. With John Seed, she created the Council of All Beings ritual.

RALPH METZNER teaches at the California Institute of Integral Studies and is president of the Green Earth Foundation, an educational organization devoted to the healing and harmonizing of relations between humanity and the Earth.

His books include *Maps of Consciousness, The Well of Remembrance, Opening to Inner Light: The Transformation of Human Nature and Consciousness,* and the forthcoming *The Greening of Psychology.*

TERRANCE O'CONNOR is a psychiatric social worker in Silver Spring, Maryland.

BETTY ROSZAK is a poet and writer and the coeditor of *Masculine/Feminine: Readings in Sexual Mythology and the Liberation of Women.* She is on the editorial board of the *Ecopsychology Newsletter.*

THEODORE ROSZAK is Professor of History and director of the Ecopsychology Institute at California State University, Hayward. He is the author of *The Voice of the Earth,* a principal influence upon the ecopsychology movement. His other books include *The Memoirs of Elizabeth Frankenstein.*

LAURA SEWALL holds a doctoral degree in visual psychology and teaches ecopsychology and Women's Studies at Prescott College in Prescott, Arizona. She is working on a study entitled *Revisioning Earth: Landscape, Perception, and Love.*

ELAN SHAPIRO is an ecopsychology educator, organizational consultant, and native plant expert. He teaches at the California Institute of Integral Studies and at the Institute for Culture and Creation Spirituality at College of Holy Names, Oakland. His classes include ecofeminism, bioregionalism, and ecopsychology.

PAUL SHEPARD is Professor of Human Ecology at Pitzer College in Claremont, California. He is a seminal thinker in contemporary environmental philosophy. His books include *Nature and Madness, The Tender Carnivore and the Sacred Game,* and *The Subversive Science.*

PAMELA SLOAN is a writer specializing in psychology, the arts, and technology. She serves as a publicist in the computer industry and has studied Jungian psychology for more than twenty years.

PHYLLIS WINDLE is a Senior Associate in the environment program of the Office of Technology Assessment, U.S. Congress, where she recently finished directing a study of nonindigenous species in the United States. She also serves as a chaplain at Alexandria Hospital, Alexandria, Virginia.